PACIFIC DESTINY

FORGE BOOKS BY DALE L. WALKER

Legends and Lies
The Boys of '98: Theodore Roosevelt and the Rough Riders
Bear Flag Rising: The Conquest of California, 1846
*Pacific Destiny: The Three-Century Journey to the Oregon
Country*

PACIFIC DESTINY

THE THREE-CENTURY JOURNEY TO THE OREGON COUNTRY

Dale L. Walker

A TOM DOHERTY ASSOCIATES BOOK • NEW YORK

PACIFIC DESTINY: THE THREE-CENTURY JOURNEY TO THE OREGON COUNTRY

Copyright © 2000 by Dale L. Walker

This book is printed on acid-free paper.

Maps by Mark Stein

A Forge Book
Published by Tom Doherty Associates, LLC
175 Fifth Avenue
New York, NY 10010

www.tor.com

Forge® is a registered trademark of Tom Doherty Associates, LLC.

Library of Congress Cataloging-in-Publication Data

Walker, Dale L.
    Pacific Destiny : the three-century journey to the Oregon country /
Dale L. Walker.
        p. cm.
    "A Tom Doherty Associates book."
    Includes bibliographical references (p.454) and index (p.463).
    ISBN 0-312-86933-9 (hc)
    ISBN 0-765-30310-8 (pbk)
    1. Northwest, Pacific—Discovery and exploration. 2. Northwest, Pacific—
History—18th century. 3. Northwest, Pacific—History—19th century.
4. Oregon—History—To 1859. 5. Explorers—Northwest, Pacific—History.
6. Pioneers—Northwest, Pacific. 7. Frontier and pioneer life—Northwest, Pacific
8. Fur trade—Northwest, Pacific—History. I. Title.

F880.W23 2000
979.5—dc21   00-027676

First Hardcover Edition: August 2000
First Trade Paperback Edition: June 2002

Printed in the United States of America

0 9 8 7 6 5 4 3 2 1

To my friend of all these years,
Elroy Bode

CONTENTS

Part Four: OUT TO ARCADIA

Part Five: MEDICINE ROAD

Westward the course of empire takes its way;
The four first Acts already past.
A fifth shall close the Drama of the Day;
Time's noblest offspring is the last.

—Bishop George Berkeley (1685–1753)

Eastward I go only by force; but westward I go free. . . .
I should not lay so much stress on this fact if I did not
believe that something like this is the prevailing tendency
of my countrymen. I must walk toward Oregon, and not
toward Europe. And that way the nation is moving, and
I may say that mankind progresses from east to west.

—Henry David Thoreau (1817–1862)

When God made man,
He seemed to think it best
To make him in the East,
And let him travel West.

—unknown pioneer poet

In my book a pioneer is a man who turned all the grass
upside down, strung bob-wire over the dust that was
left, poisoned the water, cut down the trees, killed the
Indian who owned the land, and called it progress.

—Charles M. Russell (1864–1926)

THE OREGON COUNTRY

Missouri River

Missouri River

Flathead Post

Musselshell River

Yellowstone River

Salmon River

• **Three Forks**

Gallatin River

Jefferson River

Madison River

Clark Fork River

Big Horn River

Powder River

Henry's Fork

Fort Henry ■

Pierre's Hole

• **Jackson's Hole**

Wind River

Fort Hall ■

Teton Pass

Snake River

Portneuf River

South Pass

Sweetwater River

Snake River

Bear River

OREGON TRAIL

Green River

N. Platte River

To California

Humboldt River

Great Salt Lake

Bear Lake

Fort Bridger

© 2000, Mark Stein Studios

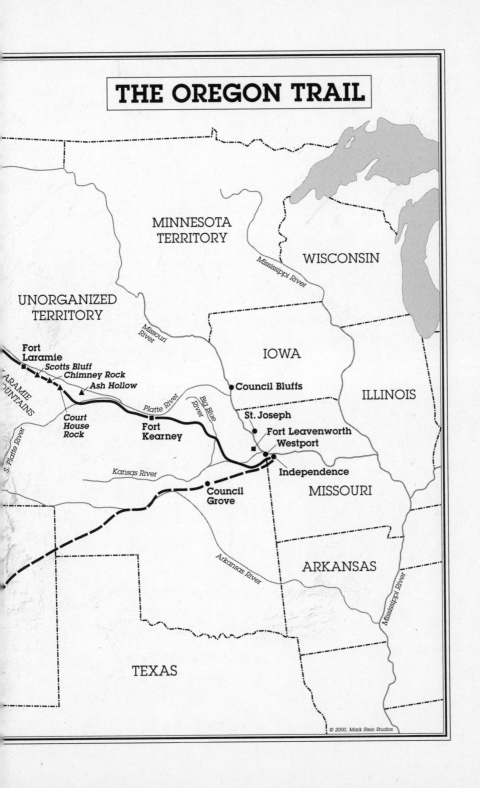

THE OREGON TRAIL

MINNESOTA TERRITORY

WISCONSIN

Mississippi River

UNORGANIZED TERRITORY

Missouri River

IOWA

Fort Laramie
Scotts Bluff
Chimney Rock
Ash Hollow

● Council Bluffs

ILLINOIS

LARAMIE MOUNTAINS

Court House Rock

Platte River

Big Blue River

St. Joseph

Fort Kearney

Fort Leavenworth
Westport

S. Platte River

Kansas River

● Independence

● Council Grove

MISSOURI

Arkansas River

ARKANSAS

Mississippi River

TEXAS

© 2000, Mark Stein Studios

PACIFIC DESTINY

INTRODUCTION

Through most of the decade of the 1840s, the Indians of the Great Plains came to the camps along the Platte River in Nebraska to witness the strange migration along what they called the White Man's Medicine Road. They sat their ponies in the noisy dawnings, caught the scent of bacon cooking, watched and listened as the camps broke, heard gunshot signals, the clank of pots and pans, the shouts and curses of teamsters, the wails and shrieks of hungry babies and skylarking children, the babble of people scurrying to their tasks. They heard the pop of white canvas sails billowing and the crack of long bullhide whips over the backs of oxen and mules drawing the creaking prairie schooners westward.

What the Indians saw we still see: trains of covered wagons headed west, the archetypal image of our archetypal American saga, and there can be little wonder why the story has such a grip on us. Those who made that epic journey toward the setting sun had all manner of reasons for going—cheap land, escape from debt, the lure of gold, the craving to teach Christianity to the heathens, the sheer adventure of it all—but whatever their motives, they acted out a dream common to all of us: the dream of a new beginning in a new place.

So captivating is this epic that there is a natural tendency in books on the subject to dwell on the pioneer "experience," to stitch together the journals and diaries of those who actually made the harrowing overland journey. For example, Merrill J. Mattes, whose *The Great Platte River Road* is among the undisputed classic works on the westering emigrants of the 1840s, listed over 1,000 sources for his work, and examined something like 700 eyewitness journal-diary narratives.

But in the research and writing of *Pacific Destiny* I kept imagining what the Indians of the Platte must have wondered: Where were these people *going*, and *why*?, and it seemed natural to me to begin where the emigrant dream really began. In this I was influenced by the lucky circumstance of having visited the end of the trail before traveling over the beginning of it.

During a trip to Portland a few years ago, I was able to visit the Fort Vancouver National Historic Site, drive south along the Willamette River to spend a few hours in Oregon City, and even travel up the Columbia, the fabled "River of the West," on a sternwheeler.

Oregon history is infectious, and I bought books at worldrenowned Powell's, collected maps and pamphlets, and caught the spirit of the place—even in the space of a week.

That trip came back to me during an October 1998 drive from Saint Louis to Fort Laramie, Wyoming, roughly following the Oregon Trail route taken by Francis Parkman in 1846.

Parkman did not reach the end of the Oregon Trail—he traveled about 40 percent of it, to a point sixty miles west of Fort Laramie—but he *saw* the trail better than anybody in his time, saw it as a symbol of the westering movement and of what that movement signified for the future. "Great changes are at hand," he wrote, "the buffalo will dwindle away, and the large wandering communities who depend on them for support must be broken and scattered. The Indians will soon be abased by whiskey and overawed by military posts; so that within a few years the traveller may pass in tolerable security through their country. Its dangers and its charms will have disappeared altogether."

With the benefit of 152 years of history and technology behind me, I traveled his route, passing in tolerable security through the Indians' country, the dangers of which are restricted to flat tires or spewing radiators on lonely roads. I had two books with me: Parkman's *The Oregon Trail*, and Gregory M. Franzwa's indispensable guide for the modern traveler, *The Oregon Trail Revisited*. I stopped frequently to consult both, especially to examine the landmarks, sites, and swales described so meticulously by Franzwa. And I daydreamed, from the Museum of Westward Expansion at the Saint Louis Arch through a tour of the Fort Laramie National Historic Site, about the people who pointed their wagons toward the Pacific Rim and rolled free of the rude civilization of Missouri to take the first tentative steps of their 2,000-mile walk to the northwest coast of America.

By the time I dropped away from the trail to the town of Wheatland and made my way south to Cheyenne and home, I was thinking of those who blazed that trail thirty years and more before Parkman traveled it, and the story of that Land of Giants, the Oregon Country, before the name "Oregon" was concocted (a fascinating tale by itself).

In *Pacific Destiny*, by taking a somewhat chronological approach to the story, starting at trail's end and ending with the trail's beginning, my ambition has been to answer the questions I imagined the Platte River natives asking: Where are all these people going and why? and Why Oregon? This book seeks to tell the story of the original Oregon dreamers and pay proper homage to them: sea dogs and explorers; *voyageurs*, trappers, and traders; visionaries and missionaries; adventurers; misfits; opportunists—all pioneers in the purest sense of the word.

In no other episode in western American history is there a more beguiling assortment of characters than those figuring in the long journey to the lands north of the 42nd parallel and west of the Shining Mountains, the people who made the Oregon Trail not only possible, but inevitable. Only history, never fiction, could give us such figures as Dr. John McLoughlin, the White Eagle laird of Fort Vancouver; Captain Jonathan Thorn, doomed skipper of the frigate *Tonquin*; that "fuming, vainglorious little man," Duncan McDougall, who cowed the Indians with his "phial of wrath"; Wilson Hunt and Robert Stuart, the original Astor overlanders; Hall J. Kelley, the half-mad dreamer who crossed Mexico to get to the Oregon Country after his followers double-crossed him; Nat Wyeth, the Cambridge iceman, and Francis Parkman, the Cambridge scholar. Not even a poet could have invented the adventures of the missionaries Jason Lee, Marcus and Narcissa Whitman, Samuel and Eliza Parker; the mountain men Jedediah Smith, Broken Hand Fitzpatrick, Ewing Young, and Joe Meek; or of such minor players as Miss Jane Barnes, the first woman to visit the Oregon coast, and Reverend Herbert Beaver ("a good name for a fur-trade station," as Peter Skene Ogden dryly observed), who had the misfortune to say something scandalous about John McLoughlin's wife.

Nor is there, to my mind at least, a more compelling tale in our Western history than that of the V-shaped ripples made by certain aquatic animals, especially *Lutra enhydris marina* and *Castor canadensis*, which aimed us toward our Pacific destiny and which bound together this astonishing mélange of early dreamers.

A final note: There are necessary anachronisms in the pages that follow. Obviously there was no "Oregon" or "Oregon Country" when Ferrelo and Drake sailed up the Pacific coast of the continent in the sixteenth century; there were no Colorado, Wyoming, Montana, Idaho, Utah, or Nevada when the Astorians crossed the Rocky Mountains, or even during Frémont's early expeditions and, as in the opening paragraph of this introduction, no Nebraska, at least as a state, until 1867. But for easy reader orientation in the often confusing geography of the era of western expansion, I have used out-of-time state and place names to avoid such tedious repetitions as "the future state of Washington" and "what would later become the state of Oregon."

Among generous friends whose assistance of various kinds made it easier to write this book, I want to thank Richard S.

Wheeler of Livingston, Montana; James Crutchfield of Franklin, Tennessee; Candy Moulton of Encampment, Wyoming; George Skanse, proprietor of the incomparable Book Gallery in El Paso, Texas; and my friends at the Village Inn, where some of the book was written: Celia Davidson, Evelyn Anderson, Tony Garza, Michelle Garza, Aldo Monterrey, Lisa De Haro, Travis Doctor, Nicole Smith, Julee Morrissy, and Marie Giger.

—DALE L. WALKER
November 18, 1999

PROLOGUE

Westering, Thoreau said, "is the prevailing tendency of my countrymen," and the movement west, inching the frontier toward that "other" great boundary, the Pacific, is as old as America. The original band of Jamestowners who reached Chesapeake Bay in the spring of 1607 were soon pulling out of Tidewater to explore and plow on the Piedmont, and within a hundred years Americans had scattered outposts along the Atlantic from Maine to Carolina.

It took a century and a half for colonists to remove from their striking distance to the sea, but the French and Indian War, proving ground for leaders on both sides of the American Revolution, pushed the frontier to the forks of the Ohio River and began a movement down the Cumberland to the valleys of eastern Kentucky and Tennessee. The Appalachians, running from Quebec to the coastal plains of Alabama, proved no obstacle, nor did the escarpments and plateaus of the Allegheny wilderness, which funneled them into Ohio and Kentucky, the Lower Mississippi, and the Old Northwest of Indiana, Illinois, and Michigan.

In March 1803, when Ohio was admitted to the Union, there were seventeen United States, but American territory had not yet crossed the Mississippi. All that changed on October 20 of that year with the ratification of the Louisiana Purchase. Suddenly the nation's area doubled—$15 million bought 828,000 square miles of land—and jumped its western boundary to the crest of the Rockies.

To the south and west of those unmapped mountains lay New Spain, including its exotic outposts of New Mexico and Alta California; to the northwest, from the Rockies to the Pacific, lay the Oregon Country, strangely alluring, as all hidden places are.

The Lewis and Clark Corps of Discovery reached the sea-slashed coast of the Oregon Country in November 1805, over 250 years after the first white men saw it. Both explorers, and their sponsor, Thomas Jefferson, knew this history, knew that Spaniards, Englishmen, Frenchmen, Russians, a Dane, possibly a Greek, and certainly a handful of Americans had already been there. Fifteen years before the advent of Lewis and Clark, Spain had signed a document that recognized British rights to trade and settle along the northwest coast of America, and in 1792 the Columbia River was named for the first American vessel to anchor there. "Bostons," the Yankee merchant captains from Massachusetts seaports, and Englishmen, and Russians, among others, had established a sea otter fur trade among the coastal Indians.

Jefferson's explorers were therefore not altogether surprised, once they reached the coast and began the work on their fort, to learn that the Indians in the vicinity had already experienced a certain level of "commercial intercourse" with whites. The Clatsops and other tribes the explorers encountered had in their vocabularies a supply of common European profanities, and knew such bartering words as *musket, powder, shot*, and *knife*.

The Corps of Discovery, stunning in its accomplishment, as "perfect" an exploration as has been recorded in history, made no claim of "discovering" Oregon, only of discovering an overland route to the Pacific, of being the first party of white men to cross the western half of North America.

Part One

SEA-LANES

1

THE PACIFIC LITTORAL

1

The first trails to Oregon were sea-lanes, the wakes left by Spanish caravels and *fragatos* with lateen sails bulging in ferocious winds and masts bent perilously as they blundered along the Pacific coast of North America in pursuit of obscure missions approved by the viceroy of Mexico.

A Portuguese soldier in the service of Mexico, Juan Rodríguez Cabrillo, led a two-ship expedition from the Pacific port of Natividad in June 1542, searching for fables: the "Coast of Cathay," believed to be a large island somewhere in the north; the seaport of Quivira and its Seven Cities of Gold; and the Strait of Anián, a northwest passage across North America to the Atlantic. Cabrillo's flagship *Victoria*, a stout and sizable vessel, and the smaller *San Salvador*, a frigate, sighted the California coast in July and in the same month sailed into a "closed and very good harbor" he named San Miguel, subsequently known as San Diego.

The bold soldier-sailor sailed on in October, threading through the Santa Barbara Channel Islands. He avoided the terrifying seas off Big Sur and led his ships north past the Farralon Islands and past the great headlands, shrouded in fog, that hid inside them a magnificent bay, to an anchorage at 38 degrees north latitude, just above the entrance to the Golden Gate. He named this cove Los Pinos for the great green mantle of pines that surrounded it, and spent some days there before sailing a short distance north to Bodega Bay.

Cabrillo hoped to proceed north along the coast but battering seas off Bodega forced him to direct his ships south to a winter anchorage at San Miguel Island in the Santa Barbara Channel. In January 1543 the former crossbowman in Hernán Cortés's conquest of Mexico died after a shipboard accident, and it fell to his handpicked successor, an Italian Levantine named Bartolomé Ferrelo, to continue the voyage.

Ferrelo led the *Victoria* and the *San Salvador* past Cape Mendocino—the westernmost point on the California coast—and north at least as far as latitude 41 degrees 30 minutes off Klamath, California. He may have sighted the Oregon coast above 42 degrees before gales drove him back, to return to Natividad in April.

Insofar as finding gold and silver, the Seven Cities, or the Strait of Anián, the expedition was a failure, but Cabrillo and Ferrelo had charted a real seacoast as fabulous as any Quivira of the imagination.

□

Francis Drake, the bold son of Devonshire and corsair of the Spanish Main, may have exceeded the *Victoria* and *San Salvador*'s northernmost mark when he brought his *Golden Hind* along the California coast thirty-six years after Ferrelo returned to Mexico.

Drake sailed from Plymouth in December 1577, with a syndicate sponsoring him as captain-general of a six-ship expedition. His backers expected him to sail through the Strait of Magellan into the Pacific and seek the Northwest Passage, the all-water route connecting the two great oceans, a lodestone that lured mariners and trade-minded politicians for more than four centuries.

Exploration, however, was incidental to Drake's work as a privateer, a pirate with governmental sanction, so he plundered Spanish ports at Valparaíso, Chile, and Callao, Peru, as he made his way up the Pacific coast. By his own account, the *Hind* approached land between 42 and 48 degrees north latitude before retreating downcoast. In *Hakluyt's Voyages*, published in 1589, Drake is credited with a northern limit of 42 degrees (the latitude of the California-Oregon boundary), which he reached on June 5, 1579. Historian Hubert Howe Bancroft, who studied the sources on Drake's voyage, concluded that the privateer "was probably, though not certainly, the first discoverer of the western coast from Cape Mendocino to the region of Cape Blanco, including fifty or sixty miles of the Oregon coast."

Drake spent five weeks in June and July on the western coast and, like Cabrillo, missed sighting the foggy entrance to San Francisco Bay as he proceeded to an anchorage north of the Golden Gate—Cabrillo's Los Pinos—subsequently named Drake's Bay.

Somewhere, at Drake's Bay, Bodega Bay, or farther north, perhaps near Cape Mendocino, the *Hind* was beached and careened, and in the process the captain-general and his men were visited by a number of Miwok Indians. The naked "sauvages" were presented with gifts of trinkets and in return brought broiled fish; a supply of a lily root they dried, ground into a meal, and ate; and such gifts as shells, sea-otter and gopher skins, and bird feathers.

Drake named the country New Albion (Albion being the Greek name for England) after passing an area of white cliffs that reminded him of the south coast of his home country.

On July 23, Reverend Francis Fletcher, a member of the expedition, said the Miwoks "tooke a sorrowfull farewell of us" and the *Hind* sailed west to Mindanao, the Indian Ocean, and home to Plymouth, arriving there, after nearly three years' absence, in September 1580, completing the first English circumnavigation of the world.

2

In 1596, a letter was published in Europe purportedly written by a Greek explorer in the service of Spain. Apostolos Valerianos, who adopted the name Juan de Fuca, claimed to have sailed a small caravel into the Pacific for the viceroy of Mexico in 1592 and to have found the western opening of the Northwest Passage, a broad inlet on the northern coast between 47 and 48 degrees north latitude. He told of "sailing inland" for more than twenty days and of finding a people who wore the skins of beasts and a land rich in silver, gold, and pearls.

His story was probably a fiction, common enough in the day, but mapmakers put his "opening" in the latitude he described. Two hundred years later, the Juan de Fuca Strait, separating Vancouver Island from the Washington mainland and leading into Puget Sound, was discovered not many sea miles distant from de Fuca's 48 degrees north.

□

Visions of the Northwest Passage continued to draw mariners along the Oregon coast of America. In 1602, the Spaniard Sebastián Vizcaíno led the *San Diego* and the *Tres Reyes* out of Monterey on the California coast as far north as the 43rd parallel, searching for Quivira and the Strait of Anián.

Nor were all the explorers Spaniards and Englishmen. Peter the Great of Russia had conquered Siberia by 1639 and reached the Pacific, and in 1741 Vitus Bering, a Dane, sailed in the *St. Peter* from Kamchatka to the coast of North America near Sitka. In the 1765–68 era, the Russians were on the move south along the coast, slaughtering sea otters and coastal Indians with equal rapacity.

In 1774, at the time when the First Continental Congress was meeting in Philadelphia, Spain sent an expedition to the Oregon coast. Among other accomplishments, it discovered Nootka Sound, on the west coast of what became Vancouver Island.

By 1812, with the consent of Spain, Russian hunters out of

Sitka founded Fort Ross on Bodega Bay in California and later another fort in the Sandwich Islands. American politicians considered these outposts dangerous in their implications, especially due to their proximity to San Francisco Bay, and in 1816 James Monroe proposed a treaty of amity in North America with the 49th parallel as the boundary between the interests of the two countries. Monroe did not mention England in his proposal, but in any event the idea was not pushed to fruition.

The Spaniards interpreted the Russian incursions as threats to her claims in the Pacific and sent new expeditions out to expand explorations of the coast of Alta California and establish missions and presidios from San Diego to Sonoma, north of the Golden Gate.

But Spain did not pursue its discoveries and, after it seemed clear that the Russians were more interested in the fur trade than in permanent settlement, it was the British who rose to challenge Spain's claims.

□

In 1778, in his third and final voyage to the Antipodes, Captain James Cook, England's greatest navigator, came to the Oregon coast with his flagship *Resolution* and the sloop *Discovery*. His mission was to conduct a thorough search for the Northwest Passage (for which Parliament was offering a £20,000 prize) by sailing above the northernmost latitude of Ferrelo and Vizcaíno, and above the latitude of Drake's New Albion exploration 200 years before. His cautionary instructions from the Admiralty were to avoid any encounters with foreigners and to respect Spanish dominions on the American coast. His orders stated, "You are also, with the consent of the natives, to take possession in the name of the king of Great Britain, of convenient situations in such countries as you may discover, that have not already been discovered or visited by any other European power, and to distribute among the inhabitants such things as will remain as traces and testimonies of your having been there."

The world had no more experienced explorer than James Cook. He had helped chart the Saint Lawrence River, surveyed the Newfoundland coast, made two previous epic voyages, that of 1772–1775 his greatest legacy: In three years he had sailed over 20,000 leagues on the southern seas—three times the circumference of the globe—with a loss of only four men (defeating scurvy with sauerkraut and meat broths), and charted the coasts of Antarctica and Australia.

In 1776, when Cook sailed from England for the last time on his square-rigged flagship *Resolution* (his sailing master was a twenty-one-year-old navigator from Plymouth named William Bligh), his orders were almost too specific. He was to proceed around the Cape of Good Hope into the Pacific, cross from Tahiti in the Windward Group of the Society Islands to the coast of North America, and proceed northward to determine the value, if any, of the theory that in arctic waters would be found the western entrance to the Northwest Passage. Failing to find it there, he was to continue through the Bering Strait and search for an open-water polar passage. Such confidence was placed in his success that the Admiralty dispatched naval vessels to meet him in Baffin Bay on the Atlantic side of the continent.

He reached and rediscovered Hawaii (which he named the Sandwich Islands after the First Lord of the Admiralty, the Earl of Sandwich), and on March 7, 1778, sighted the coast of Drake's New Albion at the 43rd parallel and charted and named such features as Capes Arago, Foulweather, and Perpetua as he sailed upcoast. He missed seeing the tumultuous mouth of the Columbia River, but on March 22 the *Resolution* and the *Discovery* stood at a cape on the edge of a strait Cook denied existed. He named the promontory Cape Flattery and wrote in his journal, "There appeared to be a small opening, which flattered us with the hopes of finding a harbor.... It is in this very latitude where we now were, that geographers have placed the pretended strait of Juan de Fuca.... But we saw nothing like it; nor is there the least probability that ever any such thing existed."

Cook's ships made their first landing at Nootka Sound, and the explorer wrote about the desolate, windblown place in his journals, which were eagerly published in England and the United States and widely read. He wrote about the furs secured from Indians at Nootka, which fetched handsome prices in the China trade (sea otter pelts, purchased for a handful of beads, sold in Canton for as much as $200 each); of savages paddling canoes, some of them forty feet long and seven wide, made from a single cedar trunk, and throwing feathers and red dust in their wake. He saw men dressed in fur-edged blankets of dog hair mixed with cedar bark and decorated with scenes of whale hunts, over which were draped capes of sea otter skins; people whose bodies were smeared with red clay mixed with whale oil, their hair long and soaked in fish oil sprinkled with bird down, their earlobes and noses decorated with bone and bits of metal, wearing wooden masks painted into grotesque visages. These amazing people had articles of iron and copper, leftovers from Spanish landings, and one native wore two silver spoons as ear ornaments. Their houses, "filthy as hogsties, everything in and about them stinking of fish," Cook said, were surrounded by racks of drying fish, piles of excrement, and strange totems.

In spring of 1779, soon after he returned to the Sandwich Islands from the northwest coast, Captain Cook, age fifty, was killed by natives at Kealakekua Bay. One of six marines from the *Discovery* and the *Resolution* fighting hand-to-hand the natives who stabbed Cook to death was an American named John Ledyard.

3

The lure of the Pacific Northwest in the last decade of the eighteenth century and the first of the nineteenth had nothing to do with its potential for settlement, or with its vast timber and fishery potential—which were obvious from the starboard rail of any ship headed north—or even with that ancient, chimerical idea of a Northwest Passage. The great enticement in those two decades was

Lutra enhydris marina, which the Russians knew as *Bobri morski*, "sea beaver," and which American and English sailors called the sea otter.

These gregarious, aquatic animals lived and bore their pups in their favorite habitats, the reefs and rocks and floating kelp beds of coastal California, British Columbia, and Alaska. The animal was prized for its thick, fine underfur, perfect for sewing into royal robes, and for the tails, which were used for decorating hats and gown borders. Like the beaver, next on the list for extermination, sea otters were "harvested" recklessly. Between 1790 and 1812 an average of 12,000 a year were clubbed to death. In fact, the animal was all but extinct on the northern coast by 1800.

English mariners to the Northwest knew the value of the sea otter from Drake's time, and the Russians were slaughtering them on Alaskan shores even before they began their poaching sorties out of Sitka down to Fort Ross. Coastal Indians had known the animals' worth from time immemorial: Two sea otter pelts would buy a slave, and when the first white explorers came, the furs could be traded for any number of iron tools, beads, and gewgaws.

In 1785 the French sent an expedition to the Oregon coast and, not surprisingly, one of its objectives was to obtain reliable information on the fur trade there. Since 1600 France had worked to establish a fur monopoly in the New World, and by 1750 its *coureurs de bois* (runners of the woods) and brigades of trappers had penetrated the continent as far west as the Mandan villages of the Missouri River and south to Santa Fé in Spanish New Mexico.

Louis XVI personally had a hand in planning the 1785 Pacific expedition. Like other European monarchs, he was interested in the China trade and therefore captivated by the idea of "some river or narrow gulf" that might communicate between the two great oceans—a Northwest Passage. He also wrote of "the possibility of a colony or at least a factory [trading post] in a region not yet occupied" on the Pacific coast of America.

A nobleman and celebrated navigator named Jean de Galaup, Comte de La Pérouse, led the expedition, commanding two vessels, the *Boussole* and the *Astrolabe*. At age forty-four he had already spent thirty years at sea, starting his career as a midshipman during the Seven Years' War. In addition to a full complement of officers and seamen, La Pérouse had aboard his ships a remarkable assortment of scientists, interpreters, and "observers" who were to gather data on the country, its people and "products," the extent of Spanish establishments ashore, and the latitude at which furs might be obtained without giving offense to Spain.

La Pérouse's ships found the northwest coast on June 23, 1786, and spent six weeks in Alaskan waters as far north as latitude 59 degrees 37 minutes, then sailed down past Nootka and the Oregon coast to California. The *Boussole* and *Astrolabe* made frequent anchorages and lowered boats, the shore parties conducting a brisk trade with Indians. The fur-shrewd Frenchmen had bartered for over a thousand sea otter "pieces" before crossing the Pacific to Macao, the Portuguese port on the China coast. There the scraps, tails, and hides were sold and the profits divided among the crews of the two ships.

"I believe there is no country in the world where the sea-otter is more common than in this part of America," La Pérouse wrote in his log, "and I should be little surprised if a factory extending its operations only forty or fifty leagues along the sea-shore might collect each year ten thousand skins of this animal." He cautioned, however, that a French factory on the northwest coast of America might cause problems with the courts at Madrid and Saint Petersburg.

In September 1787 the navigator put his Russian interpreter ashore at Kamchatka to make his way to Paris with reports and maps, then sailed south. In January 1788, now two and one half years out of Brest, the French ships battered their way into Botany Bay, the harbor on the eastern shore of Australia discovered eight years earlier by Captain Cook. There was a historical coincidence in La Pérouse's appearance there. Watching him maneuver his vessels into the bay were the crews of two British warships and nine merchant transports, which had just landed over 700 British convicts ashore after a voyage of 15,000 miles from Plymouth. This was the "first fleet" of the criminal population of Australia.

The French explorers spent six weeks at Botany Bay among the Englishmen and their prisoner-colonists before setting sail and disappearing into the maw of the Pacific. Thirty years would pass before it was determined that La Pérouse and all hands had perished when the *Boussole* and the *Astrolabe* went down among the Coral Sea reefs of the New Hebrides, 1,200 miles east of the Australian coast.

☐

In the same year as the La Pérouse expedition, Captain Charles Barkley (or Barclay or Berkeley), an Englishman, sailing from Ostende in the merchant vessel *Imperial Eagle* under the flag of a fictitious "Austrian East India Company," entered Nootka Sound, and began a trade with the Indians of Vancouver Island. His notable contribution to the history of the American Northwest occurred in July 1787, when he found the "lost" Strait of Juan de Fuca. Barkley did not venture far into it; instead, he continued south to trade with the natives.

The sailors of the *Imperial Eagle* were among the first to learn that native naïveté and docility could not always be depended upon. Four of Barkley's crew were killed after going ashore with "too much confidence and unarm'd," and the captain's report established that the attack took place at 47 degrees 46 minutes north, at a place he appropriately named Destruction Island. He ordered the burning of a village in retribution and established a pattern of violence that would last a half century.

Despite the conflict with the natives, the origin of which was not reported, Barkley's expedition made a trade bonanza among the coastal tribes, departing the coast with 4,000 sea otter pelts, which were taken to Macao in the winter of 1787 and sold at an immense profit.

2

THE RIVER OF THE WEST

"... THE MOST LOVELY COUNTRY THAT CAN BE IMAGINED."

1

From the interior of what became the Oregon Country to its thundering coast lived a diverse people who had occupied the land for centuries before Ferrelo and Drake saw it. Some of the native clans were given French or English names such as Nez Percé, Flathead, Coeur d'Alene; and there were also such tribes and subtribes as the Cayuse, Colville, Kalispell, Spokane, Yakima, Walla Walla, and Wishram; and the coastal Chinook, Chehalem, Salish, Clatsop, Puyallap, Tillamook, Coos, and Umpqua. Their cultures have been called by anthropologists the most elaborate in the world among nonagricultural native people.

All the tribes, land-bound and coastal, had a common riches: the land's lush abundance. Fish, salmon in particular, and timber for boats and homes distinguished them. Many of the coastal folk, those first encountered by Europeans, were fish-rich, status-conscious slaveholders. Their social structure was sharply divided among autocrats and commoners with a hereditary chief at the center who owned huge tracts of village lands, hunting and fishing grounds, and was served by slaves captured in raids on other tribes. This chief's status among his people and his renown among peers in neighboring clans was to a degree dependent on the elaborateness of his periodic *potlatch* (a Chinook word essentially meaning "giving away"). In this religious ceremony, after much speechmaking and feasting, to demonstrate his riches the chief would distribute gifts—from caches of dried fish to parcels of land—according to the social status of the recipients.

Among the coastal clans were accomplished artisans much admired (and soon feared) by the explorers and navigators who visited their sea-wracked shores from Nootka Sound to Alta California. In ships' logs and explorers' journals are descriptions of their longhouses and carved and painted totems, of delicately carved bowls made of alderwood, blankets of animal hair, weirs—basket-traps—of woven willow, fish lines and nets made of twisted wood fibers and grasses, hooks and harpoons made of wood, bone, and shell. They wrote of dances and rituals with much noisemaking with rattles and bells, the participants wearing wooden masks and long cloaks made of shredded cedar bark dyed with berry juices.

White chroniclers admired the native watercraft, especially the great flat-bottomed, cedarwood dugouts, some of them thirty or forty feet long, capable of carrying a crew of five and a ton of weight. Chinooks and Nootkas, among others, made such boats—rough-shaping them with stone adzes, firing them for hardness, sanding and polishing them with sharkskin—and paddled them from Vancouver Island to California waters and up the Columbia to the Indian commerce center at The Dalles rapids. They harpooned whales in them, caught sharks and seals and sea otters, netted fish, and pulled the boats ashore to collect mollusks along the beaches.

Another artistic and functional craft of the coastal tribes was the canoe. This vessel—unlike those familiar to the *voyageur*, made from birch bark and hide lashings—the Pacific Northwest Indian made his from a split log, chipped with adzes until the walls were thin and pliable, the bottom burn-hardened with heapings of hot coals, the skin painted, and the wooden prow carved into animal figureheads.

William Clark described these canoes as "butiful . . . neeter made than any I have ever Seen and calculated to ride the waves, and carry emence burthens."

The culture of the sea and river people, and even important features of their religion, were founded on fish. The Nootkas honored Salmon Beings, and the first fish caught each year was eaten ritually at an altar and its bones thrown back into the water to reincarnate. Even the inland Colvilles had a Fish Guardian Spirit. They used fish oil, which they preserved in fish- or animal-gut bags, in cooking, for flavoring, for mixing with berries, and for rubbing in their hair and on their skin.

Many, perhaps most, of the Northwest tribes were, to use the white man's word, "peaceable," avoiding wars with their neighbors and even mediating family and intertribal quarrels. Some had communal food-gathering practices and tribal assemblies in which all adults, male and female, had their say.

But there were some tribes who had waged war before the white man came and remained warlike thereafter.

2

The river rises in southeastern British Columbia and flows northwest, then south, in the Rocky Mountain trench for 465 miles before crossing the 49th line of latitude. Just below the mouth of the Spokane River lava beds force it to make a bend westward, then it veers south again, running swiftly through a narrow valley where it is joined by its chief tributary, the Snake. Now on a westward course, the river flows through the magnificent gorges it created over the millennia, through the Cascades and the Coast Ranges, reaching the Pacific, 1,210 miles from its source.

The Spanish explorer Bruno de Heçeta, probably the first European to observe its fearsome estuary, named it the San Roque.

Early geographers and cartographers, who knew of its existence before learning anything specific about it, called it the River of the West. And in 1778, an explorer who had come no closer to it than the headwaters of the Mississippi called it the Oregon River.

□

Jonathan Carver of Weymouth, Massachusetts, was nearly fifty years old when he had his brush with history. A shoemaker, and married, he enlisted in the British army in 1757 to fight the French, and was wounded during the siege of Fort William Henry in the foothills of the Adirondacks of New York.

His service must have been exemplary. After nine years in the army he had risen from the ranks to a captaincy, and in 1766 he had an important rendezvous at Mackinac Island in the strait between the upper and lower peninsulas of northern Michigan. There Carver met with Major Robert Rogers, the celebrated founder of Rogers' Rangers, the militia force he raised during the French and Indian War. Rogers had an ambition to explore. He had written a book, *Concise Account of North America*, and during a trip to England had submitted a proposal to King George that he would lead an expedition to find a route from the Mississippi to the Pacific. The "sanction," or sponsorship, of the plan was denied, but Rogers was at least given a command in upper Michigan and there determined to launch the expedition himself.

Why he chose Captain Jonathan Carver to lead it is unknown, but the two met at Mackinac, and soon thereafter Carver began what was to become the first English expedition to explore and survey the Upper Mississippi and Great Lakes region. He was specifically assigned to map the rivers of Wisconsin and Minnesota, and to determine the feasibility of an all-water passage to the Pacific.

In the summer of 1766, Carver led a small band of frontiersmen to Green Bay, at the mouth of the Fox River in northeast Wisconsin, then followed the Fox to the Wisconsin River and down to the Mississippi. He wintered at the Falls of Saint Anthony, near Saint

Paul, Minnesota, and there refined his maps and journals and anticipated continuing his journey westward.

In this, for reasons never adequately explained, he was thwarted. During the spring thaws of 1767, Carver and his crew traveled to Grand Portage on the north shore of Lake Superior. He expected to find reinforcements and supplies awaiting him there that would enable him to push west to the Pacific, but when the manpower and materiél were not forthcoming, he disbanded his men and in 1768 returned to Boston.

In London in 1774 Carver joined in a scheme with Richard Wentworth, a wealthy member of Parliament, to take fifty or sixty men up the Missouri River, explore the "Shining Mountains" (the Rockies), find the source of the River of the West, sail down it to its exit in the Pacific, and build a fort at its mouth. The plan appears to have had the sanction of the British colonial government but was buried by the intervention of the American Revolution.

Carver remained in England, married again (without divorcing his first wife in America), and died in poverty in 1780. He had one success after his Mississippi expedition, the publication in 1778 of his mixture of fact and fantasy, *Carver's Travels Through the Interior Parts of North America in the years 1766, 1767, and 1768,* which sustained a readership through thirty editions.

In the book, Carver told of his explorations of the headwaters of the Mississippi, his talks with an Indian tribe he designated the Naudowessie, and his learning of the country to the west, in particular of the Shining Mountains, a range he said began in Mexico and continued northward on a line east of Spanish California. These mountains were rich in gold, he wrote; indeed, the metal was so plentiful the Indians there made their commonest utensils from it. "Probably in future ages," he said, "they [the mountains] may be found to contain more riches in their bowels than those of Indostan and Malabar, or that are produced on the Golden Coast of Guinea; nor will I except even the Peruvian Mines." He also learned that the natives of the Shining Mountains dressed in the soft, warm covering of beasts "which skipped upon the surface" (presumably beavers), and that these natives were white.

From the Shining Mountains, Carver said, rivers flowed in every direction, these including the River of the West, which he said "falls into the Pacific Ocean at the straits of Anián."

(Of these claims H. H. Bancroft says wryly, "Brave words for one who might as well have been speaking of the Mountains of the Moon so far as actual knowledge or even probability was concerned.")

Carver wrote that the Indian name for the River of the West was the "Oregon," or as he sometimes spelled it, "Origan," and in so saying created a puzzle unsolved to this day: the source of the word *Oregon*.

He claimed he heard the name from the Naudowessie Indians near the headwaters of the Mississippi. His sponsor, Robert Rogers, may have used it—as "Ouragon" and "Ourigon"—in the unpublished "memorial" he wrote to King George asking for governmental sponsorship of an exploration of the trans-Mississippi region.

Wherever the word originated, it does not appear in any of the several dialects of the Oregon Country, and several theories on its provenance have been advanced. One of these has it that the word derives from *Origanum*, or sweet marjoram, a useful plant believed to have had medicinal properties. But it is not explained how Indians would know the Latin name of the plant, or indeed if they even knew of the plant to begin with. A writer in an 1871 issue of the *New York Ethnological Journal* proposed the more plausible idea that "Oregon" might derive from the Spanish *huricán* (hurricane), describing the shrieking winds of the northwest coast in certain months remarked on by all early-day explorers.

The word does not appear in Lewis and Clark's journals, although Jefferson used it in his instructions to the explorers. It appeared in print for the first time in Carver's 1778 book of travels, and for the second time in the 1817 poem "Thanatopsis" by William Cullen Bryant ("Or lose thyself in the continuous woods/ Where rolls the Oregon, and hears no sound"). Bancroft wrote that Jefferson and Bryant had read Carver's book and that the poet "seized upon the word that fitted best his meter, and in his 'Thanatopsis' made that word immortal."

The historian said it is doubtful that Carver understood the natives who allegedly uttered the word, but admitted, "There could have been no object, apparent to us, for him to misrepresent; he could never have dreamed that this probably meaningless sound, caught up from the wind by his too attentive ear, should ever be applied to the designation of a great, progressive state."

3

Fourteen years after Jonathan Carver's fanciful naming of the River of the West, a company of six Boston merchants financed a fur-trading enterprise to the northern Pacific, the first such American venture. The sponsors were apparently inspired by publication of Captain James Cook's journals of his 1778 voyage, especially those passages dealing with the "sea beaver" furs to be found there and their worth in the China trade. They put up $50,000 to dispatch two trade vessels from Nantucket Roads in September 1787.

In command of the expedition was the veteran privateer and trader John Kendrick of Harwich, Massachusetts, sailing on the *Columbia Rediviva* ("America Reborn"), a 212-ton, 83-foot merchantman with a thirty-man crew and armed with ten cannons. Kendrick's second was a thirty-two-year-old Rhode Islander named Robert Gray, another privateer in the American Revolution and a self-styled "sea-peddler." Gray, who commanded the *Lady Washington*, a ninety-ton merchant sloop, had a reputation as a rough and ruthless seaman with none of Kendrick's diplomacy and kindliness of character.

The ships carried a $25,000 cargo: scrap iron, 135 barrels of beef, 60 of pork, 1,500 pounds of gunpowder, 5 hogsheads of New England and West Indian rum, 2,000 bricks, tea, chocolate, copper sheets, "Barr iron," "Iron Hoops," "Chissells," and gimcracks and utensils for trade with coastal natives. These included snuffboxes, jew's harps, mirrors, buttons, cloth remnants, iron tools, cookpots, and pewter medals to be awarded to tribal dignitaries. The ships managed to maintain visual contact on the voyage from Nantucket to the Cape Verde and Falkland Islands, but lost sight of each other in a Cape Horn gale. Gray sailed on and reached "New Albion," perhaps near Cape Mendocino, on August 2, 1788. He continued upcoast to the vicinity of Tillamook Bay, above the 45th parallel, and there occurred a lamentable incident that caused Gray to call Tillamook Murderer's Harbor.

The Indians who greeted the *Lady Washington*'s shore parties were friendly and traded enthusiastically, bringing baskets of berries and crabs to Gray's famished and scurvy-ridden crewmen, exchanging furs for iron implements, assisting in gathering wood and fresh water. On August 16, nine seamen rowed ashore to gather a load of grass and shrubs for the ship's livestock. The trouble began when an Indian onlooker seized a cutlass that Gray's servant, a Cape Verde Islander named Marcos López, had left stuck in the sand. López and three others pursued the thief and caught him but in the melee López was killed and the other sailors, after slashing one attacker to death with cutlasses, succeeded in getting into a boat and to the sloop offshore. Captain Gray then directed the *Lady Washington*'s swivel gun at the pursuing canoes and drove them back to shore.

A month after the Tillamook fight and with the help of two British traders already at anchor there, Gray brought his sloop into Nootka Sound. Within a few days Captain Kendrick arrived in the *Columbia Rediviva* after a rough passage around the Horn.

The traders spent a successful winter bartering for sea otter and other skins, and in the spring of 1789 Kendrick ordered the furs loaded on the *Columbia* and turned the sloop over to Gray to sail to Canton. At Whampoa, the great traders' anchorage in the Canton River, the *Columbia* threaded its way among East India Company merchantmen, tea boats, and sampans, and in the bustling warehouses Gray sold the furs for more than $20,000—half of which he paid out in fees, bribes, and ship repairs. He took on a cargo of 21,462 pounds of tea with the remainder of the money and sailed home to Boston. On August 10, 1790, after a three-year absence, the *Columbia* anchored off Nantucket, the first American ship to circumnavigate the globe.

After less than two months ashore, Gray was rehired by the company of Boston merchants and now, as part owner of the *Columbia*, fitted his ship out for a return to the Pacific. In June 1791, after an uneventful voyage, Gray navigated his ship to its anchorage in Clayoquot Sound on the island above the Strait of Juan de Fuca and again began searching for Indians willing to trade sea otter pelts. And he was not alone. That year no fewer than twenty-eight vessels, flying the flags of France, Portugal, England, and the United States, visited the northwest coast, more than half of the number engaged in the fur trade.

Little is known of Gray's activities after he reached Clayoquot Sound except that his volcanic temper created deadly conflicts with the natives. He lost his chief mate and several seamen to Haida tribesmen in the Queen Charlotte Islands soon after he arrived, and in January 1792 one of his trading outposts ashore—its whereabouts are not precisely known—was attacked by a large force of Indians. The assault was beaten back and resulted in Gray's seamen burning a large native village.

In April 1792 Gray sailed the *Columbia* on a trade mission downcoast and in returning north on April 29 encountered the exploring ship *Discovery*, commanded by the English navigator George Vancouver. This brilliant young seaman had sailed from Falmouth, England, rounded the Cape of Good Hope to make the passage to Australia, then sailed across the Pacific. He had made a survey and mapping of the coast from San Diego to Alaska and would soon become the first explorer to circumnavigate the big island subsequently named for him.

Vancouver and his officers boarded the *Columbia* and exchanged information with Gray. On April 27, the master mariner said he had sighted the mouth of a river but, "not considering this opening worthy of more attention," had sailed on north. The *Columbia* was the first ship he had seen in eight months. Gray in turn told Vancouver that he had recently "been off the mouth of a river," in the latitude of 46 degrees 10 minutes, "where the outset, or reflux, was so strong as to prevent my entering." On that occasion the *Columbia* apparently stood out to sea and did not attempt to enter the mouth of the river first sighted by Bruno de Heçeta seventeen years before.

On May 11, 1792, Gray brought his ship back to the estuary, braved the whipping seas, and after eleven days found a passage through, crossed the bar, and anchored ten miles within the entrance. A party of thirty men sailed a cutter thirty miles upstream, found a Chinook village, and thereafter the ship was visited by numerous Indian canoes bringing furs to trade. Bad weather prevented the *Columbia* from escaping the estuary until May 20, by which time Gray named the river after his ship and claimed the territory around it in the name of the United States.

After breaking through the river's mouth in May, he took the *Columbia* to Nootka Sound and continued to trade for furs so that by the time he sailed for Canton in the fall of 1792 he had 700 sea otter skins and 1,500 other furs on board, which he traded for tea, nankeens (garments made of a natural yellow cotton), sugar, and porcelain.

George Vancouver's expedition was no less successful. His *Discovery* and armed tender *Chatham* made eighteen anchorages on the northwest coast and named such sites as Puget Sound (for its chief explorer, Lieutenant Peter Puget), Cape Dungeness, Admiralty Inlet, Port Orchard, Port Discovery, Whidbey and Vashon Islands, Bellingham Bay, and the Gulf of Georgia.

Vancouver's report to the Admiralty was lavish in its description of the lands he visited or saw through his spyglass. He wrote, "The serenity of the climate, the innumerable pleasing landscapes, and the abundant fertility that unassisted nature puts forth, require only to be enriched by the industry of man with villages, mansions, cottages, and other buildings, to render it the most lovely country that can be imagined."

On June 4, 1792, the birthday of George III, Vancouver took possession of the land from Puget Sound to 50 degrees north and named it New Georgia.

□

After Gray's departure, his commander John Kendrick took the *Lady Washington* to the Sandwich Islands, where he dreamed of developing a trade in sandalwood and pearls, then continued on to China, remaining there fourteen months. He returned to the Pacific coast in 1791, visiting Japan en route, *Lady Washington* being the first American ship to drop anchor in the waters of that forbidden land.

In December 1794 Kendrick was killed in a bizarre accident as his ship lay at anchor off Honolulu. The British trader *Jackal*, anchored adjacent to the American vessel, fired its saluting cannon to honor Kendrick, but the gun had been inadvertently "shotted"—loaded with round- and grapeshot—which pierced the side of the *Washington* and decapitated Kendrick as he sat at a mess table.

Robert Gray died of yellow fever during a voyage along the Atlantic coast in 1806. Of his accomplishments, historian Samuel Eliot Morison wrote: "On her first voyage, the *Columbia* solved the riddle of the China trade. On her second, empire followed in her wake."

4

Alexander Mackenzie of Lewis Island, the northernmost point of the Outer Hebrides of Scotland, has the distinction of being the first European to reach the Pacific Northwest coast from the interior of the continent, preceding Meriwether Lewis and William Clark by twelve years.

He seems to have had the heart of an explorer from the onset of his career when in 1779, at age fifteen, he became a clerk in a fur-trading company in Montreal. Possessed of "a vigorous mind and a fine physique," as Bancroft put it, he devoted all his free time to poring over the primitive maps of North America available to him, made a trip to London to study astronomy and navigation, and read assiduously the literature of New World explorations, including Jonathan Carver's book, and particularly the journals of Captain Cook's third voyage in 1778.

Mackenzie was also greatly influenced by the American-born North West Company fur trader Peter Pond, a former soldier and

seaman whose adventures had taken him from fights at Fort Ti-
conderoga and the siege of Montreal to the West Indies; who had
fought at least one duel (and killed his opponent), explored the
Upper Mississippi country, and had traded among the Yankton
Sioux and the Lake Superior Ojibway. Pond spent two years as a
trader in Saskatchewan and was credited with the 1780 discovery
of the Peace River, one of the chief headstreams of what was to
become the Mackenzie River.

Pond and Mackenzie seem to have met at Fort Chipewyan on
Lake Athabaska in northern Alberta in 1787, and there Mackenzie
saw a map Pond had drawn, based on his own explorations and
from what he had learned from Indian friends. The map depicted
a river flowing out of Lake Athabaska to Great Slave Lake, 250
miles to the northwest. Pond believed this river flowed on to the
Pacific and that its mouth was an inlet on the Alaskan coast described in Cook's journals.

In 1788 Pond quit the fur trade, sold his interest in the North
West Company for £800, and returned to his home in Connecticut.
Mackenzie, adopting Pond's river theory, set out from Fort Chip-
ewyan on June 3, 1789, to prove it.

With a party of four *voyageurs*, a German friend, and an Indian
named English Chief serving as hunter and interpreter, Mackenzie
reached Great Slave Lake and made swift progress down the river
Pond had described. The Scotchman soon realized that the river,
which turned out to be 1,120 miles in length, would not reach the
Pacific, but instead flowed northwest and debouched into the Arctic
Ocean. He reached its mouth on the Beaufort Sea and, after chasing
whales and paddling among the icebergs "under the starless summer sky and never setting summer sun of the hyperborean sea," he
returned by the same route, investigating along the way any tributary that might take him west to the Pacific. He arrived at Fort
Chipewyan on September 12, after 102 days on the river that
would henceforth bear his name.

The river passage to the Pacific never strayed far from Mackenzie's mind, but three years were to pass before he could undertake a
new expedition to find it. On October 10, 1792, he again embarked

from Fort Chipewyan and proceeded up the Peace River to the foot-hills of the northern Rocky Mountains, where stood the farthest-flung western trading post of the North West Company. He outfitted there and chose a trusted (and ill-fated) friend, Alexander McKay, as his second-in-command. With a twenty-five-foot birch-bark canoe loaded with 3,000 pounds of supplies, Mackenzie and his ten-member party pushed off a place called Fork Fort on May 9, 1793, and made a heroic portage around the Peace River canyon. In his search for a waterway that would carry him west to the ocean, Mac-kenzie often acted on information given to him by Indians and often on his own instinct, the latter taking him on a difficult and mistaken detour down the Fraser River. In mid-July the party crossed a 6,000-foot defile in the subsequently named Mackenzie Range, and de-scended the Fraser (which the explorer mistakenly thought was the Columbia) to the Bella Coola River and to its discharge into a narrow canal. This waterway emptied into Queen Charlotte Sound just north of Vancouver Island and by negotiating it, Mackenzie and his party reached Pacific tidewater on July 20, 1793.

He returned along the same route to caches of buried pemmican along the Fraser, reached Fork Fort on August 24, and a month later was back at Fort Chipewyan to resume his work as a fur trader. He made no further explorations.

Mackenzie's *Voyages from Montreal Through the Continent of North America*, published in 1801, was widely read and esteemed for its modesty and felicity of language. Thomas Jefferson was among the book's ardent admirers, as were the president's trans-continental agents, Messrs. Lewis and Clark, who carried the book to the Pacific on their own expedition in 1804.

For his services to the crown, Mackenzie was knighted in 1802 by King George III. Sir Alexander retired to Scotland in 1805, mar-ried, enjoyed his children, and died at his home at Mulinearn on March 12, 1820, at the age of fifty-six.

3

NOOTKA SOUND

1

John Ledyard seemed destined to make his mark in the crowded exploration decade of 1778–1788 when Cook, La Pérouse, Barkley, Gray, and Mackenzie were finding, refinding, and defining the northwestern Pacific coast. No man of his time, with the exception of his patron Thomas Jefferson, had a greater vision of what the region could mean to the United States than this half-mad seeker of a "passage to glory."

Ledyard was born in Groton, Connecticut, in 1751, the eldest of six children of a sea captain in the West Indies trade. After his father's death in 1762, he lived with his grandparents and at age twenty-one, acting on an ill-defined ambition to "minister to the Indians," undertook missionary training at Dartmouth. Not long after he began his theological studies, however, he ran afoul of certain stringent rules, and for his insolence and disobedience obliged the college by leaving it. Now disinherited by his family, he signed aboard a merchant ship out of New London bound for the Barbary Coast of North Africa, but deserted when the ship reached Falmouth, England. He was arrested in Bristol, jailed, and eventually given the choice of sailing aboard a ship departing for the Guinea coast or "taking the King's shilling"—enlisting in the army. Ledyard chose the army, transferred to the Royal Marines, and, in July 1776, as his home country launched its Revolutionary War, he learned of Captain Cook's preparations to launch his third voyage to the Great South Sea. With typical brashness, he sought an audience with Cook to ask for a billet, and the eminent navigator was sufficiently curious about the tall, powerfully built American at his doorstep to permit him across the threshold. Ledyard, an intelligent, excitable talker, explained his mission and told his history. Cook was impressed with his visitor's "ardent nature," and the Connecticut Yankee in King Cook's court left the lodging with the rank of corporal of marines on the *Resolution*, the only American in the expedition.

The *Discovery* and the *Resolution* sailed from Plymouth on July 12, 1776, and Ledyard kept a journal of the expedition's progress to the Cape of Good Hope, the outer waters of Antarctica, Van Diemen's Land (Tasmania), Australia, New Zealand, Tahiti, the Sandwich Islands, and of the voyage along the North American coast, which was reached in March 1778. At Nootka Sound on the western shore of Vancouver Island Ledyard studied the island's natives and reflected on his long absence from home. He wrote, "This was the first fair opportunity I had of examining the appearance of those unknown aborigines of North America. It was the first time too that I had been so near the western shores of that continent which gave me birth; and though more than 2000 miles distant from the nearest part of New England I felt myself painfully affected."

One of the American's notable adventures occurred when Cook guided his ships northward and anchored off Unalaska, one of the largest of the Aleutian chain. Ledyard was among the shore party that found traces of other "civilized" visitors—campfires, rusted iron traps, a black waistcoat—and he volunteered to conduct a search of the island for the white men who had abandoned the belongings. With native guides he located a camp of Russian trappers who greeted him warmly and invited him to share their meal of whale meat and broiled salmon. Using sign language and drawings, he learned that the Russians came to the Alaskan coast every year from Kamchatka to trap sable, fox, ermine, beaver, and sea otter and to trade for these skins among the natives. Ledyard learned of the Siberian and Chinese markets for the furs and the enormous profits to be made from them.

After Cook's death in the Sandwich Islands in 1779, his officers continued the expedition, returned north, sailed along the Russian Asiatic coast, called at Macao and Canton, and returned to Plymouth in October 1780 after a voyage of four years and three months.

In 1782 Ledyard returned to the United States and made his way to Groton a few weeks after the British surrender at Yorktown.

With publication of his *A Journal of Captain Cook's Last Voyage to the Pacific* in 1783, Ledyard became something of a celebrity, with newspapers referring to him as "the Great American Traveler." He was afire with schemes born from his Pacific adventures. He wanted to captain a ship that would round the Horn and sail to Nootka Sound, proceed to Alaska, and there trade in furs to take to China to exchange for tea, silks, and spices. With the profits from this venture he proposed to mount an expedition to cross the continent east to west and establish an American fur-trading post at Nootka, thus anticipating accomplishments by Lewis and Clark, and the German-born fur entrepreneur John Jacob Astor.

Supremely self-confident, vigorous, and possessing an infectious enthusiasm and the enviable history of having James Cook as his mentor and the *Resolution* as his classroom, Ledyard carried his visonary ideas to New England financiers. He earned their interest—who would not be interested, at least, in hearing the Great American Traveler recount his adventures and ideas?—but not their backing, and decided to try his luck in Europe.

Dependent on the income from his *Journal* and loans from his brother for his daily expenses, the "mad, romantic, dreaming Ledyard," as he called himself, took a room in a Paris hostelry. As a celebrated American expatriate he managed to meet such sympathetic compatriots as the American minister to France Benjamin Franklin, his successor Thomas Jefferson, the Marquis de Lafayette, and the naval hero Captain John Paul Jones. All were impressed by Ledyard's exploits, and Jefferson later wrote of him as "a man of genius, of some science, of fearless courage and enterprise."

At this time, John Paul Jones happened to be in Paris and became so ignited by Ledyard's ideas that he engaged in planning to fit out a trade ship, which he would master, to take his partner to the Pacific. Perhaps even two ships, the two decided, might be necessary, one of which would be left with Ledyard at Nootka Sound while the other carried furs to Canton and returned with a cargo of Chinese luxuries.

This scheme fell apart when Jones learned from the American chargé d'affaires in Madrid that Spain was "too jealous to permit any commercial speculation" in its Pacific lands. Ledyard also failed to interest French authorities in forming a mercantile company to engage in the fur trade in the Pacific Northwest.

Dismayed and all but penniless but still brimming with ideas and ardor, Ledyard paid a visit to Thomas Jefferson, now American minister to France, in the summer of 1786. The two had met before—it was Jefferson who introduced Ledyard to Jones—and had corresponded regularly. The future president had noted in his diary that in past talks with Ledyard, "I suggested to him the enterprise of exploring the western part of our continent, by passing through St. Petersburg, then across Russia to Kamchatka, and procuring a passage thence in some of the Russian vessels to Nootka Sound, whence he might make his way across the continent." Now Ledyard eagerly seized on this grandiose idea and in his perfervid talks about it, Jefferson noted, "only asked to be assured of the permission of the Russian Government. . . . I undertook to have the permission [from Empress Catherine II] solicited. He [Ledyard] eagerly embraced the proposition."

The Great American Traveler departed London for Saint

Petersburg in December 1786 with a letter of introduction from
Jefferson (describing the bearer as a man of "much singularity of
character") and ten guineas in his pocket. He traveled to Hamburg
and to Stockholm, and after walking halfway across the frozen
Gulf of Bothnia before finding open water blocking him, he returned to Stockholm. After a brief recuperation, he set out north
through Swedish Finland and Lapland on the 1,200-mile journey
to the Russian capital. Sheltered, and sustained by a diet of salt
herring, milk, and bread given him by strangers in hamlets and
farms along his route, Ledyard arrived in Saint Petersburg in March
1787.

Upon learning of this astonishing perambulation, Jefferson
wrote a friend, "I had a letter from Ledyard lately. He had but two
shirts, and yet more shirts than shillings. Still he was determined
to obtain the palm of being the first circumnambulator of the
earth."

In his several weeks in Saint Petersburg, Ledyard managed to
obtain a paper permitting him to proceed across Siberia to the Russian maritime provinces. Somehow—perhaps because he was an
oddity, an American carrying a letter from Jefferson, and the author of a book about Cook's last voyage—he was able to travel
the first 3,000 miles across the steppes, to Novosibirsk, in a *kibitka*,
a three-horse carriage-sleigh, accompanied part of the way by a
Scottish physician employed by Empress Catherine. From the Ural
Mountain town of Barnaul, he joined a party of government cour-
iers to Irkutsk on Lake Baikal, "driving with wild Tartar horses
over a wild and ragged country," and after a few days' rest traveled
with another governmental party down the Lena River to the fur-
trading outpost of Yakutsk. They reached the forbidding place in
September 1787, with dropping temperatures and winter winds
preventing his continuing east to the Sea of Okhotsk and his goal,
the peninsula of Kamchatka, the jumping-off spot for a crossing of
the North Pacific to Nootka Sound.

Ledyard wrote in his journal at Yakutsk, "This is the third time
I have been overtaken and arrested by winter; and both the others,

by giving time for my evil genius to rally hosts about me, have defeated the enterprise. Fortune, thou hast humbled me at last."

But then he had an experience awaiting him more humbling than the Siberian winter. In the spring of 1788, as he prepared to continue eastward, Ledyard was arrested on orders from Empress Catherine and accused, inexplicably, of being "a French spy." The accusation was in fact a ruse. The French ambassador to Russia investigated the matter at the request of Ledyard's friend from his Paris days, the Marquis de Lafayette, and reported that the empress's actions probably "disguised her unwillingness to have the new possessions of Russia on the western coast of America seen by an enlightened citizen of the United States."

Ledyard, of course, did not know this as he was hurried under armed escort to the Polish frontier. "The royal dame has taken me out of my way," he wrote as he made his way back to London, there to report his harrowing tale to the author of his journey.

Jefferson noted in his autobiography, "Thus failed the first attempt to explore the western part of our northern continent."

□

Ledyard was driven by the conviction that he was destined to make an indelible mark in history and was thus able to bear his misadventures gracefully and with honest, self-deprecating humor. His utter confidence that he would succeed in some great enterprise had an infectious quality. He was eager, daring, inexhaustible—he had proven it—and he was believed.

In London, even while he was regaining his health and strength, Ledyard cast about for some new endeavor. He visited the eminent botanist and promoter of explorations Sir Joseph Banks, who proposed that the Great Traveler's future lay not in America but in Africa. Banks told of an exploration of the sources of the Niger River being sponsored by the Association for Promoting the Discovery of the Interior Parts of Africa, and Ledyard fairly leaped on the idea.

"When can you be ready?" Sir Joseph asked.

"Tomorrow morning," his guest said.

Banks advanced him the funds to travel to Cairo, where the expedition was to be launched. There, in Turkish-controlled Egypt, Ledyard wrote apologetically to Thomas Jefferson, who had expressed disappointment that the Traveler seemed to have abandoned his ideas of exploring the American West. Jefferson later wrote James Madison that Ledyard "promises me, if he escapes his [present] journey, he will go to Kentucky, and endeavor to penetrate westwardly to the South Sea [the Pacific]."

Compared to Ledyard's incomparable crossing of Russia and Siberia, such a transcontinental journey might well have been accomplished with relative ease. Certainly no single man of his time had better credentials to attempt it.

But in Cairo in January 1789 Ledyard's impatience grew to fury at repeated postponements of the caravan that was to take him into the African interior, and he died suddenly on the tenth of the month.

Jefferson, who apparently investigated the details behind the loss of his "man of genius," explained that "Mr. Ledyard took offense at the delay and threw himself into a violent rage with his conductors, which deranged something in his system that he thought to cure by an emetic, but he took the dose so strong as at the first or second effect of its operation to burst a blood vessel—in three days he was suffocated and died."

The Traveler, Jefferson later remarked, "was a person of ingenuity" who "unfortunately had too much imagination," an extraordinary thing for a man of such ingenuity and imagination to say. Ledyard was Jefferson's agent of action, the man who saw the Pacific littoral with his own eyes, envisioned it as America's *mare nostrum* of the future, and shared his vision with the future president.

The ingenious and imaginative idea of an exploration of the western American continent with which Thomas Jefferson had inspired John Ledyard, and which he so mightily tried to accomplish, would have to wait another fifteen years.

2

Spanish claims of sovereignty over the coastal lands of western North America originated with a papal bull in 1494, fifty years before Juan Rodríguez Cabrillo's expedition actually set out from La Natividad. Subsequently, Spain sent other expeditions from Mexican ports, and galleons from the Philippines, their holds laden with silks, damasks, spices, porcelains, wax, and other exotic goods of the Far East. These vessels followed the Great Circle from Manila northeast toward Japan, then due east along the 41st parallel to the vicinity of Cape Mendocino and down the California coast.

With such voyages and its first actual land-based foothold, the *presidio* of San Diego, which was established in 1769, Spain made its presence known from Baja California to Cape Mendocino and sent occasional expeditions as far north as Vancouver Island and even into the Bay of Alaska. But in the fifteen years between Cook's voyage in 1778 and the beginning of their war with Napoleonic France, the British were preeminent in breaking the shaky grasp the Spanish held in the sea-lanes along and above the Oregon coast.

Furs, the sea otter in particular, and the riches they represented in the China trade drove the English as they had Russians and Frenchmen before them, and the Americans soon to come. The fur trade gave a new and perfect meaning to the old Spanish phrase for the mythical lands of the Pacific Northwest—the "Coast of Cathay"—and at the center of it was an obscure dimple on the ragged western shore of Vancouver Island named for the principal Indian clan inhabitating its shores.

Nootka Sound, discovered by the Spaniards, charted by Barkley and Cook, was a small detour on the sea trails to Old Oregon, but it had a significant role in the story. The place was known to Northwest explorers and fur traders for two centuries; the Indians inhabiting Nootka Island and the fringes of the Sound surrounding it posed "problems" for British and American traders that often erupted into violence, and it became the arena where contending nations fought over the sea otter, the China trade, and rights to settlement on the Pacific coast of America.

All these matters—exploration, exploitation, Indian problems, international conflict—were exemplified by the 1788 adventure of a British seaman-entrepreneur named John Meares.

□

The historical verdict on Meares is mixed: To some of his contemporaries he was a tireless, driven, intrepid figure like Ledyard, anxious to make a contribution to his nation as well as to history. To others, and to virtually all modern historians, he was an egoistic, relatively talentless rogue, full of high-sounding rhetoric but fundamentally little more than a self-promoting fortune-seeker who happened to trigger, as such frenetic blunderers often do, an international incident.

Born in 1756, Meares served as a lieutenant in the British navy and after the Peace of Paris of 1783, which settled the American Revolutionary War, entered the merchant service. He took command of a ship bound for India and in Calcutta organized a commercial house to trade on the Pacific Rim of North America. In this enterprise he was much influenced by the publication of Cook's *Voyages to the Pacific Ocean* in 1784, and by the reports of Cook's successor in command of the *Discovery* on the great value placed on sea otter skins in the Orient.

Meares learned of other voyages between England, Nootka, and the trading emporiums at Macao and Canton that resulted in immense profits for their sponsors. He acted on the information with his customary zeal. He gathered the funds to outfit two trade ships, named them after his destination and quarry—*Nootka*, a 200-ton vessel, and *Sea Otter*, at 100 tons—and put to sea in February 1786 with a consignment of opium to be delivered to Malacca on the Malay Peninsula before setting a course for the north Pacific.

Meares, commanding the *Nootka*, arrived in the Aleutian Islands in August and island-hopped around the misty shores from Attu to Unalaska, where he found a good anchorage and discovered a Russian trappers' camp. He and his crew were treated cordially by these bearded, fur-bedecked, Cossack-like hunters, and Meares, thirsty for information on the sea otter potential of the region, seems to have found ways to question the Russians at length. Like Ledyard, he was an excellent interrogator and observer.

The Russians, he wrote, came to Alaska from Kamchatka in "galleots" (small oar-and-sail galleys), each carrying from sixty to eighty men. "They heave their vessels up the same convenient station here," he said, and "hunt sea-otters and other animals whom nature has cloathed in furs. The natives of the different districts are also employed in the same occupation, and are obliged to give the fruits of their toil, as a tribute to the Empress of Russia, to whom the trade exclusively belongs." He discovered that the natives received "small quantities of snuff, of which they are immoderately fond" for their furs, "and obtaining that favorite article, they are content with their wretched condition, from whence, as far as respects any exertions of their own, they will never emerge."

Anxious to find his own fur-trade below the Russian outposts in the Aleutians, Meares took the *Nootka* into the Bay of Alaska that summer and anchored in Prince William Sound to await the *Sea Otter*'s arrival. The sister ship never came; indeed she was never seen again, presumably lost at sea.

Meares gave some thought to making a run for the Sandwich Islands to spend the winter but decided that his men, restless, some ill with scurvy, and all dreaming of loading the *Nootka* with furs and making their fortunes in Canton, might desert the ship. He preferred the rigors of a winter at latitude 60 degrees north to the possible ruination of his mission.

By January 1787 twenty-three of the *Nootka* crew had contracted scurvy (Captain Cook carried kegs of sauerkraut on his ships and thus defeated this ancient sailors' scourge) and eight men, including the ship surgeon and pilot, died. In April, with warm weather returning, local natives brought fish and game to Meares' camp and in that month another trade ship, the *Queen Charlotte*, entered the sound and, although Meares had to pay for provisions, the ship was welcomed "as a guardian angel."

With the help of crewmen and the ship's carpenter from the *Charlotte*, the *Nootka* sailors spent a month refitting their ship, caulking seams, and mending shredded sails and rigging. Meares paid for services with his trade goods and in June set sail for Honolulu. There, after more refitting and the recuperation of his crew, he continued on to Macao with the meager collection of furs he had bartered for among the natives at Prince William Sound.

By now he had a new scheme in mind. Despite his disastrous experiences in Alaskan waters, the loss of crewmen from scurvy, and the disappearance of the *Sea Otter*, Meares was aflame with the notion of establishing a British fur-trading post at Nootka Sound and building a small fleet of trade vessels to ply coastal waters from Vancouver Island down along the Oregon coast bartering for furs. He seems to have had little concern about the excellent chance that his enterprise would meet opposition from the Spaniards, who claimed the territory by right of discovery, and he knew his home country would not sanction his activities. To avoid such conflicts, he flew the Portuguese flag from his mainmast, thereby using, also without permission, the port of Macao as a front for his activities.

In Macao, through some never-explained financial prestidigitation, Meares managed to get rid of the decrepit *Nootka* and purchase a 230-ton brig, the *Felice*. At Canton he employed several Chinese "artisans" (actually carpenters) to build his factory and trade schooner. He also took aboard the *Felice* a young Vancouver Island native named Comekela, who had been taken to China the year before as a crewmen on another trade vessel. Comekela was the brother of Maquinna, chief of the Nootka people, and a compelling, if not sinister, figure in events to come.

□

In April 1788, nearly four months out of Canton, the *Felice* anchored in Friendly Cove, abreast of the village of Nootka, on the southern tip of Nootka Island, at the entrance to Nootka Sound. The *hetman* Maquinna came out to greet the ship with a great war-canoe assemblage. "They moved with great parade round the ship," Meares wrote. "There were twelve of these canoes, each of which contained about eighteen men, the greater part of whom were cloathed in dresses of the most beautiful skins of sea otter, which covered them from their neck to their ancles." He said Maquinna and his entourage wore white bird down in their hair, "and there faces bedaubed with red and black ochre, in the form of a shark's jaw, and a kind of spiral line, which rendered their appearance extremely savage."

The Nootkans fascinated Meares. They lived in sturdy wooden houses, hunted whales with bone-headed harpoons, fished for salmon and herring—their staple diet—and highly prized *olachen* oil, which was extracted from candlefish and used in cooking. They were adept with harpoons and knives in sea otter hunts, a dangerous business at close quarters when some of the animals measured six feet from nose to tip of tail and were ferocious when cornered.

Maquinna, he said, wore a royal otter-fur dress and a high, conical cap feathered at the point, and "appeared to be about thirty years, of a middle size, but extremely well made, and possessing a countenance that was formed to interest all who saw him."

That chameleonic countenance, before which traders in years to come would cringe in fear, seemed to smile on Meares. The chief was no doubt more pleased that his brother Comekela had been delivered home than by the gifts the Englishman presented to him— "copper, iron, and other gratifying articles." On the *Felice*, Meares wrote, Maquinna shrugged out of his otter garments "and threw them, in the most graceful manner, at our feet, and remained in the unattired garb of nature on the deck."

Meares negotiated with Maquinna for a parcel of land to build his factory and schooner and said the chief "not only most readily consented to grant us a spot of ground . . . but promised us also his assistance in forwarding our works." The two-story log structure was completed on the Nootka shore at the end of April. Meares would later say he "purchased" the land for a brace of pistols, a claim denied by Maquinna.

While the fort and ship were under construction, Meares took the *Felice* southward to the entrance of the Strait of Juan de Fuca and continued to Cape Flattery, the Columbia River estuary (which

Spanish charts designated as San Roque but which Meares did not
rediscover, that distinction going to Robert Gray three years later).
They sailed down as far as Tillamook Head on the north Oregon
coast, taking a jollyboat crew ashore periodically to trade among
the natives. On the return voyage along the southwestern edge of
Vancouver Island, the *Felice*'s crew enjoyed such a brisk sea otter
trade that Meares dispatched his first officer, Robert Duffin, and
several sailors in a longboat to penetrate the Strait of Juan de Fuca
to investigate the trade potential east of Cape Flattery. Instead of
finding compliant Indians eager to exchange furs for bits of iron
and copper and cheap beads, Duffin's boat was attacked by native
canoes. Four of his sailors received arrow wounds, and, said
Meares, "the rest of the people were bruised in a terrible manner
by the stones and clubs of the enemy; even the boat itself was
pierced in a thousand places by arrows."

Now the natives were the "enemy," and when Meares returned
to Nootka to supervise the building of his log fort, he "explained
his power" by ordering the throwing up of a breastwork in front
of the structure with a small ship's cannon mounted atop it.

In September, after the completion of the palisaded fort as well
as the schooner *North West America*—"the first bottom [keel] ever
built and launched in this part of the globe"—Meares sailed the
Felice to Canton with a hefty cargo of furs, leaving the Nootka
operation to be supervised by his partner, a Captain Douglas, master of the merchantman *Iphigenia*.

To Meares, his scheme was working perfectly. His experiment
with the Chinese "artisans" had resulted in the building of the fort
and schooner, he had located many profitable trading locations, he
had lorded it over Maquinna of the Nootkas, and had purchased
for a brace of pistols a factory site that would be the epicenter of
a great fur-trading monopoly.

But Meares had underestimated the Spanish resolve to protect
their interests on the Pacific Rim, and during his absence in China
his nascent fur empire fell to pieces.

During the building of the fort, a Spanish expedition returning
from investigating Russian activities on the Alaskan coast reported

to the viceroy of Mexico that the Russians were contemplating a trading post in the south to take advantage of the "commerce which the English from Canton are carrying on at Nootka." The commander of this expedition urged immediate action, and in February 1789 the viceroy dispatched two warships with a complement of soldiers "to occupy said port [Nootka] and garrison it." Several missionaries accompanied the expedition to win the goodwill of the Indians and proselytize among them. Meantime, the soldiery were to deal "with prudent firmness" with the anticipated advent of Russian traders and any English, American, or other foreign intruders.

The Spanish ships reached Nootka Sound in May. The *Iphigenia*, commanded by Meares' partner, and the newly launched *North West America* were seized. The former was later released and Douglas was permitted to sail away—which he did, to Honolulu and on to Macao. But the Spaniards claimed the *North West America* as a "prize ship," appropriated the 215 sea otter skins in its hold, placed a crew on board, changed its name to *Gertrudis*, and put it into service. Meares' factory and outbuildings were also confiscated in the name of King Carlos III.

At the time of these seizures, the American ships *Columbia Rediviva* and *Lady Washington* were also anchored in Nootka Sound but were not interned, and their skippers, John Kendrick and Robert Gray, were permitted to come and go at will. Kendrick was even allowed to take some of the *North West America* sailors on board the *Columbia* as crew members. The Americans, after all, were not forming a permanent settlement in Spanish lands while the British stood as a symbol of invidious trespassing in Spanish territory.

In China, Meares learned of the events at Nootka Sound in November 1789, four months after the fact, found a berth on a trader, and returned to England in April 1790. There he presented a report to the government on his activities in America and on Spain's "illegal" seizure of his assets.

As it happened, Meares' document came to his government's attention at a propitious time: England was attempting to negotiate with Spain for certain rights in the fur trade in the North Pacific but had reached a stalemate. The Court of Spain, according to a report made to King George III, was maintaining "exclusive rights of sovereignty, navigation and commerce in the territories, coasts and seas in that part of the world," and Spain was said to be sending armed expeditions to reinforce its claims. Parliament urged His Majesty to "act with vigor" and approved an expenditure, if necessary, of £1,000,000 to enable the king to act "as the exigency of affairs might require."

This meant England was prepared to go to war with Spain over the rights to trade and settle the northwest coast of North America and, among other, more important matters, the British government insisted that Spain indemnify Captain Meares for his seized property at Nootka Sound.

Meares was eventually paid a large restitution—said to be, in American terms, "two hundred and ten thousand hard dollars in Specie"—and with this considerable fortune he appears to have retired. His final years are difficult to trace. His book, *Voyages Made in the Years 1788 and 1789 From China to the Northwest Coast of America*, appeared in 1790, and although he had no further active service for England, he received a promotion to commander in the Royal Navy in 1795.

Meares died in 1809 at age fifty-three.

3

On August 9, 1790, the year following Ledyard's death and four months after Meares returned to England, Captain Robert Gray and his *Columbia* crew returned to Boston from their voyage around the world. They arrived in time to witness a development bothersome to all Yankee skippers and to their government: an agreement that gave England certain trading rights in the Pacific Northwest that were denied, at least on paper, to other nations.

The Meares incident at Nootka Sound was a coincidental but pivotal event in the dispute between England and Spain over territorial rights-of-way in the north Pacific. Spain's claim of discovery had been ill-attended, its realization of the value of the fur trade in the region belated. England had its own claims of discovery—Cook's voyage in particular—and had in fact rights by virtue of occupancy of Nootka Sound, where British subject John Meares purchased land from Chief Maquinna, and south along the Oregon coast to Spanish California, where British vessels had conducted trade for a decade. The stalemate between the two countries had about it the alarming potential of a call to arms, a matter that concerned the newly elected first president of the United States. George Washington worried that if England went to war it might seek access across American territory to strike at Spanish possessions in Louisiana and Florida. To refuse such access might embroil America in the conflict. Alexander Hamilton, Washington's pro-British secretary of the treasury, favored granting the right-of-way; Secretary of State Thomas Jefferson proposed to ignore such a request if it were made.

The issue never materialized. Spain could not stand alone against England and turned to Louis XVI for assistance, but France was convulsed in revolution and unable to render aid. With no alternative but to capitulate, in October 1790 Spanish ministers signed the Nootka Sound Convention, recognizing England's right to navigate, trade, and settle along the Pacific Northwest coast above San Francisco. Each nation was to have free access to the establishments of the other in those regions.

The convention strengthened British interests in the region and signaled the end of two centuries of Spanish claims.

□

Of course, the natives of Nootka Sound were not consulted in the international debate over the lands they had inhabited for untold centuries, but the Nootkans were by now familiar with the white men who came to their island. It made no matter if they were Russian, English, Spanish, French, or American; they were all of the same template. Their despicable habits had grown intolerable. The traders had always sneered at the Indians' religious rites, trampled on village customs, threatened their chiefs, and treated the coastal people as vassals. The whites were belligerent, cheated in their trading, made a show of force at the least provocation, stole, brutalized, and murdered, all without redress.

Within a few years after their first contact with the seaborne barbarians, the Indians were regarding the trespassers as useful enemies. They were not fooled by being invited aboard the traders' "floating cities," or by the strained amity as they displayed their furs on the deck to trade for bits of metal, beads, mirrors, pots, and knives. They had learned quickly the white man's wiles and had raised the ante for their otter skins; they began to barter rather than accept any gewgaw for the wares the intruders so obviously lusted after.

Magellan had been killed by natives in the Philippines in 1521; Captain Cook underestimated the Sandwich Islanders and at Kealakekua Bay in 1779 had paid for the error with his life. Countless other intruders had tried to construct native alliances for selfish gain—territorial expansion and trade being the principal motives— without understanding or respecting the natives. It seemed to be the white man's way.

Some of the trespassers on the northwest coast of America did not see Cook's or the other historical examples as instructive, but thirteen years after the Nootka Sound Convention they were taught an abrupt and bloody lesson.

4

The man who fatally exasperated Chief Maquinna of the Nootkas was Captain John Salter, and we know little about him before he brought his trading vessel to Vancouver Island in the spring of 1803. Judging from what appears to be his chronic exasperation with the natives, he was probably a veteran of the North Pacific sea-lanes and may have known Maquinna from a previous voyage.

Salter sailed from Dover in September 1802 with a crew of twenty-nine on the *Boston*, laden with trade goods. The merchantman doubled the Horn and on March 12, 1803, anchored five miles inside Nootka Sound just beyond the notch on the shore called Friendly Cove. While crew members were busy filling water casks and gathering wood for galley fires, canoes were pushed off from the beach and Maquinna and a dozen of his men made the first of several visits to the ship, bringing their furs and haggling over the trade items displayed on the *Boston*'s deck. Salter, following the tradition of presenting the chief with a special gift, gave Maquinna an old double-barreled fowling piece.

Trouble erupted on the twenty-first as Salter and his crew were preparing the ship to proceed downcoast to trade among the other coastal people. Maquinna's canoes paid a farewell visit and he and his courtiers clambered aboard. The chief brought a gift of a string of wild ducks for Salter, but he also brought the old gun with him, complaining that it didn't work, was *peshak*—bad. An armorer on the *Boston*, a twenty-year-old blacksmith's son named John Jewitt who had shipped aboard the trader at Hull and who kept a diary of the voyage, witnessed the exchange between the captain and the chief.

"Captain Salter was very much offended at this observation," Jewitt wrote, "and considering it as a mark of contempt for his present, he called the king a liar, adding other opprobrious terms, and taking the gun from him tossed it indignantly into the cabin." Maquinna "said not a word in reply, but his countenance sufficiently expressed the rage he felt, though he exerted himself to suppress it, and I observed him while the Captain was speaking repeatedly put his hand to his throat and rub it upon his bosom, which he afterwards told me was to keep down his heart, which was rising into his throat and choking him."

Maquinna knew enough English to understand Salter's words and left the trader in a rage. The next day, just hours before the *Boston* was to set sail, the chief returned to the ship amidst a small convoy of war canoes. He and twenty of his men were permitted aboard while the other canoes circled the *Boston*'s hull. Maquinna presented Salter with a bundle of salmon and suggested the captain might send some men out on a seining expedition and store the fish in the larder. Salter liked this idea and dispatched nine men in a yawl and a jollyboat to Friendly Cove, where the *hetman* said salmon were plentiful.

Despite these ominous events—the number of natives on board

his ship, the number circling it in canoes, the dividing of his crew—
Salter seems to have had no suspicion of impending trouble. Maquinna, wearing what Jewitt called "a very ugly mask of wood
representing the head of some wild beast," appeared to be in good
humor, and with his people capered and danced on the deck while
Salter waited for his fishermen to return.

Jewitt, meantime, had gone below deck to work at his vise-
bench, where he was accustomed to fashioning knives and hatchets
for the Indians, sharpening cutlasses, repairing and cleaning pistols
and muskets (of which there were 3,000 on board). He was attempting to repair Maquinna's *peshak* shotgun.

"I had not been there more than an hour," he wrote later in
his journal, "when I heard the men hoisting in the long boat,
which, in a few minutes after, was succeeded by a great bustle and
confusion on deck. I immediately ran up the steerage stairs, but
scarcely was my head above deck, when I was caught by the hair
by one of the savages, and lifted from my feet; fortunately for me,
my hair being short, and the ribbon with which it was tied slipping,
I fell from his hold into the steerage."

Still, he was stuck by an ax and gashed in the forehead and fell
senseless to the floor. On the main deck, while the yawl and jollyboat were being pulled aboard, Maquinna shouted a signal and
his men sprang on the sailors, clubbed them down, and cut their
throats. Maquinna himself grappled with Salter and threw the captain over the rail, where he was killed by those in the canoes.

Groggy and covered with blood from his scalp wound, Jewitt
struggled up the steerage ladder to the deck and was taken prisoner. Maquinna then led him to a grisly display. Along the *Boston*'s rail were arranged twenty-seven heads, those of Salter and
his crew, including the nine men who had returned from the
salmon expedition. The chief demanded that the armorer identify
each and describe his own work on the ship. Jewitt fully expected
that his head would be added to the others, but Maquinna offered
to let him live providing he was willing to become the chief's slave
and serve as his master's blacksmith. Jewitt ecstatically agreed.

The only other survivor of the *Boston* massacre was a Philadelphia-born sailmaker named John Thompson, who is described as "a powerful, fearless, violent sailor of about forty years of age"; he was found hiding in the hold, his face slashed and bloodied. When he was dragged before Maquinna his life was also spared when Jewitt claimed that Thompson was his father.

Under the two survivors' rudimentary seamanship the *Boston* was maneuvered and towed into Friendly Cove and beached so that it could be stripped of its sails, rigging, and cargo. Soon a great crowd of natives flocked to the cove to see the ship and the loot taken from it and to deck themselves out in sailcloth and the clothing found in the slopchest. Hogsheads of rum were stove in and during the feast ashore, one drunken native, rummaging in the *Boston*'s hold, set the ship afire. It burned to the waterline.

Word of the fate of the *Boston* spread quickly, and for many months traders gave Nootka Sound a wide berth. During his three years' captivity, Jewitt managed to smuggle out some letters, written, like his diary, in boiled blackberry juice. In his waiting for rescue, he took a native wife, did blacksmithing, repaired weapons, and learned the Nootka tongue. John Thompson also went native, even to the point of joining his captors in their raiding parties against neighboring tribes.

Maquinna told Jewitt he had several times been ill-treated by foreigners, that English sea captains had entered his home and stolen furs, frightened his women, and killed many of his people. This accumulation of grievances, and Captain Salter's insults, had led to the massacre.

In July 1805 the brig *Lydia* out of Boston appeared off Friendly Cove. Her captain, Samuel Hill, had come across one of Jewitt's letters appealing for rescue and decided to investigate the fate of Salter and his ship. It appears that Maquinna agreed to meet with Hill, for Jewitt was ordered to write a letter that would absolve the chief of any blame for the massacre. The armorer wrote the letter but included in it some damning words. Maquinna took the letter aboard the *Lydia*, and Hill read it and had the chief clapped in irons.

Although Captain Hill intended executing his prisoner, Jewitt interceded and spoke of his own rescue by Maquinna and subsequent kindnesses. The appeal worked: The Nootka *hetman* was released.

In the winter, the *Lydia* set sail, crossed the Columbia bar, and anchored on its north shore. After a trading cruise and the accumulation of a valuable cache of furs, Hill proceeded to the Whampoa trading center in the Canton River. Jewitt stayed with the *Lydia* until it returned to Boston in June 1807. He published his journal, *A Narrative of the Adventures and Sufferings of John R. Jewitt; Only Survivor of the Ship*, Boston, *during a Captivity of nearly three years among the Savages of Nootka Sound*, that year and thereafter disappeared from the historical record.

□

While the *Lydia* stood at anchor in the Columbia estuary in November 1805, a group of Clatsop Indians visited the ship and proudly displayed to Captain Hill some medals recently given to them. The bronze pieces were stamped with the likeness of President Jefferson and the natives said they had gotten them from two white men who had recently come downriver leading several other men. Jewitt, who understood enough of their language to serve as translator, learned that the two leaders, Lewis and Clark, had just departed the area to return home on their overland route.

Jewitt must have mistranslated. In truth, on November 25, 1805, only a few days before the Indians' representations, Meriwether Lewis and William Clark and their Corps of Discovery left the exposed northern shore of the Columbia for the more protected woods on the south bank. At the moment the Indians were talking to Captain Hill, the explorers were camped just out of the *Lydia*'s view, in the dense forest, surveying a site for the winter quarters they would name Fort Clatsop.

They all might have returned home in the *Lydia*, might at least have benefited from the ship's supplies, but neither the explorers nor the *Lydia*'s party knew the other's proximity when Captain Hill put to sea for Canton.

Part Two

ASTORIA

4

PRO PELLE CUTEM

"PERSEVERANCE"

1

Among his many professions—planter, magistrate, chancery court judge, sheriff, militiaman—Colonel Peter Jefferson was a surveyor and mapmaker, and good at both. He helped mark the boundary between Virginia and Carolina in 1749, and with another man made a map of Virginia in 1751 that was regarded as definitive for its time. He died when his son was but fourteen, but by then the gangly, red-haired boy was already poring over maps, his protean mind always exploring. He studied astronomy, navigation, shipbuilding, and the journals of the world's explorers, and held a high regard for the maxim of Henry the Navigator of Portugal: "You cannot find a peril so great that the hope of reward will not be greater."

He would never stray far west of his native Virginia, but twenty years before he became president, Thomas Jefferson had fixed his map-filled imagination on the great blank space between the Mississippi and the Pacific and was encouraging its exploration. While governor of Virginia and a delegate to the Continental Congress in the 1780s, he asked his friend George Rogers Clark, the renowned frontiersman and Indian fighter, to lead an expedition west of the Mississippi. This plan did not materialize, but Jefferson's pursuit of it continued. In 1786, when minister to France, he met John Ledyard and proposed to that fellow visionary "the enterprise of exploring the western part of our continent." Ledyard's heroic effort ended in Siberia in September 1787, but even when the frustrated Traveler turned his attention to Africa, Jefferson held out the hope that he would eventually "endeavor to penetrate westwardly" to the Pacific. In 1793, while serving as George Washington's secretary of state, Jefferson gave advice and support to the French botanist André Michaud, who was preparing to lead a party of scientists to the Pacific under the sponsorship of the American Philosophical Society. Apart from the scientific work, Jefferson urged, Michaud should concentrate on finding "the shortest and most convenient route of communication between the U.S. and the Pacific ocean." But when Napoleonic France declared war on England, Michaud's plans had to be terminated.

A decade passed before Jefferson, now president, was able to strike an epochal bargain that made his ambition for western exploration a necessity. On April 30, 1803, the president's negotiators in Paris signed a treaty, the most consequential state paper in American history excepting only the Declaration of Independence and the Constitution, by which the United States paid $15 million for the Louisiana Territory, more than a half-billion acres of wilderness five times the size of France. Although the territorial boundary would not be clarified for another sixteen years, the Louisiana Purchase roughly doubled the area of the United States, adding to the Republic the lands between the Mississippi and the Rocky Mountains and encompassing the later states of Louisiana, Arkansas, Oklahoma, Missouri, Kansas, Iowa, Nebraska and South Dakota, most of Wyoming and Montana plus portions of southwestern Minnesota and South Dakota, northeastern New Mexico, and eastern Colorado.

Three months before the Paris treaty, Jefferson, supremely con-

fident of gaining the great and largely unexplored tract and elec-
trified, as he had always been, by its potential, sent a secret message
to Congress. The letter detailed plans to explore the lands west of
the Mississippi "even to the Western Ocean, having conferences
with the natives on the subject of commercial intercourse." He
asked for an appropriation of $2,500 to finance a military expe-
dition to assert American claims to the territory and to explore a
route "across the continent, for the purpose of commerce." The
president also wanted to know about any foreign activity in the
new territory and beyond it, on the Pacific coast.

Just over a year from the signing, Meriwether Lewis, Jefferson's
private secretary and a captain of infantry, and William Clark,
younger brother of George Rogers Clark and a veteran artillery
officer, launched their Corps of Discovery into the wilderness.

□

The expedition headed out from Saint Louis on May 14, 1804,
traveling up the Missouri in a fifty-five-foot keelboat and two flat-
bottomed pirogues. In addition to the co-leaders, the party consisted of twenty-seven young, unmarried soldiers, a hunter-
interpreter, and Clark's black slave, a man named York. The
exploring party crawled up the river in the cloying heat and humidity at the rate of fifteen miles a day and wintered among the
Mandan Indian villages of the Upper Missouri. In mid-autumn they
reached the mouth of the Knife River in North Dakota and there
constructed a triangular log stockade, which they named Fort Mandan.

That winter temperatures fell to 45 degrees below zero, but the
Corps commanders made good use of their time. Hunting and
wood-cutting parties were sent out; boats, equipment, and clothing
were mended; drawings and journal entries made. Clark found a
Mandan chief who claimed to know the lands to the west and with
the expedition interpreter worked on the making of tentative
maps. Both Lewis and Clark met with delegations of Mandans,

Minatarees, and Arikaras who came in curiosity to the strange log fort on the Missouri to see the white men and to marvel over the black skin of Clark's slave.

The expedition departed Fort Mandan on April 7, 1805, to continue its journey up the Missouri, the explorers distributed among six small canoes and two large pirogues. A grueling month-long portage around the Great Falls led the expedition into the high country; in July, they reached the headwaters of the Missouri, pushed on toward a pass in the Bitterroot Mountains, and crossed the Continental Divide into Idaho. They traveled on, down the Clearwater, Snake, and Columbia Rivers, and reached the Pacific—"that ocean, the object of all our labors, the reward of all our anxieties," Lewis said, on November 8, 1805, after a journey of more than 4,000 miles. A few miles inland from the beach they built a stockade, Fort Clatsop, named for a friendly Indian tribe of the area, and settled down for the winter.

The explorers learned that the Clatsops and other native tribesmen who came to see them and their fort had become considerably familiar with white fur traders over the years and had in their vocabularies a number of common profanities and words such as *musket, powder, shot, knife, iron, copper,* and *file.* Lewis told of their bartering skills: "They begin by asking double or treble the value of their merchandise, and lower the demand in proportion to the ardor or experience in trade of the purchaser; if he expresses any anxiety, the smallest article, perhaps a handful of roots, will furnish a whole morning's negotiation." (He also took time to state that a Chinook or Clatsop "beauty" was "one of the most disgusting objects in nature," and said that in all the tribes, "a man will lend his wife or daughter for a fish-hook or a strand of beads.")

The return journey began on March 23, 1806, and in a little over three months the expedition reached the mouth of the Flathead River (Bitterroot today) at a point called Traveler's Rest. Here the commanders split up, Lewis exploring along the Missouri to probe the Maria's River, Clark south along the Yellowstone.

They rendezvoused at the juncture of the Yellowstone and Missouri, about 200 miles west of their 1805 winter quarters, and on September 23 reached Saint Louis, completing one of the most momentous explorations in history. Lewis hurried off a letter to his sponsor and benefactor: "In obedience to your orders we have penitrated the Continent of North America to the Pacific Ocean. . . ."

2

Lewis and Clark had been unable to report discovery of an all-water route from the Missouri to the Columbia, and the trail they blazed was impossible for all but the hardiest of wilderness hands, but they had begun the serious work of filling in the great blank space west of the Mississippi.

In the first decades of the nineteenth century that space was marked on maps as "Unknown" and indeed, much of what was thought to be known about it was wrong. The Great Plains—that immense tilted upland formed by the streams flowing eastward out of the Rockies toward the Mississippi—were depicted in school primers as a desert. Army explorer Zebulon Montgomery Pike, who set out from Saint Louis in 1805 searching for the source of the Mississippi, said the region had been put there by Providence "to keep the American people from a thin diffusion and ruin." He said the country was fit only for Indians, who grew no crops and lived off the buffalo who shared the plains with them.

Fifteen years later, this notion had the endorsement of Major Stephen Harriman Long of the newly created Army Topographical Engineers, sent out on an exploratory mission from Belle Fontaine, Missouri. Long and his party traveled up to the falls of Saint Anthony with orders to chart the course of the Upper Mississippi and "to exhibit the general topography of the shores, and to designate such sites as were suitable for military purposes."

The American Philosophical Society provided Long with a riverboat, the *Western Engineer*, constructed expressly to frighten hostile Indians: The vessel had a prow in the shape of a black sea serpent's head which blew steam from its mouth. (The muddy wa-

ters of the Mississippi clogged its boilers, however, and the attempt
to explore the West with it failed early.)

In his 1820 exploration, Long traveled along the Platte River to
the Rockies searching for a source of the Red River. He failed to find
it but in his five expeditions, no explorer between Lewis and Clark
and John C. Frémont was more influential, and none brought back
more a mixture of solid scientific work and wrongheaded speculation. On returning from his Red River search, Long expanded pro-
lifically on Pike's speculations by delineating a strip of land six
hundred miles wide, beginning in Texas and running to the Canadian border and from the 100th meridian to the Rocky Mountains,
as "the Great American Desert." He said this region "bore a manifest resemblance to the deserts of Siberia" and his report to his superiors in Washington contained this observation: "In regard to this
extensive section of country between the Missouri River and the
Rocky Mountains, we do not hesitate in giving the opinion that it is
almost wholly unfit for cultivation, and of course uninhabitable by a
people depending upon agriculture for their subsistence."

This myth of the Great Plains as a desert lasted fifty years and
decorated maps of the region up to the opening of the Civil War.

As for the formidable Rockies, those sprawling, ill-defined
masses of north–south ranges and valleys cut by ancient glaciers at
the Continental Divide, Long and others before him believed them
to be five miles high and a bastion as unbreachable as the Hima-
layas. They, too, seemed to represent a providential dead-end sign,
something reflected in a congressional report of the era that
warned, "Nature has fixed limits to our nation; she has kindly
interposed as our Western barrier, mountains almost inaccessible. . . .
This barrier our population can never pass."

But the barrier could be passed, indeed had been passed, by the
time of the warning, by trappers traveling up the Missouri River
to its headwaters and beyond, into the Oregon Country. French-
Canadian trappers who saw the Rockies' snowy flanks and peaks
called them *les montagnes dont la pierre luit la jour et la nuit,*
which early American fur traders translated as the Shining Mountains.

□

Among the curious features of the long story of the American journey to Old Oregon is the fact that so many of the earliest venturers
there were lured along and bound together not by any lofty motives
of exploration and discovery or by adding to knowledge, but by
the value of certain aquatic animals. *Lutra enhydris marina*, the
sea otter, drew the trade ships from New England around the Horn
to the Northwest Pacific coast; *Castor canadensis*, the beaver, lured
trappers overland from Saint Louis westward and incidentally
made explorers of them.

On its journey to the Pacific, the Corps of Discovery had encountered small parties of French-Canadians who knew the Rocky
Mountain country well as a fur hunter's paradise, and on the
Corps' return, descending the Missouri, it had encountered eleven
separate trapping parties on the river. These men had twenty boats
loaded with trade goods, and they were planning to winter among
the Arikara, Sioux, Pawnee, Crow, and other tribes and trade for
furs. Meriwether Lewis speculated on the beaver riches of the Upper Missouri in his journal, even recognizing the dangers of the
trade once the Indians of the region learned the value of the furs.

□

The commerce in furs in North America was already over two
centuries old by the time of the Lewis and Clark expedition. It had
begun with the French explorations of Jacques Cartier, which established the trade with Indian tribes in the Saint Lawrence River
valley around Montreal. In 1603, Henry IV of France sent Samuel
de Champlain to the gulf of the Saint Lawrence for the express
purpose of establishing a fur market, and until their expulsion from
North America in 1763, the French were the most successful of all
nations in the trade. They built outposts from Maine to the Great
Lakes and north into the Canadian wilderness, sending *coureurs
de bois* out among the Hurons, Ottawa, Miami, and other tribes

to barter, moving the hundred-pound packs of pelts in canoes (some so large—these called *canotes de maître*—it took a dozen men to paddle them), pirogues (hollowed-out cottonwood tree trunks, some seventy feet long and four wide), and huge keelboats capable of carrying up to twenty tons of goods along the waterways from Montreal to the Great Lakes and the Mississippi.

After navigator Henry Hudson's search for the Northwest Passage resulted in the discovery of an immense inland sea in northeast Canada in 1610, the British entered the North American fur trade with King Charles II's chartering of "The Governor and Company of Adventurers Trading in Hudson's Bay" in 1670. The Hudson's Bay Company, with a governor and seventeen noblemen as partners, was instructed to establish and maintain all the fur trade and traffic "to and from all havens, bays, creeks, rivers, lakes and seas into which they shall find entrance or passage by water or land out of the territories, limits or places aforesaid." In brief, the Company was to monopolize the fur traffic around all the lands watered by the rivers and streams emptying into Hudson Bay—a territory of about 1.5 million square miles.

The Company had as its insignia a crest depicting a moose rampant, a fox and four beavers, a Christian cross on a shield, and the scrolled motto *Pro Pelle Cutem*—"A skin for a skin."

After founding its first settlement in Prince Rupert's Land (which the Hudson's Bay territory was then called) the Company's progress was stifled by the decades of conflict between Britain and France that followed. Only after the Treaty of Paris in 1763, under which all of France's North American possessions (except Louisiana) were ceded to England, did the Company begin its true era of progress. It expanded its influence then, swarming out of Fort Garry (Winnipeg today), Mackinac, and Prairie du Chien to barter with Indians as far west as the Mandan people of the Upper Missouri, and soon into the Rocky Mountains and west to Oregon.

The Hudson's Bay Company's fur monopoly experienced its most serious challenge in 1784 when competing traders organized the North West Company—the "Nor'westers" as they were called—at Montreal. They took their coat of arms and their motto,

"Perseverance," to such trading posts as Fort Chipewyan on the Peace River in British Columbia and Fort William on Lake Superior and fought a trade war with the "Honourable Company" in Alberta and the Lake Athabasca region of Saskatchewan.

The war ended in 1820 when the rivals merged, retaining the name Hudson's Bay Company and representing British fur interests in North America.

All trappers, no matter their nationality, who ventured into Canada, roamed the shores of the Great Lakes, journeyed the continental backbone of the Rockies, or followed the Snake and Columbia Rivers into the Oregon Country eventually encountered the agents of this tightly organized and relentlessly opportunistic society, the Hudson's Bay Company.

□

By the beginning of the eighteenth century, while such furs as mink, otter, marten, sable, silver fox, weasel (or ermine as it was called when its coat turned white in the winter) were still trapped, the trade had centered on the beaver. There was a northern European–Asian variety of this aquatic rodent, *Castor fiber*, but *Castor canadensis*, teeming in the waterways of Canada and America, became especially valued in European markets. The animal had a brown, silkily rich waterproof fur prized in making felt hats, coats, muffs, linings, and other adornments; its scaly tail serving as a meat substitute in Catholic Europe, and its musky glandular secretion, *castoreum*, was extracted for perfumes and for fever and headache nostrums.

To find them and kill them, trappers had to learn the beavers' habits and history. They are social, mainly nocturnal, animals subsisting on a tree-bark diet supplemented by aquatic plants, thistles, meadow-sweet, leaves, twigs, seeds, and roots in summer. In full growth they range from two to three feet in length and weigh twenty-five to sixty-five pounds. They mate for life and live in family groups with the female birthing up to eight "kits" in each litter. The young, fully coated, can swim within hours of birth. Their tail is used for propulsion and steers like a rudder, their hind feet are large and webbed, their nose and ears seal shut when diving, and membranes protect their eyes underwater. Their life span is fifteen to twenty years.

The beaver's incisor teeth are coated with a hard orangish enamel, and a pair of the animals can gnaw through a four-inch tree or branch in fifteen minutes; a beaver family can fell 300 trees each winter. The cut logs and branches are towed underwater as stored food sources; the dams they build are reservoirs for their dome-shaped lodges of branches and mud, which have underwater entrances and a living chamber above the waterline.

They were killed by drowning. Heavy iron traps weighing five pounds each were baited with a twig smeared with the beaver's own castoreum. The trapping was ideally done in winter months, when the furs were prime, with the traps placed in the streambed at dusk and raised at dawn, and the animal was skinned on the spot. The castoreum glands and tail, a delicacy when fried, were saved, and the "peltries"—undressed hides—were scraped and stretched on a frame for drying, then folded fur side in and bundled.

The dressed hides, called "plews" (from the French *plus*, more), each weighing up to two pounds, at the peak of the trade were worth four to six dollars per pound in Saint Louis, and a bale of plews might weigh as much as 100 pounds.

Average-grade beaver furs were used by European hatters to make the surface of the tall-crowned "stovepipe" hats that were fashionable (especially after the English dandy Beau Brummell fancied them in the early 1800s) for decades on both sides of the Atlantic, and also for other hats, from tricorns to ladies' riding helmets. The long, stiff guard hairs of the pelts were picked clean and the hatter shaved the soft underfur and twanged the string of a huge bow through it, the vibrations making the hairs hook together, to mat or "felt." This matted pile was flattened, covered with wet linen, kneaded into a conical hood that was shrunken and thickened by boiling, treated with acid, and, while hot, molded into a hat shape on a wooden block. After drying and ironing, the nap was raised by brushing with a wire paddle.

The finest beaver skins were sold to furriers for capes and coats and other luxuries for the wealthy.

The French in Canada in the seventeenth and eighteenth centuries were the first to exploit and export beaver furs, followed by Spaniards, Englishmen, and Americans. The epic slaughter of this engaging animal—at the peak of the trade 100,000 beaver furs were harvested annually—would endure for 130 years.

3

The American era of the fur trade—the gaudy thirty-year adventure of mountain men—might be said to have begun when the Corps of Discovery neared the mouth of the Yellowstone River on its return from the Oregon coast. There, on August 12, 1806, the explorers, their chronometer broken and their coordinates only to be guessed at, stumbled across the camp of two Americans heading up the Yellowstone to trap beaver.

The trail-weary trappers, Illinois men named Forrest Hancock and Joseph Dickson, were as startled and delighted as Captains Lewis and Clark to see white men in the wilderness 1,500 miles from Saint Louis, and spent several days with the explorers exchanging tales and information. When the Corps departed toward the Mandan villages one of the men, a thirty-two-year-old private from Staunton, Virginia, named John Colter, was granted permission to stay behind to join the Illinoisians in their beaver hunt. By the end of the year, the three mountain men had trapped their way along the Yellowstone and taken shelter in a Rocky Mountain valley.

Hancock and Dickson endured the winter blizzards, but when the snow cleared in the spring they took their share of plews and followed Lewis and Clark's trail toward civilization. Colter stayed on alone in the mountains.

The story of this born-to-the-wilderness mountain man, a trusted hunter with Lewis and Clark, the first "free trapper" of the

American fur-trade era, and a bridge between the era of Daniel Boone and the establishment of Astoria, is worth following.

□

Colter had become what French trappers called a *hivernant* (hibernator), having spent his first winter in the Shining Mountains. He had $180 in gold, his mustering-out pay for three years' service with the Corps of Discovery; he had a small cache of furs in his canoe, and in the summer of 1807, some months after Hancock and Dickson departed for Saint Louis, he headed downriver toward civilization.

On the Platte River that June he encountered two keelboats and a fifty-man expedition out of Saint Charles heading up the Missouri to trade among the tribes. Leading this enterprise was Saint Louis businessman Manuel Lisa, the thirty-five-year-old New Orleans–born entrepreneur who had been among the suppliers of the Lewis and Clark party. Colter had met the man at the Corps' camp on the Illinois side of the Mississippi and was impressed enough with that recollection, and with the manpower and provisions of Lisa's expedition, to sign on as hunter and guide. Lisa saw in Colter a potentially valuable employee—a fine hunter and an experienced mountain man who had made friendly visits among the Crow during his winter in the mountains and had picked up sign language and a smattering of Indian dialects.

Meriwether Lewis, among others, despised Lisa for his rapacity and wrote of him and his partner, a man named Benoit, "Damn Manuel and triply damn Mr. B . . . they give me more vexation . . . than their lives are worth." A Lisa employee in Saint Louis said, "Rascality sat on every feature of his dark-complexioned Mexican face." Others saw him as a "bold and daring character, with an energy and spirit of enterprise like that of Cortez or Pizarro."

Few denied that Lisa was ruthless in his consuming ambition and search for the dollar above expenses, but he was also courageously creative. As an intinerant trader on the Mississippi and Ohio Rivers in the 1790s and barely out of his teens, he built a mercantile post at the old French settlement of Vincennes on the Wabash River in southwestern Indiana and by 1802 had established a thriving commerce with the Osage people. Following settlement of the Louisiana Purchase, Lisa set up an operation in Saint Louis to begin trading on the Missouri, particularly in its fur-rich upper country.

The Lisa-Colter party moved up the Missouri, encountering minor problems with an Arikara band that required a show of weaponry before they could continue, and they faced similar threats in Mandan and Assiniboine country farther upriver. At the confluence of the Yellowstone and Big Horn Rivers, in the midst of some of the richest beaver streams in North America, they built a timbered blockhouse and named it Fort Raymond, after Lisa's son. (It also became known as Manuel's Fort.)

The entrepreneur planned to have his men strewn among the Absaroka—Crow—villages of the Yellowstone and hoped, by displaying goods coveted by the Indians, to persuade them to bring their furs to the new fort. The Crow were adept trappers and Lisa hoped to win their loyalty first, followed by that of other tribes, including the Blackfeet, ancient enemies of the Absaroka, and build a string of outposts to establish his trade empire in the Upper Missouri country.

With his experience among the Crow, Colter was the linchpin of this plan and in the winter of 1807 he began a solitary odyssey on foot into the wilderness, traveling in a great circle south from Fort Manuel via the Big Horn, up the Wind River and its mountain range to a place later called Jackson Hole, across the Tetons, north to Yellowstone Lake, and back to Fort Raymond.

Wearing deerskins over the remnants of his "civilized" clothing from Corps of Discovery days, Colter carried a fifty-caliber musket, buffalo horns of black powder, blankets, snowshoes, a thirty-pound pack, and a "possibles" bag—a buffalo-hide sack containing such necessities as lead balls, flint, a steel striker, an awl for mending and stitching, and a folding lancet for opening abscesses and extracting arrowheads and bullets. He also carried iron traps and steel butcher knives to skin and dress hides. He lived on the meat he killed and slept in brush lean-tos under the stars wrapped in his blankets. He seems to have been welcomed into the Crow villages and was fed and sheltered there, sharing his meat as they shared theirs. He seems never to have hesitated to move on no matter how tempting it must have been to stay with Indian friends, nor does he seem to have doubted his ability to survive.

Colter wrote nothing of his journey and made no maps, but at some undetermined time, perhaps in the spring of 1808, he entered a foreboding valley of the Yellowstone, a place the Crow warned him was bewitched, inhabited by baleful spirits. He was the first white man to see, feel, and smell what they meant. There were bubbling, sulphurous tar pits all about, and steaming springs of water too hot to touch, rumblings under his moccasined feet that exploded in geysers vaulting from holes in the earth that created a scalding mist and shimmering rainbows. When he reported these things to Lisa and the men at Fort Raymond, they howled with laughter at "Colter's Hell"—what we know today as Yellowstone National Park.

On subsequent journeys into the wild, Colter explored the Green River, the valley of the Big Horn, and the headwaters of the Missouri—the Three Forks, where the Jefferson, Madison, and Gallatin conjoin—and at least three times escaped capture and torture by Blackfeet, or "Bug's Boys," as they were known to mountaineers who considered them spawn of Satan. Near the Three Forks he found himself in the midst of a battle between his Crow allies and the Blackfeet, and he took an arrow in the thigh but managed to escape. In the fall of 1808, Colter and John Potts, another Lewis and Clark expedition veteran, hunting with a party of Crow and Flatheads, ran into a Blackfeet band on the Jefferson fork of the Missouri. Potts was killed and his body chopped to pieces, but Colter was spared, stripped naked, and told to run for his life while a score of warriors chased him. He ran barefoot over brambles, stones, and pine needles, toward the Madison fork, six miles distant. In a desperate move, he stopped suddenly, turned and fought his lead pursuer, killed the man with his own spear, and reached the river. He dove in and hid for hours under a tangle of tree branches and mats of leaves and moss in the water. He made his way back to Fort Raymond, a 250-mile trek, in eleven days, appearing at the gate bleeding from a hundred cuts and shivering under a blanket he had taken from the slain Indian.

In April 1810, after again escaping a war party of Blackfeet, which killed five of his companions, Colter decided to quit the mountain country. He was a *hivernant* six times over and had the wounds, if little else, to prove it. He resigned from Lisa's service and reached Saint Louis in the summer with enough of a grubstake to start a new life.

Colter visited William Clark, provided his old chief with a wealth of information on the Yellowstone country, and learned of the tragic end of his other captain, Meriwether Lewis, dead from gunshot wounds at age thirty-five in the Natchez Trace of Tennessee. Clark thought his partner a suicide, as did their sponsor, Thomas Jefferson. Others thought Lewis had been murdered.

In the fall after Colter reached the Mississippi, he was visited by a delegation from an expedition sponsored by the New York fur magnate John Jacob Astor. The company of sixty-three men, headed by a man named Wilson Price Hunt of New Jersey, intended following the Lewis and Clark route up the Missouri to the Yellowstone, and Colter was happy to share his firsthand knowledge with them. He was probably offered a billet as hunter and guide with the Astorians, but declined.

He bought a piece of land at Charette, Missouri, close on the Mississippi. Not many miles away lived seventy-six-year-old Daniel Boone, the very embodiment of American pioneering, who had come to Missouri in 1799. Whether he and Colter met is not recorded, but one hopes they did and that these two frontiersmen spun many yarns telling what they witnessed in their years in the hinterlands. Boone was dreaming of pushing west to the Pacific when he died in 1820 at the age of eighty-five. Those last dreams might have been fortified by what Colter told him of what lay beyond the Shining Mountains.

John Colter died of "jaundice"—perhaps liver disease—at his homestead in Missouri seven years before Boone, in November

1813, age about forty. He was the original "free trapper," the link between Lewis and Clark and the fabulous era to come when mountain men would re-explore the Yellowstone country Colter knew so well, and South Pass on the Continental Divide, the Great Salt Lake, and the overland routes—the White Man's Great Medicine Roads—to Oregon and California. That era gave work and a certain fame to such men as Jedediah Smith, James Clyman, Jim Bridger, Tom Fitzpatrick, Ewing Young, Kit Carson, and Joseph Reddeford Walker, the men who followed Meriwether Lewis, William Clark, and John Colter to match the mountains and rivers of the West.

5

THE VOYAGE OF THE *TONQUIN*

"... A GUNPOWDER FELLOW."

1

On the sunny afternoon of August 4, 1810, onlookers on both sides of the Narrows separating the upper and lower bays of New York witnessed what celebrated New York author Washington Irving called "a nautical apparition." Down the mouth of the Hudson River and through the Narrows, heading for Rockaway Point on Long Island, slid a splendid flotilla of birch-bark canoes and *bateaux* filled with merrily whooping, halooing crews of French-Canadian *voyageurs* chanting boat-songs in an old patois of French and Indian tongues only they understood. Oblivious to the muggy weather and their sweaty work at the paddles, the variegated band wore beaded deerskins and blanket capotes, striped cotton shirts, moccasins and leggings; some had fur-trimmed, feather-bedecked caps on their heads, others wore feathers in their braided hair and paint on their faces. Dutch farmers along the Hudson naturally mistook them for a crew of savages. To the *voyageur* the gawkers on the riverbanks were, among kinder epithets, *mangeurs de lard* (pork-eaters).

H. H. Bancroft, in one of his flights of romantic fantasy, described the *voyageur*'s life as "wild, unfettered, buoyant, joyous, revelling, rollicking . . . full of beauty, with ever fresh and recurring fascination." He pictured them "as they sit at night eating, smoking, and chatting round the ruddy camp-fire, with weary limbs and soiled clothes, after a day of many portages, or perhaps after a wreck in a rapid, or a beating storm, their dark, luxuriant hair falling in tangled masses round their bronzed faces, and their uncouth figures casting weird shadows on the background foliage." On a frosty, hyperborean morning, he wrote, "See them as they rise from their hard though welcome bed, at the first faint streak of dawn . . . to the guide's harsh, leathern-voiced call of '*Lève! Lève!*' [wake up!] joking good-humor gradually arising out of the wheezes, sneezes, grunts, and grumbles of their somnolence. See them now, merry and musical as larks, throwing themselves with their luggage into the boats, and shoving off from a bank out upon the placid, polished water, striking up their morning song to the soft, low, rhythmic dip of their paddles, which rise and fall in unison as if moved by one hand."

These men, the backbone trappers of the Great Lakes, had come to New York from Lachine, their settlement near Montreal. They had transported their watercraft by wagon from the Saint Lawrence to Lake Champlain, crossed the lake, hoisted the boats on wagons again to travel to Lansingburgh, there pushing off on the Hudson toward the New York bays for what promised to be a grand adventure: They had enlisted as *engagés* for five years' service with John Jacob Astor's new Pacific Fur Company and were to sail from New York on the 290-ton frigate *Tonquin* to build a trading post at the mouth of the Columbia River, gateway to the fur riches of the Oregon Country.

□

Mr. Astor had no notions of "adventure" in launching his expedition to the Pacific. The scheme was purely a business matter; indeed, *he* was pure business, a financial genius all his adult life.

He was a butcher's son, born in Waldorf, Germany, near Heidelberg, in 1763, who emigrated with his family to England when he was seventeen, and to America in 1784. He had an entrepreneurial gift, selling musical instruments for a time, then, discovering the profits to be made in furs, tramping the New York countryside to buy pelts from farmers and independent trappers and from the Iroquois and other tribes. He started an import-export business and in a few years had agents trading furs in China for nankings, silks, tea, fans, cloves, and nutmegs.

After twenty years in America, Astor had his own ships in the China trade and had become the foremost fur trader in New York and one of its richest merchants. He organized the American Fur Company in 1808 and made it dominant in the Great Lakes trade, then, as Bancroft put it, "pregnant with purposes of wealth and power, Astor's mind now labored with a great conception," setting up the Pacific Fur Company for a massive assault on the fur trade of the American West. He aspired to build a chain of forts westward from Saint Louis to the Pacific with a headquarters entrepôt, to be named Astoria, near the Columbia River estuary. And he devised an overland expedition, to depart soon after the *Tonquin* set sail, which would follow Lewis and Clark's route westward and which would survey sites for forts and trading posts and blaze a trail for a migration of Americans to the Pacific coast.

Astor foresaw Astoria as the soaring American presence in the Pacific Northwest, the monopolistic center of the fur trade west of the Rocky Mountains, a place where beaver, sea otter, and other skins would be shipped to Canton, where they would fetch the highest prices.

Astoria and its satellite posts would form a commercial emporium that would strike a mighty blow against England's puissant Hudson's Bay Company and especially against Astor's greatest rival, the North West Company, which for a quarter century had dominated the Saint Lawrence valley trade.

Astor hobnobbed with the elite at the North West Company headquarters in Montreal and at the exclusive Beaver Club in the city. There he heard the stories of the rivalry between the

Nor'westers and the Company and the impossibility of either to engage in the China trade because of the monopoly there held by the British East India Company. The nabob of New York had no such restraints, and the acquisition of the Louisiana Territory and the overland pathmaking of Lewis and Clark convinced him he could construct an American fur cartel on the north Pacific Rim while the British companies were busy warring against each other.

To this end, Astor recruited seasoned agents and business partners from the discontented ranks of the North West Company to help put his plan into motion. He launched his Pacific Fur establishment on March 10, 1810, with nine partners, five of them Scotch veterans of the Nor'westers: Alexander McKay, who had been a clerk accompanying Mackenzie on his explorations to the Pacific Coast in 1793; Donald Mackenzie, who had spent ten of his twenty-seven years in the service of the Nor'westers; David Stuart, born in Perthshire in 1753, a fisherman and fur trader; Robert Stuart, David Stuart's nephew, who migrated to Canada in 1807; and Duncan McDougall a former Nor'wester described by Washington Irving as "an active, irritable, fuming, vainglorious little man, and elevated in his own opinion, by being the proxy for Mr. Astor."

The nabob signed an agreement with these men, put up $400,000 of his own money, named himself as chief stockholder and president of Pacific Fur, and agreed to bear all losses in the company's first five years of business.

McDougall and McKay were selected to lead the seaward expedition to the Pacific on the *Tonquin*, a frigate built in 1808 expressly as a trader, which had already made two successful voyages to the Pacific and which Astor purchased for $40,000 two weeks before it sailed. Donald Mackenzie and Wilson Price Hunt of Asbury, New Jersey, would lead the land-bound party. At age twenty-seven, Hunt was an established merchant in Saint Louis when he first met with Astor and learned of the Pacific plan. He became such an enthusiastic backer of it that he was selected as leader of the "Overland Astorians" with orders to take charge of the Columbia River post.

As laborers—woodsmen, carpenters, hunters, wheelwrights, packers, and the like—Astor hired many Americans "of respectable connections and of good moral character as possible" but he knew he needed the *hommes du nord* for his boats and traps. His agents were instructed to begin hiring these northmen immediately and found them in the taverns and warehouses at Lachine in the months before the *Tonquin* was due to hoist anchor and sail for the Falklands.

In June 1810 Alexander McKay led the first of three parties of fourteen *voyageurs* and several clerks to join McDougall in New York. Between June and the end of August these men had gathered and stowed their canoes and *bateaux* aboard the frigate and were ready to sail on a far greater body of water than they had known before.

2

As sole financier of the Oregon undertaking and a meticulous planner, Astor tried to cover all details and contingencies of the *Tonquin* voyage. A few days before the frigate spread its canvas, he addressed a letter to his four partners aboard the frigate, enjoining them to "cultivate harmony and unanimity" among themselves and the *Tonquin* crew and to take special care in creating good relations with "the wild people of the Oregon coast." He said, "If you find them kind, as I hope you will, be so to them. If otherwise, act with caution and forbearance, and convince them that you come as friends."

To ensure these good relations, he had financed certain precautions on the *Tonquin*. The frigate, manned by a crew of twenty sailors, carried not only the Astor partners, a number of *voyageurs*, twelve clerks, a party of workmen to build the fort on the Columbia, $50,000 in trade goods, plus tools, provisions, and even a small, dismantled coastal vessel, it also carried nearly a ton of gunpowder in its hold, was armed with ten cannon, and was "pierced" (had gunports available) for ten more.

Astor's powder-and-ball insurance, influenced by the massacre of the *Boston* crew at Nootka Sound in 1803 and rising tensions between the United States and Britain, extended to his selection of the *Tonquin*'s captain. Five years after Nelson's victory at Trafalgar, at a time when Napoleon was at his zenith but Wellington was fighting and winning battles against French generals in Portugal and Spain and William Henry Harrison was defeating Tecumseh at Tippecanoe in Indiana, the financier told friends he wanted "a gunpowder fellow" to command his ship "in fine style." He found the fellow, if not the style, in a thirty-one-year-old salt named Jonathan Thorn of Schenectady, New York. Astor was impressed by Thorn's history: He had been appointed a midshipman in the navy in 1800, served on men-of-war in the Mediterranean and on frigates against Tripolitan pirates in the Barbary Wars. So valorous was his service in these engagements, in particular the memorable expedition under Stephen Decatur to destroy the captured *Philadelphia* in Tripoli harbor on February 16, 1804, that the New Yorker had been commended by Commodore Decatur in dispatches and promoted to lieutenant. Thorn had also commanded the New York Navy Yard and its gunboats in 1806 and 1807, during which service he may have been introduced to Astor. In any event, the navy granted him a two-year leave, beginning in May 1810, to command the *Tonquin*.

Thorn had, no doubt, earned Decatur's wartime commendations, but between wars, in all the navy of the United States no worse choice could have been made to command a merchant ship than this surly, stern-visaged, acid-tongued autocrat. Even the attribute Astor must have found attractive, Thorn's sycophantic loyalty toward his employer, would prove catastrophic. In truth, Thorn had no interest in Astor's expansive, expensive fur cartel scheme. Washington Irving, Astor's hired amanuensis, wrote, "He [Thorn] evidently had but a narrow idea of the scope and nature of the enterprise, limiting his views merely to his part of it; everything beyond the concerns of his ship was out of his sphere; and anything that interfered with the routine of his nautical duties put him in a passion."

Astor saw none of the man's potential for folly when he wrote Captain Thorn a letter on the eve of the *Tonquin*'s departure urging his "strictest attention" to the health of himself and crew and the "promotion of good humor and harmony aboard the ship." The nabob's closing paragraph to Thorn would yield a bitter irony: "I must recommend you to be particularly careful on the coast, and not to rely too much on the friendly disposition of the natives. All accidents which have as yet happened there arose from too much confidence in the Indians."

Irving noted that these final admonitions were particularly pregnant and asked his readers "to bear these instructions in mind as events will prove their wisdom and importance, and the disasters which ensued in consequence of the neglect of them."

□

On September 8, 1810, the *Tonquin* and its thirty-three passengers ran down to Staten Island for a brief anchorage off Sandy Hook Lighthouse before proceeding south into the Atlantic. The presence of an escort ship, the USS *Constitution*, had been arranged by Astor. Royal Navy vessels out of Halifax, Nova Scotia, were cruising nearby and he feared that his ship, with its Canadian subjects aboard, might be boarded by press gangs. The presence of Old Ironsides also illustrated the government's interest in the Astor enterprise in the midst of growing tensions between the two powers. Two years past, Astor had written to President Jefferson of his scheme, seeking governmental sanction for it because of its "great public utility." To this appeal the president took a middle course: He made it known that while he encouraged private merchant vessels to trade in the Pacific Northwest, he opposed any official "partnership" in these expeditions. Newly elected President James Madison followed his predecessor's wishes but did extend to Astor the government's "full approbation and best wishes" for the Oregon experiment.

After striking the trade winds, on October 5 the *Tonquin* sighted the Cape Verde Islands off the West African coast and, while stores and water were low, Captain Thorn decided against an anchorage and shore party. He remained worried about British warships lurking nearby, and indeed one unidentified brigantine, mounting twenty guns, approached the *Tonquin* in what Thorn believed to be a hostile manner and followed for three days in a cat-and-mouse game until the merchantman caught a racing wind and lost its pursuer.

The sea chase was a diversion from serious problems aboard the Astor frigate. Captain Thorn's proclivity for petty tyranny seems to have surfaced the instant he climbed the boarding ladder into his floating fiefdom. From that moment he was oblivious to his civilian passengers, including Astor's partners, except as victims of his wrath. He made it known that he regarded these landsmen as "live lumber, continually in the way," and had no sympathy for their cramped quarters or their tendency to suffer *mal de mer*. "Lubberly" was his favorite word for them, including the *voyageurs*, the rivermen, who suffered as much as the partners, clerks, and workmen "the doleful rigors and retchings of sea-sickness." Throughout the voyage, Irving wrote, Thorn found it intolerable to discover the French-Canadians "lurking below in their berths in squalid state, or emerging now and then like spectres from the hatchways, in capotes and blankets, with dirty nightcaps, grizzly beard, lantern visage and unhappy eye, shivering about the deck, and ever and anon crawing to the sides of the vessel, and offering up their tributes to the windward."

Gabriel Franchére, a clerk aboard the *Tonquin* who somehow managed to keep a journal, said that Thorn, when he first addressed his passengers, "laid the foundation of rankling hatred between the partners and himself which ended only with the voyage." The captain's Bligh-like pronouncements included the news that he intended enforcing a ship-of-war discipline and therefore all cabin lanterns would be extinguished punctually at eight o'clock each night and any man proving "refractory" would be manacled. Moreover, Thorn added, he would shoot any man challenging his authority.

These decrees were clearly aimed at Astor's partners and clerks, who were accustomed to burning midnight oil as they pored over their charts, plans, and correspondence, but Thorn, described by Bancroft as "as thoroughly disagreeable a Yankee as ever crossed the path of Scotchmen," underestimated Scotch mettle. The "irritable, fuming," Duncan McDougall was having none of Thorn's insolence and after a later confrontation with the captain he seized a pistol and swore he would kill Thorn if he ever subjected him to further indignity.

After a month at sea and now approaching the equator, the skipper's annoyance with his passengers deteriorated further. He was suspicious of the Canadian passengers from the start, wondering about their national loyalties, and he now made a habit of scowling at them as they bent over the rail wracked with sea sickness, blaspheming over the squalid, stinking state of their berths, calling them the worst "lubberly scoundrels that ever broke a seabiscuit." And now, with no reprovisioning stores and fresh water for over a month, he grew especially irritated at the civilians' "keenness of appetite" and "daintiness" at the mess table.

At first, the ship's stores and galley served up what would be sumptuous meals for a sailing ship: fresh pork loins, hams, tongue, smoked beef haunches, sweetened puddings made of flour, rice, tapioca, and raisins. But the passengers complained incessantly at this fare and the furious Thorn called them "effeminate" and wrote to Astor that he would never take to sea again with such a group "without having a Fly-market on the forecastle, Covent-garden on the poop, and a cool spring from Canada in the maintop."

In the stifling heat of the slow passage below the equator, he rationed water to a quart a day—soon reduced to a pint and a half plus a half-pint of Souchong tea—and reduced the food allowance per man to fourteen ounces of hardtack, a pound and a quarter of salt pork or beef, a small portion of rice, beans, and cornmeal pudding with molasses. Even this still-considerable ration was not enough for them, he said, and he claimed that the Canadians had to be restrained from raiding the stores.

He was also irritated by the camaraderie among the Astor partners, clerks, and *voyageurs*, at their grouping together to tell tales of their lives—David Stuart was particularly loquacious in recalling his halcyon days as a fisherman off the coast of Labrador—as they cackled and sucked their pipes and sang old boat-songs. Thorn regarded such badinage as idleness, shocking to naval etiquette in general and his quarter-deck authority in particular, and beneath the dignity of Astor agents. He also regarded it highly suspicious that the clerks were incessantly scribbling in their journals, "showing literary pretensions."

The passengers were forever clamoring to find an anchorage so they could go ashore, Thorn wrote. They "insisted on my stopping at the Cape de Verds. Next they said the ship should stop on the coast of Patagonia, for they must see the large and uncommon inhabitants of that place. Then they must go to the island where Robinson Crusoe had so long lived. And lastly they were determined to see the handsome inhabitants of Easter Island."

Naturally, Thorn wrote to Astor, he turned down such requests peremptorily as "contrary to instructions." Washington Irving gave Thorn the benefit of the doubt in his dealings with the "lubberly" civilians on the *Tonquin*, admitting that the crusty seaman had some sound reasons to have "seamanlike impatience" toward the landsmen and that at least he had an "honest, trusty concern for the interests of his employer." Irving wrote that Thorn "pictured to himself the anxious protector of the enterprise, who had disbursed so munificently in its outfit, calculating on the zeal, fidelity and singleness of purpose of his associates and agents; while they, on the other hand, having a good ship at their disposal and a deep pocket at home to bear them out, seemed ready to loiter on every coast, and amuse themselves in every port."

Down the Torrid Zone, through the Tropic of Capricorn, and into cold and rainy weather as they lost the trades in advancing south, the *Tonquin* saw a few distant sails and only one up close, a Portuguese brig out of Recife on the Pernambuco coast of Brazil. In early December a lookout in the shrouds sighted the barren, reef-scattered outline of the Falklands, 300 miles east of the Strait of Magellan, and Thorn ordered his helmsman to follow a corridor through the maze of small islets and rocks to a small bay, there to take soundings, anchor, and fill water casks. The Canadians were overjoyed to set foot on dry land, and explored the bleak moorlands, visited the ancient graves of mariners who died there, swam, chased penguins and killed them by the dozens (their flesh, black and leathery, carried a strong fishy odor even when thoroughly cooked), and stole their eggs.

Thorn meantime had determined the anchorage unsafe and fresh water scarce, and stood out to sea after signaling the shore for the civilians to return to ship. To his fury, they straggled back in the jollyboats and it was nine at night before all were aboard. The next morning, after assurances from the Canadians that they would return on a moment's notice, they were again taken ashore with the water party. With the wind up favorably, Thorn was anxious to find a new anchorage and had signals made to the shore. After a half-hour with no boat seen pulling away from the beach, the captain reconnoitered with his glass and, as Irving wrote, "to his infinite vexation, saw the loiterers in the full enjoyment of their 'wild-goose chase.' " He ordered the *Tonquin* to set sail and when the Canadians saw the ship under way they jumped into the boats and pulled hard at the oars before coming alongside and aboard.

On December 7, the last act of this absurd melodrama occurred when Thorn took the ship to another Falklands bay that promised a better source of water and wood for galley fires and a safer sanctuary for repairs. The *Tonquin* remained at the place, called "Fort Egmont" on the charts, for four days, during which time the Canadians were given a boat to themselves, pitched a tent on the beach, and resumed their rambling explorations, chasing and butchering sea lions, geese, penguins, foxes, and any animal life that waddled, ran, flew, or swam.

As before, the captain warned his detested civilian supercargo not to wander far and to remain within hailing distance, for he would not detain the ship this time waiting for them to react to his signal to reboard; the Astor men, true to their custom, ignored him.

On the morning of the eleventh, the *Tonquin* signaled the shore that it was time to embark, but the civilians were scattered, some inspecting tombstone legends, others hunting and exploring, and two of the partners, David Stuart and Duncan McDougall, pursuing penguins on the south end of the island. Those closest to the anchorage heard the report of the gunshot signal and scurried about to locate the missing members of the shore party while the skipper angrily paced the deck of his ship. The landsmen had thrice defied him and he could bear it no longer: He ordered the sails spread and the ship put to sea.

The eight Canadians on the beach saw their ship stand out of the bay, and by the time they were all aboard their twenty-foot longboat the *Tonquin* was three miles offshore in surging seas. For three hours the boat tried to close the gap, thrown high on the waves as its occupants bent to the oars and bailed the water shipped by every roller. Aboard the frigate the other Canadians and crewmen implored Thorn to heave to and await the longboat, but he refused. Finally, Robert Stuart, nephew of David, "a young man of spirit and resolution," Irving said, went below and grabbed a brace of pistols "and in a paroxysm of wrath swore he would blow out the captain's brains unless he put about or shortened sail."

Stuart's proposed mutiny died out with the wind, which suddenly abated and allowed the longboat to come alongside and its sopping, exhausted passengers to board. In his account of the incident, Irving put the best face on it by allowing, "We can hardly believe that the captain really intended to carry his threat into full effect, and rather think he meant to let the laggards off for a long pull and a hearty fright." But in a letter to Astor Thorn made it clear that if not for the wind hauling, "I should positively have left them." In his blind constancy to his employer he apparently thought he would have done Astor a favor by abandoning the partners and clerks. "I cannot but think it an unfortunate circumstance for you that it so happened, for the first loss in this instance would, in my opinion, have proved the best, as they seem to have no idea of the value of property, not any apparant regard for your interest, although interwoven with their own."

The "property" Thorn referred to was certain articles of spare clothing in the ship's slopchest, which the partners asked be distributed among them. Naturally, Thorn refused to consider the request and posted the ship's mastiff to guard the chest. This pettifoggery Thorn dutifully described in his letters to Astor, as he did the feuds among the partners themselves—with unalloyed delight. Alexander McKay and Duncan McDougall, Thorn said, were particularly argumentative over their "rank" in the Astor scheme. They drew plans for the fort on the Columbia, he said, and disputed over placement of doors and windows until McDougall would produce a letter in which Astor named him his main representative and proxy, whereupon the word-contest ended and the two men "would be caressing each other like children."

On December 15, the mountains of Tierra del Fuego hove into view and on the eighteenth the ship, fifteen leagues from Cape Horn, encountered a lucky calm in the wind and a good current that carried it to the cape's stupendous rocks and seas. Thorn, excellent seaman that he was, managed to breech the Horn in a wild gale and reach the Diego Ramírez Islands—9,165 miles from New York—for a final water-and-repair stop. Six of the ship's cannons had broken loose from their carriages in the Horn gale and careened about the deck, splintering railings and tangling lines before being wrestled down and secured, and the ship was leaking and had damaged canvas and rigging, but there was time to patch and mend before the run north to the Sandwich Islands.

3

The *Tonquin* spotted the snowcapped peak of the Mauna Loa volcano on the island of Owhyee (Hawaii) on February 11, 1811, and sailed into Kamehameha Bay two days later. At anchor, the ship was surrounded by canoes filled with islanders clamoring to come aboard and exchange their yams, taro, plantains, coconuts, cabbages, and breadfruit for beads, needles and cloth, and other such treasures the vessel carried.

Great changes had occurred in the islands in the thirty-two

years since Captain Cook had been murdered there upon his return
from exploring the northwest coast of America. The archipelago
had been unified in 1810 by King Kamehameha, a crafty bargainer
who knew the value to his people of Western technology and welcomed foreign ships to his shores. The islands had already become
a trade crossroads, linking Canton with Boston, Bristol, Marseilles,
and other foreign ports.

The *Tonquin* remained in the islands two weeks, cultivating
good relations with the natives and purchasing livestock and provisions with trade items and silver coins. In planning his North
Pacific sovereignty, Astor had not neglected the importance of the
islands as a place for his ships to reprovision en route to Astoria
and in their comings and goings to China. Washington Irving said
Astor "even had a vague idea of, some time or other, getting possession of one of their islands as a rendezvous for his ships, and a
link in the chain of his commercial establishments."

As he took the *Tonquin* to Maui and back to the big island of
Hawaii, Thorn grew increasingly unhinged over what he considered the scandalous conduct of the civilians. They all stayed ashore,
dazzled by the snow-white beaches, warm waters for swimming,
the splendid hospitality afforded them, and the singing and dancing
of the native women, whose dress exposed them in a manner he
described as "very revolting to a civilized eye," but which did not
seem to injure Scotch sensibilities. Far from it, Irving said; the Canadians "were delighted with the charms and graces of the dancing
damsels."

While at Hawaii, the Astor men and a number of crew members hiked to Kealakekua Bay on the Kona Coast for a pilgrimage
to the spot where Cook had fallen under native knives in 1779. An
old islander served as their guide and pointed out the spot on the
beach where the greatest of English navigators died and where the
rocks and coconut palms still bore the marks of musket balls fired
by the marines—including John Ledyard—who formed Cook's escort, and from boats offshore. The Canadians took pieces of palm
bark and rock as precious relics back to the ship.

Thorn was unimpressed by this holy mission; indeed he threw

a fit at the unauthorized shore leave by his crewmen. Alexander Ross, a twenty-eight-year-old Astor man on the *Tonquin*, wrote in his journal of Thorn "storming and stomping the deck," and how "the captain called up all hands; he swore, he threatened, and abused the whole ship's company." The crewmen, whom the captain labeled "deserters," were rounded up and brutally flogged, Ross said. He wrote that Thorn was exceedingly angry at the Scotchmen for fomenting the desertions, for speaking in Gaelic and "making gestures toward him he construed as mutinous."

Before departing the islands, the *Tonquin* paid a visit to the village at Waikiki on Oahu, the royal residence of King Kamehameha, whose two-story "palace" of stone and wood was guarded by two dozen men dressed in long blue coats, each armed with a musket. The corpulent king, dressed in a tight regimental uniform complete with ceremonial sword, came out to the frigate in his royal barge accompanied by a large retinue that included three of his wives. Thorn permitted a three-gun greeting for the king, and while the Canadian partners appeared on deck in tartans and kilts to present greetings from Mr. Astor and engage in diplomatic talk, Thorn, ever the practical man, sought to buy hogs from the sovereign of the Sandwich Islands.

Kamehameha, Irving said, "was a magnanimous monarch but a shrewd pork merchant. . . . Several interviews were requisite, and much bargaining, before he could be brought to part with a bristle of bacon, and then he insisted on being paid in hard Spanish dollars; giving as a reason that he wanted money to purchase a frigate from his brother George, as he affectionately terms the king of England."

At length Thorn managed to buy a hundred hogs, a number of goats, two sheep, and a coop of chickens, adding these to an abundance of island vegetables.

The Astor partners were greatly impressed by the Hawaiians' singular skills at canoeing, swimming, and diving and said they had not seen their equal even among the *voyageurs* of Canada. They talked to the king about recruiting thirty or forty of these fine "watermen," but Thorn objected to the number. Eventually, with royal authorization, twenty-four natives were signed for three years' service with the Pacific Fur Company, during which time they were guaranteed food and clothing and, at the end of their service, $100 "in merchandise."

On the last day of February the *Tonquin* sailed from the warm and placid bay off Waikiki toward the sterner waters of the North Pacific. In Hawaii, Thorn had left a large packet of seething letters to his employer to be forwarded to New York on the next ship bound for the New England coast. Now, heading toward the Columbia, he wrote Astor again to describe the disgusting conduct of the agents' fraternizing with the natives, dressing in Highland plaids, loosening tongues and probably the morals of the Hawaiian women with gifts of rum and wine, making a great show of visiting the site of Cook's murder, and similar "ridiculously contemptible" acts. "To enumerate the thousands of instances of ignorance, filth, &c., or to particularize all the frantic gambols that are daily practiced, would require volumes," he said.

6

THE PHIAL OF WRATH

"I HAVE BUT TO DRAW THE CORK."

1

In the three-week voyage from the Sandwich Islands to the Oregon coast, Jonathan Thorn's enmity toward the Astor agents on the *Tonquin* deepened. He may have, as Washington Irving speculated, "picked up some information at Owyhee, possibly of war between the United States and England" and begun suspecting that the Canadians were plotting to take over the ship and alter its destination. He detected clues of conspiracy: The civilians held long conversations in Gaelic "of a mysterious and unwarranted nature," he wrote to Astor; they had their own store of firearms and distributed them among their party; they seemed furtive and silent when he made a sudden appearance among them. He saw their every utterance and act as evidence of mutinous conduct and believed that it was only his stalwart defiance of them, made clear by word and deed, that overawed them and kept them from enacting their despicable plans.

One example Thorn cited to Astor of his fortitude in dealing with this gang of disloyal Gaels was the occasion when the

Tonquin struck a violent storm in the North Pacific, one that washed much of the penned livestock overboard. During the squall the Canadians, without seeking his permission, attempted to procure rain gear from a storage locker. Thorn proudly reported that he drove them off with a pistol.

The real test of the *Tonquin*, its captain, and crew began on March 22, 1811, when the ship approached the Oregon coast and the surging mouth of the Columbia River. The estuary was four miles wide with a low sandy spit of land on the south called Point Adams, a peninsula and promontory on the north side crowned with a forest of pines and connected to the mainland by a narrow land neck. Within the cape opened a wide inlet, Baker's Bay, the entrance to which was guarded by numerous sandbars and a chain of crashing breakers. Captain Robert Gray had described the river's mouth in 1792 as perhaps the most perilous passage along the northwest coast and Thorn saw the evidence of the assertion before him. On the tossing quarterdeck of the Astor frigate he examined the hellish gate through his glass and determined that he could not attempt to penetrate it without a sounding and a close-up survey by whaleboat.

Selected to lead this perilous if not suicidal mission was Thorn's first mate, a man named John Fox. The captain ordered that he take John Martin, an old sea hand who had visited the Oregon coast before, and three of the *voyageurs* with him in the boat to sound the channel and discover a safe passage to the beach while the *Tonquin* stood three miles offshore. Fox made a mild protest over the Canadians, asking for more experienced deepwater sailors to accompany him, but Thorn refused this patently prudent request, saying that he needed his crew to help guide the *Tonquin* to anchorage. He told Fox that the Canadians were supposed to be expert small-boat men and ought to serve admirably under the guidance of two veterans like Fox and Martin.

Nothing is known of John Fox's history except that he was an experienced sailor who had a premonition that he would never return to the *Tonquin*. He sought sympathy from the Astorians, telling them pitifully, "I am sent off without seamen to man my boat, in boisterous weather, and on the most dangerous part of the northwest coast. My uncle was lost a few years ago on this same bar and now I am going to lay my bones with his." But when he protested that the mission was ill-conceived, Thorn answered, "Mr. Fox, if you are afraid of water, you should have remained in Boston."

The whaleboat was lowered at one o'clock that afternoon, and the five men rowed into the foaming breakers and disappeared in the foggy mist. The *Tonquin* searched for them all day and the next, lowering boats, which stayed on the seaward side of the bar, but no sign of them was ever found.

At the end of the second day of waiting and with the wind abating, Thorn took his ship closer to shore and anchored at a fourteen-fathom sounding north of the long peninsula forming the north side of the river entrance that was aptly named Cape Disappointment. Here a boat was lowered carrying several sailors and the Astor partners Alexander McKay and David Stuart, who hoped to find some trace of Fox and his men. But the crashing surf drove them back to the ship. Another boat, carrying an experienced crew and two of the Hawaiian outrigger experts signed aboard at Oahu, clawed its way to within a league of the shore before being tossed high on a ferocious breaker that nearly capsized it. It too limped back to the ship.

By now the *Tonquin* itself was in serious danger, riding perilously at anchor in shallow water in a roaring wind and smashing surf that threatened to splinter the ship to oak kindling on the rocks despite the extra anchors thrown overboard. Thorn had a final plan: He turned to three of his most experienced hands to guide the frigate through the passage. An old tar named Aiken, who had signed on to command the disassembled schooner on board the *Tonquin*, commanded the escort boat, with a sailmaker named John Coles; an armorer, Stephen Weekes; and two Hawaiians as crew. The plan called for Aiken to steer the boat and take soundings while the *Tonquin* followed under shortened sails. When Aiken had found the channel he was to signal with a pistol shot and return to the ship.

For a time the plan seemed to be working, but eventually Aiken's boat broached broadside to the twenty-foot waves crashing inland and was carried away. On the *Tonquin*, crewmen climbed the quaking mizzentop and saw the boat desperately trying to reach the ship, then saw it vanish in the surf. The frigate meantime had entered shallow water, scraped its hull against the rocks, and ploughed across sandbars, until at nightfall, with the help of a tidal surge, it was pushed into Baker's Bay and, at a depth of seven fathoms and with the wind lulling, cast anchor.

At daybreak, with lookouts on the masthead peering out over the wild coast for signs of the missing boat parties, Thorn sent searchers ashore. On the beach some natives who had been watching the *Tonquin* struggle into Baker's Bay came out to the ship in canoes, and were questioned with sign language about the missing sailors, but they seemed to have no information. Thorn himself led one of the search parties and a short distance along the beach he found Stephen Weekes, the armorer who had been with Aiken's whaleboat. He told a harrowing tale of the boat being swamped, of Coles, the sailmaker, and Aiken disappearing in the boiling surf. Weekes and the two Sandwich Islanders had managed to turn the boat on its keel and retrieve its oars. One of the Hawaiians died, presumably of exposure in the numbing cold before the boat beached itself; the other was found by *Tonquin* crewmen later on the morning of March 25, half dead from cold and fatigue.

The armorer and the Hawaiian were the only survivors of the ten men sent into the channel, an event, Irving wrote, "that cast a gloom over the spirits of the whole party, and was regarded by some of the superstitious as an omen that boded no good to the enterprise."

□

The natives of the lower Columbia, principally Chinook and Clatsop people, had dealt with white traders for many years and knew what they sought, and thus swarmed to the *Tonquin*'s anchorage from its first day in Baker's Bay, their canoes carrying sea otter skins and other furs. These fisherfolk were waterway artisans, and the *voyageurs* especially admired their craft, some of which were fifty feet in length, hewn from a single fir or white cedar and capable of carrying thirty men. The thwarts were thick and the gunwales flared outward, features that enabled them to stay upright in the most treacherous of waters; the bows and sterns of the boats were intricately carved into grotesque figures of men and animals, some of the prow-pieces as tall and stately as any Viking ship. The canoers sat on their haunches to paddle; one man in the stern with a paddle serving as rudder. Women were not excluded from canoe-work and were as expert as any paddler and often took the important tiller position aft. Irving, who gathered descriptions from those who saw the natives at work, wrote, "It is surprising to see with what fearless unconcern these savages venture in their light barks upon the roughest and most tempestuous seas. They seem to ride upon the waves like sea-fowl." He compared the Columbia River people with the horseback Indians of the Great Plains and said that while the buffalo-hunting tribes were "generally tall, sinewy, meagre but well-formed, and of bold and fierce deportment," the Oregon coastal tribes, "lounging about the river banks, or squatting and curved up in their canoes, are generally low in stature, ill-shaped, with crooked legs, thick ankles, and broad flat feet. They are inferior also in muscular power and activity . . . to their hard-riding brethren of the prairies."

While the natives came to the *Tonquin* camp ashore and out to the ship in their canoes, some bringing otter skins to trade, many just to gawk, and some to pilfer, Captain Thorn and a number of the Astor partners explored the Columbia estuary searching for a suitable site for the trading post. As ever, Thorn was angry. He had lost eight men in his haphazard attempt to find an entrance to the Columbia estuary, and he was anxious to be rid of his insubordinate Canadian passengers and their sinister Gaelic babble. He was particularly infuriated at Duncan McDougall, the vain and splenetic little man who made so much of being Mr. Astor's proxy. It had not escaped Thorn's notice that McDougall seemed to have a covetous eye toward the wives and daughters of the Chinook chief Comcomly, a tendency the captain found as disgusting as the women themselves. Irving admitted that McDougall "seems to have had a heart susceptible to the influence of the gentler sex," and of the Chinook women reported that they "painted their bodies with red clay, and anointed themselves with fish oil, to give additional lustre to their charms." According to H. H. Bancroft, McDougall later "took to wife a dreamy daughter of the Chinook chief."

Thorn was particularly incensed that McDougall had invited Comcomly aboard the *Tonquin* with his many wives and large retinue without so much as a by-your-leave, an event that, one of the partners later wrote, "stirred the spleen of the captain, who had a sovereign contempt for the one-eyed chieftain and all his crew."

Above all, Thorn was impatient to move on, to leave the lubberly managers and fort builders on the beach and take the ship upcoast to fulfill what he considered the most important of Mr. Astor's assignments, the investigation of the fur-trade potential of the entire Oregon coast. He ordered the building of a shed on the shore of Baker's Bay to receive the supplies, tools, and equipment needed for building the trading post, and the dismantled schooner and its rigging. He intended to relieve the *Tonquin* of this cargo and the supernumerary civilians as well and take his leave of the entire land enterprise.

Meantime, McDougall and David Stuart set out in a boat to find a site for the fort and in the first week of April selected a densely wooded point of land on the south shore of the bay. Point George, as they named it, lay opposite the site of Lewis and Clark's Fort Clatsop, twelve miles from the Columbia entrance channel and above a good harbor where trade vessels of average size could anchor within fifty yards of shore.

Work began on the fort on April 12 with axmen on scaffolds topping the biggest trees and cutting down the firs and alders. In heavy rains, laborers chopped underbrush, moved rocks, blew up stumps with gunpowder, and landed goods and livestock. Others worked to erect a twenty-by-sixty-two-foot warehouse, a powder magazine, and a "residence" of barked logs surrounded by gardens, the plots hoed and sewn with vegetable seeds brought on the ship.

As this work proceeded, two shipwrights Astor had employed began laying the keel of the trade schooner brought crated on the *Tonquin*.

At last Captain Thorn was free to take his ship to sea and search for furs along the northern coast. Aboard were twenty-nine men, including the only civilians, Alexander McKay, listed as "supercargo," with one James Lewis serving as his clerk. A Chehalem Indian named Lamanse, who had picked up some English and served vessels as interpreter to tribes along the northwest coast, was taken aboard at Gray's Harbor, after which the *Tonquin* sailed north to Vancouver Island.

Of Captain Thorn's freedom from the Astor men, Bancroft asks rhetorically if "our most sturdy captain" might not now "shake from his feet the dust of Scotch fur-traders and filthy French *voyageurs* and on the *Tonquin*'s cleanly scrubbed deck, laugh at the discordant past, laugh as with his own crew only on board she flew before the breeze, and swept gayly into the coves and estuaries of the admiring savages?" His answer: "Alas! no; with his evil temper, evil times forever attended him. Doomed to destruction, the gods had long since made him mad."

2

Jonathan Thorn, relieved of his burden of Gaelic-gabbling civilians and the detested cargo for building and provisioning of Fort Astoria, proceeded northward to Vancouver Island on June 5, 1811. He had a specific mission to fulfill: Mr. Astor wanted him to trade for furs among the coastal tribes and, having gathered a sufficient number of sea otter and other skins, to return to Astoria, check on the needs of the fort builders, and then proceed to China to sell the furs and sail back to New York. According to Astor's plan, the *Tonquin* would become one of several trade ships making a periodic run to the Oregon coast, thence to Canton and back, with Astoria as the epicenter of the Astor-Pacific emporium.

For his anchorage Thorn selected an inlet—called Neweetie by

Irving, Clayoquot or Kyuquot by the natives—opposite a large Indian village thirty-odd miles above Nootka Sound. Lamanse, the Indian interpreter on board, warned the captain that the people of the village were "of a perfidious character," but Thorn ignored the warning.

Late in the first day of the anchorage, a group of natives came out to the ship bringing bundles of sea otter hides in their canoes and were welcomed on deck. Among the visitors were emissaries of the village chief, one Wicananish, who invited the white leaders to his lodge. Thorn declined the offer, but Alexander McKay went ashore with the interpreter and was received hospitably by Wicananish and spent the night in the chief's home, sleeping in a warm bed of otter skins. As assurance of his amity toward the traders, the chief left six of his men—Irving called them "hostages"— aboard the *Tonquin*.

The next morning (the date is unknown but is believed to be about June 15), Thorn, without waiting for McKay's return to the ship, had his crewmen spread the trade goods on deck: blankets, cloths, knives, beads, fishhooks, odd pieces of iron. The captain expected a prompt and profitable sale, but as the natives boarded the ship with their packets of furs, Irving says, Thorn quickly learned that they "were not so eager and simple as he had supposed, having learned the art of bargaining and the value of merchandise from the casual traders along the coast."

The negotiations were guided by an old subchief named Nookamis, a wily bargainer with a long history of haggling with the Bostons and King George's agents and "who had grown gray in traffic . . . and prided himself upon his acuteness." Thorn, in contrast, Irving said, "was a plain, straightforward sailor, who never had two minds, nor two prices in his dealings, was deficient in patience and pliancy, and totally wanting in the chicanery of traffic."

The day's trade did not begin well, but then it got worse. Thorn pointed to the furs Nookamis' people had brought on board, pointed to the goods he would trade for them, and the old chief laughed and shook his head merrily and made a counteroffer. The captain, sorely offended from the start, sullenly paced the deck, hands thrust in his pockets, followed by Nookamis holding out a sea otter skin and pestering him to make an offer. After a few minutes of Nookamis' hectoring chatter, Thorn, "never remarkable for relishing a joke, especially when at his own expense," exploded. He snatched the pelt and rubbed Nookamis' face with it, then strode about the deck swearing, kicking the furs about, his face an ugly mask. He grabbed Nookamis by his hair and shoved the old man to the rail, grabbed another—named Shewish, one of Wican-anish's sons—and booted him toward the sallyport, and shouted to the others to leave the ship instantly. The Indians ran to the rail, "as one might recoil from a pestilence," Bancroft said, and jumped into the sea or down the boarding ladder to their canoes, Nook-amis and Shewish shouting imprecations at Thorn as their men scurried to the paddles.

When McKay returned to the ship later in the morning and learned of the incident, he and Lamanse warned of the danger and urged Thorn to make sail, as there would surely be reprisals. The captain scoffed at the panicky agent and interpreter and pointed to the *Tonquin*'s cannon and small arms locker, saying, "Do you think I would run before a lot of naked redskins so long as I had a knife or handspike?" Bancroft observed that the captain "loved to triumph, not less over those about him, than over the barbarians ashore. . . . After all, it would not sound well in polite circles to have it said that a lieutenant in the navy sailed a peddling-ship all the way round Cape Horn, and then thrashed the savages with his own hand because they were more skillful traders than he."

Accounts vary on the events that followed Thorn's tirade, but it appears that a day or two elapsed in an odd calm, as if the eye of a storm were passing over the *Tonquin* as it swung at anchor in Clayoquot Sound. During this lull the natives returned to the ship with their furs, a canoe at a time, and, as before, were invited aboard. Thorn appears to have kept to his cabin in these days, perhaps letting McKay conduct the negotiations.

The eye passed over just after dawn one morning when a large pirogue-sized canoe carrying twenty native traders and their bundles of furs came alongside the *Tonquin*. The canoe was commanded by Shewish, the chief's son Thorn had banished from the ship. He and the others held up their otter skins and the officer of the watch, determining the visitors to be unarmed, permitted them to board while Thorn and McKay slept in their quarters below the main deck. Soon other canoes appeared from shore, and more of Wicananish's villagers climbed the ladder and scattered around the deck displaying their bundled goods. The watch officer eventually sent a man below to wake the captain and the Astor partner, and by the time these sleepy gentlemen appeared on deck the *Tonquin* was swarming with Indians. McKay, with one quick glance around, told Thorn he must abandon the harbor in all haste and the captain, standing on the quarterdeck, saw the number of canoes surrounding the ship and others shoving off from shore and barked orders to his officers to weigh anchor and send men aloft to make sail, and ordered others to clear the Indians from the deck.

As hands manned the capstan and crewmen began unreefing sails, one of the natives—perhaps Shewish—gave a yelled signal and in an instant knives, hatchets, and war clubs hidden in the fur bundles were produced and the *Tonquin*'s deck turned into a killing ground. James Lewis, McKay's clerk, was standing by a bale of trade blankets, arms folded across his chest, when he was stabbed in the back; McKay himself, seated at the taffrail, was knocked overboard, where he was clubbed to death by the Indian women in the canoes; Thorn, armed only with a clasp-knife, slashed at his attackers, is said to have killed Shewish with it, and, according to Irving's unlikely account, dealt crippling blows left and right, "strewing the quarter deck with the slain and wounded" before being hemmed in, smashed down, and stabbed to death and his body heaved overboard. James Thorn, the captain's sixteen-year-old brother, a "ship's boy," was also slain.

Of the seven sailors sent aloft to work the sails, three were killed as they descended from the rigging, the four remaining, including armorer Stephen Weekes, who was mortally wounded, fighting with knives and handspikes down the steerage hatchway to a cabin where they barricaded the door. They smashed open the arms locker, loaded muskets, and came up to the main deck firing volleys at the clots of natives looting the dead and managing to force the Indians to flee over the rails to their canoes below. The four crewmen loaded the light shipboard cannon and fired grape-shot, "which did great execution among the canoes, and drove all the savages to shore," Irving claimed.

The melee had lasted only a few minutes, but the attack caught the crew unarmed and outnumbered, and Thorn, McKay, and twenty-four crewmen, half of them Hawaiians, were killed. Most of their corpses were thrown overboard, where they floated about the ship's keel.

That night, three of the four surviving sailors lowered a long-boat and rowed away from the ship, intending to make their way south along the Oregon coast to Fort Astoria. They were unable to manhandle their boat beyond the wall of surf of Clayoquot Sound, however, and were forced to beach the craft in a small cove. During the night, they were captured and tortured to death.

Weekes, dying from loss of blood, stayed aboard the *Tonquin* and survived the night. At first light the Indians returned to the ship and circled it. With them was Lamanse, the Gray's Harbor interpreter whose life had been spared and who had been taken prisoner. He recognized Weekes, who stood at the rail waving at the canoes, but the armorer quickly disappeared and was forgotten as the Indians boarded and roamed the deck, looting the blankets and trade goods. By mid-morning at least thirty canoes had reached the ship, the Indians swarming over the rails in search of plunder.

Before the first of them boarded, Weekes found the strength to get below decks to the powder magazine and there he waited, lis-tening to the whoops and shouts and the thud of running feet above him. He poured a train of gunpowder to the magazine and, before he lost the last of his strength, lit it. The explosion blew the *Ton-quin* into scraps of oak and human flesh. Lamanse, in the main-chains, was thrown from the deck into the bay and survived. He later said that "arms, legs, and heads were flying in all directions," and for days afterward the limbs and torsos of the dead were wash-ing up on the beach.

Irving described the scene: "The ship had disappeared, but the bay was covered with fragments of the wreck, with shattered canoes, and Indians swimming for their lives, or struggling in the agonies of death; while those who had escaped the danger remained aghast and stupefied, or made with frantic panic for the shore."

(Astor's author asserted that James Lewis, the clerk who was among the first men attacked on the *Tonquin*, lit the fuse, and that on the voyage out Lewis had "expressed a presentiment that he would die by his own hands; thinking it highly probable that he should be engaged in some contest with the natives, and being resolved, in case of extremity, to commit suicide rather than be made a prisoner." Gabriel Franchére, one of the Astor agents on the *Tonquin* who stayed at Fort Astoria when the ship departed north, stated that the magazine was blown up by Stephen Weekes. It seems likely that a ship's armorer, in charge of all the small arms on the vessel, would know more about the powder magazine and how to detonate it than a civilian clerk.)

As to Captain Thorn, Irving—who appears to have known him personally—wrote of him as "a frank, manly, sound-hearted sailor . . . loyal, single-minded, straightforward, and fearless" and said, "With all his faults and foibles, we cannot but speak of him with esteem, and deplore his untimely fate; for we remember him well in early life, as a companion in pleasant scenes and joyous hours."

Many months later John Jacob Astor learned of the fate of the *Tonquin* in New York and took the news stoically, although, as Irving said, he "felt it with all its force, and was aware that it must cripple, if not entirely defeat, the great scheme of his ambition." While attending a play not long after receiving the terrible news, a friend asked the financier how he could remain so calm while in possession of such dreadful information. "What would you have me do?" Astor wondered. "Would you have me stay at home and weep for what I cannot help?"

3

Six weeks passed before the first rumors of the *Tonquin* massacre reached Duncan McDougall, David and Robert Stuart, and the other Astorians preoccupied in the building of their factory and fort on the Columbia. But news of another sort reached them in July from upriver that a party of thirty white men had appeared out of nowhere and were hastily erecting buildings on the river-bank. David Stuart and eight men prepared to set out to investigate the report but were held back when, on July 15, a canoe came sliding down the river, a Union Jack fluttering at its stern and bearing a party of *voyageurs* and a distinguished passenger, David Thompson, astronomer, explorer, cartographer, and a partner of the North West Company. He was a formidable wilderness man, only thirty-one years old but already with seventeen years' experience in the Canadian back country, where he had opened trade with several Indian tribes and explored and mapped routes between far-flung Canadian forts and factories. He had crossed the Rockies in 1807, blazing a trail south of that of Alexander Mackenzie, and built a fort at Windermere Lake, the first on the Upper Columbia.

Thompson's visit to the fort seems to have been the result of his own failure to reach the vicinity before the Astorians and, in Washington Irving's words, "anticipate Mr. Astor in his intention of effecting a settlement at the mouth of the Columbia River." In crossing the Rockies with a sizable party, all but eight of his men had deserted and Thompson was now reduced to seeing firsthand his company's competition. To Irving, Thompson was "little more than a spy in camp," although welcomed by McDougall, who, the author said, "had a lurking feeling of companionship and good-will for all of the Northwest Company."

It appears that Thompson freely shared information with the Astorians on the upriver country for, on July 23, 1811, David Stuart set out for the interior with four clerks, two *voyageurs,* and two Hawaiians in three canoes loaded with provisions. During this expedition Stuart explored the Columbia River valley and the Willamette, the 300-mile-long navigable river that issued from the

Cascade Range and flowed north to the Columbia. He found the Willamette valley a region of luxuriant beauty with lakes and pools and green meadows shaded by noble copses of trees. Before returning to Astoria, he and his men made their way as far north as the Okanogan River, a Columbia tributary in the Colville Indian region, and built a fort on the east bank of the river.

□

Early in August, some sparse information on the fate of the *Tonquin* at last reached Fort Astoria, brought by a wandering band of Indians from the Juan de Fuca Strait. At first the partners treated the story dubiously, but it was soon substantiated by other natives who came south to the unfinished fort to trade and fish. Details of the massacre were eventually filled out by the interpreter Lamanse, who somehow contrived to be freed by his captors and make his way back to Gray's Harbor.

Duncan McDougall treated even the scantiest first information with gravity, and as details of the killings and loss of the ship arrived, he was devastated. There had been rumors from the time the *Tonquin* departed Baker's Bay of a conspiracy among the coastal tribes to attack white traders, and they had alarmed Mr. Astor's proxy, the more so after the dire news from Clayoquot Sound reached him. He even suspected his future father-in-law, Comcomly of the Chinooks, of complicity in the gossiped plot. In answer, the chief made repeated professions of peace and pointed to his people's history of friendly relations with white men since the time they welcomed Lewis and Clark in 1805. The chief had even saved McDougall's life in the first weeks after the *Tonquin*'s landing when a longboat had overturned in the Columbia estuary and Comcomly had plucked the terrified agent from the water and pulled him aboard the royal canoe.

To McDougall, the Astorians were now a handful of helpless men clinging to a savage coast surrounded by hostile tribes, with no means of escape by sea. Moreover, it would be months before the fort could be reinforced by the men of Astor's overland expedition, which was supposed to have started out from Saint Louis shortly after the *Tonquin* sailed. For all McDougall knew, the party may not yet have begun its ascent of the Missouri.

During this unsettling time, the Astorians set to work throwing up a primitive siege works around the still uncompleted fort—a "palisades" consisting of little more than a high picket fence and bastion-like platforms to hold the four four-pounder cannon brought on the *Tonquin* expressly to protect the fort—and posting round-the-clock vedettes and sentinels.

Still they worried. Their feeble little enclave could not long withstand any concentrated attack by a native force, even though it would be armed with only spears, knives, and clubs. No sound evidence existed that a confederation of tribes was planning a war against the whites, but the rumors alone created terror and to counter even a dim possibility of a native rising, McDougall created an ingenious stratagem.

The Astorians and all who traded among the coastal tribes knew of the Indians' greatest fear: the scourge of smallpox. Epidemics of the disease, first brought by the whites in decades past, had swept away entire tribes. The bringers of the disease seemed to survive it, but the Indians inevitably died. The specter of smallpox haunted the native people.

McDougall's design involved assembling several tribal chiefs, Comcomly among them, whose domains lay in the vicinity of Fort Astoria. These were the leaders whispered to be involved in the conspiracy against the traders, and when he managed to bring them together at Fort Astoria he told them he had heard of their treachery and that he and his men were prepared to deal with it.

"The white men among you," he said (according to Irving), "are few in number, it is true, but they are mighty in medicine. See here." At this he dramatically drew forth a small flask. "In this bottle," he said, "I hold the small-pox, safely corked up; I have but to draw the cork, and let loose the pestilence, to sweep man, woman and child from the face of the earth!" He said that so long as the whites were unmolested he would keep the "phial of wrath" sealed, but at the least hostility the fatal cork would be drawn.

Whether or not there ever was a conspiracy, the ruse had its effect; the rumors died out and thereafter the Indians called Mc-Dougall "the Great Small-Pox Chief."

(Ironically, Comcomly died in a smallpox epidemic in 1830. In his days of glory, according to the Jesuit missionary Pierre-Jean De Smet, the Chinook chief's retinue included 300 slaves and "he used to carpet the ground that he had to traverse . . . with beaver and otter skins." Father De Smet said Comcomly "had sight in only one eye, but that proved sufficient for he was all-seeing, sagacious and, in the view of some whites, unduly mercenary.")

On October 26, 1811, the Fort Astoria factory building, a structure of timber, clay, and unmortared stone, was completed and the schooner, whose frame had been carried on the *Tonquin*, assembled and given its first sea trials. Named *Dolly*, it was the first American vessel built and launched on the Pacific coast.

Now the little factory, center and symbol of John Jacob Astor's great experiment, settled down and waited for the overland expedition to join them.

7

THE OVERLANDERS

"... THE WANDERINGS OF SINBAD."

1

In October 1810, as the *Tonquin* sailed down from the Cape Verde Islands toward the equator, the overland Astorians broke camp and, with maps based on the trail followed by Lewis and Clark just seven years past, began their ascent of the Missouri River.

Astor's choice as commander of this expedition was not, as might have been expected, an experienced wilderness hand; indeed Wilson Price Hunt was "born to mercantile pursuits," his milieu the stockroom and bank, his custom to read ledgers, not maps. But the nabob of New York had cast his crafty eye on this twenty-eight-year-old businessman from Trenton, New Jersey, and saw in him an organizer, an administrator, a diplomat, a leader of men, "scrupulously upright and faithful in his dealings, amicable in his disposition, and of most accommodating manners," as Irving said. These attributes came to Astor's attention in 1809, when the two men met for the first time in Manhattan. Hunt had removed from New Jersey counting houses to Saint Louis when he was twenty-one and had built a profitable commerce there in the Indian trade.

Astor liked the man, perhaps saw in him the same ambition and scrappiness that had established the financier's fortune, and recruited him as a partner in the Pacific Fur Company. Hunt's assignment was to supersede the Scotch-Canadians who had sailed on the *Tonquin* and take over as chief factor of Fort Astoria. In that role he was to negotiate a contract for furs with the Russians at Sitka and placate the North West Company and Hudson's Bay Company traders on the coast. Astor's confidence in Hunt had a single limitation: The man had no trail experience, and this deficit had to be made up by the men selected to follow him to the Oregon Country.

While Hunt was the titular leader of the expedition, he was fortunate in having as his chief associate a keen veteran of the woods named Donald Mackenzie. This hulking former Nor'wester—by far the biggest, at over 300 pounds, of the Scotch-Canadian fraternity of "Macs" who figured in the financier's plan—was so energetic that he was nicknamed "Perpetual Motion" Mackenzie, and he had been roaming the Canadian wilds from age seventeen. While he would later be suspected of intrigue and perhaps even treachery in the Astor camp, in June 1810, when he met Hunt in Montreal, the ancient emporium of the fur trade, Mackenzie was a trusted Pacific Fur lieutenant. If he resented Hunt's superiority in command he gave no sign of it, and he fell to work with his customary energy in recruiting others for the expedition.

Since much of the journey west, would be by the Lewis and Clark designated waterways, or so it was guessed, the first men recruited were *voyageurs*, and at Montreal and Ottawa, probably through Mackenzie's knowledge of them, forty *hommes du nord* were signed on. These were the same wild breed of woods- and rivermen who called the Astor agents and clerks and all men softened by indoor luxury "pork-eaters"; the same French-Canadian brotherhood who would soon be paddling down the Hudson to Long Island in their birch-bark canoes and *bateaux* to ship out on the *Tonquin*. By late July, after stopovers at Mackinaw, the old trading post on Michilimackinac Island in the strait between Lakes Michigan and Huron at Green Bay and Prairie du Chien, most of the expedition members were in place. In Saint Louis on September 3, 1810, and on a return visit the following January after the expedition had reached its winter quarters, Hunt had sixty men to outfit and provision. He also had command of four boats, two keelboats, one barge-like flatboat, and an outsized vessel known as a Schenectady barge, which had been purchased at the old French trading post at Mackinac. All the vessels were equipped with masts and sails, and the keelboats were armed with a swivel gun and two howitzers.

In addition to the forty *engagés*, Hunt and Mackenzie had enlisted an interpreter, Pierre Dorion, son of the Pierre Dorion who had served in the same capacity with Lewis and Clark. Dorion's love of liquor, Irving said, "in which he had been nurtured and brought up, would occasionally break out, and with it the savage side of his character." Dorion was accompanied by his pregnant Iowa Indian wife and their two children. In Saint Louis another young (age twenty-three) Astor associate and Hunt acquaintance, a Glasgow-born fur trader named Ramsey Crooks, joined the party, as did Crooks' former business partner. This man, Robert McClellan, a Pennsylvania frontiersman and Indian fighter and scout, was lean and athletic, fearless and dependable, but with an ungovernable temper. Crooks had for several years worked for the North West Company among Missouri River tribes. McClellan, a one-time partisan serving with General "Mad Anthony" Wayne in his Indian campaigns in the Ohio Valley, had spent twelve years in Louisiana Territory ranging the Mississippi between New Orleans and Saint Louis as one of the earliest American fur traders in the region. Joining the Hunt expedition with these veterans came Joseph Miller of Baltimore, once an infantry lieutenant and a capable trapper and hunter on the Missouri; John Day, a tall mountain man out of Culpeper County, Virginia, thirteen of whose forty-one years had been spent in the Missouri woods where he earned a living as trapper, hunter, and gunpowder-maker; and John Reed, an Irishman whose history is lost but who, while signing on as a "clerk," had trail experience and would serve the expedition as scout.

Perhaps because of the scientific precedent set by the Corps of Discovery, and at Astor's and Thomas Jefferson's urging, two botanists were assigned to travel with the Hunt party. These were John Bradbury, a Scotchman who had come to the United States in 1809, sponsored by the Linnaean Society of Liverpool to collect American plants, had been a guest of Jefferson's in the White House and thereafter made Saint Louis his base of explorations for studying the flora of the Missouri River; and Thomas Nuttall, a Yorkshireman who had emigrated to Philadelphia in 1808 and joined Bradbury in his Missouri studies in 1810. While neither scientist would travel with the Astorians farther than the Mandan villages of the Missouri, Nuttall would return to the trail and make a journey all the way to Oregon in 1834.

On October 21, 1810, six weeks after the *Tonquin* sailed from Long Island, Hunt, Mackenzie, and their fifty-eight men began their long journey, launching their boats on the Missouri to head west and north to winter camp at the mouth of the Nodaway River.

The river work was backbreaking, the progress agonizingly slow. The boats often had to be drawn up the Missouri with grappling hooks, using roots and overhanging tree limbs for purchase, or towed by long cordelles, barge ropes, when the riverbank was clear enough of trees and brush thickets to permit men to pull along the shore. Special dangers were floating logs and "sawyers," sunken trees with sharp, jagged limbs lurking just underwater to snag and pierce the vessels. Another danger, of which the expedition leaders had been warned by Manuel Lisa, John Colter, and others in Saint Louis before they set out, were the menacing bands of Indians, Sioux in particular, who, it was said, would be watching them from the forested banks waiting to pounce on them.

The brutal work and the fear of Indian ambush caused several men to desert during the first few weeks of the journey, but others were enlisted en route to replace them. These were wandering hunters and trappers, some of them familiar with the country beyond the Nodaway. These recruits advised Hunt against following the Lewis and Clark route in favor of one more southerly for an easier crossing of the mountains ahead. This trail, they said, led to the

headwaters of the Platte and Yellowstone and avoided the murderous Blackfeet, whose domain lay in the northern reaches of the
Missouri. This advice seemed critically important to Hunt and he
acted on it, deciding to leave the river at the Arikara villages in the
Dakota country, purchase packhorses, and proceed south to the
Yellowstone, the route William Clark had followed on returning
from the Pacific.

The expedition reached the Nodaway River in mid-November,
450 winding Missouri River miles from their embarkation point,
and settled down to camp for the winter. Hunters found ample
game for the cookpots and beaver traps were set in the slushy
streams, the furs baled to await the spring thaw and the move west.

In January 1811 Hunt and eight men returned to Saint Louis
on horseback, with a stopover at Fort Osage, a government outpost
founded in 1808 by William Clark on the south bank of the Missouri, to collect the last of his expedition members, including the
two botanists. On the return trip he stopped at the village of Charette and spent some enjoyable hours with Daniel Boone, then in
his seventy-sixth year, and also visited John Colter's nearby homestead. The Lewis and Clark corpsman rode several miles alongside
the Astor lieutenant, providing valuable information on the Missouri and Rocky Mountain tribes, before returning home.

Hunt rejoined his party at their Nodaway River camp on April
17.

At the time Hunt and his men departed Saint Louis, Manuel
Lisa, practical ruler of the Missouri River fur traffic, mounted a
trapping expedition, and nineteen days after Hunt's departure led
his twenty-five men upriver in a barge with a swivel-gun mounted
at the bow. The two parties intersected at the Arikaras' domain, a
scattering of lodges above the mouth of the Grand River that Lisa
considered his domain as well—and were instantly at loggerheads.
Vague old feuds resurfaced. Pierre Dorion, who appears to have
departed Saint Louis a few steps ahead of his debtors and the law,
was plied with liquor and urged to quit Hunt and join Lisa's party
but grew incensed at Lisa's threats to have him arrested. Irving says
Dorion "snatched up a pair of pistols belonging to Mr. Hunt, and

placed himself in battle array." Robert McClellan, who held a grudge against Lisa over some unhappy past business dealings, also threatened violence against his former employer, and Ramsey Crooks announced that he was prepared to help McClellan. Hunt tried to act as intermediary and calm tempers, but "an impression was made use of by Lisa derogatory to his honor," and the Astorian, normally the most sanguine of men, was driven to challenge Lisa to a duel.

Somehow the disputes were salved over and Lisa, who well knew the "Rees" (as the Arikaras were known by mountain men), assisted Hunt in purchasing horses from the tribesmen. He also exchanged fifty animals of his own, sent down from his fort near the Mandan villages 180 miles upriver, for the boats Hunt had decided he must abandon. In the spring and early summer the Astorians camped among the Rees, hunted and trapped and pieced together a herd of eighty-two horses to serve as pack animals excepting riding mounts for the partners and Pierre Dorion's pregnant wife and their two children.

On July 18, 1811, Hunt, now with sixty-five men, broke camp and left the Missouri, bound south and west for the Grand River and thence to the Little Missouri. Upon their leaving, according to Washington Irving, "the veteran trappers and voyageurs of Lisa's party shook their heads as their comrades set out, and took leave of them as of doomed men; and even Lisa himself gave it as his opinion, after the travelers had departed, that they would never reach the shores of the Pacific, but would perish with hunger in the wilderness, or be cut off by the savages."

2

One of the Lisa men who joined Hunt's party and who would serve as guide into the Absaroka country west of the Black Hills was Edward Rose, mulatto son of a white father and a Cherokee-Black mother. He was about twenty-five, had grown up in Kentucky, and had roamed the Missouri River country since age eighteen. In some obscure Indian fight he received a face wound and the name "Cut Nose," and in his trapping forays into the Big Horn Mountains had earned the friendship of the Crow, had fought with them against the Sioux, and was said to have collected five scalps in one battle. He was a colorful, reckless character with a shady past, but came highly recommended by Lisa, who shared many of Rose's wilder attributes. Hunt, who had learned something of Rose's unsavory history in Saint Louis, was nonetheless grateful to have such a knowledgeable pilot to take him through the dangerous lands ahead.

(Irving speaks of a "plot" by Rose "to rob and abandon his countrymen when in the heart of the wilderness, and to throw himself into the hands of the savages." The author described Rose as "one of those desperadoes of the frontier, outlawed by their crimes, who combine the vices of civilized and savage life, and are ten times more barbarous than the Indians with whom they consort.")

In August Hunt's party skirted the Black Hills and struck westward along the arid divide to the Big Horns and crossed Crow lands, during which time Rose stayed behind with Indian friends. Proceeding to the Wind River, Hunt and his men crossed the Continental Divide to the Green (called then the Spanish) River. In camp on the Green, a band of Snake—Shoshoni—Indians sold Hunt a large supply of buffalo jerky and through sign language and dirt-drawn maps provided help for the next leg of the journey.

The party crossed the Big Horn River and the lower Wind River Range in September and reached the headwaters of the westward-flowing Snake, which the trappers accurately called the Mad River. Known from Lewis and Clark reports to be a tributary of the mighty Columbia but unknown to Hunt and his party, the Snake was a writhing, death-dealing 1,038-mile waterway filled with narrow, rock-walled canyons and deep, timber-choked gorges with miles of churning rapids between. It was a mad river in every respect, and Hunt intended to negotiate it to the Columbia and Fort Astoria. The partners voted unanimously to attempt the river route and in early October turned most of their horses over to their Shoshoni guides, presumably in exchange for labor in constructing the fifteen canoes and pirogues required to carry downriver the party, their supplies, and the furs they had gathered. The necessary trees, big cottonwoods, were found at Henry's Fort in Idaho, a deserted trappers' stockade where a deceptively tranquil bend of the Snake widened to 150 yards.

Joseph Miller, the Marylander, could not go on, due to what Irving mysteriously called a "bodily malady," and stayed behind at the fort with a group of trappers detached from the party. These men, provided with some of the remaining horses, were to occupy the fort, continue to trap beaver that fall and winter, and bring their furs on to Fort Astoria in the spring.

Hunt and the fifty-four members of his expedition remaining pushed off the banks of the Snake on October 19 and spent the rest of the month and the first week of November attacking the river and losing the battle. One *voyageur* drowned; several canoe-loads of provisions and furs were lost in the seething, bitter-cold water; and progress was agonizingly slow, every yard of advance gained in peril and exhaustion. At night, hunkered at their camp-fires, they made plans for the dawning: Detachments were sent out under various partners and by the clerk John Reed to hunt game, explore ahead, find possible new routes along the Snake's banks, find Indians who might serve as guides, and barter for horses.

At one point near what became Twin Falls in south-central Idaho, the river was abandoned and the expedition split into two parties. Hunt led the main force of thirty men and Dorion's wife and children; Ramsey Crooks took charge of the others. Furs and other impediments to fast travel were cached, and the detachments set out on opposite sides of the Snake on November 9, still 700 miles from Fort Astoria, hoping to find Shoshoni camps, horses, and food. Both parties suffered as they trudged northwestward along the general course of the Snake in blizzard weather. Game was scarce, and all were reduced to eating roots and berries. One of Crooks' party said that during one nine-day period the men subsisted on "one beaver, one dog, a few wild cherries and some old mockason soles." Another of Crooks' contingent, a *voyageur* named Jean Baptiste Prevost, went insane from starvation and drowned in the river. In Hunt's camp, Marguerite Dorion gave birth and although her baby died after a few days, she managed to keep up with the line of march.

On December 15, Hunt and his people stumbled on a Shoshoni village of a dozen lodges near the merging of the Snake and Boisé Rivers, where the Hudson's Bay Company would subsequently erect a trading post. By the end of December, with three Shoshoni guides and with segments of the parties now rejoined, the expedition proceeded northwesterly, crossed the Grande Ronde valley and the Blue Mountains, and on January 6, 1812, struck the Umatilla River and located a large Indian camp. The party rested there six days before proceeding to the banks of the Columbia and following the river on purchased horses to The Dalles rapids, where they obtained canoes for the last miles of the journey. They arrived at Fort Astoria on February 15 with the stragglers coming in over a period of several weeks, each with a harrowing tale to tell. Crooks and John Day, wandering west from the banks of the Snake, would not be found and rescued until April.

□

Upriver from the fort, Hunt had received sketchy information from Chinook informants on the *Tonquin* disaster, now eight months past, and in conference with the other Astorians learned the chilling details. As dismayed as he was at the news and while still recovering from the privations of the sixteen-month trek from Saint Louis, Hunt undertook his duties as factor-in-chief at Fort Astoria. He sought to follow Astor's instructions on negotiating with the Russians and cementing friendly relations with the British fur traders on the coast, dispatched trappers upriver, assigned duties at the post, and took the resignations of partners Ramsey Crooks and Robert McClellan, who joined Robert Stuart in the summer for an overland journey back to Saint Louis.

The opportunity to begin Astor's diplomatic work came in May with the arrival in Baker's Bay of the *Beaver*, a 490-ton brigantine commanded by Captain Cornelius Sowle of Rhode Island and carrying reinforcements and tons of foodstuffs, supplies, and trade merchandise, some of which was transferred to the fort's warehouses. In the fall, Hunt boarded the ship and sailed with Sowle to Sitka, the flourishing capital of Russian America, 600 miles north of Vancouver Island. Sitka, and the island on which it lay, was ruled by the fierce, erratic, vodka-loving Count Alexandr Andreevich Baranov, and at Hunt's advent in his miniature kingdom the nobleman had spent forty of his sixty-five years in the fur trade in Siberia and Alaskan waters. He was as tough a customer as any Astor man was likely to encounter, but the New York financier's confidence in Hunt, and Hunt's tenacity, paid dividends as the Astorian traded to Baranov all the *Beaver*'s cargo of food, arms, powder, and trade merchandise, except for the portion that had been necessary to provision Astoria, in exchange for 75,000 seal skins. In Canton, by Hunt's calculations, the furs were worth four or five times the value of the cargo exchanged for them.

Baranov's furs were stored in a fishery in the Pribilof Islands, and Hunt remained aboard the *Beaver* as it sailed to the Bering Sea for the six-week detour required to get there, load the skins, and return to Astoria to pick up the baled furs awaiting the China trade. Hunt decided to omit the Astoria stopover and instructed Captain Sowle to drop him off at Oahu, then to sail on to China with the Baranov furs. It was now early in 1813, and the chief factor hoped to make passage back to the Oregon coast in the spring on the *Lark*, the resupply ship Astor had dispatched to the Pacific.

News of the American war with Britain reached the Sandwich Islands shortly after Hunt's arrival there, and all his plans—and those of his employer—went awry. The *Lark* arrived in the islands on schedule, but she was wrecked in a gale off Maui in March, at a cost of seven men drowned. The surviving crew members and their captain were rescued after a harrowing twelve days in the splintered and dismasted hulk of the vessel, living on a small ration of salt pork and wine that had been saved. Hunt was forced to purchase a Boston brig, the *Pedlar*, to return him to Astoria. He arrived there on August 20, just in time to witness the sale and abandonment of the fort.

3

Astor's proprietors had witnessed signs of deteriorating relations between the United States and England even before the *Tonquin* sailed in September 1810. The ship had been escorted from Long Island into the open sea by the *Constitution* to prevent its being boarded by British press gangs ostensibly searching for deserters from their navy—but, lost to the world in their tiny enclave on the Oregon coast, the Astorians knew virtually nothing of the war's cause and progress. What little news seeped into the fort told nothing of Britain's seizure of American merchant ships in European waters; President James Madison's trade embargo against England; the fall of Forts Michilimackinac, Detroit, and Dearborn to the Americans; the battle at Queenston in the Niagara campaign; the capture of York, capital of Upper Canada; or Perry's defeat of the British fleet at Lake Erie.

To John Jacob Astor, the war meant potential ruin for his Pacific enterprise, and he begged the Madison administration for protection. He sent urgent letters asking for a minimal force of forty soldiers to be dispatched to Astoria to protect his interests, which he felt were American interests, but his entreaties to Secretary of State James Monroe were ignored. In March 1813 he sent the supply ship *Lark* to the Columbia, but it was lost at sea. And, fearing that a blockade of New York Harbor would prevent departure of a second supply vessel that autumn, he managed to get a dispatch to Captain Sowle of the *Beaver*, then at Canton selling the Baranov furs, to return to Astoria with his ship's hold filled with supplies.

While these measures were being taken, the partners at Astoria were measuring their anomalous situation: They had learned of the war in January 1813, probably via North West Company trappers who came visiting, and now they were British subjects trading under the flag of the United States, unable to bear arms against their own country. They were isolated on a wild coast with a warehouse full of furs, cut off from Astor supply vessels, faced with dwindling food reserves and the imminent possibility of takeover by any armed British ship arriving on the coast or any British land force traveling down the Columbia.

The threats were real. While the Astor agents were nervously conferring on their plight, their great rival, the North West Company, "clearly perceiving this to be their time to strike, and plant thorns beneath Astor's pillows," Bancroft says, dispatched the twenty-gun man-of-war *Isaac Todd* to the Columbia to "plant a fort and dominate the region." Many months would pass before this ship reached the Oregon coast, but the North West Company paid a visit in the meantime, and the Astorians saw no recourse but to make terms with them.

Wilson Hunt was still at Oahu on April 11, 1813, when his fort was confronted by a convoy of canoes and pirogues led by a Nor'wester named John George McTavish. This man was welcomed, somewhat too warmly, some thought, by Duncan McDougall, senior partner at Astoria and now both Astor's and Hunt's "proxy." McTavish notified McDougall, Donald Mackenzie, and the others that the war now presented certain "difficulties" for the Americans. He told of the expected advent of the *Isaac Todd* and notified the Astorians that since the Oregon coast was now in British hands he was authorized to take control of the fort and purchase its stores, buildings, and furs. At some point in the discussions McTavish appears to have made certain other representations and incentives to those Astorians who were former North West Company men.

In August, Hunt returned at last to Astoria on the *Pedlar*. He argued against selling or quitting the fort but was voted down by the other partners.

After the negotiations that summer, the Astorians agreed to sell the fort's goods "at cost" and the furs housed there at the current London market price. The sale was completed on October 12, 1813, with McTavish presenting bills of exchange in the name of the North West Company. The selling price was $58,191.01, a fraction of Astor's investment and of the value of the property and goods.

There was a tense moment during the negotiations, reported by Alexander Ross, one of Jonathan Thorn's hated "scribbling clerks" who kept a journal on the voyage to the Columbia. A twenty-eight-year-old Nairnshire, Scotland, native, Ross had been fortunate in staying with the fort-building party while the man who had hired him, Alexander McKay, sailed north to his death on the *Tonquin*. Ross witnessed the sale of Astoria to the North West Company agents and wrote that near the conclusion of the negotiations, McTavish seemed to be buying time: He had learned that the *Isaac Todd* and perhaps other British warships were due to arrive on the coast at any moment, whereupon the American fort and property would "be seized as a prize," costing his company nothing. McDougall and Mackenzie, Ross said, "saw through this piece of artifice" and insisted that the bills of exchange be signed immediately. While McTavish stalled, "full of commercial wiles," the partners summoned all seventy-two of the Astorians and ordered the fort manned, the cannons shotted and pointed—presumably at McTavish's camp, which was situated a short distance from the fort—and slow matches lit. "In an instant," Ross said, "every man was at his post, and the gates shut. At eight o'clock a message was sent to McTavish, giving him two hours, and no more, either to sign the bills or break off the negotiation altogether and remove to some other quarters." This offensive move seems to have convinced McTavish not to wait for his warships: He signed the bills and the fort was delivered up.

One month later, the Nor'westers formally took possession of Fort Astoria, raised the Union Jack over its factory building, and christened the place Fort George. Many of Astor's Pacific Fur Company employees, including some of the *voyageurs*, who had come out to Oregon on the *Tonquin*, entered the service of the Nor'westers. McDougall, suspiciously, some of the Astor faithful thought, accepted a partnership with the British company. A few of the Astor overlanders decided to stay in Oregon, thus becoming among the first permanent settlers in the Willamette River valley.

In April 1814 Wilson Price Hunt sailed out of Baker's Bay in the *Pedlar*, which he had purchased for Astor in the Sandwich Islands, and spent two years in the Pacific coast trade trying to recoup some of his employer's investment. He ended his tour with a voyage to Canton and sailed home with the *Pedlar* loaded with chinaware, silks, and tea. He reached New York in October 1816, after a seafaring adventure "that might have furnished a chapter in the wanderings of Sinbad," Irving said.

Hunt resumed his former life as a merchant in Saint Louis, prospered in his business ventures, married a widow with three children, and died peacefully on April 13, 1842, on the eve of a great migration to the Oregon Country.

□

On November 29, the British sloop-of-war *Raccoon* anchored in Baker's Bay and its main passenger, another of the ubiquitous Macs of the Astoria saga, one John McDonald, a senior partner in the North West Company, assumed command of Fort George and the entire Columbia River fur enterprise. The skipper of the *Raccoon* took one look at the fort's split-board "palisades," pitiful bastions, and earthworks and said to McDonald, "This, then, was your enemy's stronghold, requiring a navy to conquer? Damn me! With a single four-pounder I would have battered it down in two hours!"

And, in April 1814, the long-awaited *Isaac Todd* crossed the Columbia bar and anchored before Fort George, thirteen months out of England, bringing with it another North West Company eminence, another Mac, another McTavish, another Donald, all in the person of Donald McTavish. Another noteworthy passenger on the warship was a certain Miss Jane Barnes, and H. H. Bancroft found it a pity "that the first European woman to stand upon the banks of the Columbia should have been of so questionable a character."

According to the historian, "One of the Macs [presumably Donald McTavish], doomed to the perils of western life yet loath all at once to relinquish every creature comfort, had brought with him some bottled porter, canned beef, cheese, and a blue-eyed, flaxen-haired female companion." Miss Barnes was a "daughter of Albion," who, "at the solicitations of this Mac had resigned her position as bar-maid in a Portsmouth hotel, and had come to this land of doubtful pleasures and profits, where at once she became an object of deepest interest to all." The more carnal-minded on the wild coast, the historian said in an abundance of superfluous language, "were scandalized that this lecherous Mac should so far break the laws of God and of the Honorable Northwest Company, as to form an unholy alliance with a frail fair one whose father was no chief, when fur-trading interests demanded duskier relationships. Make as many unmarried wives as you please of native maidens, and the great interests of commerce shall guard your good name, but to bring hither a white mistress—what will the savages say?"

Duncan McDougall's Chinook wife was envious, Bancroft said, "for pretty Miss Barnes flaunted a new frock almost every day," and McDougall's father-in-law, Chief Comcomly, was "curious, and one of his sons who had now but four wives, was amorous, wishing immediately to marry her." This young warrior, arrayed "in the richest robes, well painted, and redolent of grease, came and laid at her feet the offering of his heart. One hundred sea otter skins her owner should have, and she should never carry or dig. She should be queen of the Chinooks, and all his other wives should humble themselves before her. Elk, anchovies, and fat salmon should be heaped upon her lap, and all the livelong day she should sun herself and smoke."

But Miss Barnes declined these royal overtures and, indeed, found the society of the Columbia unsuited to her taste. She quickly determined to return to England and bartending by the ship that brought her out "but at Canton where the vessel touched, she fell in love with a wealthy English gentleman of the Honorable East India Company, and consented to grace a splendid establishment which he offered her."

Donald McTavish, however, had little time to enjoy the company of Miss Jane. His factorship at Fort George lasted barely a month. On May 22, as he crossed the river in a longboat, a sudden squall struck the channel and the boat filled and sank in a few minutes. McTavish and five other men from the *Isaac Todd* drowned.

Part Three

WILDERNESS CROSSINGS

8

TO THE TETONS

"INDIANS! INDIANS! TO ARMS!"

1

Among the heroes of John Jacob Astor's little band of Scotch fur traders at Fort Astoria, none stood taller than the Perthshireman Robert Stuart. He was born on his father's small farm in 1785, of a lineage that seems to have been more affluent than the ordinary crofter family of the southern highlands. The family had a crest bearing the legend *Nobilis ira est leonis* ("Noble is the anger of lions") and his father, John Stuart, known locally as *Ian Mair na Coille*, "Big John of the Woods," saw to it that his nine children were well educated. In his youth, "Little Robert of the Woods" made plans to join the Honorable East India Company as a clerk, sailing to Calcutta and seeing the world beyond the Stuart farm. He probably shared this dream with his uncle David. Twenty years older than Robert, David Stuart had emigrated to Canada in 1800 with no special prospects, had worked as a fisherman and trapper, and soon became a trusted North West Company trader. He saw promise in Robert, understood the lad's need to quit the farm and make his own life, and urged him to come to Montreal, where employment in the Nor'westers awaited him. Robert sailed and in 1807 joined the company as a clerk, and in 1810 followed his uncle to New York where John Jacob Astor's new Pacific Fur Company was organizing a ship to carry the enterprise to the Columbia River.

We have a photograph of Robert Stuart taken thirty-five years after he sailed on the *Tonquin* to the Oregon coast as a raw "junior partner" in Astor's magnificent scheme. The *carte de viste*, although taken in about 1845, when he was sixty, corroborates certain contemporary impressions of him in the early years of his quarter-century career as Astor's ablest lieutenant. In that time, when he received a salary of $500 or $600 a year from Astor, Stuart was the best of bargains. In the daguerreotype he gives the impression of a man who has fulfilled the promise in Bancroft's phrase for him: "a most promising young man." He seems tall even though the image is of him from the waist up, his arms folded across his chest, stern and statesmanlike in a frock coat with velvet lapels and a stock-like collar. He is high of forehead and clean-shaven, his curly hair (which one imagines was a rusty, maybe fiery, red in his youth) graying at the temples, and he is the living representation of *Nobilis ira est leonis*, leonine and fiercely handsome—and impatient if not angry. His flared nostrils and clamped jaw give the sense of a man unaccustomed to waiting, certainly of one unused to smiling. He seems to have required no instructions on freezing for the moment it took for the daguerreotypist to capture him on film; indeed, one has the sense that he scarcely flinched when the powder flashed. He stares at the lens with irascibility, resoluteness, and utter self-confidence. Many saw and remembered Robert Stuart's dour and grimly purposeful aspect: the starving, fever-stricken, hope-abandoned men he led through the western wilderness; the natives of over twenty tribes and bands, from Walla Wallas to Missouris, he encountered on his expedition from Astoria to Saint Louis; businessmen in boardrooms, politicians in legislatures, Presbyterian ministers in their pulpits.

One who had cause to remember those deep-set blue eyes and unblinking gaze, and the coiled ferocity lying within the tall, thin, clerkly frame hovering over him, was Captain Jonathan Thorn of the *Tonquin*. In December 1810, as the Astor brig bobbed at anchor off an island in the Falklands, Stuart had taken a stand, a flintlock pistol in one hand, the other a fist shaking in the choleric captain's face as he threatened to blow Thorn's brains over the compass box. The would-be Bligh looked into this Covenanter's eyes and had enough of his sanity remaining to realize that there were some men he could not tyrannize.

□

After Wilson Hunt reached Fort Astoria in February 1812 and took command of the post, he had the urgent duty of sending dispatches to Mr. Astor in New York to apprise the financier of the details he had gathered on the *Tonquin* calamity and the state of affairs on the Columbia. With no ship to carry the papers home, he arranged an overland expedition back to Missouri that would follow the rough and meandering trail he had blazed to the Pacific.

The original expedition, a two-month fiasco, consisted of three small parties under Stuart's generalship that set out late in March 1812. One of the detachments was to proceed east to the Snake River to salvage the furs, traps, and provisions cached by Hunt the previous November. The second group, which included Hunt's Irish clerk John Reed and five other men, would carry the important dispatches to Mr. Astor and locate and assist two of Hunt's men who had as yet not reached Fort Astoria. Before starting east the third group, headed by Stuart, was to take two *bateaux* loaded with supplies to a subsidiary trading post established by his uncle on the Okanogan River, a tributary of the Columbia 250 miles northeast.

The three parties, seventeen men in all, paddled upstream from Astoria to rapids of The Dalles (from the French for "flagstones," the name deriving from the basaltic rocks of the canyon walls), the site of an old Indian commerce center and a "notorious plundering place," Irving said. There the parties unloaded their canoes and recruited a number of Cathlasko natives—a small band related to the Chinooks—whose village lay nearby to provide horses and

assist in the portage around the rapids. In a rocky defile, several of
the Cathlaskos bolted up a narrow path, taking with them two
bundles of provisions. When Stuart, who was riding behind, heard
of the theft, he moved to the front of the column to keep an eye
on the "impudent villains."

After passing the rapids, Stuart and his men and Indian portagers reached the fishing village of the Wishram people and, Irving
says, "found themselves benighted in a strange place, and surrounded by savages bent on pilfering." Guards were posted, and
at dawn the party pushed off from shore in their reloaded canoes
to "gladly bid adieu to this abominable den of robbers," Stuart
said. But his problems had just begun. Along the banks above The
Dalles the Wishrams were gathered in force, whooping and bran-
dishing their spears and war clubs and with arrows nocked and
ready. The Indians pretended to offer help in the next portage, but
Stuart believed they were bent on further plunder and when the
canoes came ashore below the Great Falls (so named by Lewis and
Clark), they were surrounded by several hundred of the "river ruf-
fians." Stuart promised to employ them as portagers next day if
they conducted themselves peaceably.

During the night, Stuart attempted to steal a march on the Indians. He roused his men in the moonlight, gathered the canoes,
gear, and provisions, and led the portage afoot while the natives
slept. Reed and Robert McClellan, the temperamental Ohio Valley
Indian fighter, brought up the rear.

The ruse lasted until dawn, when some of the Wishrams on the
opposite bank of the river pushed their canoes off and paddled
toward Stuart and his portagers. They were quickly joined by others, and by the time they struck the shore numbered at least a
hundred. Reed, with his dispatch case on his back, seems to have
been a special attraction. "Shining afar," Irving said, "like the brilliant helmet of Euryalus," the tin box became a glittering prize.
The Indians fell on McClellan first, throwing a buffalo robe over
his head while attempting to stab him. He wrestled free, raised his
musket, and shot one of his attackers through the heart. Reed,
meantime, was also under attack. As he fumbled for his rifle he

was clubbed senseless and stripped of his weapons and the dispatch case. McClellan ran forward, killed one of Reed's assailants with a pistol, and then was wounded by a tomahawk blow. Stuart and the other men now came forward to the fight, firing their weapons into the Indian force and scattering it into the woods.

Later in the day, as Reed's and McClellan's wounds were being tended, a Wishram chief approached Stuart's camp. This elder announced, apparently through sign language, that his people demanded vengeance for the deaths of two of their brothers. Stuart stood his ground and made it clear that his guns would kill many more warriors if he and his men were attacked again. Eventually, after much awkward diplomacy, an agreement was negotiated. Stuart said the compromise cost "3 Blankets to cover the dead, and some Tobacco to fill the Calumet of Peace, on condition they should immediately cross the River and leave our passage free, which was Soon complied with and we saw no more of them."

The tin dispatch box was never recovered, but Stuart allowed no time to search for it. He led his party back to the Okanogan and was returning downriver toward Fort Astoria when at least one of the missions of the original three parties was fulfilled. Below the forks of the Columbia, Stuart's canoes were hailed from shore by two wraith-like figures. They were white men, thin, long-bearded, and entirely naked, and when the canoes reached the shore, Ramsey Crooks and John Day, the "lost" members of Wilson Price Hunt's expedition who had been left on the banks of the Snake River in December last, fell at their feet.

The entire party reached the fort on May 11, and by the end of June Stuart was ready to restart his expedition to Saint Louis.

2

The Astor brigantine *Beaver* rammed into Baker's Bay a few days before Stuart and his men reached the fort after their near disaster at The Dalles rapids. The ship brought supplies and reinforcements, and since as yet there was no news of war with Britain, Astoria rejoiced in its new prosperity. Among the newcomers were five clerks, fifteen American laborers, six Canadian *voyageurs*, and twelve Hawaiians who signed on for service on the Columbia during the ship's stopover in the Sandwich Islands. In charge of the civilian contingent aboard the *Beaver* was a new partner and distant relative of Astor's, John Clarke, an American with long service in the fur trade, including six years with the North West Company.

The reinforcements breathed new life into the Pacific outpost and six weeks after they were landed, the senior partners launched four new expeditions to extend the fort's operations up the river and one to carry dispatches east. Two of the parties set out on foot, led by Donald "Perpetual Motion" Mackenzie and John Clarke, to locate sites and establish new trade posts above the forks of the Columbia; a third headed north for Fort Okanogan with supplies; and the fourth, "one of peril and hardship," which "required a man of nerve and vigor," Irving said, was designated to convey dispatches to Saint Louis, thence to New York for Mr. Astor, replacing those carried by John Reed in the tin box recently lost to the Wishrams. This mission was confided to Robert Stuart, who, Irving said, "though he had never been across the mountains, and a very young man, had given proofs of his competency to the task."

Bancroft provided a prose poem to describe the leave-taking of the parties:

> It was a beautiful sight and one which would have warmed the blood of Astor . . . see these sixty-two men on the Thirtieth of June, 1812, set out in ten canoes and two barges from the fort which was now to become the Mother of Forts and a great city on these broad Western waters, and with paddles flying, with shout and song, and the ringing of artillery, strike boldly from their several posts.

Stuart had six men with him when he departed Fort Astoria with the other parties. Ramsey Crooks and Robert McClellan, both having resigned from Astor's service, were eager to return to Saint Louis, as were François LeClairc and André Vallé, both Canadian *engagés*, and Benjamin Jones, a Virginia backwoodsman. This latter valuable man had left home at age sixteen, spent time in Kentucky, and drifted to Saint Louis in 1802, where he and a partner, Alexander Carson (a distant relative of Christopher "Kit" Carson), began trapping along the Upper Missouri. Although his history is sketchy, Jones, and Carson as well, may have served with Lewis and Clark in 1804, at least as far as the Mandan villages. The Virginian had been canoeing down the Missouri when he encountered Wilson Hunt's westbound expedition and joined it to Astoria. He was an excellent hunter and a crack shot, had been in the thick of the fight with the Wishrams at The Dalles, and had Stuart's complete trust.

The sixth man was John Day. He had barely survived the privations of Hunt's party and with Crooks had been rescued by Stuart less than two months past. Irving described him as about forty years old, six-foot-two in height, and "straight as an Indian; with an elastic step as if he trod on springs, and a handsome, open, manly countenance." But his vigorous step and strong physique dated back to the time he joined Hunt's overlanders in their winter camp on the Nodaway River at the end of 1810. The seven months he and Crooks had wandered the country between the Snake and Columbia—sick, starving, and lost—had beaten Day down. Now he was thin, tired, and delusional, and it became clear soon after the departure from Astoria that he would not survive the journey ahead. Stuart, who had no experience with trail fevers and no patience with sick men, observed Day's babbling and noted in his journal that the man "spoke in the most incoherent, absurd and unconnected sentences." After four days on the river, Day put a pair of loaded pistols to his head and pulled the triggers but fired high and was wrestled to the ground, bound, and placed under guard. Stuart had him escorted back to the fort.*

---

*He recovered enough to join the North West Company's service but seems never to have conquered his infirmities and died, "infirm of body," in a defile in the Salmon River Mountains of Idaho in February 1820. One of his trapper companions wrote, "He appeared to die the good death of a good man."

Most of July was occupied in portages and slow advances in ascending the river to the mouth of the Walla Walla, a shallow stream that debouched into the Columbia. The natives of the region were a hospitable horseback tribe and greeted the Astorians with a huge bonfire on the riverbank and, after camp was established, conducted a dance in their honor. Stuart purchased twenty horses from the Walla Wallas, most of them to be used as pack animals, and on the last day of July he and his men set out with their string of ponies to the southeast over the open plains toward the Blue Mountains.

The trail they blazed roughly followed Wilson Hunt's route, but Stuart hoped that traveling it in summer would avoid the privations Hunt and his men had experienced. Game ought to be plentiful now, the weather agreeable for a fast passage of the mountains and the approach to the Snake River. But as the little party entered the arid wastes, naked and sandy hills, and crossed sunbaked and cracked ravines and streambeds, the search for water consumed them and slowed their pace to a crawl. The waterskins they carried were too soon exhausted, and horse and man became tortured by thirst, trudging forward in stifling, dust-bearing winds on sunburned sand and clay "without the least appearance of having experienced any share of the dews of heaven since the time of Noahs Flood," Stuart wrote.

They were four days crossing forty-five miles of desert before spying a fringe of forest in the distance and, upon approaching it, heard the water. The horses needed no goading and led the party to the bank of the Umatilla River, the same lifesaving stream Hunt and his men had fallen on after crossing the Blue Mountains seven months past.

After a camp on the gravelly beach and a skimpy meal, and with the skins filled and the horses watered and fed, Stuart and his men left the Umatilla on August 1. They followed a grassy plain to another stream, which Stuart identified as the "Glaise" (Clay) River (subsequently called the Grande Ronde), and on the seventh entered the dense forests at the foot of the Blues. They led their

horses in crossing and recrossing rocky streambeds, through
wooded defiles and narrow paths shouldered by great promontories
and drop-aways. On August 12 the party broached the mountains,
crossed a fertile meadowland, and arrived on the shore of the tumultuous Snake, 400 yards wide, its frothing waters running below
high, shrubby sandbanks.

The men recuperated on the riverbank for two days, and on the
evening before they pushed on they were visited by a solitary Shoshoni who rode into the camp and through laborious signing told of
a white man living with his band a day's journey upriver. Stuart figured that the man was probably one of Wilson Hunt's trappers who
had remained at Fort Henry to hunt beaver and had vanished into
the wilderness. Finding one of them would be the key to learning the
fate of the others, as well as the location of the several caches of furs,
saddles, and supplies left behind by Hunt's Astorians.

After two days' travel upstream with no sighting of the mysterious straggler, the journeyers reached what Stuart called "a renowned Fishing place," a junction where another large waterway,
apparently the Boisé River, flowed into the Snake and where Shoshonis in great numbers gathered to collect the salmon teeming in
the confluence. At a streamside village inquiries were made about
any white men seen in the vicinity, and the party was directed to
another Indian camp on the opposite shore. Stuart found a Shoshoni willing to canoe across to seek out any white men and bring
them across the river.

The Astorians spent a miserable night in the Indian camp,
galled by clouds of mosquitoes, which, Stuart wrote, "assailed us
in innumerable hosts, and completely deprived our eyelids of their
usual functions; even after the dew had fallen those infernal Pests
Still continued their music to our no small annoyance." In the
morning they were disappointed to learn that the Indian messenger
had returned alone in his canoe. There were no white men across
the river or, so far as could be determined, anywhere else in the vicinity. As the morning wore on, disquieting news came to them
when an elderly Shoshoni rode into their camp, dismounted, ran

directly to Stuart's horse, flung his arms around the animal's neck, and hugged and kissed it. The horse, purchased from the Walla Wallas, Stuart had so grown to love as a "noble animal, admirably shaped, of free and generous spirit" that he intended taking it to New York as a gift for Mr. Astor. Now he learned from the Indian elder that the beast had been stolen from him and that he wanted it back.

While this uncomfortable sign-and-word conversation was proceeding, Crooks, McClellan, Ben Jones, and others who had been in Wilson Hunt's party came forward and recognized the old man as one of the "trusty Snakes" who had served as guide the preceding autumn when they all reached Fort Henry. They questioned the elder closely and learned much bad news: The horses Hunt had left in the care of the Shoshoni guides had been stolen by an Absaroka war party; all of Hunt's caches had been plundered; and the missing trappers had been attacked by the Crow marauders, stripped of their weapons, horses, and goods, and left to wander along the river.

One piece of intelligence that had great implications for the future was given to Stuart that August 16, 1812. The Snake elder told the Astorians that he knew a shorter and safer route across the Rocky Mountains than that taken by Wilson Hunt. Stuart noted in his diary that upon "learning that this Indian was perfectly acquainted with the route, I without loss of time offered him a Pistol a Blanket of Blue Cloth—an Axe—a Knife—an awl—a Fathom of Beads, a looking glass and a little Powder & Ball if he would guide us from this to the other side, which he immediately accepted." The Indian, who had seemingly forgotten the matter of the stolen horse, said he was tired of eating salmon and longed to hunt buffalo and so rode off to retrieve his arms and equipment for the journey across the Rockies—the shorter "trace," as Stuart called it, which lay south of the Wind River Mountains.

He rejoined the Astorians the next morning and after the horses were collected, all tormented during the night by flies and mosquitoes clouding up from the river, the party "journeyed quite harmoniously together," Irving said, "though now and then, the Snake would regard his quondam steed with a wistful eye." They had made a late start and had traveled only about nine miles when they came to a great bend in the river. The Shoshoni guide advised that they make camp there and get an early start for the next full day's travel. That day, he said, would take them across a hilly stretch of country that would save many miles in the approach to the western foothills of the Rocky Mountains.

At the dawn muster of his party, Stuart discovered the guide and the noble horse missing. Tracks showed that the Shoshoni had ridden off, and taken his other horse as well. Irving wrote, "It was plain the Snake had taken an Indian mode of recovering his horse, having quietly decamped with him in the night. . . . New vows were made never more to trust in Snakes, or any other Indians." Sentries, three each night, were assigned to watch the remuda.

The march proceeded in sultry weather across the prairie lands paralleling the Snake, with "Mosquitoe Serenades" and hordes of sand flies—"Imps of Darkness," Stuart called them—continuing to devour the party during the day and thirst driving them again and again to the willow-rimmed edge of the river, where they fell in its cooling waters to drink and wash away trail grime.

On August 20, during one of these respites, they stumbled upon a gaunt white man in ragged clothing fishing at the river's edge. It turned out to be John Hoback, one of the missing Hunt men. After Stuart and his men greeted this specter of the forest, three other of the missing trappers emerged from the willows—Joseph Miller, Jacob Reznor, and Edward Robinson. All had served in Andrew Henry's fur brigade before joining Hunt's overlanders and were among those who, the previous autumn, had elected to remain at Fort Henry to trap. Miller was the former infantry lieutenant from Pennsylvania; of Hoback, Reznor, and Robinson nothing is known except that they were Kentuckians and that Robinson, who may have been the oldest of the group, had been scalped in some past Indian fight and wore a handkerchief knotted about his head.

The men told of their desperate experiences over the past ten months. They had twice been robbed—by Arapahoes, not Crow—of their furs, horses, provisions, and most of their weapons, and had wandered hundreds of miles, not straying far from the Snake, where they could at least subsist on fish. "Nothing could exceed their joy on thus meeting with their old comrades," Irving wrote, "or the heartiness with which they were welcomed. All hands immediately encamped; and the slender stores of the party were ransacked to furnish out a suitable regale." Stuart jotted in his diary, "After regaling our half famished friends with the best our small pittance of luxuries could afford, we proceeded along the banks of the river, for 3 miles, to a good fishing and grazing place, where we took up our lodgings for the night."

3

The expedition, now numbering ten men, continued to follow the course of the Snake for several days, encountering small Shoshoni fishing camps en route and a large one of over 100 lodges at a falls on August 25, where they gorged on salmon and purchased a quantity of dried fish before moving on. Soon after, they reached the vicinity of Hunt's caches and located nine of them. Six had been dug up from ground covered with wolf tracks. Stuart concluded that the ripe buried beaver hides had brought the scavengers and that Indian scavengers followed, taking everything remaining except the books, which lay scattered about. The three unmolested caches contained some clothing articles, ammunition, and beaver traps. With clothing, arms, and traps, and with their strength returned, Robinson, Reznor, and Hoback decided to stay on in the Snake River country. Thus, Irving said, "fitted out for a campaign of beaver-trapping," the men "forgot all that they had suffered, and determined upon another trial of their fortunes; preferring to take their chances in the wilderness, rather than return home ragged and penniless."*

On September 7, the seven-man party left the banks of the Snake to head for the Teton Range in western Wyoming, still following Wilson Hunt's route. Joseph Miller, who had had enough of Indian country and stayed with Stuart "to return to the bosom of civilized society," volunteered to serve as guide but proved "indifferent," Irving said, and the travelers were soon lost on the game-barren plains and, having used up their supply of dried salmon, had to eat roots and serviceberries mashed into cakes and a dog purchased from a forlorn Shoshoni lodge. They struck the Bear River after five days' travel, averaging twenty to twenty-five miles a day, and on the last day of their rest, while fishing the stream discovered a dozen Absarokas prowling their camp. The Crow chief, whom Irving described as "a dark Herculean fellow, fully six feet four inches in height, with a mingled air of ruffian and rogue," was at first friendly, even sending some of his people to their nearby village to bring buffalo meat for the white men. But by midnight, with over twenty of the native band around the camp, Stuart and his men grew apprehensive, more over "the adroitness of these fellows in stealing Horses," Stuart said, than for their own safety.

Watches were doubled, and after an uneasy night the Astorians repacked their animals and prepared to push on. The Crow signed and pointed to Stuart's muskets and indicated that they wanted to trade horses for powder. Stuart declined and the big Crow leader grew belligerent, slapped himself on the chest, and announced his power as a great chief. He signed that it was customary for chiefs

---

*In January 1814, all three were killed by Shoshonis at the mouth of the Boisé River, together with the Irishman John Reed (who had lost the Astor dispatch box at The Dalles rapids) and Pierre Dorion, the liquor-loving interpreter with Wilson Hunt's party. The only survivors of the massacre were Dorion's Indian wife, Marguerite, and their two children. Marguerite married thrice again and died in 1850, at age eighty, at her home on the Willamette River.

to give each other gifts. He pointed to Stuart's horse and when it was denied him he grasped Stuart and shook him as if to pull him out of the saddle. Irving reported, "Mr. Stuart instantly drew forth a pistol and presented it at the head of the bully-ruffian. In a twinkling his swaggering was at an end, and he dodged behind his horse to escape the expected shot." Stuart ordered his men to level their rifles at the others but not to fire unless he gave the order. The ploy worked. The Crow scrambled into the brush. Not long after, the chief emerged from cover affecting to laugh off the affair, and Stuart gave him twenty charges of powder as a gift.

They moved on uneasily, heading east over a chain of hills, watching columns of smoke in the mountain foothills around them, and made a hard twenty-five-mile march before setting up a closely guarded camp, hobbling their horses, setting the sentries, and sleeping fitfully with their rifles.

On September 18, six days and 150 miles from the Bear River confrontation, the party reached the "Mad River," Henry's Fork of the Snake, just west of the Tetons. At dawn, as an antelope-meat breakfast was cooking, Stuart was standing at the riverbank when he heard the cry "Indians! Indians! To arms!" at the camp. A Crow raiding party swooped down on the small horse herd and proceeded to drive them off, and as the Astorians ran to their rifles the main body of raiders, about twenty men, crashed out of the brush and began carrying off the packs of provisions and supplies lying about the campfire. The leader of the Crow party rode past the panicking Astorians—he was the same bulky leader Stuart had encountered the week past—and, rising from his horse's back, slapped himself on the buttocks ("clapping his hands on the most insulting part of his body" in Washington Irving's delicate phrase) and yelled some jeering words.

Lapsing into a style adopted by dime-novelists many decades later, Irving re-created the scene that followed:

Sharpshooter Ben Jones leveled his rifle and caught the big chief in his sights.

Stuart shouted, "Not for your life! not for your life! You will bring destruction on us all!"

Jones replied, "O, Mr. Stuart, only let me have one crack at the infernal rascal, and you may keep all the pay that is due me."

"By heaven, if you fire," cried Mr. Stuart, "I'll blow your brains out!"

Jones was angry to be prevented from making his clear shot, but Stuart knew instinctively what the consequences would be had he permitted it: He told Irving that the Indians believed in a life for a life and the whole Crow nation would have risen in vengeance. He said signal fires would have directed war parties to their camp to slaughter them; they were but seven men, now afoot, at the mercy of the Indians—Crow, Blackfeet, even the ostensibly friendly Snakes—the land, and the elements. He had to admire the savages and their leader and wrote in his journal, "On the whole it was one of the most daring and intrepid actions I ever heard of among Indians, and convinced me how determined they were on having our Horses, for which they would unquestionably have followed us any distance."

The party was now in desperate straits, heading toward unmapped mountain passages and unknown hazards, without pack animals and able to carry only what they could mount on their backs, facing the coming winter and the necessity of finding a camp and game to sustain them for the months of immobile isolation. But they had little time to despair and spent the day after the raid making their backpacks, burning in a bonfire the goods they could not carry, and cooking a scanty meal from a beaver Ben Jones had trapped in the river.

They followed the Mad River through a mountain defile to a point below Fort Henry where it emptied back into the Snake. They lived on fish, built two crude rafts, and floated on the Snake's currents for six days, poling ashore at each dusk to set up camp, hunt, and fish. Jones eventually killed a deer and they gorged on the meat, jerked what remained, and made moccasins of the hide to reinforce their tattered boots.

Stuart hoped to find a Shoshoni village where he might barter for at least one packhorse, but none were found. They were now on dangerous ground—Blackfeet territory—and grew fearful of hunting since a gunshot might attract these intractable white-hating warriors. The nights turned bitter, a sharp reminder of the need to find a winter hideaway, and after floating over ninety miles on the south fork of the Snake, Stuart took his men ashore. They quit their rafts and struck east toward what Stuart called the "Pilot Knobs," the Tetons (which French *voyageurs* had named *Trois Tetons* for their perceived resemblance to three female breasts). They tramped over an alluvial bottom thick with cottonwoods, hawthorns, and willows and across a series of stony hills and ravines, skirting sulphurous hot springs.

Ramsey Crooks took a fever in this stretch of the march but struggled on with the others, after a day's rest, to the foothills of the Snake River Range. Here, on the last days of September, near a place under the Tetons later called Pierre's Hole, Stuart consulted with his men on the question of climbing the low chain of mountains or detouring around them to the south. Since it was decided that the longer route might put them among Blackfeet hunters, six of the seven Astorians decided to climb. The dissenter was Robert McClellan, the forty-two-year-old Indian fighter, "hot-headed and impatient at all times," Irving said, who "had been rendered irascible by the fatigues of the journey, and the conditions of his feet, which were chafed and sore." He swore he would rather face the Blackfeet than climb another mountain and soon fell back, deriding the others, and disappeared—"a braggart spirit, that took a pride in doing desperate and hare-brained things," in Irving's estimation.

Crooks' fever flared violently during the crossing and a willow bower was thrown up for him to lie in. He was dosed with castor oil and made to endure an "Indian Sweat," made with hot coals in water. Some of the members thought he was dying and apparently talked of leaving him behind. Stuart would not hear of it and noted in his diary that such an idea was "too repugnant to my feelings to require long deliberation." He used the occasion to write philosophically of men daring the "unknown and untravelled wilderness." The artificial solitude of parks and gardens, he said, is apt to give humans "a flattering notion of self-sufficiency" but "the phantoms which haunt a desert are want, misery, and danger," and the wilderness reminds that "man is unwillingly acquainted with his own weakness, and meditations shew him only how little he can sustain, and how little he can perform."

9

SOUTH PASS

"... HARBINGERS OF THE WISHED-FOR LAND."

1

Robert Stuart's party crossed the low hills west of the Teton Range on October 1, 1812, the passage made difficult by snowdrifts and the weakened state of Ramsey Crooks, who was still suffering the effects of his fever. He could not eat, but there was little to eat for any of them, and Stuart said they were all "reduced to their last extremity, nor had they strength to make use of their rifles, although now and then some deer were seen."

From the summit of the hills could be sighted a grassy plain stretching at least twenty miles in width with a meandering river bordered by willows at its edge. Those who had traveled with Wilson Hunt recognized the place and pointed out to Stuart the route they must take to Henry's Fort, the deserted trappers' post where Hunt had abandoned his horses and proceeded on the Snake in canoes. As they descended to the plain, Robert McClellan was spotted in the distance making his solitary, sullen way toward the stream. They halloo'd to him but he did not respond.

They camped in the willows on the edge of the river. Crooks was so weak and despaired that some of the party again spoke of leaving him behind. They were in Blackfeet country, winter was approaching fast, the Tetons were probably snowbound, they were starving, and no game had been seen in many days. But Stuart was aghast at such a suggestion, said they must give the ailing man time to recuperate, and sent Ben Jones out along the river with a beaver trap and rifle despite the continuing fear that a gunshot might attract hostiles to their camp. Jones shot but only wounded a grizzly bear, which vanished into the brush, but six miles from the camp he came upon a number of grazing elk and was able to kill five of them. The camp was moved to the meat, with Crooks supported between two of the party, and by the end of three days his fever had eased and he was able to eat and regain some of his strength. The elk meat that remained was smoked and dried, and later a grizzly was killed and added to the larder. The fat on its rump, Stuart said, was three inches thick.

They pushed on, with Crooks now able to walk alone and carry his rifle, and crossed Teton Pass through nine inches of snow, bending their course eastward as much as possible through a succession of rocky heights, deep valleys, and rapid streams. Their path lay along the margins of perpendicular precipices several hundred feet in height with the rocky bed of the river roaring below. Their food supply, the elk and bear meat they were able to smoke and pack, disappeared even after careful rationing, and they found no game and only a few trout in the Teton River. When a small deer was killed, Stuart eked out a three-day meat allowance from it.

On October 11 they stumbled upon a camp McClellan had made, found the remains of a wolf he had eaten, and the next day spotted a plume of smoke in the distance, which François LeClairc was sent out to investigate. Stuart and his men were starving and had forgotten their fear of the Blackfeet, and they hoped the smoke was issuing from an Indian camp. Stuart wrote that he and his men "sat up late waiting his [LeClairc's] return in expectation of getting something to eat, but at last despairing of his coming we went to bed about 11 o'Clock, again supperless."

In the morning they resumed their march and en route were hailed by LeClairc as he made his way back to the night's camp. He reported that the smoke had risen from McClellan's campfire on the banks of the river, where he had tried and failed to find fish. They reached the Pennsylvanian in an hour and as Stuart dispassionately described the scene, "We found him lying on a parcel of straw, emaciated and worn to a perfect skeleton & hardly able to raise his head or speak from extreme debility."

In the twelve days since he had angrily struck out on his own, McClellan had fared worse in finding game or fish than the others, and while Stuart said "our presence seemed to revive him considerably," the older man said he would as soon die on his pallet than go on. Nevertheless, they dragged him to his feet, distributed his pitiful belongings into their packs, and were able to proceed to a new riverbank camp after plodding on seventeen miles.

Weak with hunger, three days since the last scrap of jerky had been consumed, Stuart and those who could summon the energy to hunt spent the afternoon of October 14 foraging for anything edible. They found no fish, and the few antelope they saw were too far away to kill. They returned to the camp, Stuart said, "with heavy hearts but I must confess we could not enter the same complaints against our stomachs." He wrote in his journal that "one of the Canadians" (Irving said it was LeClairc) came to him that evening and suggested they drew lots, proposing, "It is better one should die than that all should perish." Stuart wrote, without mentioning the cannibalistic implications of the proposal, "I shuddered at the idea & used every endeavor to create an abhorrence in his mind against such an act, urging also the probability of falling in with some animal on the morrow but, finding that every argument failed and that he was on the point of converting some others to his purpose, I snatched up my Rifle, cocked and leveled it at him with the firm resolution to fire if he persisted." He said, "This affair so terrified him that he fell upon his knees and asked the whole party's pardon, swearing he should never again suggest such a thought—after this affair was settled I felt so agitated and weak that I could scarcely crawl to bed."

The day after this incident, eleven miles along their route they found an old buffalo bull wandering alone and succeeded in killing it. They were so ravenous they ate some of the meat raw, then butchered and carried the remainder to the camp, where Stuart instructed they boil some of it and drink the broth before gorging on the steaks.

Now "somewhat recruited and refreshed," they moved on, left the river, and traveled another fifteen miles, heading toward the foot of the Wind River Range, a bulking, unbroken wall of snow-capped mountains running toward the northwest and forcing the Astorians southward. After fording a tributary of the Green River they came upon an abandoned Indian camp strewn with buffalo bones and lying within a copse of pines. They stopped to examine it and found at its center an enormous lodge 150 feet across. The tepee-shaped structure was composed of twenty pine logs, each twelve inches in diameter and forty feet long, the whole covered with pine and willow boughs. Inside it, opposite the entrance, three bodies lay on pallets, at their heads a branch of red cedar and at their feet a large black-painted buffalo skull. From the conical ceiling were suspended "numerous ornaments" and many children's moccasins. While Stuart gave only a clinician's description of the sacred place, he knew its significance. The time and labor taken to assemble it, he said, gave a hint "that the personages on whose account it was constructed were not of the common order."

On the eighteenth, the men crossed a ridge of the Wind River Mountains, waded a branch of the Green River, and coming up from the bank encountered six Shoshonis in a hunting party who escorted them to their streamside encampment. There were four pine-branch huts in the camp and Stuart found the people "poor but hospitable in the Extreme," and traded a pistol, an ax, a knife, a cup, two awls, and some beads for the single horse they had with them, some deerskin for moccasins and a bit of buffalo meat. The natives explained that they had been ravaged by Crow raiders who had stolen all but one of their horses and most of their food and effects and had abducted several of their women. Stuart told them that "the day was not far distant when we would take signal vengeance on the perpetrators of those deeds," and smoked a pipe with them.

On October 19 the seven Astorians packed their horse with enough buffalo jerky to last six days and left the Snake camp to follow the river branch southeast. They were grateful to the Indians, and justly so: They had a horse to ease their burdens, they were reasonably fit now and well fed, and even McClellan and Crooks had revived their strength and were anxious to push on. They found a beaten path, which Stuart surmised was a trail the Crow used in their forays along the river, and followed it all day. LeClairc and André Vallé, hunting ahead of the others, killed a buffalo calf toward dusk and they had a camp feast that night, with a kettle full of meat on a roaring fire as the wind whistled and snow fell around them.

The next day they quit the Crow trace, which seemed to wind too far north for their purpose and was too dangerous in any event. Keeping to it, Irving said, "they might be described by some scouts and spies of that race of Ishmaelites, whose predatory life required them to be constantly on alert." Instead of taking such a chance, they tramped southeast through new-fallen snow, across undulating country with the ridges of the lower Wind River Range on their front and left, and crossed a salt plain to camp in a cutting wind on another stream bank. At twilight, as they sat huddled before their fire, McClellan set out with his rifle and killed a buffalo, which they would skin and slaughter the next morning.

□

October 21, 1812, had no special significance to Stuart or his men beyond the fact that on that day they were able to cover only a paltry fifteen miles of ground in the face of a wind driving needles of snow. The expedition leader noted the snowfall and biting cold in his diary "soon after we left the drain which compelled us to encamp at the end of 15 miles E N E on the side of a Hill [which he later called "a handsome low gap"] which we must inevitably traverse where we found a sufficiency of dry Aspen for firewood, but not a drop of water." Washington Irving, writing from Stuart's notes and journals and presumably from interviews with Stuart, Crooks, and others of the expedition, said the seven men "set forward on their bleak and toilsome way" on the twenty-first "towards the lofty summit of a mountain, which was necessary for them to cross."

The camp that day was made on a hillside at the approximate latitude 42 degrees 26 minutes, not far above the line that would later establish the California-Oregon border, and the "handsome low gap" was the western entrance to a twenty-nine-mile-wide, gently sloping saddle of the Wind River Range. Stuart and his party of seven had discovered, without their slightest knowledge of it, the corridor through the Rocky Mountains that thirty years hence would enable the American settlement of Oregon and California.

The gateway, located where the Continental Divide debouched into a wide, arid plain of sage and sand forming the eastern boundary of the Oregon Country, would come to be called South Pass ("south" because it was south of the mountain passes followed by Lewis and Clark). The Astorians' camp lay two miles southwest of the 7,412-foot-high summit of the pass, squarely on its western terminus.

2

At daybreak on the twenty-second the Astorians ascended the pass three miles, found a spring, and made a fire beside it to cook breakfast. After five more miles they scrambled upward to a level ground strewn with pumice stones and strange shells—"evidently the production of the sea," Stuart noted, "and which doubtless must have been deposited by the waters of the deluge." This "top of the mountain . . . in the midst of the principal chain" lay at the Continental Divide, the North American backbone running from northern Alaska to Mexico and in the Rocky Mountains marking the point separating westward- and eastward-flowing rivers.

Over the next five days winter closed on them as they descended the pass, a northeast wind harrying them as they plodded on through intermittent but blinding snowstorms, making tortuously slow progress and early bivouacs. There was little grass, and time had to be spent searching for forage for the faithful packhorse as well as for hunting for meat and wood for the campfire. Two bighorn sheep were shot and the men feasted on the "mountain mutton," but as often they rested huddled together with no meat and no fire. They followed an eastward-bearing stream and drank from it; Stuart was convinced of its "great similarity of taste to the muddy waters of the Missouri." They found a great supply of dried "Buffaloe dung," which solved their campfire problem for a time, and on October 28 entered what Stuart called "a handsome Plain" with a meandering river sixty feet wide running through it. This was the river that came to be called the Sweetwater, one of the headwaters of the Platte River, which flowed in turn into the Missouri.

Winter now barred their progress, and the need to find a place to survive it preoccupied the Astorians. They were less than 900 miles from Saint Louis, but six months would pass before they reached it.

□

They followed the Sweetwater, camping in the willows along its banks. One of their bivouacs was set up four miles east of a 128-foot-high turtle-shaped granite boulder overlooking the river. This was an unremarkable formation from their vantage point, but to the emigrants who would see it coming from the east, it would have a special significance. The boulder lay 814 miles from the Missouri frontier and came to be called Independence Rock.

For the first time in many weeks, game and water were plentiful. Three buffalo cows were shot one morning ("the hump meat is by far the most delicious I have ever tasted," Stuart said), and bighorns, black-tailed deer, and elk were often seen feeding at the base of the mountain or at the water's edge.

On November first the Astorians crossed the Platte and on a bend found a low point of land covered with willows, firs, aspens, cedars, and cottonwoods. It seemed a perfect place for winter habitation: plenty of wood for fuel and constructing a hut, game abounding, and water nearby. Stuart's only apprehension was a visit by the "villainous and rascally Poncas." They were a small band of Missouri River Indians normally on friendly terms with whites but whose propensity for thievery had been witnessed by Crooks, McClellan, and the other Wilson Hunt veterans.

With their winter site selected and their camp established, Ben Jones and the two *engagés*, LeClairc and Vallé, set out to hunt. In three days they had killed twelve buffalo and stored the meat in a frozen cache near the river. By the tenth, the Astorians had killed, butchered, and cached the meat of thirty-two buffalo, twenty-eight deer and bighorn sheep. After Ramsey Crooks had a dangerous encounter with a grizzly that he found whuffling in a pile of buffalo guts, Ben Jones bagged the animal and added the meat to the cache.

When not hunting and transporting the meat and hides to the campsite, all hands worked at constructing their winter quarters, an eight-by-eighteen-foot hut six feet high made of cottonwood logs and buffalo hides with a fire pit in the middle and a hole in the roof over it, Indian style. The party now reveled in abundance. They had a snug cabin, plenty of meat, water, forage for their packhorse, and deerskins to scrape and soak and soften to replace tattered shirts, trousers, leggings, and moccasins. They "looked forward to a winter of peace and quietness," Irving wrote in a poetical reverie:

> . . . a time of roasting, and boiling, and boiling, and feasting upon venison, and mountain mutton, and bear's meat, and marrow bones, and buffalo humps, and other hunter's dainties, and of dozing and reposing round their fire, and gossiping over past dangers and adventures, and telling long hunting stories, until spring should return; when they would

make canoes of buffalo skins and float themselves down the river.

But these dreams were rudely interrupted a few days after the hut was completed, its log walls chinked with river clay, its fire pit dug and fueled, the communal kettle cooking meat. At daybreak on December 10, "savage yelps" woke the men and they sprang up and grabbed their weapons. From the low entrance to the cabin they saw Indians, armed and painted, in the fringe of trees and brush bordering the camp. Joseph Miller, the one-time infantryman from Wilson Hunt's party, was first to speak. "We are in trouble," he said to Stuart. "These are some of the rascally Arapahays that robbed me last year."

The seven men slung their powder horns and ball pouches. Mc-Clellan, who had taken his rifle apart to clean it during the night, now fumbled to reassemble it and proposed to Stuart that they knock the chinking from the walls for loopholes to fire on the Indians. Stuart cautioned for the moment against bringing any weapons into play. "We must first hold a parley," he said, and, accompanied by one of the Canadians, walked from the hut, rifle in hand, the other held palm-out to signify peaceful intent.

The leader of the Indian band emerged from the brush thicket and shook hands with Stuart. Through signing, pointing, and what few words the *engagé* could translate, Stuart picked up their errand. The Arapahos were from a village several days to the east that had been attacked by Absaroka raiders who had made off with most of their horses and had taken some of their women captive. The warriors facing the Astorians' camp were of a war party, armed with bows, arrows, war clubs, skinning knives, and a few ancient firearms, and had been sixteen days trailing the Crow. They had heard the gunshots of Stuart's hunters, found the remains of the deer and buffalo killed, and followed the tracks to the white men's camp.

The Indians were hungry, and Stuart invited the "chief" and another warrior, seemingly a "lieutenant" in the band, into the hut to help themselves to the haunches of meat hanging from the roof-

beams over the smoking fire pit. The chief and his aide needed no
urging, and the venison and buffalo quarters quickly disappeared,
being passed out the doorway to those waiting outside. There were
twenty-three warriors in the Arapaho band and Irving wrote that
"a scene of gormandizing commenced, of which few can have an
idea, who have not witnessed the gastronomic powers of an Indian,
after an interval of fasting."

The Astorians soon realized that the Arapahos were in no hurry
to pursue the hated Crow raiders and for two days were content
to raid the white man's meat supply. They threw up what Irving
called "breastworks," into which they "retired at a tolerably early
hour, and slept like overfed hounds" while the chief and his lieutenant stayed in the hut, getting up two or three times at night to
carve meat and eat. Irving maintained that it was Stuart's policy to
overfeed his rapacious hut-guests and keep the chief and his aide
as unknowing "captives" to ensure the "good conduct" of those
outside.

At last, on the third day since their encounter, the Arapaho
party prepared to leave. They had a six-day journey, the chief said,
before they would find the Absarokas, and since they would be
traveling through country lean of game asked for provisions for the
journey. Stuart complied, noting in his diary that they "departed
peaceably about 10 A.M. carrying with them a great proportion of
our best meat." The chief also requested powder and ball but, the
Astorian wrote, "a peremptory refusal soon convinced them that
all demands of that nature were unavailing and they laughingly
relinquished their entreaties."

(Irving's story had the chief saying, "We are poor now, and are
obliged to go on foot, but we shall soon come back laden with
booty, and all mounted on horseback, with scalps hanging from
our bridles. We will give each of you a horse to keep you from
being tired on your journey." To this Stuart replied, "Well, when
you bring the horses, you shall have the ammunition, but not before." The author does not explain how the Arapaho was able to
convey all this in such courtly language, nor, apparently, does he
think it strange that Stuart, with six men in his command, would

speak so rudely to a chief with twenty-two well-armed warriors behind him.)

They were relieved to be rid of the Arapahos but knew their meat-hungry guests would return and so held a council. They were in a vise, caught between freebooters and freeloaders, the Crow within a six-day ride on stolen Arapaho ponies, the Arapahos bound to come again, probably with more people from their village and this time probably not amused to be refused ammunition. Stuart and his men agreed on their only course of action and he entered in his journal that "we determined to abandon our Chateau of Indolence" after dressing enough deer and buffalo skins "for Mogasins etc." and "extricate ourselves out of the paws of our rascally neighbors by going a very considerable distance down the river." He hoped to make their next cantonment on the Missouri River.

On December 13 they set out in the crusted snow, their bony packhorse laden with as much frozen meat as it could carry, and managed to travel twenty-five to thirty miles a day. The country turned barren after the first few days; the horse had to be fed cottonwood bark and willow twigs, and finding fuel for their fires required tedious work. Footsore from breaking through miles of frozen ground, Stuart early on noted that they were so anxious to find new winter quarters that they were willing to face hostile Indians and "rather than die on the march, fall valiently on the field of Mars."

On the thirty-first they set up their second winter quarters on the North Platte River in far eastern Wyoming in a grove of big cottonwoods and devoted the early days of 1813 "solely to the gratification of our appetites." Buffalo were so plentiful that seven were killed in one day, and the Astorians "destroyed an immoderate quantity" of hump meat and tongue. Stuart also described exhausting the party's tobacco supply, "but in commemoration of the new year we cut up as a substitute and smoked Mr. Miller's Tobacco Pouch."

They completed their cabin on January 6, dug their fire pit, laid in the meat as they had six weeks before, and felled two trees to hollow for a trip down the river in the spring.

The two months they spent in their cabin passed uneventfully. They were troglodytes but they had plenty to eat, plenty of work, and no Indian visitors.

3

On March 8, with the river running free of ice, the Astorians launched their rough canoes. Two men were left behind to follow the Platte bank with the packhorse while the canoe experiment got underway. After only a few miles of labored travel it became clear that boat travel, at least on this segment of the Platte, was impossible. The river ran so shallow, was laced with so many sandbars, sinuous, sandy channels, fallen trees, "sawyers," and boulders that the canoes had to be dragged downstream as often as floated. They were soon given up and after a camp to wait out a sudden reversal of weather—a terrible wind that froze any foot progress—the party resumed its march on the twentieth, following the river as it wound a mile wide and knee-deep east by northeast across the undulant prairie. The nights remained bitter and they shivered at their bivouac fires, but buffalo, wild geese, ducks, and grouse abounded. The flatlands, sparse of trees even at the riverbanks, grew rich in grass and the lovable horse fattened on it. The grass was of a variety the Hunt veterans recognized as being native to a region close to the bottoms of the Missouri. As well, some of the driftwood gathered for their fires bore ax marks, another tantalizing clue that they were nearing the white man's habitat. "Thus they went on," Irving wrote, "like sailors at sea, who perceive in every floating weed and wandering bird, harbingers of the wished-for land."

Toward the end of March they passed through three deserted hunting camps, Pawnee or Oto, it was guessed, littered with buffalo skulls, bones, and forlorn, hide-denuded tepee poles. A day or two later they discovered a hut in the midst of another Indian camp in which three old women were waiting to die. "It is a common practice with the Pawnees, and probably with other roving tribes," Irving said, "when departing on a distant expedition, which will not admit any encumbrance or delay, to leave their aged and infirm with a supply of provisions sufficient for a temporary subsistence. When this is exhausted, they must perish."

Stuart made gifts of buffalo meat to the women, but they were so terror-stricken at the sight of the white men that no information could be gleaned from them, and they had to continue overland another day before coming upon the first landmark that gave them their bearings. This was an enormous island on the Wood River near its junction with the Platte, its features recognized by the Hunt veterans as a mere 150 miles from the Missouri. Soon after this comforting sighting, the Astorians encountered a solitary Oto hunter on the riverbank and the man greeted them warmly and escorted them to his Platte-side village. There they found two white men, the first they had seen since plunging into the wilderness nearly ten months past. The men, François Derouin and Jean Baptiste Antoine Roi, were trappers and Indian traders out of Saint Louis and they were brimming with news and had an audience voracious for it. From the traders Stuart and the others learned of the war with Britain, now a year old and begun before they had pushed off the banks of the Columbia to begin their wilderness sepulture.

Stuart struck a bargain with Derouin. He provided a sound canoe in exchange for their venerable and much-loved packhorse and after a few days of convivial information exchange, the Astorians set out on April 16 for the penultimate fragment of their march.

The Indian-constructed canoe, actually a canoe-shaped bullboat, was a godsend: Twenty feet long, four wide, and eighteen inches deep, it was a sturdy vessel with a willow frame covered by sewn and stretched elk and buffalo hides, the seams caulked with "unctuous mud." They paddled it effortlessly down the Platte thirty miles from the Oto camp to reach the swiftly flowing Missouri, then were borne along briskly another hundred miles where they beached at an old trappers' camp. There they found a larger, wood-and-bark canoe, transferred their gear and provisions into it, and rode the river another fifty miles to a bend and a glorious scene on the south bank: the ramparts of Fort Osage. There Wilson Hunt and his eight companions had been cordially received before their return to their winter camp on the Nodaway River.

Lieutenant John Brownson was still in charge of the post and was delighted to welcome the ragged Astorians and treat them to a meal including pork and bread, the first they had tasted since leaving the Columbia.

They set out again on the twenty-seventh in good spirits and with "a sufficiency of Pork & flour," compliments of Fort Osage. At just before sunset on April 30, Stuart wrote, "we reached the Town of St. Louis all in the most perfect health after a voyage of ten months from Astoria during which time we underwent many dangers, hardships, & fatigues, in short I may say, all the privations human nature is capable of."

He calculated that the journey covered 3,768 miles counting all the numerous detours and wanderings, and estimated that he and his men had encountered thirty Indian tribes, bands, and hunting parties, including Cathlamet, Chinook, Walla Walla, Clatsop, Absaroka, Arapaho, Pawnee, Ponca, Oto, and Shoshoni.

□

Stuart spent three weeks in Saint Louis before embarking for New York for an audience with Mr. Astor, but except for the details of his overland adventure he had no news not already known to his employer. The war with England had begun on June 19, 1812, ten days before he and his party embarked on their mission, and by journey's end Fort Astoria was an isolated American enclave in the midst of the enemy—the North West Company—and was destined to fall as a casualty of the war. Many months were to pass before either man learned of it, but as Stuart reached Saint Louis that spring of 1813, a convoy of Nor'wester canoes was already headed downriver to begin the takeover of Astor's Pacific Fur emporium.

The New Yorker had a high regard for the Perthshireman and had employment for him. Beginning soon after his marriage in New York to Elizabeth Emma Sullivan in July 1813, Stuart became Astor's fur-trade representative in Montreal. In 1817 he joined his overland partner Ramsey Crooks as a co-agent at the Michilimackinac post, the center of Astor's Great Lakes and Upper Mississippi operations, where he supervised 200 clerks and 2,000 *voyageurs*. (One of his employees said he was "one of those Scotchmen who gave his orders abruptly and expected them obeyed to the letter, yet a man of a deal of humor and fond of fun.") He held this post until 1834, when Astor sold his northern fur enterprise to Crooks and other investors.

The other five members of the Stuart expedition scattered once they reached Saint Louis.

Robert McClellan, the irascible old Indian fighter, was imprisoned briefly for debt, opened a store in Saint Louis, and died there after a brief illness on November 22, 1815, at the age of forty-five. He was buried on the farm of his friend William Clark.

Benjamin Jones bought land on the Mississippi after he returned from Astoria but became restless and went to Santa Fé in 1825 and remained in the Southwest four years. When he returned to Missouri he settled on a tract of land on Gravois Creek near Wilson Hunt's homestead. Jones died of cholera in 1835, leaving a wife, five children, fourteen slaves, fifty-four books, and considerable property.

There is no record of the lives of former army lieutenant Joseph Miller of Baltimore, and the two *engagés*, François LeClairc and André Vallé, after they reached Saint Louis.

In 1856, three years before his death in New York at age seventy-two, Ramsey Crooks took exception to certain newspaper stories lauding the western explorations of John Charles Frémont, then the Republican Party presidential candidate. Crooks was particularly disturbed by claims (which Frémont himself did not make) that the explorer-politician had "discovered" South Pass. In a letter to a friend that was subsequently published in the *Detroit Free Press*, Crooks wrote that "even if the Colonel *had* discovered the

'South Pass,' it does not show any more fitness for the exalted station he covets than the numerous beaver hunters and traders who passed and repassed through the noted place full twenty years before Col. Frémont had attained a legal right to vote." These men, he said, "were fully his equals in enterprise, energy, and indomitable perseverance, with this somewhat important difference, that he was backed by the United States Treasury, while other explorers had to rely on their own resources." He stated, as if to make a formal record of it, that he was among the seven men "who left Astoria toward the end of June, 1812, crossed the main chain of the Rocky Mountains, and through the celebrated 'South Pass' . . . reaching St. Louis the following April."

In a splendid stew of metaphors, the *Free Press* editor preceded Crooks' letter with his own comments, saying that the letter "quite dissipates the halo of glory sought to be woven around Col. Frémont's brow as the alleged discoverer of the 'South Pass,' and plucks the stolen plume with which his supporters have adorned him."

Robert Stuart lived to witness the Great Migration to Oregon and California along the trail he helped blaze and over South Pass, which he and his little expedition stumbled upon on October 21, 1812. After retiring from Astor's service he purchased land in Detroit and built a home, became an elder in the Presbyterian Church, a bank director, state treasurer of Michigan, and the United States superintendent of Indian affairs for Michigan.

He died in Detroit on October 29, 1848, leaving an estate valued at over $78,000, and upon his death, his widow, Elizabeth Sullivan Stuart, wrote in his Bible, "He leaveth the incense of a good name."

4

When the news reached him in New York of the fate of his beloved fort on the Columbia, Astor said, "Had our place and our property been fairly captured, I should have preferred it; I should not feel as if I were disgraced. . . . The very idea is like a dagger in my heart."

His dream of empire ended with a financial loss estimated at $150,000* and while at first he blamed the war for the failure of Pacific Fur, he later adopted the idea that he had been betrayed by certain of his partners, chief among them Duncan McDougall, who had, Washington Irving said, received the Nor'westers "with uncalled for hospitality, as though they were friends and allies," and supplied them with stores from the fort. In Astor's view, were it not for McDougall's largesse, Donald McTavish and his North West Company minions would have been starved off for want of provisions, or driven off by the Chinooks "who only wanted a signal from the factory to treat them as intruders and enemies."

In 1823, at the request of John Quincy Adams, then secretary of state in the James Monroe administration, Astor gave an account of his lamented enterprise and of the sale of Fort Astoria. Of McDougall he wrote, "From the price obtained for the goods, etc., and he himself having become interested in the purchase, and made a partner in the North West Company, some idea may be formed of this man's correctness of dealings." Another view was held by Alexander Ross, one of the Scotch partners who had sailed to Oregon on the *Tonquin*. He maintained that "M'Dougall had been with the nabobs of the North West before, and did not leave them without tasting of the bitter cup of disappointment; he could, therefore, have had no predilection in their favour." On the other hand, Ross also had transferred *his* allegiance back to the Nor'westers after the sale of Astoria.

The loss of his investment meant less to Astor than the loss of his dream, and he drew little comfort in viewing the establishment of Astoria as strengthening American claims to the Oregon Coun-

---

*And the lives of sixty-one men, according to Alexander Ross, who listed eight men lost "on the bar" of the Columbia, five in Hunt's overland expedition, twenty-seven on the *Tonquin*, eight on the *Lark*, and another thirteen in miscellaneous mishaps between Astoria and the Snake River country.

try. He wrote to Wilson Hunt that his spirit had been "aroused" by the conduct of the North West Company. "After their treatment of me," he said, "I have no idea of remaining quiet and idle." In fact, he said, he was determined to resume his Pacific enterprise upon the end of the war with Britain.

In the summer of 1814, that opportunity seemed in the offing with the news that Adams, Henry Clay, and other American commissioners were conferring with their British counterparts in the Flemish town of Ghent to reach a peace accord. Five months passed before the document emerged that ended the war, and not until February 11, 1815, did details of the agreement reach New York. Of principal interest to Astor was the provision of *status quo ante bellum* under which all pre-war territorial claims were restored. This meant that Fort Astoria and the adjacent Columbia River lands were once again American property. Moreover, in the winter of 1815, Congress passed a law prohibiting all traffic of British traders within the United States' claims.

But all this diplomatic and legal paper lay 3,000 miles from the Columbia, where the facts were quite different. The withdrawal of the Astorians had left the Pacific Northwest in the hands of the well-armed and belligerent agents of the North West Company who were already engaged in a trade war with the Hudson's Bay Company, and to dispossess them would require more than a cadre of Scotch partners, clerks, and *voyageurs*. Astor above all was aware of this and made an "informal overture" to President James Madison, through his Treasury Secretary Albert Gallatin, offering to renew his Oregon enterprise and reestablish Fort Astoria providing it would be militarily protected by the American flag. He estimated that the force required for its protection "would not exceed a lieutenant's command."

Gallatin approved the idea and recommended it to the president, but Madison chose not to respond to it. Said Irving, "Discouraged by this supineness on the part of the government, Mr. Astor did not think fit to renew his overtures in a more formal manner, and the favorable moment for the re-occupation of Astoria was suffered to pass unimproved."

The failure of Astor's scheme, Irving said, was ascribable to a series of "cross purposes, disasterous to the establishment." These included the loss of the *Tonquin* ("which clearly would not have happened had Mr. Astor's earnest injunctions with regard to the natives been attended to"); Wilson Hunt's long detainment in the Sandwich Islands, during which Astoria was sold to the Nor'westers; the loss of the supply ship *Lark* off the island of Maui; the War of 1812, which "multiplied the hazards and embarrassments of the enterprise"; and the failure of President Madison to support the idea of a military reoccupation and protection of Astoria.

And so the financier turned his brilliant business mind to more profitable, settled, matters—his fur business in the Upper Mississippi and Great Lakes—and watched discontentedly while certain diplomatic efforts surfaced that affected his late Oregon dream. In 1818 President James Monroe's secretaries of state, Richard Rush and John Quincy Adams, negotiated an agreement with Britain that established the Canadian-American border at the 49th parallel between Lake of the Woods, in the pine forests of northern Minnesota, southern Manitoba and Ontario, and the Rocky Mountains. Both nations claimed the lands west of the Rockies, the Oregon Country, and since no boundary could be agreed upon, a compromise was reached: That territory was declared "free and open" to both England and the United States, a quasi-solution called "joint occupation." Meantime, Adams sought to pressure Spain to relinquish its claims on lands north of its province of Alta California, this part of the sweeping Adams-Onís Treaty signed in February 1819. In it Spain, weakened by its colonial problems in South America, ceded the Floridas to the United States and defined the western limits of the Louisiana Purchase. The 42nd parallel became the boundary separating northern California from the Oregon Country, to which Spain relinquished its claims.

Two years later Russia gave way. In the late eighteenth and early nineteenth centuries Russian traders had moved south of Alaska and established outposts as far down the Pacific Rim as San Francisco. In 1821 Czar Alexander I rattled a saber by issuing a proclamation prohibiting the ships of foreign nations from coming within 100 miles of the 51st parallel of the North Pacific coast of America. Since this latitude encompassed lands claimed by Britain that were still a subject of dispute with the United States, both nations pressured the czar. As a result, in 1825 Russia disclaimed all territories below the latitude of 54 degrees 40 minutes, a pairing of numbers that would reverberate in years to come.

John Quincy Adams, one of many political figures who viewed the United States and North America as synonymous, saw these developments as leading to a time when "the remainder of the continent should ultimately be ours" and, citing the Monroe Doctrine, considered the entire hemisphere "closed to any new European colonial establishments."

Thus by the mid-1820s, only the old establishments—England and the United States—remained to contest the territory between 42 degrees north and 54 degrees 40 minutes. Britain's claims rested on the Nootka Sound Convention of 1790 and various explorations from the time of Captain James Cook and the establishment of fur-trading posts by its Hudson's Bay Company. The United States had its own declarations: explorations by Robert Gray, discoverer of the Columbia River, and by Lewis and Clark; the acquisition of Spanish claims in the Adams-Onís Treaty; and the fact that Oregon was contiguous to American lands gained in the Louisiana Purchase.

The joint occupancy accord between the vying nations was renewable as long as each signee agreed to renew it. Either signee had the right to renounce it, giving the other a one-year notice.

Twenty years would pass before the "Oregon question" was finally settled.

10

FORT VANCOUVER

"... THE OARS BRIGHT FLASHING LIKE TOLEDO BLADES."

1

George Simpson preferred to travel in a big, white birch-bark *canot du maître*—master's canoe—paddled by six or eight black-bearded *voyageurs*, and at a fur-trade outstation have a bagpiper in full tartan regalia announce his arrival. On such occasions he would wear a tall beaver hat to improve his 5½-foot height, a scarlet-lined black cloak over a buttoned-up, expensively cut frock coat with matching trousers and waistcoat, a boiled white shirt and black cravat. This outfit, severe against the filthy but brightly beaded deerskin shirts, leggings, and moccasins of his oarsmen, was purposeful: He would never be mistaken for a mere trader, factor, or petty bureaucrat but would be instantly recognized as possessor of the impressive and sonorous title of governor of the Northern Department and Columbia River District of the Honourable Hudson's Bay Company.

There were times when Simpson's ostentation had the reverse effect, when onlookers greeting him on the beach at some far-flung Company factory gathered from his show and ceremony, and from his dark raiment and dour visage, that he was precisely what he looked like: a vainglorious politician, or a porer over ledgers, more at home among pallid boardroom colleagues or barricaded behind a tower of paperwork than in the wilderness amongst trappers and traders and bales of beaver furs.

If the "Little Governor," as he was called, gave these impressions when he stepped ashore at Fort George, formerly Fort Astoria, on November 8, 1824, they did not last long. He *was* a politician and ledger man, but in its history of a century and a half the Hudson's Bay Company never had a high-ranking officer to match Simpson's physical vitality. His stature belied a strength and endurance that matched that of any of his *voyageurs*, and he proved it in pushing these woods-wise roughnecks overland from the Company's headquarters at the York Factory on Hudson's Bay to the Pacific. In eighty-four days they crossed Manitoba, Saskatchewan, Alberta, the Rocky Mountains, and the Selkirk range and paddled down to the mouth of the Columbia. The linear distance was about 1,500 miles, but the actual miles traveled, on winding, wandering waterways, in portaging, walking, and climbing, may have been a thousand miles more.

Simpson did not yet have a piper to skirl notice of his coming— that fine touch would be added when he began his inspection tours—but the unheralded occasion of his arrival at Fort George on that crisp winter forenoon had great portent for the future of British-American relations in the Oregon Country. Simpson was only thirty-seven and had risen swiftly in the Company's service since he ventured to Canada from his birthplace of Ross-shire, Scotland. He was a well-knit, broad-chested man with blazing blue eyes, an imposing mode of speech, and an affable manner. He possessed other qualities, including something called "redundant animal spirits," that his superiors adored: He had an educated, orderly mind, a driving ambition, a work ethic that shamed the most tireless of his colleagues, and a penny-pinching profit philosophy. He had, a contemporary said, "the imagination of a Clive," the reference, electrifying to Englishmen of the era, being to Robert Clive of Plassey, the soldier-founder of the British empire in India.

Simpson was regarded as such a pragmatic visionary and was sent to the Pacific Northwest to take advantage of the fall of Astoria and Astor's failure to persuade his government to provide military support for reopening his fort on the Columbia. The governor was to consolidate Fort George's strength and wage a campaign to solidify the Company's fur empire: send trapping brigades east into the Snake River and Rocky Mountain country, north into Canada, and south to Mexican California; prosecute the fur trade vigorously; monopolize it by fending off American trappers venturing across the Rockies; and make a profit for the directors and stockholders in London. He was also authorized to abandon Fort George and build a new trade center on the north bank of the Columbia.

This intimidating mission was made possible by the merger, after thirty-seven years of vicious rivalry, of the North West Company with the Hudson's Bay Company. The Nor'westers had been organized in 1784 specifically to compete for a fur monopoly in Canada and fought—often literally—for trapping rights throughout "Rupert's Land" (named for King Charles II's cousin Prince Rupert, first governor of the Honourable Company), that is, all the lands that drained into Hudson's Bay, 1.5 million square miles of North America. The competition turned brutal in the second decade of the nineteenth century in the Red River country of Manitoba and in what later became northern Minnesota and North Dakota. In these rich trapping grounds the rival companies built well-armed forts, broke up traplines, stole each other's furs, and conducted guerrilla warfare in the rivers and forests around the frontier town of Winnipeg. In this region occurred a particularly destructive episode that sealed the fate of the warring competitors.

In 1811, Thomas Douglas, the Fifth Earl of Selkirk and a major stockholder in the Company, was granted 116,000 square miles of territory in the valley of the Red River. Lord Selkirk intended to set up an agricultural colony in his wind-scoured wilderness and succeeded in attracting his first settlers there in 1812. The titular governor of Selkirk's colony soon alienated the local descendants of *voyageur* fathers and Indian mothers—who were called métis— and the Nor'westers joined in the conflict with these families. The

factions engaged in outright battle in 1816, with twenty white settlers killed by the métis at Fort Douglas in the colony. After the
failure of Selkirk's struggling domain the Hudson's Bay Company
transferred his territory back to their control and in 1820, the year
his lordship died, the British colonial secretary launched negotiations for the merger of the adversarial companies.

The result of these negotiations was the issuance in 1821 of a
"deed of co-partnership" amalgamating the two companies under
the Hudson's Bay Company name and extending the Company's
fur-trade hegemony. The area covered was no longer limited to the
territory prescribed in the 1670 charter—all the territory draining
into Hudson's Bay—but now embraced the entire Canadian west,
including the Oregon Country, "Westward of the Stony Mountains."

While the British were thus consolidating in the Pacific Northwest, American influence there seemed waning despite certain ominous stirrings between the fall of Fort Astoria and George
Simpson's arrival there in the winter of 1824. These portents, recognized by the politically astute and American-wary governor and
his associates, began surfacing in February 1815 with the treaty
that ended the Anglo-American war. The nettlesome *status quo
ante bellum* stipulation of the Ghent diplomacy and the subsequent
agreement between the nations for "free and open access" to and
"joint occupancy of" the Oregon Country would eventually have
to be confronted.

After Astoria, the Hudson's Bay Company had an almost exclusive Columbia River fur-trade foothold, one that would endure
fifteen years. The Americans, however, had not forgotten the
Oregon Country and while the march back began slowly, it gained
momentum every year of those fifteen.

2

A week or so before he set out from York Factory for the Pacific,
Governor Simpson sent ahead his appointee as chief factor for the

Columbia District, John McLoughlin, a man who needed no beaver hat to tower over his employees nor London cut of clothes to impress them. He was formidable in stature, physical strength, and endurance, protean in intellect and temperament, one of those singular men who seemed born to be a liege lord of some great remote domain. Through the sheer, blunt force of his presence he left an impression, not always positive but always indelible, on everyone who came in contact with him. "Once seen, he was never forgotten," H. H. Bancroft said of him.

Simpson, who would quarrel often with his colleague and eventually scheme against him, stood in awe of McLoughlin, never quite knowing what to make of the man. On September 26, 1824, the governor and his *voyageurs* caught up with McLoughlin's Columbia-bound vanguard party near the Athabaska River north of the future town of Edmonton, Alberta. At this rendezvous Simpson recorded in his diary an impression of the man whose character he would recognize, from the beginning of their relationship and over twenty years to come, as bearing no resemblance to his own. "He was such a figure as I should not like to meet in a dark Night in one of the bye lanes in the neighborhood of London," he wrote with an amusing hyperbole that barely hid his condescension, "dressed in Clothes that had once been fashionable, but now covered with a thousand patches of different Colors; his beard would do honor to the chin of a Grizzly Bear, his face and hands evidently Shewing that he had not lost much time at his Toilette, loaded with arms and his own herculean dimensions forming a *tout ensemble* that would convey a good idea of the highway men of former days."

Bancroft wrote that McLoughlin "was of an altogether different order of humanity from any who had hitherto appeared on these shores. Before or after him, his like was unknown; for he was far above the mercenary fur-trader, or the coarse, illiterate immigrant."

He was born Jean Baptiste McLoughlin in 1784 in the parish of Rivière du Loup, 120 miles down the south shore of the Saint

Lawrence from Québec, his father an Irish farmer, his mother a Fraser of the great Scotch clan. In 1803, when he was nineteen and after a period of study with a Québec surgeon, McLoughlin received his certification as a physician and joined the North West Company, rising from post surgeon to chief trader in the Sault Sainte Marie area of Ontario. At some point in his service there he married a Cree Indian woman who bore him a son but died in childbirth.

In Ontario, McLoughlin became acquainted with Alexander McKay, the Nor'wester trader who had accompanied Alexander Mackenzie on his explorations to the Pacific Coast in 1793 and, as one of the original Astor partners, sailed for the Columbia on the *Tonquin* in September 1810. McKay was murdered by Indians at Clayoquot Sound on Vancouver Island the following June and soon after this McLoughlin married McKay's widow, Marguérite Wadin McKay, the half-Cree daughter of a Swiss trader. She was nine years the young physician-trader's senior, had four children fathered by McKay, and would bear another four by her utterly devoted second husband.

At the time he reached Fort George with Governor Simpson in November 1824, McLoughlin was forty years old and, says Bancroft, "as he appeared among his pygmy associates, white or red, there was an almost unearthly grandeur in his presence. Body, mind, and heart were all carved in gigantic proportions." Everything about him did seem majestic. Six and a half feet tall, a full foot taller than Simpson, McLoughlin was lean and tough as a lath, wide-chested, long-limbed, and thick-necked, with a massive head crowned by an unruly mass of shoulder-length white hair, mid-parted and swept back behind his ears. When he shaved the grizzly bear's beard Simpson had noted, he uncovered a squarish, handsome face with a hawk's nose, a wide mouth, and deep-set, palely luminous blue eyes.

From his mane of white hair, Columbia River natives gave him the name White Eagle and in the years ahead he became their personal King George. To others, including the Americans he befriended, the names for him were always regal—"Emperor of the West," and "King of Old Oregon"—befitting the benevolent autocrat of a 670,000-square-mile wilderness realm.

Bancroft, given to few panegyrics in his massive histories, was captivated by the man: "His life should be written by the recording angel and pillared at the crossing of the two chief highways of the universe. Search these shores from Darien to Alaska, and you will find none such. . . . His life though quiet and untrumpeted was full of glory."

□

Governor Simpson's plans for construction of a new factory on the Columbia River and installing McLoughlin there to run it were elements of a scheme aimed at warding off any American interference in the Hudson's Bay Company's fur monopoly in the Northwest. The new fort would serve as the hub of the Company's commerce in the Oregon Country and from it and other, smaller, posts in the region Simpson intended having his brigades fanning out west to the Rocky Mountains and south to Mexican territory to trap beaver to extinction. The idea was to create a "fur desert" between American lands and the southern approaches to the Columbia that would discourage American traders and, as a consequence, discourage American emigrants.

To implement this brutal strategy, Simpson selected as his chief brigade leader for the Columbia district Peter Skene Ogden, age thirty when he came down from the Spokane post and joined Simpson and McLoughlin at Fort George in the winter of 1824.

A contemporary described Ogden as "humorous, honest, eccentric, law-defying, short, dark and exceedingly tough," and it was said that he had "a taste for violence." He was born in Québec City, the son of a Canadian admiralty court judge, and ran away from legal studies to join the North West Company as a clerk. He was a prodigious, ambitious worker and by age twenty-four, after commanding a fur post at Lake Athabasca, he earned a transfer to the Columbia, which in 1818 was the remotest of the Nor'wester's many remote fur interests. There, in two years' time, he had led trapping parties from Fort George to Puget Sound and all the waterways of the Columbia and was promoted to brigade leader. He had a single black mark on his record, a time when his meteoric career plummeted to earth. In 1821 Ogden was among the most outspoken opponents of the merger of the North West Company with Hudson's Bay and proved such an irritant that his name was excluded from the list of Nor'westers to be retained in service. During this period of unemployment he traveled to London to appeal to Hudson's Bay officials and apparently made a good impression on the Company sirs and lords. They saw the value of his experience in the raw Columbia River country, as did the new governor of the district, George Simpson, who reinstated Ogden as clerk of the first class and brigade leader at the Columbia factory.

Ogden's return to the Oregon Country did not begin auspiciously. From his headquarters at the Spokane fort he followed Simpson's orders to begin the campaign to "trap out" the competition by sending a brigade east into the Snake River beaver streams. The leader of this expedition was Alexander Ross, one of the former Nor'westers who had come to the Columbia on the *Tonquin.* He was a capable administrator but proved overcautious in Blackfeet territory and returned with an unsatisfactory cache of furs. Simpson was not happy at the outcome of this first foray and wrote Ogden: "The Snake River Expedition has hitherto been considered a forlorn hope [a British army term for a suicidal mission], the management of it the most hazardous and disagreeable office in the Indian country. . . . This important duty should not be left to a self-sufficient and empty-headed man like Ross who feels no further interest therein than that it secures to him a Saly [salary] of £120 p. Annum and whose reports are so full of bombast and marvellous nonsense that it is impossible to get any information that can be depended on from him."

A month after he arrived at Fort George, Simpson fixed the problem: He saw in Ogden a man who could best serve the

Company on the trail, Ross best in a clerkly capacity, and so appointed Ogden to command the Snake River brigades and Ross to take over Ogden's duties at the Spokane post.

In his first expedition east, Ogden set out in December 1824 with a heavy brigade of over 70 trappers, each with five heavy, iron-jawed and chained traps, plus 372 horses, 80 guns, and an unwieldy party of camp followers—wives and children of the trappers, clerks, and interpreters. He also had seven Americans in his company who had returned with Ross to Spokane after being separated on the Green River from a band of traders organized by William Henry Ashley. Among the seven was a twenty-five-year-old New Yorker, Jedediah Smith, a name soon to be familiar to Hudson's Bay authorities in Oregon.

This cumbersome company miraculously crossed the Continental Divide to the headwaters of the Missouri, doing so in the dead of winter without serious incident. Near the Three Forks of the Missouri they found a region rich in beaver and buffalo but one also haunted by Blackfeet and the clear realization that they were trespassers in American territory. Ogden led them west again and they spent much of the winter trapping, hunting, and camping on Salmon River streams and byways in Idaho and, in April 1825, on the Salmon's juncture with the Snake. The fur hunt that month was "tolerable," Ogden scrawled in his journal, but of "short duration"; the principal hindrance, as it had been with Ross and countless other expeditions, was again the Blackfeet. (The enmity of these natives began, some said, after two Piegans—a Blackfeet band—were killed by Meriwether Lewis and his men on their return journey from the Columbia in 1806.) A small band of these nomadic buffalo hunters killed and scalped one of Ogden's trappers and caused "unrest" among the others; this event was followed by an encounter with Americans that came close to a territorial battle and the near ruination of his first expedition.

In May Ogden led his party southward along the foothills of the Wasatch Mountains of Utah to the Bear River and a point where, Ogden noted, it "discharged into a large Lake of 100 miles in length." (The Great Salt Lake had first been seen by white men only the year before, by the twenty-year-old Virginian James Bridger and his trapping party.) The Bear River and its streams and feeders swarmed with beaver, so many that Ogden's men dressed 600 skins in under two weeks—then lost them.

This disaster began on May 25, 1825, while Ogden's party camped on the Weber River, east of the Salt Lake. He was working on papers in his command tent when he was paid an unfriendly visit by an American named Johnson Gardner who coolly informed the brigade leader that Hudson's Bay men had no business on United States soil and said they must "return from whence they came without delay." Ogden left no record of his reaction to this abrupt command, but it can be assumed that he greeted it with less diplomacy than he reported.* He informed Gardner that he and his brigade were on lands "jointly owned" by Britain and the United States and that therefore he was no trespasser. The American was adamant, ordering Ogden to collect his men and depart, Ogden countering that only upon receiving orders from his government would he do so.

During this edgy colloquy Ogden's trappers were mixing with Gardner's and were being educated on the difference between "free" trapping and working for the Company: The Americans were being paid significantly more for their furs than the British paid. This lesson learned, twenty-three of Ogden's men decamped to Gardner's side and took with them 600 beaver skins—most of the catch to date.

With his brigade depleted by a third, Ogden took his remaining men north and west before he lost more of them. By the time he brought the remnant into Fort Nez Percé in November he had only 400 furs on his packhorses, a trifling number for an expedition so well manned and mounted.

No one was more furious over the outcome of his first Snake River expedition than Ogden, nor more unwilling to admit to

---

*Nor did Gardner make a record of the encounter. Nothing is known about him except that in 1831 he was killed by Arikaras on the Yellowstone River.

failure. He rested twelve days before starting out again, this time with a compact company of thirty-seven seasoned *engagés* and "freemen" (trappers contracted for a single season). The demi-brigade struck out across the Blue Mountains to the Snake in November and by the end of March 1826 had 1,000 furs, and 3,800 by the time it returned to Fort Vancouver in July.

"M'sieu Pete," as his men called him, led four other trapping-exploring parties through 1830 searching out new fur territories for the Company. In 1826 he marched south from Fort Nez Percé to Klamath Lake, just above the border of Mexican California; in 1828 he returned to Utah, explored the northern shores of the Great Salt Lake, and upon his return became the first white man to trace the Humboldt River (then variously called the Mary's, the Unknown, the Swampy, and Ogden's River) to its sink in northern Nevada and to put to rest the long-standing notion of the "Bonaventura River," a mythical waterway believed to flow from the Salt Lake to the Pacific.

On his sixth and final expedition in 1829, Ogden led a brigade south out of Fort Vancouver through the Great Basin to the Colorado River and down through Mexican territory to the Gulf of California, fighting one pitched battle with Mojave Indians en route. He returned up the length of the San Joaquin and Sacramento valleys of Alta California, having heard stories of the trapping opportunities in the region spun by Jedediah Smith, who came through them in 1828. Another informant was a Tennesseean named Ewing Young, whom Ogden met near Yerba Buena, the town subsequently named San Francisco, who was on his way to the Oregon Country.

Ogden went on to serve the Company in British Columbia and in the fastnesses of the Canadian Northwest Territories, but as a factor rather than an explorer-trapper. That life, he said, "makes a man sixty in a few years," and he managed to live only four years beyond that age. It is said that he "mellowed with age," developing a certain tact and charm that were not noticeable in his early years with Hudson's Bay brigades.

3

As Ogden's first brigade worked its way toward the beaver streams of the Snake, Governor George Simpson and Chief Factor John McLoughlin were supervising the construction of Fort Vancouver on Belle Vue Point, ninety miles southeast of Fort George on the north bank of the Columbia near the mouth of the Willamette River. The new "grand mart and rendezvous for the Company's trade and servants on the Pacific" lay in territory claimed by both the United States and Britain. It was trapezoidal-shaped, 750 by 450 feet in size, surrounded by hewn-log palisades twenty feet high with a bastion at its northeast corner armed with twelve-pounder cannons. There were several eighteen-pounders inside the compound as well, and the massive log gates of the main stockade were manned by armed sentries.

All of Fort George's supplies, furniture, furs, and men were ferried upriver early in 1825, and the new fort was officially opened and christened with a bottle of rum on March 19 by Governor Simpson. He paid honor to its namesake, explorer George Vancouver (who died in 1798) and claimed the site "on behalf of the Honorable Hudson's Bay Company and King George IV." After the ceremonies Simpson departed for York Factory headquarters and left Fort Vancouver in his chief factor's charge.

Over the twenty years that McLoughlin had its command, the fort would evolve into a true "nerve center of British trade west of the Rockies," eventually housing a bakery, a chemist's shop (pharmacy), warehouses and fur stores; workshops for mechanics, carpenters, blacksmiths, coopers, tanners, tinners, and wheelwrights; houses for officers and their families; a chapel, a schoolhouse, a powder magazine of brick and stone, and a governor's house with dining hall and public sitting room. This "veritable hive of industry" was surrounded by saw- and gristmills, orchards, gardens, cultivated fields—cleared by idle trappers in summer months—which eventually produced wheat, oats, peas, corn, barley, buckwheat, and potatoes, and maintained herds of cattle and horses from

California, sheep from Canada, and hogs from the Sandwich Islands. When Lieutenant Charles Wilkes, the American naval explorer, visited Fort Vancouver at the peak of McLoughlin's stewardship, the officer remarked on the industriousness of this "large manufacturing, agricultural, and commercial depot," and said he found "few, if any idlers, except the sick. Everybody seems to be in a hurry, whilst there appears to be no reason for it." He and many others before and after him recalled the big fort bell calling cooks, teachers, and shop and field hands to work, calling people to church and school, heralding the arrival of Company boats and ships and, like a bo'sun's pipe, welcoming visiting Company dignitaries aboard Fort Vancouver.

The fort gates were thrown open in the summer months to receive the trappers with the year's fur harvest, their boat-songs heard two miles from the fort. The canoes and *bateaux*—some of the latter pine-constructed, thirty-two feet long, and seven feet amidships—each bearing the Company's crest and *Pro Pelle Cutem* motto, came downstream, "the oars bright flashing like Toledo blades" Bancroft said. The big boats, carrying fifteen or twenty tons of furs, swept down the current in perfect order amidst the shouting and cheering from the shore and the clanging of the fort's big bell. The *voyageurs*, "in gala dress, ribbons fluttering from Canadian caps and deerskin suits ornamented with beads and fringes," contracted trappers, and brigade leaders came ashore where the big Union Jack fluttered in the breeze above the fort's ramparts. There they off-loaded their cargos and filed into the huge dining hall where Kanaka (Sandwich Islander) cooks and servers laid out steaming platters of meat and bread.

McLoughlin rose before dawn and did not quit his workday until after dark. He supervised all trapping operations at the Company's headquarters, which annually shipped out furs valued at $150,000, and managed all the fort's subsidiary businesses: selling smoked meat and salmon, lumber, hardware, vegetables, and grains to the Sandwich Islands, Russian Alaska, China, and even England. He was also responsible for opening new trade centers in the Columbia Department: Fort Walla Walla (also known as Fort

Nez Percé) north of the Umatilla River, Forts Okanogan and Colville in British Columbia, Forts Boisé and Hall in the Snake River country, and even a post at Yerba Buena in Mexican California. He once described his territorial responsibility as running "from San Francisco . . . to Latitude Fifty-Four North [Russian Alaska] and the Interior as bounded by the Rocky Mountains."

The factor and his family had a fine nine-room white home at Fort Vancouver surrounded by grapevine trellises and with an outbuilding for laundry and cooking. He became famous for his hospitality at the "Big House" and at the fort's great dining hall, where dinner was always a dignified social affair, the men and their ladies in their best finery and military visitors in full uniform ablaze with medals and orders. Sumptuous meals were served during which McLoughlin relaxed his own abstemiousness, permitting wine to be served (but no liquors) and even taking a glass himself while he led the after-dinner talk. There were mariner's tales of beating around Cape Horn and circumnavigating the globe, of battles and travels in exotic lands, and of wilderness adventures where fights with savages contended with the catastrophic whims of Mother Nature. McLoughlin loved books and talked about them, and spoke as well of his studies in botany and anthropology and other natural sciences.

During these memorable times glasses were filled and pipes were lit. McLoughlin, who did not smoke, did allow himself a pinch of snuff now and then and shared his snuffbox with his guests. One who shared one of these banquets with him recalled, "The doctor at the head of the table suddenly pulled the bell-tassel. 'Bruce!' and in a few minutes Bruce would be on hand with an open mull, from which a pinch would be taken, without a word on either side." (The fort did stock and sell tobacco, most of it from Brazil, which was twisted into a cord an inch in diameter, coiled, and sold by the foot. American settlers in the area called it "trail-rope.")

Marguérite McLoughlin shared her husband's love for these social occasions and always appeared at the table resplendent in her scarlet shawl, blue broadcloth petticoat, beaded and quilled leggings, and mocassins decorated with tiny bells, her hat trimmed in gay ribbons. Bancroft said "she presented a picture, if not as elegant as that of a lady of the sixteenth century at a hawking party, yet quite as striking and brilliant." And another favorite at the table was Eloisa, the McLoughlins' only daughter residing at the Big House, who often joined her father on his inspections. Many kept a fond image of her: a tall, pretty blond girl on a beautiful tan mare riding alongside her hulking father in his dark blue cloak, their manes, white and blond, flowing in the wind.

□

Yankee trade ships continued to come to the Oregon coast periodically after the abandonment of Astoria, and an occasional Yankee trapper appeared out of nowhere to find succor at Fort Vancouver. The New Yorker, Jedediah Smith, for example, stumbled into the fort in the summer of 1827, his trapping party having been massacred by Indians on the Umpqua River, his furs and horses stolen.

Americans supposedly "shared" the riches of the Oregon Country under the 1827 joint occupancy agreement, but the Company gave no sign that they were pleased with the arrangement and forbade all but rudimentary assistance to the Americans who wandered into their Columbia River domain. McLoughlin was realistic, perhaps even fatalistic, on the subject, but he was also of a practical mind. As chief factor for the Hudson's Bay fur enterprise in the Oregon Country, his responsibility lay in protecting that interest, widening it, and making a profit. Even though he built Company forts to the south on the Umpqua and, with Mexican sanction, even at Yerba Buena, and Fort Walla Walla and Fort Hall to the east, he became convinced that the future of the Company's business lay north of the river. Thus, while he saw the American push toward Oregon as inevitable—they would come, to trap and trade, to preach and teach among the Indians, to settle and to farm—he would shrewdly point the settlers toward the Willamette Valley south of the Columbia, and the missionaries to the east.

In truth, the Americans vexed him: He liked most he met, treated them hospitably, helped those in need, and in return, too often, they showed no gratitude.

11

CAPTAIN SMITH

1

In January 1822, Jedediah Strong Smith of Jericho, New York, landed in Saint Louis with a few coins in his pocket and everything he owned on his back. His treasured possessions were the two books that inspired him: the Bible and the heavy 1814 edition of the Lewis and Clark journals.

He had come to the Gateway to the West aimlessly, but he seemed to be have been making his way there from childhood.

Jedediah was the fourth of eleven children of Sally Strong, who was from a pioneering Massachusetts family, and Jedediah Smith, Sr., of New Hampshire, and was born on January 6, 1799, in the Susquehanna valley of southern New York. His and his father's surname had significance among strict Methodist farm folk: In Samuel II of the Old Testament, Solomon, the second son of David and Bathsheba, who would become the last king of Israel, was called at birth Jedediah, "beloved of the Lord."

The Smiths moved to Erie County in northwestern Pennsylvania in the early 1800s, and at about the age of twelve the boy was taken under the tutorial wing of a local physician and received a good frontier education.

In 1812 the family occupied farmland on the southern shore of Lake Erie, and Jedediah, now a gangly, God-fearing lad of thirteen, found work as a clerk on a Lake Erie freighter. In this period his mentor introduced him to the newly published journals of the Lewis and Clark expedition, and he pored over this book almost as assiduously as he read his Scriptures.

His movements between 1814 and 1822 are uncertain. The Smith family had permanently settled in the farm country of the Western Reserve of Ohio by 1817, and Jedediah apparently continued to work on Lake Erie while hinting to his family of his ambition to travel somewhere west and become a geographer. Sometime in the spring of 1821 he made his way to Illinois, spent the winter near the Rock Spring rapids of the Mississippi, and after the New Year crossed the river.

His appearance in Saint Louis, population about 5,000, was weirdly propitious for a yearner to walk the wilderness steps of Meriwether Lewis and William Clark. He scarcely had time to find cheap lodgings in the teeming town when he read a notice in the *Missouri Gazette & Public Advertiser* that seemed to have been written with Jedediah Smith in mind:

TO
Enterprising Young Men
The subscriber wishes to engage ONE HUNDRED MEN, to ascend the river Missouri to its source, there to be employed for one, two, or three years. For particulars enquire of Maj. Andrew Henry, near the Lead Mines, in the county of Washington, (who will ascend with, and command the party) or to the subscriber at St. Louis.

The subscriber was William Henry Ashley, a forty-four-year-old Virginian who had migrated to Missouri in 1802 and become a mine operator, a colonel in the War of 1812, and a brigadier general of militia. His hasty life knew few disappointments and many triumphs, the latest his election as lieutenant governor of the new, twenty-fourth, state of Missouri.

Smith, at age twenty-three a rangy six-footer with soft blue eyes and a self-possessed, somewhat pious manner, found his way to the entrepreneur's busy office. "I called on Gen'l Ashley to make an engagement to go with him as a hunter," he later wrote of the encounter. "I found no difficulty in making a bargain on as good terms as I had reason to expect."

Smith and the other men recruited as "hunters," a varied, scruffy lot, a good many of them Saint Louis waterfront toughs and sweepings from the taverns and mean alleys of the town, were to be paid $200 per annum to trap beaver in the Rocky Mountains.

□

Manuel Lisa, the man Wilson Hunt met on the Missouri River in 1811 and challenged to a duel, had led the first organized American trapping party up the Missouri River in 1807, and mounted thirteen expeditions between that year and his death, in his forty-seventh year, in August 1820. His brigades ranged as far upriver as the merging of the Yellowstone and Big Horn Rivers, and his Missouri Fur Company trappers, while few in number, had scattered along the rivers, making peace and trade with the Mandans, Assiniboines, and Arikaras (but not the Blackfeet) and building forts in their territories. One of Lisa's partners in the Missouri Fur Company was Andrew Henry, a Pennsylvanian who served as Lisa's field captain and took his trappers as far afield as the Snake River in the Idaho wilderness. The fort he built on a bend of the Snake had been useful to both Wilson Hunt's and Robert Stuart's Astorians in their journeys out to the Columbia and back to Saint Louis.

Andrew Henry and William Ashley were neighbors, veterans of the late war with England, comrades in the Missouri militia, and after Lisa's death they pooled their money to invest in the Missouri beaver trade. Ashley began with the recruiting effort, hoping to engage 100 men for an expedition to the Upper Missouri country that would depart from Saint Louis in the fall.

The *Missouri Gazette* notice turned up a good number of likely men—some of them more likely than either organizer could realize. Among the first of the Ashley-Henry contingent were Jedediah Smith, James Bridger, and Thomas Fitzpatrick, who would have consequential connections with the Oregon Country.

□

The Ashley-Henry plan borrowed and modified Hudson's Bay Company tactics. The partners intended to move a trapping brigade into beaver country, build a fort, and stock it with goods that would attract the native trade. Ideally the Indians would do most of the trapping and exchange their catches for such inexpensive commodities as gunpowder, scarlet cloth, traps, alcohol (illegal in the Indian trade but much in demand), vermillion powder, knives, tobacco, beads, mirrors, and the like. The hunters were at first salaried but later contracted for a season's hunt, emulating and improving on a system devised by Donald Mackenzie, the former Astorian who had traveled overland to the Pacific with Wilson Hunt in 1811. "Perpetual Motion" Mackenzie, in the years before the Nor'westers and Hudson's Bay Company merged, was instrumental in opening up the rich Snake River country to the fur trade and in this work took his brigades into the mountains, supplied them with horses, equipment, and provisions, and arranged to meet them at a prescribed rendezvous in the summer where he would buy their furs.

Ashley and Henry combined their resources to do much the same thing: supply their trappers with a string of packhorses and outfit and provision them for half of the plews they brought back, agreeing to purchase the balance of the furs at the market price. The money paid the "free trappers" would finance them another year in the mountains and another fur catch. And the harder they worked, the farther they journeyed to explore richer beaver streams, the more cash they would earn.

Another Ashley innovation was the "rendezvous," a prescribed place—the Siskadee (later Green) River valley, Bear Lake, the

Cache Valley of northern Utah—where the hunters would gather
in the summer (off-season for beaver trapping) and meet with the
trade wagons out of Saint Louis or Independence. These caravans
were loaded with traps, guns, ammunition, knives, tobacco, and
liquor, useful to the white as well as the Indian, and "foofuraws"—
cheap goods attractive to Indian women, such as mirrors, needles,
bells, beads, ribbons, and cloth.

The first rendezvous was held in midsummer 1825 on the Green
River in Wyoming, and they continued for fifteen years thereafter.
At the peak of the trade, when beaver furs fetched five dollars a
pound in Saint Louis, hundreds of mountain men, traders, and Indians at rendezvous held horse races, wrestling contests, duels, and
buffalo chases before heading back into the mountains or another
year of working their traplines. Called by Bernard De Voto "the
mountain man's Christmas, county fair, harvest festival, and
crowned-slave carnival of Saturn," the rendezvous came to exem-
plify the unfettered life of the free trapper, spending his time living
off the land and coming down from the mountains for a few summer days of roistering with his comrades. Bancroft called the rendezvous "Olympia, with Dionysius enthroned," "a fair in the
wilderness . . . the tournament of the prairies" where "Extravagant
and depraved habits were pandered to . . . with whiskey at three
dollars a pint, and gunpowder at six, with tobacco at five dollars
a pound, and fancy articles at fancy prices." The gathering of
mountaineers, he wrote, was "as motley in character as it was numerous, embracing every class and race. The Indian was represented
in all stages, from the degraded, root-eating, naked Bannock, with
humble yet cunning mien, to the chivalrous Nez Percé in gaudy
trappings, dashing to and fro on caparisoned steed. . . . The half-
breed was there, the connecting link between Indian and white
man, despised by the one for his blood, admired by the other for
his superior intelligence and appearance." The Mexicans, the voyageurs, the free trappers in attendance, he said, were "independent
of all save his horse and rifle."

Nathaniel Wyeth, a New England ice merchant who came west
in 1832 and attended a rendezvous that year, had a less romanticized

view. He took one look at the filthy, loud, frightening crowd of drunks gnawing buffalo meat around a roaring fire and pronounced them "a great majority of scoundrels."

2

In his first year as an Ashley-Henry trapper, Jedediah Smith distinguished himself in a fight with Arikaras and disfigured himself in a fight with a bear.

The Ree incident took place on June 1, 1823, when something like 500 Indians battled an Ashley brigade between two of their Missouri River villages in the Dakotas. Concentrated fusil fire by the Arikaras killed thirteen Ashley men and wounded another dozen in a quarter-hour before the Americans could escape in keelboats and canoes.

After reaching the safety of a wooded shore some distance downriver, the two dead men they had managed to wrestle aboard the boats were buried and, with sentries posted, the party bedded down for a few hours of uneasy sleep. At dawn, Smith volunteered to take a canoe north through the Arikara pincer to the Yellowstone fort to notify Andrew Henry of the attack and bring back reinforcements. A French-Canadian boatman accompanied him, and after they departed Ashley had the other dead and wounded loaded on the keelboat *Yellowstone Packet* and dispatched it down to Fort Atkinson on the Nebraska-Iowa border, the administrative center and fur-trade base for the Upper Missouri.

Two months passed before a sufficient punitive force could be gathered for a counterattack on the Rees. From Fort Atkinson, Colonel Henry Leavenworth brought 230 of the Sixth U.S. Infantry in three keelboats and on foot and horseback upriver. Andrew Henry, after receiving the dispatch carried by Jed Smith, left twenty men to protect the Yellowstone fort and took the balance of his force down the Missouri to join Ashley, giving them eighty men between them (forty of Ashley's crew, mostly *voyageurs*, had deserted). The Missouri Fur Company contributed another fifty men led by Joshua Pilcher, who had become president of the company after Manuel Lisa's death, and eventually over 300 Sioux—Yanktons, Tetons, and Hunkpapas, all long-time enemies of the Arikaras—joined the expedition after being promised all the plunder they could gather at the villages.

Leavenworth's force reached Ashley on July 30, and in two days the Sioux and other stragglers arrived to join the "Missouri Legion." The attack on the lower Ree village began on August 9 with Jed Smith, whom Ashley had appointed a captain at the head of a company, in the midst of the fight, but the Sioux volunteers outdistanced all the others, charging impetuously into the village, killing anything that moved, cutting up the dead, and dragging dismembered arms and legs over the ground behind their horses.

After a five-day battle, thirty Arikaras were killed, with but a small number of American casualties. The Indians abandoned both villages during the night of August 13, stealing off into the woods without alerting Leavenworth's pickets. Joshua Pilcher said the only living things found in the two villages were the aged mother of a Ree chief, forty or fifty dogs, and a single rooster.

In September 1823, a month after the Arikara fight, Captain Smith led a crew of Ashley-Henry men in a venture across the plains south of the Yellowstone in search of new beaver grounds. Among the fourteen men with him were James Clyman of Fauquier County, Virginia, hired as a "clerk" by Ashley; Thomas Fitzpatrick of County Cavan, Ireland, who had trade experience among midwestern Indians before enlisting with Ashley; James Bridger, another Virginian, son of a surveyor and innkeeper, who came west in 1818 with his family and apprenticed to a blacksmith in Saint Louis; and Etienne Provost, a Québec-born trapper who, on a trade venture to Santa Fé, had been arrested as a foreign interloper and jailed by Spanish authorities.

After about a month of trapping, Smith had an encounter with a grizzly west of the Black Hills and in a few desperate seconds of the mauling had his ribs broken and his scalp torn away at the hairline, exposing the bone of his skull and leaving his ear hanging loose at the side. Clyman sewed the scalp and ear back in place and later wrote, "The bear had taken nearly all his head in his capacious mouth close to his left eye on one side and close to his right ear on the other and laid the skull bare to near the crown of the head, leaving a white streak where his teeth had passed. One of the captains ears was torn from his head out to the outer rim. . . . Then I put my needle stitching it through and through over and over, laying the lacerated parts together as nice as I could with my hands."

Smith recovered after a few painful days in camp, although he carried the scars from his injury the rest of his life and thereafter wore his hair long to cover the mutilated ear.

He and his crew worked and wintered on the Wind River and in the early spring moved on, drifting north, setting their traps and searching for fresh beaver country. In March 1824 they crossed South Pass, by September reached Hudson's Bay territory in north-western Montana, and spent the winter of 1824–25 at the Company's Flathead post just before Peter Ogden arrived to take over the Company's trapping operations there.

They rejoined the other Ashley-Henry men on the Green River in July 1825 for the first of the annual rendezvous. Smith's personal take from the season's hunt was 668 beaver furs, a record catch for a single trapper at the time.

At the end of the rendezvous he had become a partner with Ashley and when the two departed for Saint Louis they took with them nearly 9,000 pounds of furs worth $50,000.

□

In August 1826 Smith set out from Cache Valley, Utah, heading south of the Great Salt Lake with seventeen trappers. He led his party south to the Sevier River, then on to the Colorado, crossing it into the Black Mountains of northwestern Arizona. Two of his party deserted, half his horses died, and Smith and the fifteen others were starved and nearly out of water when they emerged from the mountains into a broad valley and made their way to a Mojave village where they rested for two weeks. In November they moved on westward across the Mojave Desert and the San Bernardino valley and arrived in the San Gabriel Mission near Los Angeles, completing the first overland crossing of the southwestern route to Alta California.

They were at first welcomed by Mexican authorities but trappers were unknown in California at the time and Smith, who traveled on south to San Diego to meet the governor-general of the province, had difficulty explaining his mission and profession. The governor ended up listing him as a *pescador* (fisherman) and considered imprisoning him in Mexico until they could figure out what he and his ruffian-like crew were up to, coming uninvited to their country. Only the intervention of Captain William H. Cunningham, master of the Boston trade ship *Courier* anchored in the harbor of San Diego, prevented this, but the Mexicans had seen enough of the American *pescadores* and in the spring of 1827 Smith and his men were ordered to leave California.

Captain Cunningham took Smith north to San Pedro Bay, where he was reunited with his fourteen-man trapper party and, equipped with new provisions and horses, retraced his route over the San Bernardino Mountains, fulfilling the governor's orders. But instead of returning to American territory, he led his men north along the Mojave Desert to the southern margin of the San Joaquin River valley, which proved to be rich beaver grounds, and wintered there.

In May, after trapping along the Stanislaus River and amassing a season's haul of 1,500 pounds of furs, Smith and his men tried to cross the Sierra Nevada via the American River but were turned back, losing five horses along the way, by heavy snow in the passes. Leaving his main party behind, Jedediah and two others made a second attempt and succeeded in crossing the range, becoming the first white men to traverse the Sierra Nevada range and adding another record by completing a passage through the Great Salt Desert. Their journey of 600 miles ended in July 1827, in time for the rendezvous at Bear Lake.

After the summer gathering and with a party of eighteen other trappers, Smith headed south, picked up their California trail, and on August 15, 1827, reached the Mojave village on the Colorado. This time they were not welcomed. The Mojaves, tired of being victimized by white hunters who had found them easy marks for theft and abuse, attacked the Americans as they crossed the river and killed ten of them, capturing their horses and supplies. Smith and the eight survivors managed to escape, making their way across the desert on foot.

In mid-September, Smith, who had traveled alone to the San José Mission to buy provisions, was arrested and jailed briefly before posting bond and agreeing, again, to vacate Mexican territory. As before, he did not leave—his righteousness did not, apparently, apply in keeping his word with Mexican authorities—but rejoined his men and spent the winter of 1827–28 in southern California. The deaths of ten comrades had not dampened their trapping ardor, and the furs gathered in his absence, and those accumulated in the winter season, were sold to a sea captain and the proceeds used to buy 250 horses and mules. Smith and his men planned to sell the animals at a profit at the 1828 rendezvous.

But instead of riding eastward across the Sierra Nevada, the trappers, including new recruits gathered along the way, moved north along the California coast through unmapped country and reached the Klamath River in July 1828. This expedition, the first to travel California south to north into the wilds of Oregon, resulted in the third of Smith's four Indian fights—Arikaras in 1823, Mojaves in '27, and now the Kalawatsets on the Umpqua River.

With two other men, Smith set out by canoe on July 14 to discover a route northward to the Willamette River, and during his absence, about 100 Indians entered the American camp and butchered eighteen trappers. Only one man, Arthur Black, described as a "Scotchman," escaped wounded into the woods and made his way to the coast and north 100 miles to Fort Vancouver. When Smith and his two companions returned to the Umpqua camp on

August 10, they were fired upon from the shore and beat a retreat to a high point on the opposite bank, where the deserted camp could be seen in full view. Smith sadly—and correctly—concluded that his men were dead. He had also lost 780 beaver, 50 sea otter, and miscellaneous other skins valued at over $20,000.

With his companion and after much suffering, Smith made his way to Fort Vancouver.

When John McLoughlin heard the story of the Kalawatset ambush from Smith, he took off his spectacles, threw them on the mess-hall table, snatched his cane, and marched to the mess-building porch shouting for his stepson, "Mr. McKay! Thomas McKay! Tom! where the devil is McKay?" McKay, a tall, dark-skinned, powerful man of noted courage who had commanded many trapping parties into Blackfeet country for the Hudson's Bay Company, at last made his appearance. According to Bancroft's re-creation of the moment, McLoughlin quit his angry pacing and said, "Here, Tom, this American has been robbed, his party massacred. Take fifty men. Have the horses driven in. Where is La Framboise, Michel, Baptiste, Jacques; where are all the men? Take twenty pack-horses; those who have no saddles ride on blankets; two blankets to each man; go light, take some salmon, pease, grease, potatoes—now be off, cross the river tonight; and if there be one of you here at sunset I will tie him to the twelve-pounder and give him a dozen lashes."

During the bustle of preparations for the punitive raid, McLoughlin dictated instructions to his clerk and handed them to McKay at the door. "Take this paper and be off," he said, clapping his devoted stepson on the back. "Read it on the way; you'll observe the place is beyond the Umpqua. Good-by, Thomas; God bless you. Be off! be off!" He later wrote angrily of the Kalawatsets in his diary, "such barbarians . . . have no horror or compunction of Conscience at depriving a fellow Man of Life."

(It appears the expedition was commanded by long-time Nor'wester and Hudson's Bay Company brigade leader Alexander McLeod, who had led a similar raid against Puget Sound Indians.

It is possible that Thomas McKay asked McLeod, fourteen years his senior, to lead the party, or to serve as co-commander.*)

The expedition set out along the Willamette early in October 1828, with twenty-two *engagés*, fourteen Indians, Jed Smith and his three surviving party members, and a string of packhorses. At the Umpqua River the pitiful remains of the American camp were found. McLeod wrote in his journal of the traps, kettles, shirts, lead pencils, and similar oddments the Indians had left behind, and of the dead found scattered about the camp. It was, he said, "a sad spectacle of Indian barbarity," with "the skeletons of eleven of those Miserable Sufferers lying bleaching in the sun." By the end of the month they returned safely to Fort Vancouver. Twenty-six horses and mules and most of the stolen furs had been recovered without a fight. For the Company's services McLoughlin charged Smith a modest four dollars each for the horses lost during the mission and prorated the *engagés'* time at the rate of sixty dollars per annum. Governor George Simpson, who during the expedition was visiting Fort Vancouver, paid Smith £486.18s.5d. Sterling—$2,369.60 American—for the recaptured furs.

3

A year after the Arikara misadventure the Ashley-Henry partnership dissolved. Andrew Henry, after bringing in a good fur catch to Saint Louis in the fall of 1824, retired to his home in Washington County, Missouri, and died there in 1832. Ashley continued to direct trapping operations on the Upper Missouri for another year, but at the end of the 1826 rendezvous in the Cache Valley he gave

---

*However, Oregon historian Horace S. Lyman states, "Thomas McKay was the military leader of these expeditions, and was naturally disposed to treat the Indians with severity, saying he would revenge his father (Alexander McKay, killed in the *Tonquin* massacre) upon the red race—although perhaps expressing more ferocity in his language than he actually felt, as he is not known to have killed Indians wantonly or without orders."

his farewell speech and sold out to Jedediah Smith, William Sublette of Kentucky, and David Jackson, an older man said to have
fought with Andrew Jackson at the battle of New Orleans in 1814.
All three of the new partners had fought in the Arikara battle.
Between 1823 and 1827 Ashley is believed to have brought to Saint
Louis 500 bales of beaver furs and made an average profit of
$50,000 for each year. In Saint Louis he continued for a time to
serve as a *bourgeois* (agent and outfitter, called a "bushway" by
mountain men) until reentering politics. He was twice elected to
Congress, twice defeated for the governorship of Missouri, thrice
married, and when he died on March 26, 1838, at age sixty, he
left a substantial estate.

He was, as a contemporary said, "a thoroughly honest and
good-natured man, and to his Yankee shrewdness, with one eye
ever on the main chance, he united thoughtful intelligence engen-
dering independent action."

□

Hudson's Bay governor George Simpson's plan to fend off fur trade
competition with his Columbia River Department was something
his superiors in the Hudson's Bay Company must have admired as
a model of ruthless simplicity. Trapping beaver to extinction, creating "a fur desert" buffer zone between American territory and
the southern approaches to the Columbia, would preserve the
Oregon Country for the Company and eliminate Yankee traders
and the immigrants who followed in their tracks.

This scheme, as it happened, was both too ambitious and too
late. By the time Peter Ogden's brigades made their first forays in
Snake River lands to implement the governor's orders, the detested
competition was already in place. Ogden met Johnson Gardner's
trapping crew in northern Utah in March 1825, and that rude encounter served notice that no number of Hudson's Bay trappers
could stop the American march. In little more than a generation
the Americans, in an unwitting partnership with the British and
with the unforeseen assistance of Chinese silk merchants, would

accomplish what Simpson's people could not have done alone: create a fur desert vaster than either competitor ever imagined.

□

The thirteenth rendezvous, the last memorable one, took place in the summer of 1837 in the Green River valley, a favored site remembered as the place where a pack of rabid wolves attacked the trappers' camp in '33, where Kit Carson fought (and won) a duel with a French-Canadian bully named Shunar in '35, and where that same year a New York physician-missionary named Marcus Whitman dug an old Blackfoot arrowhead from Jim Bridger's back. In 1837 fur profits were down, but 100 trappers congregated to welcome the American Fur Company's wagon caravan with its cargo of trade goods and whiskey. Among visitors to the Green that year were the soldier-hunter-adventurer William Drummond Stewart of Scotland, who had become a familiar figure at rendezvous, usually traveling with Tom Fitzpatrick's men. This time he brought a guest, Alfred Miller, a Baltimore artist. Stewart met Miller in New Orleans and commissioned him to produce sketches and paintings of the 1837 hunt and rendezvous to be displayed in Murthly Castle, the Stewarts' ancestral home in Perthshire. Miller kept busy. Besides the mountain men, the Astor supply train, and its traders, there were hundreds of Indian lodges along the looping river and throughout the valley, and the largest of the Indian contingents, the Shoshoni, filled Miller's sketchbooks.

But for all the flashing color and carefree carousing Miller witnessed, the end was in sight and the last rendezvous, in 1840, produced a sadly low number of trappers, traders, and Indians; the beaver pelt that fetched five or six dollars in 1832 was now valued at a dollar. Shiny silk hats were now the fashion and, fortunately for the beaver, the demand for its hide was disappearing quicker than its slide toward extinction.

For the American mountain man, the fur trade had endured a generation, and at the end its vestiges were confined to a desultory business at Fort Laramie and a scattering of other old posts on the eastern edge of the Rocky Mountains. The old trappers still trapped, but there was no wage in it and they had to turn to other sources of income born of their wilderness skills. They had broken the trails, the Oregon Trail among them, to and across the Rockies, prepared the way for others looking westward. Now they would guide the others.

□

Jedediah Smith, who had stood above and apart from his comrades from the beginning of the mountain-man era, who had seen more of the western wilderness than any man of his time and filled in more of its blank spaces in his journeys, did not live to see the era end.

After his deadly experience with the Kalawatsets in Oregon in 1828, he rejoined his partners and continued to trap the Upper Missouri and the Yellowstone. In August 1830, seemingly tired of the hardships of life on the trail and stating that he "missed the care of the Christian Church," he sold his trapping interests and, now a man of moderate wealth and but thirty-one years old, returned to Saint Louis in retirement.

But he chafed at inactivity and, within a few months, with his former partners William Sublette and David Jackson pooled funds for a venture in the booming Santa Fé trade. The men bought twenty-four wagons of trade goods and in April 1831 Smith, his old crony Tom Fitzpatrick, and seventy-four men departed Saint Louis bound for New Mexico.

In late May, after several days' travel in the arid country between the Arkansas and Cimarron Rivers, Smith and Fitzpatrick rode ahead of the caravan to find a streambed in which to dig for water. The two men took separate trails and, as later evidence indicated, on May 27, 1831, Smith found a water pocket in an old buffalo wallow in the Cimarron. What he could not know was that the wallow was closely watched by a band of Comanches. Legend has it that Smith was able to get a single shot off from his Hawken rifle, killing the leader of the Comanche band, before he was overwhelmed and probably stabbed to death with lances.

His body was never found.

Josiah Gregg, who wrote a book titled *The Commerce of the Prairies* in 1844 about his experience as a Santa Fé trader, first set out with a trade caravan in May 1831 from Missouri to seek relief for his lifelong frail health. On that journey, a Mexican *cibolero* (buffalo hunter) rode up to his caravan and brought news that a famous *Americano* had been killed by Indians on the Cimarron. Later Gregg learned that the American was the celebrated mountain man and explorer Jedediah Smith, a man who, Gregg said, "would surely be entitled to one of the most exalted seats in the Olympus of prairie mythology."

The eulogy that appeared in the *Illinois Monthly Magazine* in 1832 described Smith as "modest, never obtrusive, charitable, and without guile . . . a man whom none could approach without respect or know without esteem." Others spoke in similar terms. Jed Smith was a prototypical Yankee puritan—grim, celibate (his biographer Dale L. Morgan points out that Smith was never known to have had an interest in women, least of all in taking an Indian wife or mistress as so many of his trapping cohorts did), highminded, and without fear. He was "a bold, outspoken, professing and consistent Christian," a trapper friend named William Waldo said.

A modern historian of the mountain men, Win Blevins, wrote of Smith's "Love of wild places," which "had rooted into him and become a deeper religion." Blevins says Jed Smith's "altar was the mountaintop, his place of meditation not the pew but the wilderness, his sacraments his mountain skills."

12

KELLEY'S ODYSSEY

"... A GREAT AND CRAZY VISION."

1

In the winter of 1820, while Stephen Harriman Long of the Army Corps of Topographical Engineers was mapping the Great American Desert and describing it as a retardant to westward migration, Congressman John Floyd, M.D., of Virginia, took up the Oregon question. He said England was stealing the Pacific Northwest from America and advocated annexation of it and filling it with settlers.

Dr. Floyd had grown up in Kentucky, and Bancroft wrote that he "understood the character of the Western states," where everyone was "a pioneer of the Alexandrian type, sighing for more worlds to conquer, more wilderness to redeem to civilization by the sheer strength of brawny arm and independent will." The congressman counted among his friends several prominent Astorians and the explorer William Clark. (Floyd's cousin, Charles Floyd, had served as a sergeant in the Lewis and Clark party and died of a ruptured appendix in August 1804, the only casualty of the expedition.) The idea of Oregon inspired the Virginian, and the British presence there as the sole occupant of the "joint occupancy" angered him. "With two oceans washing our shores," he liked to say, presaging the tenets of Manifest Destiny, "commercial wealth is ours and imagination can hardly conceive the greatness, the grandeur, the power that await us."

On December 19, 1820, Dr. Floyd presented to his colleagues in the House of Representatives a petition for the appointment of a select committee to "inquire into the situation of the settlements upon the Pacific Ocean and the expediency of occupying the Columbia River." The document was adopted and Floyd named chairman of the panel. The committee's report, introduced on January 25, 1821, was praised by Senator Thomas Hart Benton of Missouri, one of the most influential expansionists in Washington, who said that with it "the first blow was struck; public attention was awakened, and the geographical, historical and statistical facts set forth . . . [the report] made a lodgment in the public mind." But the report carried with it a bill, considered overly radical, which authorized the president to occupy "the Origon country," extinguish whatever Indian title to the lands existed, and provide for the establishment of a government there. The measure failed but Floyd reintroduced it in 1822, revised to provide that when the settlement in the region reached a population of 2,000 it should become "the Territory of Origon," and a possession of the United States.

Floyd made an impassioned speech on his bill on December 17, 1822, but it aroused little interest other than a discussion of the northwest coast as a fur and whaling station, a fishery and timberland. Some congressmen dreaded the potential of war with England over the region and wondered whether such remote lands were worth such a danger.

Still, the Virginia legislator did not yield. On January 19, 1824, he presented yet another bill—another revision of the old one—that would authorize occupation of the Columbia River by the United States, establish a military post and a territorial government there, and hold out as an enticement a section of land to each new settler.

The War Department reported that transportation by the Missouri and Columbia Rivers of sufficient numbers of troops and horses to man a military post in the Pacific Northwest would cost $30,000, and transportation by sea of the heavy baggage, ordnance, and supplies would amount to another $14,000.

The issue was debated and, while no questions were raised on the validity of the American claims to the region, Floyd repeatedly tried to refute claims that mountain barriers made colonization of the Oregon Country impossible, that the lands west of the mountains were "bleak and inhospitable" with "impenetrable forests" and a climate so forbidding as to "preclude cereal crops." Some said that the Columbia was too distant to attract settlers, but Floyd reminded his fellow representatives that in 1775, Kentucky was considered "too far away to be a part of the Union." He found supporters such as Congressman Baylies of Massachusetts (who assailed the "Gentlemen who are talking of natural boundaries" by asserting, "Sirs, the natural boundary is the Pacific Ocean") and others among New England's merchants. These monied men saw the potential for fishing and whaling in North Pacific waters and for a timber industry in the forests stretching from the 42nd parallel to Russian Alaska and inland from the Pacific to the Cascade Range; there were fortunes to be made in pine, spruce, hemlock, fir, and cedar.

On December 23, 1824, after four years of effort and in defiance of such influential opposition as that of Representative John Quincy Adams (who damned the proposal as a "tissue of errors; there was nothing could purify it but fire"), Floyd saw his bill for the occupation of the Columbia River and establishment of the Territory of Oregon pass the House by a vote of 113–57.

In February 1825 the bill arose in the Senate, where it was batted down by Senator Mahlon Dickerson of New Jersey, who contended that the military occupation of Oregon would lead to war with Britain, and that it would never become a state of the Union or accrue to any advantage to the United States. He said the proposed $50,000 for implementing the bill was a bagatelle, that a sum ten times that amount would actually be needed. He ridiculed the idea of a territorial representative coming to Washington and returning to Oregon via an overland route or around Cape Horn in under a year's travel time. Moreover, he said, in a clear echo of the Long expedition report, the region between Council Bluffs and the Rocky Mountains, which would have to be traversed by the military party and by any settlers venturing to the Oregon Country, was sterile, without wood or water, its mountains inhospitable—fit only as "a retreat for red men."

Floyd's colleagues were clearly not yet ready to share his dream of a Pacific commonwealth and his bill was tabled, consigned to Congress's paperwork perdition. In Bancroft's words, the subject of the occupation of the Columbia "was suffered to lie perdu in the minds of the people of the United States, except as attention was called to it by the writings of Hall J. Kelley, or by some more obscure person."

□

"In the long story of our nation's westering there are few adventures more curious or difficult to assess," historian David Lavender wrote of Hall J. Kelley's half-century-long Oregon obsession.

"He is neither a great hero nor a great rascal," Bancroft said of Kelley. "He is great at nothing, and is remarkable rather for his lack of strength, and in staggering for fifty years under an idea too big for his brain. He was a born enthusiast and partisan, one of a class of projectors more capable of forming grand schemes than of carrying them to a successful issue."

Bernard De Voto said Kelley was "a man of a great and crazy vision."

Of his contributions to the 300-year journey to the Pacific Northwest Kelley himself said plainly, "The colonization of Oregon was both conceived and achieved by me, and all for the hope of laying a foundation for the advancement of religion and the kingdom of Christ." And the prolix titles of the abundant books and tracts he published (works Bancroft said were "no less voluminous than peculiar") told his faithful armchair adventurer-readers precisely whose single-handed travails and triumphs were responsible for the American presence in the North Pacific littoral. One example: *A History of the Settlement of Oregon and the Interior of Upper California, and of Persecutions and Afflictions of Forty Years' Continuance, Endured by the Author, Hall J. Kelley.*

One hundred and sixty years after he made his mad hegira to the land of his dreams, Hall Jackson Kelley remains the most vexatious character in the story of the Oregon Country. While he annoyed his contemporaries by making too much of his contributions, his contemporaries annoy us by making too little of them. In David Lavender's memorable phrase, Kelley was "cursed with the unfortunate propensity for getting on the nerves of everyone with whom he came in contact"—a propensity that still lingers. He was precisely what his peers said of him: a waspish, humorless, pious, self-aggrandizing, overbearing pest, and a likely lunatic. But even his cruelest critics had to admit he saw things and did things beyond their dreams, and even beyond his own.

Before he clasped to his heart the notion that he had been selected by God to lead a great congregation to the banks of the Columbia, Kelley had other obsessions, among them Christian religion and educating himself and others. Born in New Hampshire in 1789, his family had the resources to see that he received a fine formal education. He earned an undergraduate degree at a Middlebury, Connecticut, college, and a master's degree at Harvard, where he is said to have ruined his eyesight by studying Virgil by moonlight in the Cambridge hills, and he became a surveyor and a proficient teacher of mathematics. Until 1824 he seems to have been content in the worthy, if mundane, life of a Massachusetts grammar-school teacher (during which tenure he may have introduced the first schoolroom slate blackboard), dedicated churchgoer (he is credited with the founding of the first Sunday school in Boston), and active and probably vociferous member of the Boston Young Men's Education Society and the Penitent Female Refuge Society. He had a facility with the pen even in these early years, publishing in 1820 a book on elementary education titled *The American Instructor.*

The precise moment Kelley caught the Oregon fever is not

known, but he caught it early, before most people had heard of the place, even before the name "Oregon" caught on. As had Jedediah Smith, Kelley became mesmerized by the Lewis and Clark journals. He studied accounts of Astor's failed venture on the Columbia, collected clippings on the renewal of the joint occupancy agreement with England, and seems to have followed assiduously the debates in Congress over Congressman Floyd's bill. Bancroft states that by 1824, Kelley had given himself over to study of the Columbia River country: "Nor did he cease writing and raving, until at the ripe age of eighty-five he was transferred from his New England hermitage, where after his fruitless excursions he had retired to brood in poverty over the wrongs inflicted by a soulless corporation and an ungrateful republic."

He devoured exploration journals, tracts, pamphlets, newspaper stories, and congressional publications, and pored over the pathetic maps then existing of the lands beyond the Rocky Mountains, most drawn by cartographers who had never been close to them. Slowly accreting in his brain, a plan took shape, "the first thin strands of Manifest Destiny did twine together in his frantic, half-crazed hands," as Lavender wrote. This scheme, devised by a man who never led anybody anywhere, who had traveled out of New England no farther than Washington, was curiously premonitory. He threw himself fanatically into the idea of American settlement of the Oregon Country, envisioning the formation of an emigration society and taking 3,000 New England farmers to the banks of the Columbia River.

After throwing over his teaching duties, Kelley began the work God had assigned him by composing broadsides and making speeches to anyone willing to listen. Churchgoers were inspired by his ardor, as he put it, to "promote the propagation of Christianity in the dark and cruel places about the shores of the Pacific," and it was impossible not to be impressed with his encyclopedic knowledge of these places he had never seen. He made a good appearance: He was handsome, with a squarish, clean-shaven face, high forehead, dark hair cropped short and brushed forward in Napoleonic style, and expressive eyes; he was dignified and well dressed. His screeds and tracts, his voluminous letters to Boston newspapers, and his impassioned speeches gave the impression that he had tramped over all of the dark and cruel places and the sun-dappled and friendly ones of the Oregon Country. He dwelled on the positive, wrote and spoke of the land out there as an Eden, a pristine, fecund region of farmlands so rich they would require "but little labor" to raise grain, vegetables, and cattle; a place teeming with beaver and other precious fur-bearing animals and game of every known species and many unrecorded ones; and a trove of fish and timber beyond mortal calculation. As for getting there, he said, warming to the real heart of his plan, the journey would not be taxing: People would ride comfortably in wagons, and the materials needed to set up a colony would precede them in ships sailing out of Boston Harbor and following the Cape Horn route to the Pacific. Congress would underwrite most of the expenses. Each emigrant might need as little as fifty dollars for incidental expenses on the trail, and perhaps five dollars for each accompanying child.

He gathered money in small donations wherever he spoke and, like citizens of the late twentieth century signing on to colonize a space station, his listeners placed their names on his petitions as they dreamed of a place as remote then as the moon, the Eden awaiting them on the lush and friendly banks of the Columbia.

In 1828, Kelley began petitioning Congress, each paper submitted carrying new numbers, longer and more ambitious blueprints for his settlement, and new proposals and budgetary requests to carry them out. The original document he drafted outlined the general Kelley plan and stated that the undersigned and 3,000 others were prepared to start west on short notice. A year later, he refined his congressional request, asking that a modest twenty-five square miles of the Columbia valley be granted him for colonization. He listed 500 members of his American Society for Encouraging the Settlement of Oregon Territory, and in 1831 incorporated the group under the laws of Massachusetts. Among his original members were some influential citizens, such as the impatient Cambridge ice merchant, Nathaniel Wyeth, but, as Bancroft summed up the matter, "This society was Hall J. Kelley. He was the body and brains, the fingers and tongue of it."

While awaiting favorable response from Washington, Kelley and his society members met in Boston churches and lecture halls, debated, drew up bylaws, recruited new members, collected funds, and scrapped over the details of founding a town in Oregon, to be built in New England style, which would "repeat, with appropriate variations, the history of the Puritan Colony of Massachusettes Bay."

The thrill of all the meeting, debating, planning, and petitioning waned early, and Kelley was faced with the inevitable duty of setting a date when the vanguard of the society membership would actually start west. He had no congressional commitment but he had some funds, a host of anxious emigrants-to-be, and a handful of associates willing to join him in taking the first real steps toward the Pacific.

He appears to have traveled to Saint Louis in 1828, perhaps alone, or more likely with a few close society advisers, to investigate an overland route to the Columbia. In this mission he failed and returned angrily to Boston with vague threats against the minions of the Hudson's Bay Company and certain American fur traders, who he said had thwarted him. By now he was confident that powerful enemies were arrayed against him, some of them identifiable, others unseen but no less mighty, and all devoted to causing him to fail.

He took comfort in pinning his reverses on them.

2

For another four years there were fits and starts—mostly fits—while Kelley proceeded to make maps, write his copious and strident letters to newspapers, hold society meetings, cadge donations, and besiege the Jacksonian-era Congress for land allotments and official sanction for his scheme. Kelley's plans for an emigrant invasion of the Oregon Country were ever-changing. He seems to have realized that an overland trek to the Columbia River would probably be taxing after all, especially for a Boston congregation for whom a trip to Cape Cod or Poughkeepsie was a long haul, and that the answer was to travel by merchant ship along with the cargo necessary for setting up the colony. Astor had set up his Columbia River enterprise by sending his first agents out there by sea, and American traders had been sailing out of Massachusetts Bay for the Pacific for fifty years. To be sure, the voyage would be tedious, and even occasionally uncomfortable—Cape Horn and all that—but these were minor considerations.

In 1832, by now the nation's chief Oregon boomer, Kelley made a frenetic effort to get his expedition underway. He increased the tempo of his fund-raising—adding to his familiar appeal the idea of taking missionaries with him to work among the Oregon "savages"—and actually chartered a ship as proof that his was no armchair dreamer's scheme, something a good many of his supporters had begun to suspect. But he was arrested that summer, probably for nonpayment of debts, before he and a handful of his faithful could sail. He used the occasion of his brief tussle with the law to rail at his "wicked adversaries," notably the Hudson's Bay Company and Astor's American Fur Company, whose hirelings "watched every movement of mine, pursuing me from city to city, laying every plan to vex and worry me." The falsehoods, calumnies, and "vile sayings" of these shadowy nemeses "panic-struck my followers and turned them back," he said.

The arrest, and the furor he made of it, seems to have revived Kelley's faltering campaign. In some miraculous way he paid his debts and in the winter of 1832 made his way out of Boston to New York. There he found new converts waiting and obtained contributions of cash and credit sufficient to engage a merchant vessel to carry himself and a few of the society elite to New Orleans—where they promptly deserted him.

There are many possible motives behind the exodus of Kelley's people. Thrust in with him in a confined space, they must have grown weary of his nagging, irascible self-absorption. In New

Orleans they must have realized at last that only a shore-to-ship gangway separated them from the start of a crack-brained undertaking from which there might be no return. Perhaps the passage to the mouth of the Mississippi wrung from them in its first installment the dream of a pioneering adventure. Very likely, the idea of continuing on, six weeks or more to Rio de Janeiro, another two months via the Horn to Valparaiso, untold months crawling northward along the Pacific coasts of South America and Mexico, Baja and Alta California, in a stinking, wallowing, merchant sailing ship chased them back to their New England comforts.

Under the protection of whatever spiritual force is in charge of lunatics, Kelley was undaunted by the mutineers who fled his ship. He proceeded alone in the spring of 1833 to Vera Cruz, experiencing "incredible hardships," he said vaguely, and overland to the Mexican capital, where he somehow gained an audience with President Antonio López de Santa Anna. At the time of Kelley's visit, this august personage, then newly elected in the first of his five scattered administrations, was facing civil war in his country and unrest among the American settlers in Mexican Texas. While Kelley was permitted to proceed in his journey across Mexico, much of his baggage was seized. Americans were anathema in Mexico, and Kelley no doubt made of himself a particular nuisance. The baggage may have been taken as payment for having to put up with him, the permission to travel given in the belief that he would die en route to the Pacific.

He added Mexico to his list of thwarters and set out across the country, joining a pack train part of the way, traveling alone much of the time. In a month or two (everything is vague about this journey) he struggled into San Blas near the eastern shore of the Gulf of California, presumably made his way north to the Sonoran capital of Hermosillo, thence to Puebla, a town near San Diego in Alta California. What battles he fought against the elements, fever, hunger, thirst, hostile Indians, and Yankee-suspicious Mexicans are not recorded. He may have had a rudimentary command of the Spanish language, but how this vociferous, cantankerous man got across Mexico alive is a question that Kelley, for all his voluminous writings, left unanswered.

In the spring of 1834, in San Diego, Kelley contrived to meet with the governor of Alta California, José Figueroa, perhaps seeking permission to travel upcountry to Monterey, Yerba Buena, and on north. His eyes were trained on the Oregon Country, and he must have assured the governor that he did not intend to remain in the Mexican province. Permission was granted. He then offered his services to survey the Sacramento River valley and after this strange overture was politely declined, Kelley moved on north to the Los Angeles pueblo, and there had the first of three encounters with an American trapper named Ewing Young. This burly frontiersman had twice before ventured to Alta California on trapping expeditions and had a firsthand knowledge of the country from tramping it from San Diego to Klamath Lake on beaver hunts. At the time Kelley met the man, subsequently so troublesome not only to Kelley but to John McLoughlin and the entire Hudson's Bay enclave at Fort Vancouver, Young was already among the most seasoned of mountain men.

Born about 1792 in the wilderness near Jonesboro, Tennessee, he had training as a carpenter and cabinetmaker but, according to Bancroft, was "a man of fine intelligence and nerve united to a grand physique, and too restless and fond of new experience to remain beside a turning-lathe all his life." He moved to Missouri in 1822 and accompanied one of the first American commercial caravans to reach Santa Fé, a year after Mexico's independence from Spain and the opening of New Mexico (and Alta California) to a trickle of American traders. After this profitable enterprise, Young recruited a few partners and trapped beaver on the Pecos and San Juan Rivers, dealt in Missouri produce and Mexican mules, and survived fights with Osage, Papago, Yuma, Apache, and Mojave war parties.

In 1829, just a year after Jedediah Smith's adventure in California and on the Umpqua River in Oregon, Young led a trapping party (which included "Kit" Carson, a nineteen-year-old runaway from a Missouri saddle shop) out of Taos, New Mexico, to the San Gabriel River, a few miles northeast of Pueblo de los Angeles. He returned to California in 1832 with ten trappers and again in 1834 by the Gila River route.

In Los Angeles, Kelley collared Young and belabored him on the wonders of Oregon, among which were its beaver riches, and seems to have been lobbying for a billet in Young's party, which was then preparing to march north to Monterey. Young was wary, Kelley overinsistent. The two proceeded separately.

In June Kelley arrived in Monterey, the most cosmopolitan town on the Pacific Seaboard, and tarried, basking in the beauty of the place, investigating taking passage on a trader headed for the Columbia River estuary. He was in no hurry. He had survived, or so he thought, all the worst of his journey, had crossed Mexico on foot, arriving unconquered in this semblance of civilization, a mere 600 miles from the Columbia. He was practically home.

The capital of Alta California was situated on a commanding headland south of a magnificent bay first seen by Portuguese explorers 300 years before. Its whitewashed and red-roofed adobes were scattered between piney hills and a wide strip of white beach, the town and its setting as invigorating as the sea breezes that cooled it. In 1834, scarcely a decade before American annexation, Monterey thrummed and jostled with trade. (Alta California's greatest export treasures were its cowhides, sought for shoemaking and other leather goods, and tallow, sold in rawhide bags, twenty-five pounds for two dollars, for soap and candles; it imported everything, including the shoes, soap, and candles made from its hides and tallow.) The waterfront swarmed with a heterogeneous collection of foreigners—mostly trade-ship captains and their crews, trappers, and hunters—and Mexican soldiery, customs officials, and clerks. Monterey Bay was forested by the masts of merchant vessels from seaports as distant as Genoa, Marseilles, Rio, and Boston, and by visiting ships-of-war, mostly British, that cruised Mexican waters from Acapulco and Mazatlán to Yerba Buena and on to the Oregon and Alaskan coasts.

It must have been a relief for Kelley to discover that there were

other "Bostons" among the brigantine and schooner crews lounging near the Customs House and wandering the dirt streets of the
town. No doubt he harangued them with his grand plan to reclaim
Astoria and populate the Oregon Country with righteous American
emigrants. He may have paid a visit to the most eminent American
residing in Monterey, Thomas O. Larkin (from Charlestown, Massachusetts), who had come to Monterey in 1832 and with a capital
of $500 opened a a flour mill and a small store dealing in such
things as furs, horses, and lumber. He had married a widow on
shipboard en route from the Sandwich Islands, and Rachel Hobson
Holmes Larkin was said to be the first American woman to reside
in Mexican California and their child, Thomas, Jr., the first American baby born there. Larkin had political connections in New England and Washington and in a few years would become United
States consul in Monterey.

Kelley and Ewing Young talked again in the seacoast town.
This time Young listened as Kelley extemporized. The trapper knew
there was some truth in the stories of Oregon's untapped fur
riches—he had seen the potential when wandering the upper
reaches of the Sacramento River in '33—and finally agreed to take
Kelley along with him.

Young's plan was to buy horses and mules en route north and
take the herd into Oregon to sell, grubstaking himself and his sixteen men—"adventurers, deserted seamen and others," Bancroft
said of them—to a season in the beaver streams. A hundred of the
animals were collected in Monterey and San José, and on the journey to Yerba Buena the party was joined by nine other men with
their own herd of fifty-six horses. At least two of these suspicious
newcomers were Americans. Kelley later called them "marauders"
and he suspected, as did Young, that their animals had been stolen.

In August, Young, Kelley, and the others reached the Umpqua
River valley, near the site of the massacre of Jedediah Smith's party
in '28. In camp near the river, while the other men were rounding
up strayed animals, Kelley fell desperately ill with malaria and was
unable to walk a step or mount a horse. While Young ministered
to him as best he could, the expedition was stalled several days.

Then, in a lucky circumstance, a band of Hudson's Bay trappers, returning from Sacramento River hunting grounds, came upon Young's camp. The leader of the party was the French-Canadian Michel Laframboise, who had been among the *voyageurs* who had sailed from New York to the Columbia on the *Tonquin* in 1810. His employment as an intrepid "utility man" in the Company, meaning that he was assigned dangerous missions to uncover new fur grounds, was accompanied by a reputation as a thief and "womanizer"—George Simpson, Hudson's Bay governor of the Pacific Northwest, called him "a lying, worthless blackguard." His checkered history notwithstanding, Laframboise saved Hall Kelley's life by agreeing to take him on to Fort Vancouver, where he could receive medical care and assistance from Dr. John McLoughlin.

Thus assisted by representatives of the entity that topped his list of enemies in all his Oregon schemes, traveling by Hudson's Bay mule and Hudson's Bay canoe, Kelley saw for the first time the land of his letters, tracts, petitions, and fantasies. At the same time others who knew of his obsession saw him. In the Willamette valley, after Ewing Young and his motley group of horse herders caught up with the Laframboise party, Kelley met Québec-born Jason Lee and his nephew Daniel Lee, who had come out to do Methodist religious work among the Flathead Indians. While there is no record of their conversation, Kelley certainly took the opportunity to preach to them on his Oregon dream and his original idea of taking missionaries to this Eden. The Lees no doubt listened patiently. Daniel later recalled Kelley as "a New England man, who entertained some very extravagant notions in regard to Oregon."

Laframboise brought Kelley into Fort Vancouver in late October, and his party was followed a few days later by Ewing Young's and its horse herd.

They were not welcomed; indeed, the gates of the customarily hospitable place were closed to them.

3

Six weeks before Young and Kelley appeared in Fort Vancouver, the Hudson's Bay schooner *Cadboro* returned to the Columbia from a trade voyage to Monterey and delivered to John McLoughlin an angry communiqué from Governor José Figueroa of Alta California. The letter denounced the two Americans as horse thieves and cautioned the factor to have nothing to do with these outlaws, least of all to buy the horses and mules stolen from Mexican ranchos.

Confronted with the charges, both men protested their innocence. Young admitted he had allowed some suspicious characters to join him north of Yerba Buena but said he paid for every animal he had brought in. Moreover, he said the Mexicans were the real thieves, claiming that he had been "plundered" of thousands of dollars in furs by California customs authorities in payment of fines for unauthorized trapping in the province.

McLoughlin remained dubious of this upstart American, and when Young tried to trade some beaver skins collected on the journey to Oregon the factor refused them, although he sent the supplies Young requested to his camp. This charity infuriated the trapper and he ordered the goods returned. In effect, McLoughlin was saying the furs were as tainted as the horses, to Young a choice example of hypocrisy since the Company was also poaching furs in Mexican territory. He rode to the factor's headquarters to demand an explanation. McLoughlin listened patiently—he was never a man to be cowed by another's anger—and invited Young to address a protest to Governor Figueroa, which would be sent to Monterey in the *Cadboro*, soon to depart for Mexican waters, with the factor's own request for details and proof of the horse-thievery charges.

Young wrote a letter but was not mollified by McLoughlin's suggestion and left Fort Vancouver sullenly, taking his horses and mules with him. He eventually settled near Champoeg, an old Indian camp on an open, sandy peninsula on the east side of the Willamette River. He built a cabin there, hired workers to erect a sawmill, and within two years was also proprietor of a whiskey distillery—an immensely disturbing development to teetotaling Mc-Loughlin—and a cattle company, and was claiming over fifty square miles of territory for his enterprises.

A few months after McLoughlin received the damaging letter, Young and Kelley were exculpated of the horse-theft charges, but Young never forgave the factor for treating him as an outcast. In 1836 William A. Slacum, an American "private merchant" on a tour of Oregon, reported a conversation with Young at Champoeg in which the Tennesseean claimed that "a cloud hung over him so long through Dr. McLoughlin's influence, that he was almost maddened by the harsh treatment of that gentleman."

These words might have been written by Hall Kelley; indeed, in slightly different language, were so written, countless times. While Ewing Young was taking the brunt of the punishment for the crimes alleged by the California governor, Kelley had his own stories of "maltreatment" at the hands of McLoughlin, and they dovetailed perfectly with the theories he devised before he ever set foot in Oregon: that the Hudson's Bay Company had contrived to ruin him.

In the beginning of his barrage of letters to newspapers back east, and in personal correspondence, Kelley wrote of arriving in Oregon "much depressed in spirits and under great bodily weakness, then recovering from a violent attack of fever and ague." He said he was received in Fort Vancouver as "an unwelcome guest" and without being specific about the horse-thievery charges said "calumnies and slander were propagated" against him, and that "bloody men" had more than once threatened his life.

In fact, Kelley was the author of all his problems. He had fallen in with outlaws but was as innocent of any crime as Ewing Young—and probably more innocent. But his reputation as a haranguer of the Hudson's Bay Company had preceded him. From reports in eastern newspapers and from such Americans as Jason and Daniel Lee and Nathaniel Wyeth, who had preceded him to Oregon, McLoughlin knew of Kelley's intemperate and irrational accusations against the Company, and his grandiose ideas of "driving the British out of Oregon."

Even the handful of Americans coming in and out at Fort Vancouver shunned him. Wyeth, who had been inspired to come to Oregon by Kelley's writings and oratory, paid him only a perfunctory visit. (Kelley surmised that Wyeth had "crossed over" to the Hudson's Bay intriguers, even to embracing their policies of discouraging emigrants.)

McLoughlin, exasperated at having this difficult and foolish man at his fort, remained great-hearted. Kelley was shaken by fever, gaunt and weak, and "out of humanity" the factor assigned him a servant's hut, saw to it that he was attended by the post surgeon and that food was delivered to him regularly as he recovered his strength. Kelley, while spending the winter of 1834–35 at Fort Vancouver, demonstrated his gratitude for McLoughlin's largesse by demanding his "rights" as "an American on American soil . . . pursuing the avowed purpose of opening the trade of the territory to general competition."

One visitor to the fort who saw Kelley that winter described him as "five feet nine inches high, wearing a slouched hat, blanket capote, leather pants, with a red stripe down the seam, rather *outré* even for Vancouver . . . penniless, and ill-clad, and considered rather too rough for close companionship, and was not invited to the mess."

Kelley appears to have recovered enough from his debilitations that winter to write voluminous journals and make extensive notes on his surroundings. In an 1839 publication, he claimed to have surveyed the Columbia from Fort Vancouver to its Pacific estuary and provided convincing proof of his wanderings with data on the topography, climate, and soil conditions of his surroundings and observations on the Columbia bar and entrance, harbors and mountain ranges, timber and mineral potentials. He even claimed to have discovered deposits of gold, silver, copper, and coal in the vicinity of Fort Vancouver.

But for all his activity that winter, Kelley was anxious to return home. He was without funds or friends, at the mercy of the charity of his enemy, and his health was weakened. He still believed passionately in his Oregon dream, saw all his research and sumptuous descriptions, written in the comforts of Massachusetts, beggared by the actual place. For all the despair he experienced in getting there, his meager five months at Fort Vancouver steeled him. Now he could say out of experience and observation that Oregon must be American territory; he could use the personal pronoun in the lecture hall and in his writings: I have been there and this is what I saw.

McLoughlin, no doubt delighted to be rid of his resident ingrate, made him a gift of £7 and passage to the Sandwich Islands on the Company ship *Dryad*, and Kelley departed the Oregon coast in March 11, 1835, never to return. Bancroft says he remained true to his propensities to bite the hand that fed him: "The rude manners of the sailors with whom he was forced to associate in his feeble state of health were a sore annoyance to him, operating yet more to prejudice his diseased imagination against the company to whom he was indebted for this means of getting out of the country of his misfortunes."

McLoughlin wrote later that he had provided Kelley with shelter and victuals "until he left . . . when I gave him passage to Oahu. On his return to the states, he published a narrative of his voyage, in which, instead of being grateful for the kindness shown him, he abused me, and falsely stated I had been so alarmed with the dread that he would destroy the Hudson's Bay Company's trade, that I kept a constant watch over him."

From Oahu, Kelley was able to take passage to Boston on an American whaling vessel and arrived home early in 1836. He was then forty-six years old and had a long life yet to live. He wrote even more voluminously than before his Oregon odyssey, "planned and prayed, and blessed his friends, and cursed his enemies by the hundreds of pages," Bancroft wrote. "Besides pamphlets and newspapers, he wrote letters literally by the bushel." His books and treatises bore such titles as *A Geographical Sketch of that Part of North America called Oregon, A General Circular to all*

Persons of Good Character who Wish to Emigrate to the Oregon Territory; Embracing some Account of the Character and Advantages of the Country, the Right and the Means and the Operations by which it is to be Settled; and all Necessary Directions for Becoming an Emigrant, and *History of the Colonization of the Oregon Territory.*

While he wrote often of his struggles and persecutions and took credit for not only the settlement of Oregon but also of California, not all his writings were foolish. Among influential politicians who were educated by Kelley's work were Senator Lewis Linn of Missouri, who subsequently introduced bills to extend American laws to Oregonian settlers and to give generous land grants to emigrant families; Senator Thomas Hart Benton, also of Missouri and a powerful expansionist voice in Congress; and Senator Daniel Webster of Massachusetts, who upon reading Kelley's *Geographical Sketch of Oregon* wrote the author, "I think much of your project; I will do all I can to sustain it."

Not long after his return to Boston, Kelley married and hoped to have a career as a respectable businessman. He enlisted some partners and built a cotton mill in Three Rivers, Massachusetts, counting on his share of the income from the business to finance his continuing Oregon work. But the mill failed and he lost what remained of his meager finances—and his sanity. Thereafter, he thought, talked, and wrote of nothing but his Oregon expedition and the oppression and inhumanity of the Hudson's Bay Company, imagining that every annoyance of whatever kind he suffered was attributable to its "hirelings." Bancroft wrote, "So great was his suspicion of every one, and so irritable had he become, that he drove his wife and children from him, and afterwards resided alone on a small piece of land heavily mortgaged, at Three Rivers... where he was designated as The Hermit, and from which the entreaties of his friends were unable to draw him."

Kelley died "of paralysis" on January 20, 1874, at the age of eighty-five.

"To the very last he remained the warm friend of Oregon," Bancroft said, "indignantly denying that he had ever entertained 'extravagant notions' of that country, which he still contended was 'the finest on which the sun shines.' " The historian was saddened by the end of Kelley's life, as were many of the old man's contemporaries. "Had I been in Congress," Bancroft said, "I would have given the old school-master something to sweeten his second childhood's cup withal, and I would have praised and petted him somewhat in an official way, for he did more than many a well paid officer of the government."

13

THE ICEMAN

1

Among the 500 members of Hall Kelley's American Society for Encouraging the Settlement of Oregon Territory was an outspoken Bostonian named Nathaniel Jarvis Wyeth, an impressive business-man with broad shoulders, thick chest, and an open, clever face, the lower portion framed in straggly chin whiskers, the middle of it unmasked even by a mustache. He was big-nosed and large-headed, and his mouth was shaped into a perpetual grin—not a smirk or affectation but the slight smile that success, and the prospect of more of it, brings. He was dynamic, brim full of ideas, and impatient to shake Kelley from his perpetual dreams. Wyeth's tenure as a Kelley man would be brief; after all, how much oratory, tract-writing, and planning would it take to make a start for the Columbia?

Patience was no virtue to Nat Wyeth, nor did he profess any lofty motives in his own plans to get to the Oregon Country. No patriotic or spiritual needs haunted him; indeed, one of his religious-minded acquaintances called him "a perfect infidel." He wanted to make a fortune in the Pacific Northwest fur trade and the fact that he knew nothing of the fur business from experience was no deterrent. He had known nothing of the ice business, either, when he got into it in his early twenties and accumulated a modest wealth from the frozen ponds around his native Cambridge, Massachusetts.

Nat Wyeth's love of ice had no poetry in it. He looked upon the beauty of ice with a clear commercial vision, just as John Jacob Astor looked upon the beauty of furs. Ice was seasonal, and thus not everyday common; it was free for the taking; there was an eager market for it in places where it was treated as a luxury. While working for the Frederick Tudor Ice Company in Boston, Wyeth acted on these alluring facts by inventing a horse-drawn machine that grooved pond ice so that it could be cut into huge blocks to be hoisted upon wagons and stored under mounds of sawdust in warehouses. Tudor's ice was sold locally and shipped everywhere, including an especially lucrative market in the West Indies and eventually as far away as Calcutta.

Wyeth saw no great leap from the ice business to the fur trade. Beaver were seasonal, free for the taking, luxury items fetching handsome profits. But he could not wait for Hall Kelley to start walking, and so, late in 1831, he launched his own Oregon-bound organization by putting up $3,000 of his own money and raising another $5,000 by mortgaging his ice patents. With this cash backing he formed the joint-stock, imposingly named Pacific Trading Company and enlisted twenty-four "industrious and temperate men" who anted up forty dollars each to join him. Among these "investors," most of them interested in making their fortunes in Oregon in other endeavors than trapping beaver, were his brother, Jacob Wyeth, M.D., who agreed to serve as the company physician; a nineteen-year-old cousin, John B. Wyeth; a gunsmith; a blacksmith; two carpenters; two fishermen; a cooper; a founder; and an assortment of farmers and tradesmen.

Wyeth planned as carefully as his chronic impatience permitted. His was to be an overland expedition, not across Mexico in the

Kelley mode but a plunge from the Missouri frontier across the Rocky Mountains to the Columbia. Faced with a 2,000-mile journey, most of it on foot, some of it on horseback, and some by boat crossings of rivers, he determined that his company would travel light, buying the necessary provisions, horses, and mules en route. He bought space on the merchant brig *Sultana*, which was sailing from Boston early in 1832 for the Pacific, and loaded the hold with foodstuffs, traps and supplies, and a consignment of goods from Boston merchants to be used in trading with Indians for furs. The ship would rendezvous at the Columbia bar with Wyeth's overland party.

Some of his ideas were more imaginative than practical. He outfitted his recruits in spiffy uniforms—woolen jackets, canvas-like pantaloons, striped cotton shirts, brogans—and armed them with muskets, bayonets, knives, and axes. He hired a bugler to call the men to parades and mess, and to blow tattoo and reveille. He upset his own "travel light" plans by buying heavy, cumbersome tents. He devised and had constructed a thirteen-foot-long "amphibious machine" consisting of three small wagons in tandem, their gondola-like boxes to serve both for mule-drawn cargo and as boats to cross any waterways on the trail west. This contraption was dubbed the "Nat-wyethium" by Cambridge wags who saw it, and much else in the iceman's preparations, as "extremely notional."

On March 11, 1832, at a time when Hall Kelley was under arrest as a debtor, Wyeth got his two-dozen-man "Band of Oregon Adventurers," as the local press called them, aboard a merchant steamer, each man paying his own way, and out of Boston Harbor for the passage to Baltimore, Pittsburgh, Cincinnati and Saint Louis.

In the Mississippi metropolis, old trailsmen told Wyeth that the boat-wagon was too flimsy and awkward to portage across the Rockies, that in any event it wouldn't work even on the Platte, the least problematical of the rivers he would be crossing, much less on the Sweetwater, the savage Snake, and the Columbia. He considered this advice and got rid of the Nat-wyethium, finding a buyer interested in trying it out and who paid half of what it cost to construct.

A much more serious disappointment was the defection of six of his company, men who decided they had more of the pioneer-adventurer in them in the planning than in the actuality. They apparently found, after taking in a day or two of the riotous, stinking, mud-filthy Saint Louis waterfront, that their Cambridge comforts beckoned them too strongly to resist. Wyeth bid them farewell and good riddance and trooped the others aboard the steamer *Otter* for the 300-mile drift up the serpentine Missouri to Independence. This settlement, scattered across high ground in rocky, well-timbered country about three miles from the boat landing, lay only a few miles inside settled territory. In 1832, five years after its founding, it was a ramshackle congeries of log huts, tent-taverns, and outfitting shops, but for all its forlorn appearance was already a principal staging area for trade caravans outward bound to Mexican lands on the Santa Fé Trail, and for fur traders provisioning for the summer rendezvous in the Rockies.

Wyeth and his company spent ten days in Independence. He bought three horses for each of his men, fifteen sheep, two yoke of oxen, and reached an agreement with Kentuckians William and Milton Sublette, who had been among Ashley's original "enterprising young men" of the 1823 expedition up the Missouri. The Sublettes were partners with Jim Bridger, Tom Fitzpatrick, and others in the Rocky Mountain Fur Company and were taking a sixty-two-man fur brigade to the trappers' rendezvous at Pierre's Hole in eastern Idaho. The brothers permitted Wyeth to attach his Oregon Adventurers to their company.

The trail to the rendezvous was a trial, with a signal error of Wyeth's authorship. Under the Sublette brothers' steady and knowledgeable guidance, the brigade, with the tenderfoot component bringing up the rear, made good progress, averaging twenty-five miles a day, to the Platte River, conduit to the fur country. There the trappers set about fashioning bull boats of buffalo hides sewn over willow frames and caulked with a mixture of elk tallow and campfire ashes, to ferry men and supplies across the shallow but swift river. Wyeth observed this activity, and Bill Sublette urged him to get his men busy building their own boats but, as one of the Cambridge tenderfeet observed, "Captain Wyeth was not a man easily diverted by the advice of others." This stubbornness proved costly: Wyeth and his party built a raft, and as it was being poled across the Platte's unpredictable current, valuable stores, the blacksmith's equipment, and several kegs of gunpowder were washed overboard and lost.

One incident scarier even than the Platte crossing was a night raid on the brigade's horse-string by a Blackfeet band. Five horses were lost but no human casualties resulted.

The only other memorable experience en route to the rendezvous occurred near South Pass when the Sublette party encountered twenty wagons loaded with trade items, the train led by Benjamin Louis Eulalie Bonneville, a Paris-born army captain on leave to trap and explore the Rockies and the Oregon Country. Bonneville's wagons were making history as the first to cross the Continental Divide and to reach the Green River valley. Later the captain would give serious thought to an American occupation of Oregon, and in a letter to Army Adjutant General Roger Jones on July 29, 1833, he wrote, "The information I have already obtained authorizes me to say that if the Government ever intend taking possession of Oregon the sooner it shall be done, the better." He said the Hudson's Bay Company "are too much exposed by their numerous small posts even to offer the least violence to the smallest force."

The brigade reached Pierre's Hole on July 8, and within a few days Wyeth lost another seven men, including his physician brother Jacob and nephew John. All had experienced quite enough of the wilderness and arranged to turn back to Independence with Bill Sublette, who was returning to Missouri with pack animals loaded with beaver plews. Nat Wyeth, now with eleven men remaining in his company, joined with Milton, who was preparing to move on into the Snake River country. On July 18, a short distance west of the rendezvous, Wyeth and his remnant found themselves on the fringe of a bitter fight against a Gros Ventre war party. The New Englander and his men suffered no casualties but five white trappers were killed in the battle.

By contrast at least, the rest of the journey was uneventful. Wyeth and his men were able to do some amateur beaver trapping, and on October 29, 1832, eight months after departing Boston, he brought his tenderfeet into Fort Vancouver, making them the first westbound party of Americans to travel along what came to be called the Oregon Trail. But Wyeth was not a man looking at the historical record; bringing the first emigrants overland to Oregon was incidental to his real mission—to make a fortune in the fur trade—and in this, struggling with his forlorn and foreshortened party into Fort Vancouver that fall day, he had failed. The crowning blow was the news trickling into the fort of the fate of the *Sultana*, the merchant vessel he had commissioned to precede his overland party and carry his traps, trade goods, and equipment for his Columbia River scheme. The ship, he learned, had sunk in a gale after striking a reef east of Tahiti. The ship's captain and most of its crew had survived, making a miraculous sixty-eight-day voyage in a launch to Valparaiso.

As would be the case with Hall Kelley two years hence, Wyeth and his men had to depend upon the generosity of John McLoughlin to survive the winter.

Being beholden to the man representing the company he intended to compete with was not what Wyeth had in mind. Nor were those who came with him overjoyed at their prospects for the future: In the spring, eight of them, with McLoughlin's assistance, found passage to return to Boston. Of the three who remained to become among the first Americans to settle in the Oregon Country, one became a teacher to the Indian wives and half-breed children of the French-Canadian trappers at the fort, and two took up farming in the Willamette valley, where a small vanguard of retired Hudson's Bay men and their families were clearing land and planting crops.

□

Wyeth returned to the Rockies in March 1833, traveling with a Company pack train to the Portneuf River in southeastern Idaho, where he retrieved a cache of furs left there the previous summer. His mind boiled with ideas for a second expedition to the Oregon Country to reverse the bad luck that dogged him. He proposed to McLoughlin a plan whereby the Company would outfit him and a party of trappers to hunt beaver south of the Columbia, in exchange for which he would sell his furs exclusively to the factor at Fort Vancouver. He sought out Benjamin Bonneville for a partnership. And before returning home he made arrangements with Milton Sublette and Tom Fitzpatrick to supply their Rocky Mountain Fur Company with $3,000 in trade goods from Boston at less cost than they would pay for them in Saint Louis. He also harbored an idea of shipping kegged salmon from the Columbia to Boston at a handsome profit, and proposed to build a trading post on the Portneuf that would become the center of an American fur monopoly in the northern Rockies.

Wyeth had never experienced failure and had no space in his mind for such a concept. He was certain something in his grab bag of ideas to conquer the Oregon Country would succeed. He had monied friends in the East who would help finance such costly matters as hiring cargo space on another merchant ship bound for the North Pacific; buying trade goods to be shipped to Saint Louis and Independence; hiring trappers, teamsters, laborers, fishermen, and stevedores; and financing construction of a fort. He had his own resources to draw on, such as his ice-cutting and storage patents, which he leased to his employers. He had his reputation as a sound man of commerce and, unlike some Oregon boomers, he had *been* there; he knew the country and its resources.

2

In 1832, the precise date unknown, four native chiefs from the Oregon Country appeared in Saint Louis with a fur caravan and found their way to the home of General William Clark, superintendent of Indian Affairs for the city. The chiefs, Spokanes, Nez Percé, Flatheads—it is not clear—explained that their fathers had told them of Clark's visit to their nation a quarter century past with Mr. Lewis and a great party of other whites. From travelers and trappers they had learned of the white man's God and holy book, and they had a hunger to know more about this "Great Spirit." They had journeyed 2,000 miles to ask the White Chief Clark to send religious men to their country to point the way to Heaven.

There are various accounts of the fates of these Indian emissaries. Two are said to have sickened and died in Saint Louis soon after their meeting with Clark, one may have died on returning to his tribe, and one is said to have reached home and spread the news that white men of God were coming. Clark appears to have summoned three Methodist elders to his home and reported on the Indians' visit. According to John W. York, one of those present, Clark explained that while he was a Roman Catholic, "Methodist traveling preachers were the most indefatigable laborers, and made the greatest sacrifices of any men in the world" and that while "Catholic priests could teach the mysteries of religion . . . Methodist ministers taught practical piety and husbandry, and the two united would be the best arrangement he could think of." The elders agreed and promised, if possible, to send a missionary to Oregon.

To the Indians, it did not matter whether the missionaries were Protestant or Catholic, since they probably did not know the difference. They had learned about the "black robes"—Jesuit priests—from French-Canadian trappers and from Catholic Iroquois who worked for the North West Company and taught some of the Flatheads and Nez Percé about prayer.

The Indians who visited Clark may have represented a very

practical idea among their people: "To the Indian mind it was quite clear that the white man's guns, knives, cloth, burning glasses, and talking paper were the product of extra powerful medicine," David Lavender wrote. "Mastering the white man's medicine, it followed, would lead to mastery of the white man's power."

Of course, no such speculation was made when a highly wrought version of the Clark visitation story appeared in a letter published in the March 1, 1833, issue of the New York–based *Christian Advocate and Journal*. The Methodist convert who wrote the letter described the Indians as "three Nez Percés and one Flathead" and said that no sooner had they arrived at General Clark's doorstep than two of them dropped dead from exhaustion and privation, the first martyrs to the cause of spreading the Word of God to the heathens of the Pacific Northwest. The letter was accompanied by a drawing by an educated Wyandot Indian named William Walker showing the manner in which Flatheads deformed the shape of their children's heads in infancy by lashing them to a cradle-board. (Actually none of the Indians visiting Clark had this deformity; nor, for that matter, did the Nez Percé have pierced noses. The name came from a clumsy French translation of Indian sign language.)

The inspiring letter and the editorial peroration in the same issue of the *Christian Advocate* ("Let the Church awake from her slumbers and go forth in her strength to the salvation of these wandering sons of our native forests") created a small sensation among churchly New Englanders. The Missionary Board of the Methodist Episcopal Church was galvanized to call for a mission "among the Flatheads," and the celebrated Oregon fanatic Hall J. Kelley, then still stumping around New England trying to get a start toward his imagined Eden, was aided by the clarion call. "His schemes multiplied," Bancroft wrote, "his pen worked with new vigor; he urged the preachers of the Word not to confine their efforts to the mountains, but to descend the broad River of the West to the Canaan there awaiting them, and unite earthly empire with heavenly enlightenment."

With uncommon alacrity, the Missionary Board chose a thirty-year-old newly ordained Methodist minister named Jason Lee as its candidate to lead the church into the wilds beyond the Rockies. He had been among the first to step forward and volunteer, and he had perfect credentials: He was a former farmer; he was a native of Stranstead, Québec, which gave him something in common with many of the Hudson's Bay agents in Oregon, including John Mc-Loughlin; he had an impeccable record as a church deacon and elder. Lee possessed other striking qualities as well. He *looked* as if he could survive any of the vicissitudes of the trail, clear a forest and build a mission house with his bare hands, and convert Indians to Christianity by the sheer strength of his character and physical bulk.

Lee was a brawny, shambling man, six-foot-three in height, powerfully chested and shouldered, with a massively jawed face featuring a shaggy black beard, a prominent nose, and eyes described as of a "superlative, spiritualistic blue." He carried himself awkwardly, as if his brain's instructions took an extra millisecond to reach his faraway limbs, but still he had a certain sureness, was frank, affable, and inspired confidence. "Strong in his possession of himself," Bancroft said, "there was nothing intrusive in his nature. . . . Some would have said he lacked refinement; others that his brusque straight-forwardness was but simple honesty, unalloyed with clerical cant, and stripped of university gown and sectarian straitlace."

Daniel Lee, who had joined his uncle Jason in volunteering for the Flathead mission, was hardly identifiable as a Lee relative. He was thin and bony, in Bancroft's words, "a pious Pierrot, a man in stature, but a child in mind and manners," and possessed of a face "beaming in happy, good-natured unconsciousness of his lack of knowledge, particularly of knowledge of the things of this world."

Two lay preachers and a schoolteacher were selected to accompany the Lees, and in October 1833 the Missionary Board came up with $3,000 to finance the expedition. The expectation was that additional funds would be raised as the men made their way to

Saint Louis, there to join a fur caravan heading to Independence and the Rocky Mountains.

By perfect happenstance, as the Lee party was preparing to leave New York news reached the city that Nathaniel Wyeth had arrived home after a journey to the Oregon Country and was preparing to return. Jason Lee hurried down to Boston to meet with the iceman. The "perfect infidel" may have cringed at the notion of shepherding Lee's divines through the wilderness, but he needed the money to help finance his new venture and Lee needed Wyeth's expertise to get him, his followers, and his baggage to the Columbia. By the end of their meeting, they had made a business arrangement: Lee would send his mission supplies ahead on the *May Dacre*, the merchant vessel Wyeth had commissioned to precede him to the Pacific, and Lee would rendezvous with Wyeth in Saint Louis in the spring.

□

The expedition got underway at the end of April 1834, with Wyeth and Milton Sublette in the lead, and 70 trappers and 250 horses loaded with the supplies Wyeth hoped to sell at the Pierre's Hole rendezvous. Jason Lee's party brought up the rear with their own horses and a small cattle herd.

For Wyeth the rendezvous was a financial disaster. William Sublette had beaten him there with a pack train out of Independence and by the time the iceman arrived with his, the trappers had already purchased their winter's supplies from Milton's brother. Wyeth, in a fury, decided to push on to the Portneuf River and build a cottonwood-log trading post, from which he hoped to sell his surplus goods. Lee and his followers went along, and in July, as Wyeth's men cleared some ground for building the fort, the minister held his first Sunday service. He had a strange congregation: Wyeth and his trappers ("the most profane company I think I was ever in," Lee later said of them); a number of Hudson's Bay fur traders and *voyageurs* under Thomas McKay; some Nez Percé and Flathead Indians, all of whom had drifted down to the grassy meadow along the Portneuf to investigate the goings-on at the place Wyeth was calling Fort Hall (after one of his prime backers). Bancroft painted a memorable word picture of Jason Lee's sermon in the wildwood: "It was a grand and solemn sight, these rough and reckless children of the forest, gathered from widely remote quarters, with varied tongues and customs, here in the heart of the mighty wilderness, the eternal hills their temple-walls, and for roof the sky." He added, "What these same devout worshippers were doing an hour afterward, drinking, trafficking, swearing, and stabbing, it is needless to detail. Man is oft an irrational animal, and we are least of all to look for reason in religion."

On July 30, with Wyeth and his men remaining behind to complete Fort Hall, Lee and his party pushed on to the west with McKay. After some tribulations, including the loss of much of their baggage at The Dalles rapids, Lee brought his bedraggled party into Fort Vancouver on September 16, 1834.

John McLoughlin treated the Americans with great cordiality, opened his home to them, and even provided Lee with a temporary place to preach. His first Sunday sermon was expounded to a motley flock, stranger even than the one gathered at Fort Hall, consisting of Englishmen, Irishmen, Scotchmen, French-Canadians, Indians of several tribes, Sandwich Islanders, and three Japanese shipwreck survivors.

McLoughlin also slyly redirected Jason Lee's plans to erect a mission house some distance south of the Hudson's Bay headquarters. The Flatheads, he told Lee, were not disposed to religious conversion. Their tribal lands were an exceedingly wild and dangerous country hundreds of miles to the east. They had an ancient tradition of warring against the Blackfeet. They were a nomadic people, difficult to pin down, impossible to gather up and funnel toward any mission church. He suggested that Lee settle in the nearby Willamette valley and proselytize among the natives in that region, the Calapooyas, Umpquas, Clackamas, and Tualatins, among others.

With horses, provisions, and men provided by McLoughlin, the

Lees explored the valley and fell in love with it. Along the river they found a dozen French-Canadian families. The men, retired Company fur hunters working new farms, generously welcomed the Americans to stay over. One man, Joseph Gervais, even set up a tent for the Lees in the midst of his melon and cucumber garden. Jason Lee was reminded of the passage in the first chapter of Isaiah about "a lodge in a garden of cucumbers."

He selected for his mission house a tract of richly grassed alluvial plain on the east side of the Willamette, sixty miles below its mouth. The site, two miles above the Gervais farm, was bordered by copses of oak, fir, cottonwood, white maple, and ash trees.

Lee returned to Fort Vancouver full of hope and plans and ready to work. The *May Dacre*, Wyeth's brig, had survived the Horn passage and South Pacific storms and arrived on the Columbia, and McLoughlin supplied boats and crews to transport the American's mission goods ashore; horses, ox teams, and canoes to transport the supplies to the Willamette, and teamsters to drive the mission stock to their new home. By October 6, six weeks after the Lee party arrived at Fort Vancouver, they were sleeping in tents among the oaks and firs along the river. Some of the Canadians farming nearby, together with a Calapooya boy, a Kanaka volunteer, and later several of the horse-drovers who came to Fort Vancouver with Ewing Young and Hall Kelley, helped the Lees saw planks and split shingles for cabin building and stake out thirty acres of rich ground for spring planting of wheat, oats, corn, and garden vegetables.

3

In February 1835 Jason Lee wrote to his Mission Board and told of the progress he had made in the Willamette valley. He made a lengthy appeal to the board to send more men, with their families, to the Columbia. He said female schoolteachers were especially needed, and other "White females" because he had learned they "would have more influence among Indians than males," and could relieve the menfolk who he said were "doing too much household work."

The mission grew in direct ratio to the number of able-bodied men and women who planted and tilled the fields; built cabins, a schoolhouse, and outbuildings; and found time to teach and proselytize among the Indians. In the latter effort they had limited success. Most of the Indians in the region were reluctant to leave their children at the mission school, and those who did come were mostly orphans. The prospect of laboring in the fields while receiving religious instruction was also unappealing to the natives, who were unaccustomed to any kind of regularized labor. An attempt to locate a branch mission among the Calapooya people failed, Lee reported, because of the indolence and apathy of the natives.

Over two years passed before his letter home had the effect Lee hoped for, but in July 1836 the merchant brig *Hamilton* sailed from Boston Harbor bound for the Sandwich Islands with a "reinforcement" for the Willamette mission of thirteen Methodist men, women (three of them unmarried), and children. This small contingent arrived on the Columbia in June 1837, after a long delay in Honolulu, and within two months Jason Lee married Miss Anne Maria Pitman of New York, described as a "prepossessing woman," in the first Methodist wedding ceremony in Oregon. Additional church people arrived on the *Sumatra* that fall, giving the Willamette mission a population of sixty, about half of that number native children.

By then Lee was spending more time at his administrative duties and less at his religious ones. He had explored the whole region south of the Columbia and found no prospect of success working with or teaching, much less converting, the natives. Many of the tribes he regarded as hopelessly depraved and diseased, others—such as those of The Dalles, Umpqua, and Rogue River valleys—as unredeemable banditti. It was impossible for Lee to think the Lord intended him to minister to a handful of orphans. His personal mission had to be bigger: Perhaps it was that of a colonizer.

□

In the winter of 1837 Lee paid a visit to the handful of pioneers in the Umpqua River valley. They, like all the Americans in the Oregon Country, were eager to talk about encouraging settlers to come west. They wanted "good people"—hardworking, God-fearing folk. All were fearful of an influx of unprincipled adventurers, deserting seamen, and other flotsam washing ashore from such refuse dumps of humanity as Botany Bay.

Lee began thinking of the Willamette valley as the perfect place to draw respectable, God-loving Americans, a colony that would enjoy the guidance of the Methodist Church and the protection of the United States government. In March 1838 he recruited a few men and started out on an overland journey home. He hoped to collect funds and enlist new settlers en route and then meet with the Missionary Board and seek its assistance to deliver a "memorial," signed by fifty colonists, to the Congress of the United States. The petition gave the history of the Willamette settlement from 1832 to the present and stated that the American people were ignorant of the riches of the lands beyond the Rocky Mountains and its limitless potential for commerce with China, India, and the islands of the Pacific. The paper urged that the United States take immediate formal possession of the Oregon Country south of the Columbia River for the benefit of the nation at large and the protection of the settlers already there, who regarded themselves as the nucleus of a great new state of the Union.

Faced with such mighty responsibilities, Lee could not be deterred, not even by the crushing blow he received while resting at Pawnee Mission, near Council Bluffs, Iowa. There an express rider delivered a letter sent out from Fort Vancouver by John McLoughlin notifying Lee that his wife Anne Maria had died on June 26 past, three weeks after the birth and death of their son. She had been buried near the mission house, the grave site shaded by fir trees.*

Nothing could be gained by going back, so Lee went on and began lecturing in churches from Independence to New York, often to large audiences but more often to small ones, on the subject of Oregon, its riches and opportunities, and its certain future as a territory of the United States. He was a persuasive orator, filled with ardor and righteousness, presenting to his audiences his unromanticized views of the potential of the great land in which he had labored, experienced joys and sorrows, and had grown to love. Elijah White, a physician from Tompkins County, New York, who had been among the first reinforcements at the Willamette mission, said that Reverend Lee's only concern was that his heated oratory might draw to Oregon an undesirable element, men "from the western frontier of the states, of a restless, aspiring disposition."

In New York in November 1838, Lee appeared before the Board of Managers of the Methodist Episcopal Missionary Society and was so persuasive that a "call" was published in the *Christian Advocate and Journal* for missionaries, church laymen, physicians, farmers, mechanics, and young women to serve as teachers. Lee's petition was turned over to Congressman Caleb Cushing of Massachusetts and presented to the House of Representatives together with Lee's voluminous correspondence and supporting papers from Nathaniel Wyeth, Hall Kelley, and other notable Oregon enthusiasts. One of the newest of these was a government agent named William A. Slacum who had just returned from Oregon, where he spent time with Lee at the Willamette mis-

---

*Later her remains were reinterred in the mission cemetery in Salem, where a marker told her story: "Beneath this sod, the first ever broken in Oregon for the reception of a white mother and child, lie buried the remains of Anne Maria Pitman, wife of Rev. Jason Lee, and infant son. She sailed from New York in July 1836, landed in Oregon June 1837, was married in July 1837, and died June 26, 1838, in full enjoyment of that love which constrained her to leave all for Christ and heathen souls. So we have left all, and followed Thee; what shall we have therefore."

sion. His voluminous report to Congress merged perfectly with Lee's petition.

All the submissions were published as a Report of the Twenty-Fifth Congress in a printing of 10,000 copies and were widely distributed.

In all, thirty-six adults and sixteen children sailed from New York for the Oregon coast on the *Lausanne*, a ship chartered by the society and carrying $42,000 in supplies and equipment. Lee, who had by now remarried, joined the contingent with his new wife, and they all reached the Columbia in May 1840. The new colonizers, called the Great Reinforcement, firmly established the permanent American presence in the Oregon Country.

Over the next five years, Lee continued his labors for federal recognition of the Methodist settlement in the Willamette. In that time he also weathered the repeated frustrations of ministering to the Indians, the peak moment of which was a camp meeting in 1841 where he reported 130 baptisms. But, he admitted, most of the conversions to Christianity would likely not be permanent. He said many of the Indians asked to be paid for attending services.

In 1844 he returned to New York to visit the missionary board and to work on soliciting funds. Two months before his forty-second birthday he died, on March 2, 1845, at Lake Memphremagog in the province of Lower Canada. His remains were reinterred in Salem in 1906.

Lee had lived to see the first stirrings of an American colonial government in Oregon and the first organized emigrant wagon trains reach the Willamette valley. He died in the month and year of the inauguration of President James K. Polk and the push to settle the Oregon boundary question.

"He certainly saw how grand a work it was to lay the foundation of a new empire on the shores of the Pacific," Bancroft wrote of Lee, "and how discouraging the prospect of raising a doomed race to a momentary recognition of its lost condition, which was all that ever could be hoped for the Indians of western Oregon. There is much credit to be imputed to him as the man who carried to successful completion the dream of Hall J. Kelley and the purpose of Ewing Young."

□

Except for guiding Lee's party to the gateway to the Oregon Country, Nat Wyeth's second Oregon expedition failed miserably; his confidence, fall-back schemes, and superhuman efforts arrived at nothing but frustration. The arrangement he had proposed to Mc-Loughlin, for the Hudson's Bay Company to outfit him and his trappers in exchange for exclusive rights to all the furs he brought in, was turned down by Governor George Simpson. The partnership he suggested to Captain Benjamin Bonneville did not advance beyond the discussion stage. By the time Wyeth arrived at the summer 1834 rendezvous, the Rocky Mountain Fur Company had gone under. Worse, Bill Sublette had beaten him to Pierre's Hole with a pack train of supplies, and those Wyeth brought so laboriously from Boston to sell to the Rocky Mountain outfit were no longer wanted. He wrestled them by pack train to his Fort Hall site but was able to collect only $500 for them, a small fraction of their cost.

The salmon scheme proved to be an even greater financial disaster, and the crowning blow came when he was forced to sell Fort Hall to the Hudson's Bay Company, again at a huge loss.

Wyeth returned to Boston in the fall of 1836, having devoted five years of his life and $20,000 of his own money (a substantial fortune in the era) to his Oregon labors. He had no regrets; he let others blame the Hudson's Bay people for thwarting his designs on the Oregon Country. (One of his prolix contemporaries wrote that the Company "preceded him, followed him, surrounded him everywhere and cut the throat of his prosperity with such kindness and politeness that Wyeth was induced to sell his whole interest, existent and prospective, in Oregon, to his generous, but too indefatigable, skillful and powerful antagonist.")

Wyeth returned to the Tudor Company at triple his former salary and patented new devices for ice gathering, and when he struck out on his own in 1840 he made a new fortune shipping refrigerated fruit and vegetables to the tropics.

His beloved Oregon remained in his thoughts. For congressional reports he wrote accounts of his Northwest ventures, provided his observations on the potential for commerce there, and urged governmental support of American efforts to settle the Pacific Northwest. Like Jason Lee, Wyeth lived to witness the emigrant migrations to the Oregon Country, but he also lived to see it declared a territory of the United States.

He died in Cambridge on August 31, 1856.

Bancroft memorialized Wyeth by writing that "The flag of the United States was planted by him simultaneously in the heart of the continent and on the seaboard of the Pacific. He it was who, more directly than any other man, marked the way for the ox-teams which were so shortly to bring the Americanized civilization of Europe across the roadless continent."

Part Four

OUT TO ARCADIA

14

THE MACEDONIAN CRY

1

The story of the Indians who came to William Clark's home in Saint Louis to find out about the white man's Book of Heaven created many an armchair dream among readers of the *Christian Advocate and Journal*. Pious imaginings of taking leave of cozy hearthfires and braving the rigors of the wilderness were commonplace, many listened when the *Advocate* editor wrote "Hear! Hear! Who will respond to the call from beyond the Rocky Mountains?", and many read every stirring word of the *Advocate* article by Dr. Wilbur Fisk, the celebrated divine, educator, and founder of Wesleyan College in Middletown, Connecticut. He wrote: "Let two suitable men, unincumbered with families, possessing the spirit of martyrs, throw themselves into the [Indian] nation—live with them—learn their language—preach Christ to them. . . . Who will go? Who? Were I young, healthy, and unincumbered, how joyfully I would go! But the honor is for another. Bright will be his crown, glorious his reward."

Marcus Whitman, like Jason Lee, never seems to have hesitated to respond; indeed, when the idea came to him, probably through the writings of Fisk, Hall Kelley, and Lee, he would not be denied. In 1834, when he made a fervent application to the American Board of Foreign Missions in Boston for an assignment in the Oregon Country, he was thirty-two years old and still searching for his life's niche. His parents, descendants of colonial New Englanders, were citizens of Rushville, New York, where Marcus was born, and provided him with a comfortable Congregationalist upbringing and a good education. In his twenties he turned to medicine, riding the lumber camps of western New York state as a physician's apprentice. He studied for two sixteen-week terms at a medical school in Ohio and received an M.D. degree in 1831, but he was not fulfilled by buggy travel over the back roads of New York state lancing boils, splinting broken limbs, and tending to sick, wounded, and dying farm folk. Nor was he satisfied by Sunday school and temperence teaching or the sweaty labor at the sawmill he operated with his brother in Rushville. All he learned seemed destined for some higher purpose, and when he asked to be sent to Oregon he listed his qualifications—"physician, teacher, or agriculturist"—and hoped one or more of these valuable skills would earn him an assignment.

The Mission Board clearly liked his application. Here was a man in the prime of his life, from a good and Godly family, a physician and a teacher. He had an excellent church record. He was unmarried. If Whitman made a personal appearance before the committee he would have impressed them the more. He fairly radiated energy, enthusiasm, and *bonhomie*. He was of medium height, thin but sinewy, with big but not unhandsome facial features, iron-gray short-cropped hair, muttonchop whiskers, and deep-blue, soul-searching eyes. His habitual slovenliness of dress and outspokenness the members would have dismissed as the products of an outdoorsman's life. This was a man who had bent his back in physical labor, not in hovering over a desk and paperwork. He had what the Boston mission people imagined were the characteristics of a real "Western man," no actual specimen of which they had ever really seen.

He had but one serious drawback, his lack of divinity training, and on this basis he was initially rejected as a missionary. Formal Christian religious training, it was felt, was absolutely necessary if one were to preach, teach, and proselytize among savage races. But Whitman's application came at a propitious time: The Mission Board had been studying the feasibility of opening an Oregon mission and had commissioned a seasoned Presbyterian divine, Reverend Samuel Parker, to make an overland tour of the "Flathead country" beyond the Rocky Mountains and report on potential mission sites. Parker had been to Saint Louis once before, in the spring of 1834, six weeks after Jason Lee and his Methodists had departed with a fur caravan for the frontier. He ran out of money and was forced to return home, but he was regarded as a veteran trailsman, and Whitman, distressed at his rejection, was thrilled when he received notification from the board that he could accompany Parker to the Oregon Country as physician-missionary.

Theirs was a strange pairing; they seemed to have only their religious zeal in common. Parker, born in Ashfield, Massachusetts, held degrees in theology from Williams College and the Andover Theological Seminary and had been ordained a Congregational minister in 1812. At the time of his commission, the fifty-five-year-old church wheelhorse was working as a teacher in a girls' school in Ithaca, and had a reputation for erudite oratory and a much-appreciated talent for fund-raising. He was handsome, prim, mannered, fastidious, and authoritarian—never a man to be called "Sam"—the very picture of the studious, sedentary preacher. He was perceived as having forceful leadership qualities, a physical vitality, a scientific and linguistic bent, and a churchly dignity and flintiness that would serve well in a wilderness setting.

For all their differences, Whitman was beholden to Reverend Parker for speaking on his behalf to the board—and for being the instrument by which Marcus met the woman of his dreams.

In November 1834 Parker made a speech at a small Congregational church in Amity, in Allegany County, New York, on the need for missionaries to serve among the savage tribes of the far West. In the audience sat a particularly enthralled young woman named Narcissa Prentiss who, after hearing his sermon, sought out the visiting theologian. She was twenty-six at the time, tall, golden-haired, "buxom," a contemporary said of her, and "symetrically formed," with a strikingly pretty oval face. She made a good impression on Parker, especially after he learned her unusual history.

The third of nine children of Stephen and Clarissa Ward Prentiss, Narcissa (named after the amaryllis-like flower) was born in Prattsburg and afforded a formal education unusual for a young female of the era. Her father, a fourth-generation descendant of a Massachusetts Bay colonizer, had made a prosperous business as a builder and was respectfully called "Judge" Prentiss for the single term he served as a probate court magistrate. He and his wife were devout in their Congregational religion and devoted to the idea that a good education leavened, rather than diminished, the Christian faith. As a teenager, Narcissa, third of the nine Prentiss children, was sent off to the Academy for Women in Troy, and later came home to Prattsburg to attend Franklin Academy, a coeducational religious school her father had helped endow.

(In the course of her studies at Franklin, Narcissa met a polite, broodingly serious theology student named Henry Harmon Spalding, who was bowled over by her good looks and vivacity and startled by her honest humor. Some of these attributes were considered suspect by the gravely pious of the 1830s, people who, in Henry L. Mencken's definition of Puritanism, seemed to have "the haunting fear that someone, somewhere, is happy." Spalding was smitten but mistook Narcissa's naturally gregarious, friendly nature for affection, and when he made a sudden proposal of marriage she gently turned him down.)

After graduating from Franklin Academy, Narcissa and one of her sisters opened a kindergarten in the town of Bath, but she felt she was merely marking time and must have conveyed her frustration to Samuel Parker, a man preparing to embark on a great, meaningful journey of faith, one she had dreamed of all her life, to Christianize Indians. She had studied assiduously the *Missionary Herald*, organ of the Presbyterian Congregational and Dutch Reformed Churches, and the Methodist *Christian Advocate*. She had been utterly captivated by the story of the Flathead and Nez Percé suppliants in Saint Louis, the accounts of Jason Lee's mission to the Columbia, and had what the religious journals called "the Macedonian Cry"* echoing in her brain.

Samuel Parker was won over by Narcissa's ardor to be of service "among the savage races" and in a communication to the Mission Board wrote, "Are females wanted? A Miss Prentiss . . . is very anxious to go to the heathen. . . . Her education is good, her piety conspicuous, her influence good. She will offer herself if needed." He understood that she could not accompany his quick exploratory journey but hoped she might be a part of some actual mission party in the future.

Having performed one signal service each to Marcus Whitman and Miss Prentiss, Parker may have even brought the two anxious evangelists together.

Toward the end of 1834, Whitman, then practicing medicine in the town of Wheeler, a short distance south of Prattsburg, met Narcissa Prentiss. He doubtlessly learned of her ambition to serve in the Oregon Country through Parker. Whatever the occasion of their meeting, he fell in love with her in the moment and let her know his feelings. She no doubt was gracious and appreciative of the sentiment, but sudden professions of love, as in the case of Henry Spalding of sad and recent memory, made her cautious. She found Whitman curiously attractive—rugged, honest, forthright, rather charming in his awkwardness—and could imagine their doing God's work together in the wilderness. He was a man a woman could learn to love.

In January 1835 Whitman presented himself to the Prentiss family, then living in Amity, and there he and Narcissa made a

_____

*The reference is apparently to the passages in Acts 16, in which the Apostle Paul has a vision of a Macedonian coming in the night asking for prayer and saying, "Come over into Macedonia, and help us." In biblical times, Macedonia, a land often visited by Paul, lay north of Greece in the Balkans and had been ruled, three centuries before Christ, by Philip II, and later by his son, Alexander the Great.

pact before he set out for Saint Louis ahead of Samuel Parker. The arrangement seems to have been a betrothal of sorts.

In February, as Whitman was en route to the Mississippi, Narcissa made a formal application to the Mission Board for service among the Indians of the far West. Her bid was enthusiastically endorsed by the pastor of her church in Amity. Reverend Oliver S. Powell and his wife were making plans of their own for a mission in the Flathead country and hoped to have Miss Prentiss accompany them. He wrote to the board, "I am happy in the prospect of having so efficient a fellow-laborer in the missionary service," then gave a clue as to the arrangement his parishioner had recently made: "As it is probable that Miss Prentiss will hereafter become the companion of Doctor Marcus Whitman (should he be established as missionary beyond the Rocky Mountains), it may be proper to add that he expressed a desire that she might accompany us on our mission."

Narcissa's application was accepted by the board in March 1835, but because the Powells were unable to carry out their expedition plans, she had to wait. Marcus had departed for Saint Louis ahead of Reverend Parker, and it would be many months, perhaps a year or more, before he returned for her.

2

Samuel Parker left Ithaca on March 14, 1835, and reached Saint Louis three weeks later via Buffalo, Pittsburgh, Wheeling, Cincinnati, and Louisville, staying with church families, distributing tracts, holding services in the ladies' cabins of steamers, talking to whoever would listen about his forthcoming journey.

Whitman was awaiting him and had made preliminary arrangements with the help of local churchmen to attach Parker and himself to a party of trappers heading up the Missouri to the summer rendezvous on the Green River. Leading the brigade was a capable if somewhat boozy trader named Lucien Fontenelle. This man, a Louisianan, had twenty years' experience trapping along the Missouri and in the Rockies; skirmishing with Blackfeet, Snake and Crow horse raiders; and confronting Hudson's Bay agents over "rights" to certain rich beaver streams. He was not enamored of the idea of escorting church folk to rendezvous, but he was persuaded, probably by Whitman, who could be quite persuasive.

They traveled upriver by steamer to Liberty, the Missouri frontier town just above Independence, and were delayed there three weeks. Fontenelle used the time to enlarge his trapping party to fifty men and put together a pack train of horses and mules, three yoke of oxen, and six light wagons. The wagons were to carry trade goods and supplies to rendezvous and furs and buffalo hides (which were fetching more on the market than beaver hides) back to Missouri. Parker and Whitman occupied themselves by visiting a nearby Mormon settlement and riding "twenty miles out of the United States" to Cantonment Leavenworth in Kansas, where Parker preached to the garrison.

At first, Fontenelle and his rough-hewn mountaineers treated both New Yorkers with contempt. Parker in particular seemed an easy target for their sneers. To the filthy, foul-mouthed, buckskinned trappers sucking their pipes at the campfires the reverend cut a comic figure in his plug hat, black suit, white neck stock, and nose-in-the-air manner. He seemed to think he was in charge of the expedition, and it was galling to watch him standing aloof and unhelpful, never bending his back to any camp labor, parceling out chores to his companion then finding fault with everything done, including the doctor's "unskillful management" of their horses and the single mule they had purchased in Liberty. Whitman took everything in stride. He felt fortunate to be at the brigade camp waiting to jump off into savage lands, soon to see the Indian country of the Upper Missouri, the great Shining Mountains, and the mysteries that lay beyond them. He was learning from Fontenelle and his men, felt he was fulfilling his destiny, knew that he would be useful.

Whitman's utility was proven sooner than he expected. The caravan departed Liberty on May 15 and made its way upriver to Council Bluffs, crossed the Missouri in bull boats, and camped at

Bellevue, a few miles below Omaha. There in the rain-soaked bottomlands Fontenelle and several of his men fell ill with cholera. The Asiatic strain of the disease had ravaged Europe in the 1830s and came to America on passenger ships, struck the Eastern Seaboard (killing 3,000 people in New York City alone), and spread inland, thriving in crowded campgrounds amid fetid sloughs of garbage and the excrement of men and animals. Whitman knew the awful symptoms of the disease: the clayey appearance of the skin, bluing of fingernails and face, the violent diarrhetic attacks, ceaseless vomiting and sweating (cholera killed by dehydrating its victims), and had treated it with the accepted remedies of the day and with the same mixed results. Many died of it, some recovered, some never contracted it even in the most plagued areas.

He took charge of the stricken, administered the recommended apothecary doses of sixty drops of laudanum in half a glass of cold water followed by thirty more drops every half hour. He prepared clysters (medicinal enemas) by mixing three teaspoonfuls of laudanum in a thin, warm gruel, and mustard poultices, and cold cloths to bathe foreheads and limbs. He bled his patients, and purged them with tepid water and salt, or with ipecacuanha. He also recommended that the camp be moved from riverside to higher ground, and this was done. Three men died of the disease but Fontenelle and several others recovered, and Whitman's labors earned him the respect of the brigade, a reputation that preceded him as the caravan moved west to Grand Island to pick up the Platte and follow it across Nebraska.

At Fort Laramie, Fontenelle turned over the brigade to his partner Tom Fitzpatrick, who would lead it to the rendezvous. From the white-haired, Irish-born mountain man Samuel Parker and especially Marcus Whitman got a wilderness education. "Broken Hand" had twenty years in the Indian trade. He had been with Ashley in 1823 and, of more interest to the New Yorkers, had traded among the Flathead people northwest of the Rockies. He was wise, patient, and admired; the churchmen questioned him incessantly. Whitman had heard of Captain Bonneville's party taking a number of freight wagons across the Continental Divide and

South Pass to the Green River just three years past and quizzed the guide on the feasibility of emigrant wagons making their way across the mountains to the Oregon Country. On this matter Fitzpatrick was not sanguine, but his doubts did not dampen Whitman's enthusiasm on the subject. He studied the fur traders' wagons and felt that similar conveyances were the key to success in establishing missions in the far West, and to attracting families of settlers who would set up their households in the wilderness.

Samuel Parker had a moment of triumph at Fort Laramie in late July when a band of Oglala stood in silence while he, with his plug hat clapped across his heart, preached to them and sang "Watchman, Tell Us of the Night." He told Whitman the Indians had asked for an encore and noted in his journal that "the expression on their countenances seemed to say, we want to know what all this means."

Fitzpatrick, true to his wagon doubts, left them behind at Fort Laramie and had all the equipment, provisions, and trade goods packed on horses and mules. Thus unencumbered, he led his party westward to the Wind River Range and South Pass, arriving there on August 10, and a week later at the Green River rendezvous.

The churchmen were wide-eyed in wonderment during the week they spent with the traders and trappers, and particularly among the Indian lodges crowding the hillsides along the river. Parker expressed disappointment that the Flatheads and Nez Percé appeared to have neither flat heads nor pierced noses, but his wanderings among them, and among the Arapaho and Sioux camps, convinced him that they were all conducive, if not eager, to receive the Word. Whitman, naturally sociable, enjoyed the friendship of Fitzpatrick's trapper-trader comrades, many of whom had heard of his good work among the cholera victims at Bellevue camp and sought him out for medical advice. One who came forward was the mountain man Jim Bridger, who was bothered by a Blackfeet arrowhead he had carried in his back for many years, the point now embedded in bone with cartilage grown around it. Whitman deftly extracted it without anesthetic (except for whatever whiskey Bridger took internally beforehand) in front of a crowd of mountaineers and Indians, and when he expressed amazement that the wound had not festered, Bridger opined, "Meat don't spoil in the Rockies."

The missionaries picked up heartening news from soldier-hunter William Drummond Stewart of Perthshire, Scotland, who was traveling with Fitzpatrick's trappers. He was an experienced rendezvous hand who had shot game all the way to Fort Vancouver with Jason Lee's party the previous year and told Whitman and Parker that Lee had set up his mission on the Willamette and had thus bypassed Flathead country. The field among this tribe was still open.

Whitman also met Bridger's friend Kit Carson at the rendezvous and may have witnessed, or at least been nearby during, one of the most celebrated episodes in Carson's colorful career, a favorite of dime-novel writers ever after. Fitzpatrick, Bridger, and other traders had set up their camp adjacent to an Arapaho village, and as the days passed Kit's eye is said to have fallen on an Arapaho girl named Waa-nibe and he went so far as to make a preliminary courtship present of powder and ball to her father. Accounts vary widely on precisely what happened after this, but it appears that in the camp was a French trapper named Shunar (or Chouinard or Shunan), a huge, bullying drunk much disposed to ragging and threatening the Americans. One of Carson's biographers claims that Shunar insulted or tried to rape the Arapaho girl and that Kit confronted the Frenchman, a foot taller and a hundred pounds heavier, in his lair.

Most sources agree on the result of the challenge. Both men fetched their sidearms and horses and rode up to one another. Both guns were fired simultaneously; Shunar's wrist was shattered by Kit's bullet, and Kit's hair was "parted" by Shunar's shot and his face burned by the powder.

Carson "married" Waa-nibe before the rendezvous ended.

3

The Green River turned out to be the temporary end of the trail for Marcus Whitman. While Parker was to proceed to the Columbia River with a number of Flathead and Nez Percé guides to scout mission sites, Whitman would return east for "reinforcements," Narcissa Prentiss among them. A year hence, he would return to the rendezvous and reunite with Parker, who would come out from Fort Vancouver to the Green to intercept him. The plan may have been agreed upon during the course of the journey out of Saint Louis, but the clear motive for it was that the two men were becoming alienated. The minister was not a compatible companion for Whitman or anyone else, and Parker's conduct at their separation makes Bancroft's assessment—"it is most probable that the want of congeniality made it acceptable to both of them"—seem excessively euphemistic: The reverend appropriated their mule and the others purchased en route and gave Whitman five dollars to buy a horse for himself. Since horses were selling for a minimum of seventy-five dollars at the rendezvous, Whitman dug deep and scraped up enough to buy a scrawny animal—"a disgrace to any man to pack on account of his extreme sore back," he said—and hired two men, one to act as interpreter and guide, the other to cook and mind the horse, each to be paid eighteen dollars for the two months they were to serve him.

On August 22, 1835, Parker accompanied Jim Bridger and sixty men riding out from the Green River to Pierre's Hole at the headwaters of the Snake. There the trappers took a course toward Blackfeet country and left Parker with his escort of ten Nez Percé to proceed to the Oregon Country. The reverend suffered greatly in the Salmon River mountains, weakened and dizzy with fever, but heroically pushed on, falling from his saddle at day's end, often unable to eat and with barely enough strength to bleed himself, as he'd been taught by Doctor Whitman, add new pages in shaky hand in his journal by campfire light, and crawl into his blankets. By late September, when he and his Nez Percé escort crossed the Salmon and climbed the Kooskooskie (Clearwater) range, he found his health improving in the "wild, cold mountains" and his strength regained by the time he reached Fort Walla Walla on October 6.

Parker rested two days among Hudson's Bay people, then with three husky Walla Walla Indians embarked by Company canoe on the Columbia. He visited a Cayuse village on the south side of the river, and on the twelfth, near The Dalles rapids, met Nathaniel Wyeth, the one-time ice merchant then en route to his fort on the Portneuf River, and home.

Parker reached Fort Vancouver on October 29, 1835, and spent the winter enjoying John McLoughlin's hospitality and "the society of gentlemen, enlightened, polished, and sociable." He was provided half of a newly built and furnished house, dined with the factor, was given books from McLoughlin's library and horses to explore the Oregon coast and Willamette valley. He met and was greatly impressed by Jason Lee and the Methodist minister's mission house and gardens on the east side of the Willamette River. He especially admired Lee's work in setting up a temperance society, and if he experienced any disappointment as Lee's guest, it was upon learning that the sheer physical labors of building and maintaining a mission had kept the minister from attending to his spiritual work. In any event, Lee told the chagrined Parker, Christianizing the savages was exasperating, impossible work, and he had written his superiors that "we have no evidence that we have been instrumental in the conversion of one soul."

Parker shared with Lee the conviction that more women were needed in the Oregon Country and endorsed the idea contained in a letter Lee had written home in March 1835: "I have requested the Board not to send any more *single men*, but to send men with families. . . . A greater favor could not be bestowed upon this country than to send to it pious, industrious, intelligent females." Parker later wrote, "Christian white women are very much needed to exert influence over Indian families." Clearly they had differences on the issue: Lee wrote more as a settler than a missionary; Parker's only interest was Christianizing Indians.

On April 14, 1836, the reverend bade farewell to McLoughlin

and Fort Vancouver. He planned to explore the Upper Columbia, scout sites for mission stations, then, with his Nez Percé as guides, move on to the Green River for the summer rendezvous. There he expected to meet with Marcus Whitman and whatever party his erstwhile partner was able to organize in the East.

Parker reached Walla Walla on the twenty-sixth and remained there two weeks, preaching to a number of Nez Percé and Cayuse Indians who came to the fort and learning firsthand what Jason Lee meant about the frustrations of converting the savages. The Cayuse chief could not accept that doctrine of monogamous marriage as the Nez Percé people seemed willing to do, explaining to the missionary that he could not dispense with any of his wives, was too old to turn away from the ways of his people, and preferred "the place of burning" if that was the only recourse.

On May 9 Parker set out for the Green with his Nez Percé faithful. He dreaded taking the terrible Salmon River Mountain route to the rendezvous site—he had narrowly escaped dying there the year before. He tried to persuade his escort to take the Grande Ronde and Snake River route, but the Indians preferred the Salmon since it avoided hostile Blackfeet country, and they could not be persuaded otherwise. Parker may have fallen ill again on the trail, or he may have had a change of heart about returning east over such arduous country, for he sent letters ahead addressed to Whitman, then turned back to the Columbia to await a merchant ship that would take him home.

He scouted mission station sites on the return to Fort Vancouver and was particularly enamored of a spot twenty-two miles from Fort Walla Walla near the mouth of a small stream and in a pretty valley amidst high rolling hills covered with dark green grass. The Cayuse people, in whose country it was located, called it Waiilatpu, "Place of the Rye Grass."

He traveled as far north as Fort Colville, the northernmost Company post on the Walla Walla River, and preached among the Palouses, a people related to the Nez Percé, and the Spokanes. He explored the Spokane River and made extensive notes in his journal

in which he envisioned a mission that would minister to the Nez
Percé, Palouse, Spokane, Coeur d'Alêne, Pend d'Oreille, and Shu-
yelpi tribes.

Parker returned to Fort Vancouver in early June and found the
Hudson's Bay Company's new steamship *Beaver* recently arrived
on the coast from England. A sidewheeler of 110 tons with a crew
of thirty and armed with four six-pounder cannons, the *Beaver* was
the first steam-powered vessel to reach the Pacific coast. Parker
booked passage on the steamer and on June 18, 1836, embarked
for Honolulu and New York.

He reached home on May 23, 1837, and calculated that he had
traveled 28,000 miles, counting his sea voyage, in the twenty-six
months that had passed since he set out for Saint Louis. In 1838
he published in Ithaca his *Journal of an Exploring Tour Beyond
the Rocky Mountains*, the first detailed account of the Oregon
Country and its Indian tribes since Lewis and Clark's journals and
the miscellaneous writings of Hall Kelley. The volume was immensely popular, selling 10,000 copies.

In the book Parker mused "upon the probable changes which
would take place in these remote regions in a very few years" and
told of his dream of "a new empire to be added to the kingdoms
of the earth."

4

His unhappy experiences with Samuel Parker forgotten, Marcus
Whitman returned to New York anxious to tell of his adventures
on the trail from the Missouri frontier to the trappers' rendezvous
on the Green River. He wanted nothing more than to marry Miss
Prentiss and return west and conveyed both these ambitions to the
Board of Missions. The board members were impressed by the report he made to them and by the two Nez Percé boys, Tackitooits
and Ais—their Christianized names Richard and John—he brought
home with him. There remained a stumbling block. The board was
satisfied with Whitman's plans for the return journey: using wag-

ons at least as far as Fort Laramie, having a small cattle herd to supplement whatever game they were able to kill en route, purchasing horses, pack animals, flour, and similar stores from Missouri outfitters. But the unresolved question had to do with the non-negotiable requirement that an ordained minister must accompany his party. Whitman was a mere physician, after all, and did not have the requisite training to elevate the heathen heavenward.

For the doctor, everything hung in the balance. If a certified church servant did not accompany him, there would be no mission; if there was to be no mission, Miss Prentiss would not marry him— such was their agreement—and his life would fall in a shambles. He sought her out in Amity and learned that she was aware of the problem, and had even thought about prospective ministerial candidates for the mission. She had reluctantly landed on the name Henry Harmon Spalding, a man she suspected was embittered and probably vindictive over her rebuffing his marriage proposal when they were classmates at Franklin Academy in Prattsburg in 1828.

Spalding, now thirty-two and as gloomily pensive as ever, was only recently returned to New York from Missouri, where he and his wife had conducted mission work among the Osage Indians. He had not forgotten Narcissa's rejection; indeed he seemed still to be nursing the wound and wondering about her motives in declining the offer of such a prize catch, as he wrote the board that he did not wish to travel to Oregon with her: "I do not want to go into the same mission with Narcissa," he said cryptically, "as I question her judgement."

But after receiving certain assurances from the board, perhaps that he would be "senior" in the expedition, perhaps that in Oregon he would have a separate station from the Whitmans, he was persuaded to reconsider and even paid a courtesy call to the Prentiss family in Angelica a few days before Narcissa's wedding.

Soon after his rebuff by Miss Prentiss, Spalding had married Eliza Hart, the daughter of an Oneida County, New York, farmer. She was described by Bancroft as "a tall, slender, plain, dark woman, sympathizing, and faithful" who "won the confidence of all about her." What she lacked in personal charms, he said, "she made up in the excellence of her character, taking for her own standard that of the highest in pious life." She was a talented artist and linguist, a frail and shy spinster when she fell in love with Spalding and his missionary dreams through the correspondence they conducted during his theological studies. She waited patiently while he completed his preliminary degree work, and the two married while he was attending a seminary in Cincinnati, she taking in boarders to supplement their meager income. Spalding, in his limitless capacity for caddish expression, wrote the Mission Board that he had married Eliza "for the express purpose of giving my wife the opportunity of pursuing the same Theological studies as myself."

After completing his studies, the couple returned to Utica to await the birth of their first child and a response from the Mission Board to Spalding's application for a "foreign" appointment. He was ordained a Presbyterian minister in the summer of 1835, and in October Eliza's baby was stillborn. Spalding's reaction to the tragedy was that "the Lord most righteously chastised us for our sins." In this he might best have spoken only for himself, for in recommending the couple to the board for a mission appointment, one reference stated that Eliza was beloved by a large circle of friends and was "one of the best women for a missionary wife with whom I am acquainted." The writer also seemed to know her husband well, stating that Henry Spalding "can turn his hand to almost any kind of handy work, is not remarkable for his judgment and common sense . . . is sometimes too much inclined to denounce and censure those who are not as zealous and ardent as himself." The correspondent also used the word *jealous* to describe the man "so fortunate as to have married Eliza Hart."

Eliza and Narcissa were to become friends, but of Spalding Narcissa wrote her father during their journey, "The man who came with us is one who ought never to have come. . . . My dear husband has suffered more from him in consequence of his wicked jealousy, and great pique towards me, than can be known in this world."

They arranged to join forces in Cincinnati.

□

Marcus Whitman and Narcissa Prentiss married in Angelica, Allegany County, New York, on February 18, 1836, two months after his return from the Rocky Mountains.

Since much of the courtship had taken place before he left the state the previous year, Whitman had only to make certain she wanted to accompany him to the Oregon Country. He described the rigors of the trail, much of it arduous and dangerous, and reminded her that she would be separated from her family for an indefinite period; indeed, she might never see them again.

"It is God's will," she said. "I will go."

She wore a handmade black bombazine dress at the wedding where the minister led the party in a hymn by Reverend Samuel F. Smith, author of "America," the last stanza of which, it was reported, "was sung by the sweet voice of Mrs. Whitman alone—clear, musical and unwavering":

In the deserts let me labor
  On the mountains let me tell
How he died—the blessed Savior—
  To redeem a world from hell!
Let me hasten,
  Far in heathen lands to dwell.
Yes, my native land, I love thee,
  All thy scenes I love them well.
Friends, connections, happy country,
  Can I bid you all farewell?

Narcissa made other dresses of gaily colored calico for the journey and purchased a pair of small "gentleman's riding boots" to wear while, she anticipated, riding sidesaddle to Oregon. She bought an inflatable life preserver for crossing the streams and rivers her husband had mentioned, and for the two of them made a spacious conical tent of mattress ticking waterproofed with oil. She also packed a considerable trunk with clothing, books, and similar necessities.

The day after the wedding, the Whitmans and the two Nez Percé boys set out by wagon and sleigh from Elmira to Hollidaysburg, Pennsylvania, where they would board a canal boat bound for Pittsburgh and Cincinnati. In these earliest days of the long journey ahead, Narcissa sustained a loss that would become commonplace on the Oregon Trail: She wrote home that her trunk fell off the sleigh into a creek, ruined her books, and had to be abandoned. On her honeymoon, long before passing the last outposts of civilization, she had arrived at a sad emigrant truth: "The custom of the country is to possess nothing, and then you will lose nothing while traveling."

The Spaldings had gone ahead and in Pittsburgh had a meeting with the artist George Catlin, who in 1832 had traveled to the mouth of the Yellowstone River and along the way made sketches and paintings of Mandans, Assiniboines, Sioux, and Blackfeet. He regarded himself as an authority on the far West and told Spalding bluntly that it was a mistake to take a white woman into that unforgiving wilderness.

The four missionaries came together for the first time in Cincinnati, where the Spaldings tarried several days while Henry visited his former classmates and professors at the seminary. Narcissa said nothing about seeing him again but wrote of Eliza, whom she met there for the first time, "I like her very much. She wears well upon acquaintance. She is a very suitable person for Mr. Spalding—has the right temperament to match him. I think we shall get on well together."

Since they planned to travel to the Green River rendezvous with Tom Fitzpatrick's trade caravan, which was jumping off from the Missouri border in mid-May, Spalding made the arrangements for the party to travel by steamer to Liberty, and in that frontier town their party expanded in numbers and encumbrances. Whitman took charge of a third Nez Percé lad who was waiting to return to his home country in Idaho, and assigned the three to take charge of the livestock he and Spalding purchased. Two white teenagers were hired for camp chores. The final member of the party who joined them in Liberty was William H. Gray, appointed by the Mission Board as "secular agent" for the Oregon missions. He was a cabinetmaker from Utica, age twenty-six, described somewhat ominously by Bancroft as a "good-looking young fellow, tall of stature, with fine black eyes . . . having pronounced natural abilities, of quick feelings, and a good hater where his jealousy was aroused." Gray had applied to the board for missionary service but his sponsor, who said he was a skilled craftsman, and abstinent, stated bluntly that Gray had "a confidence in his own abilities *to a fault*" and described him as "a slow scholar."

On the basis of Captain Bonneville's example and his own limited experiences in traveling from Liberty to the Green River, Whitman was convinced, despite Fitzpatrick's doubts, that wagons could negotiate the tortured trails and mountain paths and be floated across the waterways to Oregon. Wagons seemed especially essential to convey the women, providing them with at least some comfort and protection in bad weather. Eliza Spalding was "sickly," so Henry had purchased and sent ahead a light Dearborn wagon for her and their possessions. Since Narcissa insisted that she preferred to ride horseback beside her husband, a heavy farm wagon was obtained in Liberty for the party's belongings, and the trade goods, camp gear, medicines, blacksmithing tools, plow, grain, seeds, and provisions purchased from Liberty outfitters. In all, with the thirteen-head beef herd, six mules, fourteen horses, and equipage, Spalding and Whitman spent nearly $3,000 in Mission Board funds to launch themselves toward the Rockies.

After sending the wagons ahead, they crawled up the Missouri by ferry to Fort Leavenworth, then afoot and on horseback followed the North Platte, broke a church rule by traveling on Sunday, and reached the Loup Fork of the Platte. There they overtook Fitzpatrick's caravan, an immense column of 400 horses and mules, seven big freight wagons each drawn by six-mule teams, and seventy men.

The missionaries fell into the caravan's daily routine. In her journal Narcissa wrote: "We encamp in a large ring—baggage and men, tents and wagons on the outside and all the animals except the cows fastened to pickets inside the circle. . . . In the morn as soon as the day breaks that first that we hear is the word 'arise, arise'; then the mules set up as much noise as you never heard, which puts the whole camp in action. . . . You must think it very hard to have to get up so early after sleeping on the soft ground. When you find it hard work to open your eyes at seven o'clock, just think of me." While the horses and stock were feeding, she said, "we get our breakfast in a hurry and eat it. By this time the word 'Catch up, catch up' rings through the camp, for moving. We are ready to start usually at six, travel till eleven, encamp, rest and feed; start again about two, travel until six, or before if we come to a good tavern [her word for campsite], then camp for the night."

In the scheme of the caravan, her party ate dust. She wrote on June 3, 1836, "The fur Com[pany] is large this year. We are really a moving village. . . . If you wish to see the camp in motion, just look ahead and see first the pilot and the Captain, Fitzpatrick, just before him; next the pack animals, all mules loaded with great packs. Soon after you will see the wagons, and in the rear our company. We all cover quite a space."

She adapted, learned to "dine" on the ground on an India-rubber tablecloth that doubled as a cloak when it rained; scrubbed tin dishes, cups, knives, and spoons with sand; gathered buffalo chips for fuel. Of this latter chore she noted in her journal, "Our fuel for cooking since we left timber (no timber except on rivers) has been dried buffalo dung. . . . I supposed Harriet [one of Narcissa's sisters] will make a face at this, but if she was here she would be glad to have her supper cooked at any rate, in this scarce timber country."

Crossing the Platte and any other waterway on the route tested everybody's patience and endurance. Wagons had to be converted into boats by covering the box with waterproof hides and worrying them across with towlines; the women crossed in bull boats or on horseback; the cattle were swum across tended by their drovers, who stripped naked and tied their shirts around their heads.

At Fort Laramie, to Whitman's disappointment, the heavy freight wagon had to be left behind with all the other fur company rolling stock. Fitzpatrick insisted on it but gave in to the physician's insistence on proceeding with Spalding's wagon, the little Dearborn, which would carry Eliza Spalding and, after jettisoning what was agreed to be non-necessities, the missionaries' combined gear. One other wagon in the caravan, actually a two-wheel cart, carried Broken Hand's partner Milton Sublette, whose leg had been amputated the year before and whose cork substitute allowed him to stand and walk on flat ground but not to negotiate mountain trails. To help move the two wagons across the Laramie Mountains, an old buffalo trail was cleared of boulders and cottonwoods to create a rude roadway. Even so, the Dearborn spilled over once, and Sublette's cart twice, before they cleared the passes. Spalding was depressed over their agonizingly slow progress and in his letter to the board wrote, "Never send another mission over these mountains if you value life and money." Whitman, even though enslaved by the Dearborn, was more optimistic. "I see no reason to regret our choice of a journey by land," he wrote.

Eight hundred miles out from Liberty, the caravan camped at Independence Rock, a granite formation on which the names of passersby were scratched or daubed in axle grease. Fitzpatrick sent a rider ahead to the Green River to let the trappers know his party was coming in, and the express apparently also reported that the caravan was bringing along some missionaries, including two white women. A wild celebration awaited them after they crossed South Pass on Independence Day 1836, and as they pushed through the sagebrush along Little Sandy Creek, a Green River tributary, the travelers were greeted by an advance party of trappers, Nez Percé, and Flathead Indians from the rendezvous encampment. "Their approach was like the rush of a tornado down a mountain side," Bancroft wrote of these welcomers, "the cracking of their rifles and their terrifying yells like the snapping off of the branches of trees before the wind, and the fierce howlings of a tempest."

The raucous greeters were led by a barrel-chested, black-bearded mountain man and bear hunter from Virginia named

Joseph Lafayette "Joe" Meek. He wanted to catch an early glimpse of the first white women to cross the Continental Divide and also deliver a message to the missionaries that some Indians had brought to the rendezvous from Oregon. The letter was from Samuel Parker and in it he informed Whitman that he would not be joining them as planned. He was worn out and could not even consider making the overland journey from Fort Vancouver. He said he had explored the Oregon Country from Jason Lee's spread on the Willamette to Spokane and Fort Colville on the north, and gave a rambling discourse on potential mission sites.

This was devastating news. Spalding and Whitman, and indeed the Mission Board in New York, had counted on Parker to lay the groundwork for establishing their mission, gather information, not only locate ideal sites but begin the clearing and building work, and serve as guide from the Green River to the Oregon Country. Now they learned that he had spent a comfortable winter at Fort Vancouver, and he hinted that he would return home by sea. He had left them stranded with no place to go but ahead, likely to reach Oregon in the winter with no prospects except to accept, like mendicants, whatever charity was available from the Hudson's Bay Company.

15

SPIES

"... TO CONTROL THE DESTINIES OF THE PACIFIC."

1

In his letter to the Whitmans, Samuel Parker dilated excitedly on the explorations he had made out of Fort Vancouver but failed to say what these ramblings meant to the missionaries he left stranded on the Green River. Marcus Whitman was angered at Parker's unexplained and inexplicable reversal of their plan and wrote, "We cannot say how much good Mr. Parker's tour will do others. It has done us none, for instead of meeting us at the Rendezvous as he agreed, he neglected to write a single letter containing any information concerning the country, company, Indians, prospects or advice whatever."

The Whitmans had faith that the Lord and Tom Fitzpatrick would solve their problem of getting on to the Columbia; meantime, there was nothing to do but wait for the solution and enjoy the spectacle around them.

Nothing in their lives, before or after, would surpass the experience of the twelve days the missionaries spent among the 400 fur traders and 1,500 Indians scattered in the camps and lodges along the lush banks of the Green that July of 1836. The women were special celebrities, and Narcissa was ecstatic over the blunt stares and crude chivalric attention paid her as she mingled, wearing her bright calicos, with the rough crews, chatting, shaking hands, hugging, and passing out church tracts. The Indians, mostly Nez Percé, Flatheads, Shoshoni, and Bannocks, were stunning in their paint, feathers, beads, breechcloths, and moccasins, carrying their lances, shields, and war clubs and dancing to chants, drums, and rattles. They staged a wild horseback show for the newcomers, then came forward to inspect the ladies, hoping for a kiss, a foreign practice they heard was commonplace among white men and women. The trappers, the trail-filthy, shag-bearded Sons of Saturn whose drunken "sprees," knife fights, and horseback and marksmanship contests were standard rendezvous fare, came shyly to have a close look at the "Bible-toters." Some even asked for the Good Book and any Christian literature available to take on the trail for any literate comrade to read aloud. Narcissa wrote home excitedly that she and Eliza could have dispensed two mule-loads of books and tracts had they been available.

Eliza, who had a gift for languages, began learning the Nez Percé tongue and compiling a vocabulary. Narcissa helped, but William Gray, the Utica woodworker and would-be missionary who was ever alert for any faint sign of what he considered inappropriate conduct, said Mrs. Whitman spent too much time flirting with Fitzpatrick, Joe Meek, and the Scotsman Stewart. "In consequence of these attentions or interruptions," he wrote, "she did not acquire the native language as fast as Mrs. Spalding."

Narcissa, in fact, drank in the spectacle of the rendezvous precisely as might be expected of a woman cloistered all her life, and saw in the savages—Indian and mountain man alike—the quintessence of her Christianizing dreams. "This is a cause worth living for!" she wrote in her journal, and her exuberance continued until they departed their roistering company to continue their journey into the grim and rocky sage-lands to the west.

Midway in their stay at the rendezvous, the missionaries were heartened by the arrival of Nathaniel Wyeth, on his way to the states after his failed enterprises in Oregon. He rode into camp with a brigade of Hudson's Bay men led by Thomas McKay and brought additional news from the lately unrevered Samuel Parker. The reverend urged his colleagues to come directly to Fort Walla Walla under the Company's protection, and before they could ponder how they were expected to get there, McKay and his partners graciously offered to escort them. Their hope now was to reach Oregon before Parker departed for home and obtain from him first-hand, specific, critical information on where they should build their missions and how they would sustain themselves through the winter.

They followed McKay's brigade out of their camp on July 18, bound for Wyeth's fort on the Portneuf River. Narcissa was in the early stages of pregnancy, the baby probably conceived at Fort Laramie in June when the couple found some rare privacy. Although she never mentioned her condition in her journal (it would have been unthinkable to do so), she probably suffered from morning sickness—the odor of sagebrush nauseated her—yet she did not seek Eliza Spalding's company in the Dearborn. Instead, she continued to ride the "excellent sidesaddle and very easy horse" with the Nez Percé boys, the "cow column," and the man she called "Husband" at the rear of the column.

She did not complain, but Marcus' bullheaded coaxing of the wagon down along the Bear River sorely tested her. "Husband had a tedious time with the waggon today," she wrote. "Waggon was upset twice. I do not wonder at all at this. It was a greater wonder that it was not turning a somerset continually. It is not very grateful to my feelings to see him wear out with such excessive fatigue. . . . All the most difficult part of the way he has walked, in his laborious attempt to take the wagon over." On one occasion the wagon was stuck fast in creek mud and Whitman spent most of a day waist-deep in water levering and muscling it free. Narcissa had a momentary hope that Marcus would relinquish the wagon when at Soda Springs the axle broke, but he managed to dismantle the forward wheels and rig it as a cart so he could belabor it on toward Fort Hall.

She noticed her Job-like mate "not as fleshy" as when they'd started out from Missouri. In truth, none of them were. On the wicked trail and under cloudless skies and the pitiless sun, the party endured a diet of buffalo jerky and little else. She wrote in a letter home, "I can scarce eat it, it appears so filthy, but it will keep us alive & we ought to be thankful for it." She said to her sisters, "Girls do not waste bread, if you know how well I should relish even the dryest morsel you would save every piece carefully."

But she bore up. "Do not think I regret coming," she wrote. "No, far from it. I would not go back for the world. I am contented and happy notwithstanding I get very hungry & weary. Have six weeks steady journeying before us. Will the Lord give me patience to endure it. . . . Long for rest, but must not murmur."

Wyeth's Fort Hall provided them with a rest and a chance for laundering and to add turnips and fried bread to their buffalo-jerky diet. When they departed the fort and crossed the Portneuf, heading for the Hudson's Bay post at the confluence of the Snake and Boisé Rivers, the misery started again. McKay's hunters brought in some elk meat and fresh salmon, but such delicacies could not divert them long from the oppressive heat, the incessant stink—to Narcissa at least—of sagebrush, "so stif and hard as to be much in the way of our animals and waggon," and the clouds of mosquitoes that nearly drove them, their pack animals, and cows mad.

Marcus continued to heave the wagon-cart forward, even after it turned over in the mud of the Boisé taking its mule team down with it, tangling cart, harness, and drowning animals in a frothing mass that required two horse teams and two men to help turn it aright. Only when they reached Fort Boisé on August 19, after 1,500 miles of tribulations, was Whitman persuaded by McKay and his men to surrender the infernal wagon at long last.

As they forded the Snake on horseback and on rope-towed rafts made of willows and rushes toward the Burnt River and the Blue Mountains beyond, the missionaries decided they must split up. The Whitmans and William Gray were to push on with some of McKay's men to reach Fort Vancouver before Reverend Parker shipped out for home. The Spaldings and the Nez Percé wards were to follow, bringing along the cattle and pack animals, with the balance the Company's brigade.

On August 29, the advance party reached the western slopes of the Blue Mountains—which reminded Narcissa of the Catskills—and glimpsed the great white cone of Mount Hood in the hazy distance. Three days later they sighted the timber palisades of Fort Walla Walla, the eighteen-year-old Hudson's Bay post on the east bank of the Columbia and at the mouth of the river from which it derived its name. That night Narcissa wrote in a letter home, "You can better imagine our feelings than I can describe them. I could not realize that the end of our journey was so near. We arose as soon as it was light, then dressed for Walla Walla. . . . If you could have seen us now you would have been surprised, for both man and beast appeared alike propelled by the same force. The whole company galloped almost all the way to the Fort."

They reached it at rooster's crow on September 1, 1836, six months and thirteen days after Narcissa packed her black bombazine dress, her calicos and books, and embarked with her husband by sleigh for Pennsylvania.

The post factor, Pierre Pambrun, a Québec veteran of the War of 1812 and one of John McLoughlin's most trusted agents, welcomed the Americans into his drift-log stockade's inner gallery and led them to guest quarters where they could bathe and ready for breakfast. Narcissa breathed in the fort's civilized trappings—clean water, soap, a soft bed, chinaware, cutlery. "No one knows the feelings occasioned by seeing objects once familiar after long privation," she wrote.

The Spaldings and their escort joined the Whitmans two days later. Together they were the first emigrant families to travel overland to the Pacific, more than 3,000 miles from home.

Nothing had been accomplished by the Whitmans' rush across the Blue Mountains to Fort Walla Walla, since the Spaldings, who had been expected to arrive at a later date after inspecting potential mission sites en route, had also proceeded apace without inspecting anything. None of them as yet knew if Samuel Parker had departed the Columbia, but the urgency of determining that fell below

resting and gaining lost strength under the hospitable care of Factor
Pambrun.

They lingered several days at the fort before embarking for the
Company's great fortress on the lower river. Pambrun personally
escorted them downstream in a thirty-foot *bateau*, the oars pulled
by Company *voyageurs*. The only discomforts of the journey were
the high winds, which forced the boat ashore to wait until they
abated, and an incident that occurred during a portage around The
Dalles rapids. In a Chinook village Narcissa, apparently inspecting
it too closely, became infested with fleas. Her hair and dress, she
said, were "black with these creatures, making all possible speed
to lay siege to my neck and ears." She fled to Husband, who
brushed her off as best he could and set up a protective arbor so
she could wash and change her clothing.

In the forenoon of September 12, with the *voyageurs* singing
and with a bite of fall in the air, the *bateau* swung around a piney
point of land and the missionaries caught their first view of what
Narcissa called "the New York of the Pacific Ocean." On the Fort
Vancouver landing stood Dr. McLoughlin with his second-in-
command, James Douglas, to greet them.

They learned at once that they were too late to interdict Samuel
Parker. He had sailed on the steamship *Beaver* for the Sandwich
Islands three months past, about the time his colleagues had
reached Fort Laramie, and had left no messages or instructions.
After the earlier Parker disappointments, the Whitmans and the
Spaldings seem not to have been overwhelmed by the news and fell
quickly to planning the exploration of mission sites—plural. At
some point in their travels, probably long before they reached the
Columbia, they agreed to separate, ostensibly to spread the Gospel
farther by establishing two missions but as much because they were
never comfortable together. Parker, in the letter from him received
at the rendezvous, advised that a site might be established among
the Nez Percé, perhaps near the junction of the Clearwater and
Snake Rivers in Idaho, and suggested also a station among the
Cayuse people east of Fort Walla Walla.

These ideas seemed sensible to both families, both eager to put miles between themselves, and they were probably endorsed by McLoughlin as well, who saw such stations as pleasingly remote from the Hudson's Bay main theater of operations. He urged that while the menfolk set out on their explorations the ladies be left in his care; then, when the sites were selected, the men would gather their wives, the building materials, and the laborers they would require. This was agreed upon, and Whitman, Spalding, and William Gray set out on September 21 with some Nez Percé helpers and a few other men on loan from McLoughlin, promising to return within a month.

The wives were treated royally at the fort during their husbands' explorations; Narcissa became especially close to the half-breed Cree wives of McLoughlin and Douglas. Two other white women were residing at the fort, one married to a Hudson's Bay agent, the other the wife of Reverend Herbert Beaver, the post's recently arrived chaplain. A special attraction for the Americans was meeting Jason Lee, up from his Willamette mission to visit McLoughlin and welcome the newcomers to Oregon.

Meantime, following Samuel Parker's suggestions, Whitman found what he considered an ideal mission site on the north bank of the Walla Walla River, twenty-two miles east of Pambrun's fort in a lush meadow the Indians called Waiilatpu. William Gray and some workers were left behind to bring in tools and supplies purchased at Fort Vancouver while Whitman, Spalding and their escort rode on 100 miles northeast of Waiilatpu to the juncture of the Clearwater and the Snake, a place Parker had recommended. There they met a party of Nez Percé who, when told of the mission plans, led the white men another ten miles east to Lapwai Creek. Spalding had found his site.

While Whitman, Gray, and their workers began the labor of cutting timber for a cabin at Waiilatpu, Spalding returned to Fort Vancouver, arriving there on October 18, to fetch the wives, load two *bateaux* with a winter's supply of provisions, and, with a Company escort, return upriver. Narcissa, now four months into her pregnancy, was landed at Fort Walla Walla to await completion of the Whitman cabin while Spalding and Eliza, with the help of a force of 100 Indians, loaded twenty horses with supplies and set out for Lapwai Creek. They would live in a tent until better shelter could be erected.

The 110 miles separating the missions seemed a perfect distance. The men were frequently at odds; the wives, so different in temperament to begin with, were so wedded to their husbands' views on their work among the natives that their own relations were strained. Spalding, trained and ordained, hoped to change the pattern of Indian lives to make them more susceptible to Christian teachings. He regarded Whitman as an upstart, not even a minister, who seemed to take his lead from Jason Lee's approach, acting as a promoter more of settlement than of Christ and believing that the way to convert Indians was by submerging them among a large white, preferably white American, population.

2

With a few exceptions, John McLoughlin liked Americans and even broke some of the Hudson's Bay regulations in assisting them. His brigade leaders helped Jason Lee, Nat Wyeth, the Whitmans and the Spaldings in their journeys from rendezvous to the Columbia, and he was always a generous host when such Americans, and such troublesome ones as Hall Kelley, reached his domain. His magnanimity extended to the missionaries, though he was wary of them and dubious of their chances of success in Christianizing the native tribes. He had, in fact, no great regard for churchmen, and even less after a particularly hateful episode involving one sent out to him to serve as chaplain at Fort Vancouver.

Herbert Beaver—"an appropriate name for the fur trade," Peter Ogden dryly observed—crossed the Columbia bar on the *Nereid*, out of England via Cape Horn and the Sandwich Islands, early in 1836. He stepped up on the landing below the fort, surveyed its primitive surroundings, shook hands with McLoughlin and his welcoming delegation, and thereafter fell afoul of almost all who came in contact with him. Reverend Beaver was a Church of England divine who had served as a regimental chaplain at Saint Lucia and must have viewed his new assignment as similarly beneath his station as the West Indies. He began his tenure by demanding better quarters and agonizing over the log cottage that was set aside to serve as his parsonage. Worse than the lodgings was his realization that here he was thrust among several hundred French-Canadian *voyageurs* who were Roman Catholics and surrounded by Indian tribes whose heathenish "religions" perplexed and angered him.

Beaver fancied himself a great maker of humorous *mots* and a greater orator, but contemporaries at Fort Vancouver described him as a small, pale man with a high-pitched "feminine" voice, an air of pretension, and an undisguised disdain for all he saw and all he met. Bancroft said, "He was of the fox-hunting type of English clergyman, and had been much diverted by the manners of his fellow passenger from Honolulu, especially Mr. Jason Lee, whom he was constantly in the habit of quizzing." As to the "inmates of the fort," Bancroft said, these grave, dignified, disciplined men, "accustomed to respect, did not always escape the reverend gentleman's sallies of wit." Indeed, "his ideas of clerical dignity were such that he felt himself defiled by association with the gentlemen at Fort Vancouver. McLoughlin was uncivil, the clerks boors, the women savages. Here was a fine beginning of English missionary work!"

Beaver found many of the Hudson's Bay "practices" among the Indians reprehensible and dutifully reported these to the Aborigines Protection Society in London, saying that his work among the savages and his attempts to introduce civilization and Christianity to them were constantly thwarted by the Company. He found a special abomination in the practice among "the gentlemen of the fort" of consorting with native women, and in this discovery he made a terrible mistake.

To his horror, Beaver learned that many of the traders at Fort Vancouver were married to Indians without the blessing of clergy, and then he discovered, through some species of moccasin telegraph never disclosed, that John McLoughlin and his half-Cree wife Marguérite had cohabited before the death of her first husband, Alexander McKay, in 1811. In a letter home, Beaver referred to Marguérite as "a female of notoriously loose character . . . the kept Mistress of the highest personage in your service at this station."

In his moral certitude and God-given abstruseness, Herbert Beaver did not count on the chief factor having so many Hudson's Bay friends in England and at the York Factory, and thus had no concern that the contents of his letter might come back to McLoughlin. But they did, and, predictably, the chief factor exploded. It was dangerous enough to spread rumors about McLoughlin, but it was positively suicidal to involve his beloved Marguérite in them.

When the White Eagle got the news, he marched out into the fort's courtyard, found Beaver, and braced him. The scene must have been delectable for any onlooker: Here stood the man whom Governor George Simpson said was "such a figure as I should not like to meet in a dark Night," his formidable six-and-a-half-foot height looming and rigid as an old oak, his great expanse of chest working like a bellows, his white mane of hair flowing, his face suffused with wrath, his icy eyes narrowed, one fist clenched at his side, the other strangling a stout cane. And here stood poor, cringing Herbert Beaver, paler than usual, looking up, snared in a trap sprung by his own folly and from which there was no escape.

McLoughlin demanded an explanation of the vile rumors contained in his worship's letter.

Beaver, nervously searching his mind for a *mot* by which he might wrench his foot from the snare, replied, "Sir, if you wish to know why a cow's tail grows downward, I cannot tell you; I can only cite the fact."

At this astonishing response, Bancroft reports, "Up went the cane of its own volition, and before McLoughlin was aware of it, he had bestowed a good sound blow upon the shoulders of the impudent divine."

Beaver made a full, if quite preposterous, record of what ensued in his encounter with "this monster in human shape." He wrote that McLoughlin "came behind me, kicked me several times, and struck me repeatedly with his fists on the back of the neck. Unable to cope with him from the immense disparity of our relative size and strength, I could not prevent him from wrenching out of my hand a stout stick with which I was walking, and which he . . . inflicted several severe blows on my shoulders." Beaver reported that the factor then "seized me from behind, round my waist, attempted to dash me on the ground, exclaiming 'You scoundrel, I will have your life.' In the meantime, the stick had fallen to the ground; my wife, on impulse . . . picked it up; he took it . . . very viciously from her hands and again struck me with it severely. We were then separated by the intervention of other persons."

If McLoughlin was ever reprimanded for his conduct toward the chaplain, it was done verbally by Governor Simpson and, one imagines, quite diplomatically.

Reverend Beaver, apparently concluding that his salary of £400 per annum was insufficient to include canings, decamped from the Columbia soon after the incident and in 1838 returned to England.

The Hudson's Bay Company sent no more chaplains to Fort Vancouver.

□

The trickle of American missionaries into Oregon did not go unnoticed by McLoughlin's superiors, and in June 1836, three months before the arrival of the Whitmans and the Spaldings and about the time Samuel Parker was sailing home, the factor received a warning from the Company's headquarters at York. "Were we satisfied that the sole object of those Missionaries were the civilization of the Natives and the diffusion of moral and religious instruction, we should be happy to render them our most cordial support and assistance," the minute read, "but we have all along foreseen that . . . the formation of a Colony of United States citizens on the banks of the Columbia was the main or fundamental part of their plan, which, if successful, might be attended with material injury, not only to the fur trade, but in a national point of view."

The suspicion that these Americans were more interested in

colonization than converts to Christianity came as no news to Mc-
Loughlin. Missionaries were historically precursors of colonizers,
and he viewed all the Americans who came to Oregon as the vanguard of a settler invasion and held that belief even before the
arrival of Hall Jackson Kelley, as blatant a stumper for American
"occupation" of the Pacific Northwest as Fort Vancouver ever endured. He followed reports in the American press, knew of the
congressional work of Dr. John Floyd of Virginia and his bills to
claim Oregon for the United States; he knew of Hall Kelley and his
agitations before that peculiar man ever reached the Columbia; he
had talks with such Americans as Jedediah Smith, Ewing Young,
Nat Wyeth, Jason Lee, and Samuel Parker.

McLoughlin's hospitable treatment of the Americans who came
to Fort Vancouver was the product of his shrewdly realistic assessment of his and Hudson's Bay's presence in Oregon. By 1836
he had twelve years in the Pacific Northwest. He enjoyed a virtual
monopoly in the fur trade and had expanded the Company's enterprises to the north, south, and east, making good profits for his
employer. But he knew that the British foothold was fragile, the
1827 joint occupancy treaty toothless, the fur business precarious
and already showing signs of playing out. He was alert to the
changes on the wind. The Americans were returning to the river
they had discovered and never relinquished—the missionaries were
harbingers of a great migration of them—and those who had arrived, the churchmen among them, were talking of farms, industry,
settlements, and of pushing the British out.

McLoughlin dealt with them cleverly. He had an honest affection for most Americans and assisted them, at times beyond the
boundaries of Hudson's Bay policies. He was hospitable and generous, at times to a fault; and would later reminisce woefully about
how certain of the beneficiaries of his largesse thanked him by stabbing him in the back. He also did the best he could to protect the
Company's interests. When possible, he shunted the missionaries
off to the Willamette valley and other locations remote from Fort
Vancouver; he loaned and sold, but did not give, supplies and labor
to those intending to stay; he was aggressive in keeping the Com-

pany paramount in the fur trade—this, after all, being his chief responsibility.

An example of McLoughlin's acumen toward the Americans who sought him out at Fort Vancouver was his use of a man named William A. Slacum.

This gentleman arrived on the Columbia in the last week of December 1836, the single passenger on the American brig *Loriot*, which he had chartered for $700 a month at Honolulu. He identified himself as a "private merchant" who had traveled from Washington via Cape Horn, Guaymas in Baja California, and the Sandwich Islands, to investigate trade possibilities on the Pacific coast. McLoughlin, who learned that Slacum had been an obscure purser in the United States Navy, suspected from the moment he met his overly inquisitive guest that he was neither merchant nor gentleman traveler but an intelligence agent of some kind, and in this he was correct. The visitor had been commissioned by John A. Forsyth, President Andrew Jackson's secretary of state, to visit Oregon to ascertain the truth of Hall Kelley's vituperations that American settlers were being "oppressed" by Hudson's Bay agents, and that the British were thus in flagrant violation of the Anglo-American agreement.

Slacum expressed an interest in meeting Jason Lee and other Americans who had preceded him to Fort Vancouver, and in this request McLoughlin saw the opportunity to utilize the spy in his midst. He told Slacum of the case of the American Ewing Young, who had come to Oregon more than two years past with a horse herd said, by no less an authority than Governor José Figueroa of Alta California, to have been stolen in his province. McLoughlin had banished Young from the fort and refused him trade; then, a few months later, Governor Figueroa exculpated the trapper from the charges. McLoughlin had been instrumental in urging Young to seek redress from Figueroa, but Young had become an enemy, refusing to trade at the fort after McLoughlin lifted the ban, and with a partner had established a farm and sawmill in the Chehalem Valley north of the Columbia.

None of this bothered the factor; what did were the reports

that Young had built a still on his farm and was brewing alcohol, using a huge copper salmon-pickling cauldron salvaged from Nat Wyeth's Fort Hall. This was a disturbing development with a high potential for mischief, and McLoughlin asked Slacum to serve as an emissary to entreat Young to abandon the still in exchange for open privileges to trade at the fort stores. Slacum must have thought this a reasonable request and an appropriate assignment for one American to negotiate with another. He remained with McLoughlin until January 10, then, with six *voyageurs* as escort, began his tour by visiting the old Indian camp called Champoeg on the east side of the river, where McLoughlin had a warehouse. There he met with Jason Lee and several others eager to tell him, or any other visiting American, their problems, especially their complaints of subservience to the Company's monopoly on food-stuffs, seeds, supplies, tools, building materials, and virtually every-thing else needed to build and settle.

While spending two weeks with Lee at his Willamette valley station, Slacum learned that Lee's temperance society had already visited Ewing Young on the whiskey issue. The Methodists had offered sixty dollars and twelve bushels of wheat to offset what Young had already invested in the still if he would tear it down. The trapper rejected the missionaries' offer and that of McLoughlin as well, but he told Slacum he had abandoned the distillery for the present. He said he had turned his attention to a sawmill he had recently built.

Bancroft's assessment of the whiskey issue was that "Young's distillery speculation had been like the labor of Cleanthes, who supported himself by drawing water at night in order that he might indulge in plucking the flowers of philosophy during the day; it was not appreciated by the Willamette Areopagus."

3

The more-or-less secret agent William Slacum crammed as much travel and talk as he could into his brief visit to the Oregon Country. Probably before he reached Fort Vancouver, the *Loriot* had taken him as far north as Juan de Fuca Strait. He was awed by the great sound that connected to the Pacific, named in 1792 by its discoverer, Captain George Vancouver, for his aide, Peter Puget; he met with delegations of Canadians and assured them that they would not lose their farms when (not if) the United States took possession of Oregon, and cheered them further by saying that under American protection they would receive as much as three times more than the fifty cents a bushel Fort Vancouver was paying for their wheat.

During Slacum's visits with Jason Lee and Ewing Young, the Americans dwelled on beef cattle—their scarcity in Oregon, their importance for colonization—and Young, who had tramped Alta California from San Diego to Klamath Lake as a trapper, daydreamed about the abundance of cheap cattle there. The issue so impressed Slacum that he offered his chartered *Loriot* when Young said he wanted to mount an expedition to buy and bring a beef herd back to the Willamette.

In a report he wrote later the agent said, "I found that nothing was wanting to insure comfort, wealth, and every happiness to the people of this most beautiful country, but the possession of neat-cattle, all of those in the country being owned by the Hudson's Bay Company, who refused to sell them under any circumstances whatever."* The idea gained such momentum that even McLoughlin participated when the Willamette Cattle Company was organized in a meeting at Champoeg. In all, about $2,500 was gathered to float the enterprise. Slacum loaned Jason Lee $624 for the mission's share and put in another $100 of his own; McLoughlin anted up $558 of his own money and $300 more in the name of two of

---

*Actually, there were so few head to begin with that they went unslaughtered in order to multiply, and McLoughlin refused to sell them not only to Americans but to anyone, including the British. This simple explanation did not prevent the cattle issue from becoming one of the many bones of contention between the missionary-settlers and Hudson's Bay agents.

his traders. (His contributions were never mentioned by the Americans.) Young gathered up thirteen men, two of them Indian guides; Slacum packed his kit, intending to return home after disembarking the cattle hunters, and they all boarded the *Loriot* on January 21, eager to reach California.

However, from the first day to the last in what became a tortured nine-month expedition, nothing went smoothly. First, the Columbia threatened to scuttle them before they could cross the bar. In Baker's Bay they found that two Hudson's Bay fur vessels had been detained nearly a month by high seas, and the *Loriot* had to join them. Tossed and battered in the estuary, the brig's mooring cables parted, its sails were shredded to rags, and its decks and bilges were awash before it could batter a path into the open sea on February 10. They reached Fort Ross, the Russian trading post fifty miles north of San Francisco Bay, nine days later, and on March 1, 1838, Young and some of his men were disembarked at Yerba Buena, after which Slacum sailed south toward the Horn and home.

Young met with Mexican officials at the tiny settlement and learned that it was illegal for foreigners to remove live cattle from the province. Three months were lost shuttling on horseback from the bay to San José, Monterey, and even as far south as Santa Barbara and north to Sonoma before the rules were slackened and Young was permitted to buy 800 head of cattle at three dollars each. The stock was anything but prime; the Mexicans fobbed off wild, skinny animals hazed out of the brush and into corrals.

Young spent the last of his Willamette Cattle Company start-up funds by buying forty horses and hiring five footloose Americans found wandering about Monterey to help the others put the cattle into a semblance of a trail herd. The drive began by skirting the animals around San Francisco Bay on the south toward the San Joaquin River. There were no cowboys in Young's party, and no one had experience in moving cattle across land, much less water. The terrified animals, already maddened by the flies and mosquitoes infesting the river bottoms, refused to budge from the San Joaquin banks; even when calves were dragged across the river by horse and rope their mothers bawled and dug their hooves into the mud or ran off into the brush. Pens were rigged to contain them but were quickly reduced to rubble as the animals stampeded, and days were devoted to hunting them down and dragging them back to the crossing. Then, when a sizable number were cursed and goaded into the river, they ignored the far shore and swam out in all directions. Seventeen drowned in one such sortie. Finally, Young and his exhausted, exasperated drovers built rafts of bulrushes and with a rope strung across the river ferried the cattle one at a time to the opposite bank.

Toward the end of August they reached the mountains at the head of the Sacramento valley and on September 12 arrived on the Rogue River (also called Les Coquins and sometimes the Rascal River, after the "rascally," unpredictable Indians living on its banks) in southern Oregon. This was dangerous country. Not far to the north, on the Umpqua, Jedediah Smith's trapping party had been attacked by a Kalawatset war party ten years past, and some of Ewing Young's men had been in fights with Rogue River raiders and had learned to hate the sight of any Indian in the vicinity. Trouble was assured when one drover shot and wounded a native boy shortly after the herd splashed across a shallow river fording. Each day afterward, arrows flew into the cattle camp and gunshots rang out, and on September 18 there was a fleeting massed attack on the drovers that resulted in the wounding of one white man, several cows, and Young's horse before the Indians were driven off by gunfire.

The cattle company straggled into Jason Lee's Willamette Mission grounds in mid-October, nine months after boarding the *Loriot* and having traveled 700 miles in eighteen weeks from San Francisco Bay, with 600 of the original 800 head of stock still alive, still skinny, and still wild. The drovers were paid off in cattle at the rate of twenty dollars a month, and the remaining stock was prorated among the investors.

□

William A. Slacum sailed from Alta California on February 10, 1837, arrived in New York that summer, and submitted a report to the Twenty-fifth Congress in December of the year. The document became influential for its strategic recommendations, its lengthy description of Fort Vancouver, and its condemnation of the Hudson's Bay Company. The document also contained random remarks on the Indians and the physical features of the country; firsthand glimpses into the lives, and problems, of the missionary-settlers of the Willamette valley; and recommendations on what was being called "the Oregon Question," the issue of extending American hegemony from the Rocky Mountains to the Pacific.

Slacum wrote of the importance of Puget Sound as a deepwater port and sea-lane into the Pacific, writing, "In a military point of view, [Puget Sound] is of the highest importance to the United States." So important, in fact, that he urged the government to insist upon the 49th parallel as the northern boundary in any settlement with England in order to bring the sound into American control. He added the notion that a large colony of American settlers in Oregon might assist if there should be resistance in obtaining it.

As to the state of the missionaries and other Americans already in Oregon, Slacum had brought their woes, real and imagined, home with him. "Some steps must be taken by our government," he wrote, "to protect the settlers and traders, not from the hostility of the Indians, but from a much more formidable enemy . . . the Hudson's Bay Company."

Slacum's work was perfectly timed with that of his missionary friend Jason Lee who, within weeks of the agent's submission to Congress, arrived in New York with his memorial, signed by fifty settlers describing themselves as the nucleus of a great new state of the Union and urging the United States to take formal possession of the lands south of the Columbia River.

4

A year after Slacum reached Washington, the six-ship United States Exploring Expedition sailed from Norfolk, Virginia, for the Pacific under the command of navy lieutenant Charles Wilkes, a forty-three-year-old New Yorker. With him were an impressive scientific contingent that included naturalists, botanists, mineralogists, a philologist, and even taxidermists. The expedition was to make extensive scientific, commercial, and strategic studies from the South Seas to Alta California and what his orders called "the territory of the United States on the seaboard," the Columbia River country.

The ships made stopovers on the South American coast, at the Paumotus, Samoa, New South Wales, the Antarctic coast, Fiji and the Sandwich Islands, and lingered several weeks in Mexican California before some of them reached the mouth of the Columbia in April 1841.

Wilkes was an imperious naval officer with scientific pretensions ("His impudence was greater than his talents," Bancroft said) who had inexplicably been given the command over many senior officers desiring it. He spent several months exploring the country from Puget Sound to the Willamette valley, from Fort Vancouver as far east as the Spaldings' Lapwai Mission, and was unimpressed by the handful of American settlers he met and dismissed the missionaries as more interested in money than in converting Indians. After he lost one of his vessels, the sloop-of-war *Peacock*, on a sandbar at the entrance of the Columbia (its crew was rescued by Chinook Indians), he wrote, "Mere description can give little idea of the terrors of the bar of the Columbia; all who have seen it have spoken of the wildness of the scene, and the incessant roar of the waters, representing it as one of the most fearful sights that can possibly meet the eye of the sailor," and encouraged the occupation of the coast above forty-nine degrees where safer harbors could be found.

Of the anchorages farther north Wilkes said, "Nothing can exceed the beauty of these waters, and their safety; not a shoal exists within the Straits of Juan de Fuca, Admiralty Inlet, Puget Sound, or Hood's Canal, that can in any way interrupt the navigation by a seventy-four-gun ship. I venture nothing in saying there is no country in the world that possesses waters equal to these."

Later, after he visited Alta California, Wilkes predicted that within a few years that province would probably be separated from Mexico and united with Oregon and "will perhaps form a state that is destined to control the destinies of the Pacific." This future state, he wrote, "is admirably suited to become a powerful maritime nation, with two of the finest ports in the world—that within the Straits of Juan de Fuca and San Francisco."

In October 1841, about a month before he departed Oregon to sail to Japan before returning home, Wilkes met with Hudson's Bay governor George Simpson at Fort Vancouver. Sir George (he had been knighted that year) learned from Wilkes that he intended recommending to his superiors in Washington that the United States should claim the Oregon Country to the line of 54 degrees, 40 minutes north latitude. Simpson, upon the American's departure, wrote a memorandum to the British Foreign Office stating that the lands south of the Columbia were not worth fighting for, that the dangers of the Columbia estuary and the "unhealthfulness" of the south augured against British interests in that region. But he urged the government "not to consent to any boundary which would give the United States any portion of the Territory north of the Columbia River."

□

The four-year expedition resulted in an eighteen-volume *Narrative* under Wilkes' name, which the *North American Review* described as "a work of oppressive dimensions . . . crushed under the weight of irrelevant matter." Even so, as Bancroft wrote, "Meagre as was the knowledge gathered by this expedition, its influence upon the affairs of the Pacific territory of the United States in their then incipient state was important."

In the period of 1838–41, Slacum, Lee, and Wilkes, two spies and a missionary in John McLoughlin's thinking, were the new reigning Oregon authorities, supplanting if not replacing such old ones as Hall Kelley, who was still writing and bemoaning his fate in Three Rivers, Massachusetts, and Nat Wyeth, still working for the Tudor Ice Company in Boston. Kelley and Wyeth shared platforms occasionally to speak on the glories of the Arcadia of the Pacific Northwest, and their orations and writings, and the work by Slacum and Wilkes, oiled the engine moving the government, and trains of certain citizens seeking a new life, to provide answers to the "Oregon Question."

CHAMPOEG

"... FREE CITIZENS OF OREGON."

1

The annexation petition Jason Lee delivered to Washington anticipated the need for governance in the growing American colony in the Willamette and had influential support in Congress. Massachusetts Representative Caleb Cushing, perhaps inspired by the voices from the wilderness, wrote a combative, twenty-seven-page discourse on the Oregon question for the *North American Review* in January 1840. The congressman questioned the "blindness and supineness of the Federal Government" toward the Hudson's Bay Company's "monopoly of commerce of that wide-spread and noble domain of the United States situated on the Pacific Ocean." He said that "this foul blot on our national honor" must be wiped out "if there is one spark of true patriotic feeling left in the breasts of Congress or the Federal Administration" and urged that the government would be "impelled forward by the irresistible voice of the people."

Senator Linn of Missouri, in 1838, 1841, and annually until his death in 1843, introduced bills to extend American laws to

Oregon settlers and to give generous land grants to families who
would risk the journey out there. He proposed grants of 640 acres
to every male citizen over eighteen years of age, and 160 acres more
for each wife and child, this in a time when a subsistence-sized
patch of farmland east of the Mississippi cost $200 or more. Linn's
bills were invariably voted down or tabled as too severe an affront
to the British, and while the Oregon colonists waited for congressional legislation to guide them, they banded together to make
some of their own.

The lawmaking occasion was the death of Ewing Young, that
"excellent old captain" and "audacious pioneer" Bancroft admired,
in early February 1841, after he fell into a delirium at his Chehalem
Valley homestead. He had long suffered from some undiagnosed
ailment, probably peritonitis from a stomach ulcer, and gave up at
the age of forty-nine. At the fevered end of his life Young may have
been dreaming of how far he had come from his native Tennessee
in his allotted half century; of trapping, wandering, and fighting
Indians along the Santa Fé Trail and along western rivers from the
Gila to the Rogue. To the end he smarted over the accusation that
he was a horse thief, still held John McLoughlin and the Hudson's
Bay Company in contempt, and remained proud of the great cattle
drive he led out of Mexican California to the Willamette in '37,
his 137-head share of which had grown to 600 when he died. He
was a cantankerous, lonely figure to the end, never married, and
had few friends, but he managed in less than a decade in the Northwest to become wealthy, at least by Oregon standards, with land
holdings, cattle, a sawmill, and a homestead.

Since Young died intestate, with no heirs or legal claimants,*

---

*At least until 1854 when a young man named Joaquín Young came out to
Oregon from Taos, New Mexico, with papers seeming to prove that he was
the son of Ewing Young and María Josefa Tafoya of Taos. Kit Carson was
among those who provided paper testimony on the authenticity of the young
man's parentage, and others swore that Ewing Young spoke of having a son
in New Mexico. The Oregon Territorial legislature found Joaquín Young's
claim to have merit and awarded him nearly $5,000 in settlement of his claim.

the American settlers south of the Columbia decided to gather to liquidate his property and other assets. The process began with a series of public auctions conducted by one of Young's few friends, Joe Meek, "his splendid figure clad in the ragged habiliments common to the improvident mountain man," Bancroft said. The auctions netted a healthy $4,000 (Young's prized, and pristine, two-volume set of Shakespeare, brought $3.50), but the property presented a more complex problem, and to deal with it a call was issued for all Americans in the Oregon Country, and any interested Canadians, to congregate at the Methodist mission on February 17, 1841, to serve as an ad hoc probate court.

Beginning with the matter of Young's estate, this meeting and the others following at Champoeg, in a grassy, timbered place on a bend of the Willamette called French Prairie, gave rise to the first series of "wolf meetings" dealing with predators—wolves, coyotes, mountain lions, even bears—killing the settlers' stock. The attendees also formed a committee to draw up a legal code and constitution, and a miniature provisional government that would press for annexation of the Oregon Country by the United States.

A few months into this process, Lee and others instrumental in the Champoeg meetings approached the naval explorer Charles Wilkes for advice. If the settlers hoped for his endorsement of their efforts they were sorely disappointed, for Wilkes, who had the highest regard for his own importance, worked hard to dampen their ardor. He suggested that the whole governmental scheme was unnecessary, that it was a poor and uninforceable substitute for a moral code such as that preached by the missionaries. He said it would be wise to wait and not to disturb the Hudson's Bay people until the United States officially extended its jurisdiction over the Pacific Northwest. He assured the Americans that he intended to recommend this course in his report to his superiors in Washington.

The settlers pressed on, regardless of Wilkes' admonitions, and created their constitution, calling it their "First Organic Laws" of the "free citizens of Oregon." The document contained a religious freedom article; others on habeas corpus, the right of trial by jury; and a prohibition against cruel and unusual punishment and against slavery. A "voluntary subscription" of funds was to take the place of taxation. As to the natives of the country, the signers pledged that the "utmost good faith shall always be observed towards the Indians. Their lands and property shall never be taken from them without their consent." Voting rights were granted to those age twenty-one and older (males only), and those eligible to vote were also eligible for public office. Provisions were made for a legislative body, a supreme court, a treasurer and "recorder"—a clerk to make records of governmental proceedings. Rights of marriage were reserved to male persons age sixteen and older and females fourteen years and older.

The preamble of the constitution employed the name "Oregon Territory" to describe the lands south of the Columbia even though, when it was signed and adopted by the American enclave on July 5, 1843, there would be a five-year wait before territorial status became federal law. In the meantime, two years after its creation, John McLoughlin, acting on behalf of the Hudson's Bay Company, recognized the Americans' provisional government "for the security of the Company's property and the protection of its rights."

2

In March 1841, a month after Ewing Young died in Oregon, William Henry Harrison became the ninth president of the United States. He was a frail sixty-eight—the last president to have been born before the Revolution. He rode horseback to his inauguration without a coat or hat in cold and stormy weather, spent an hour and forty-five minutes reading his 8,500-word address, and, a month later, at thirty minutes after midnight on Sunday, April 4, died, of "pleurisy fever"—pneumonia—in the White House.

During the administration of John Tyler, Harrison's vice president and fellow Virginian, the United States and Great Britain signed a boundary agreement. It fixed the border between Maine and Canadian New Brunswick, added 7,000 miles of disputed land to the United States, and made minor adjustments to the U.S.-Canadian boundary from the Atlantic to the Rocky Mountains. This "settlement" seemed an excellent opportunity to reconcile the Oregon boundary matter, but neither nation was as yet ready for anything so radical, and left the question unresolved.

In 1841 the American nation of 17 million citizens was still reeling from the effects of the financial collapse of '37, the greatest economic depression ever experienced, that followed the end of the Jackson administration. Bad banking policies and feverish speculation in public lands during the Jacksonian era lay at the root of the disaster, but among the hardest hit were those who had no money in banks nor any interest in land other than what they could grow on it. Farmers, who had to scrabble hard to eke out a living in the best of times, were devastated by falling prices for their agricultural products and the surpluses clogging the marketplace. Farms were foreclosed and families rendered homeless and impoverished as surely, and in some instances as fatally, as the cholera epidemic that was creeping westward.

The anthem of the dispossessed—"There *has* to be something better out there"—in many cases referred to free land. All the best farmlands east of the Mississippi had been claimed; even in Missouri, with its 400,000 settlers in 1841, an acre of mediocre land was selling at a dollar and a quarter, and a foreclosed dirt-farm family couldn't afford a tract big enough to subsist on.

The far West propagandists made an impression on such desperate people in the first half of the decade of the forties, the tub-thumpers ranging from those who had been to the Pacific—trappers, traders, travelers, government agents—to those like Linn of Missouri and Cushing of Massachusetts who had not seen, nor would ever see, the places west of Independence about which they wrote and orated.

They all talked about free land—that they had in common, and there was no greater lure for westering than free land—and most spoke of a second chance, a new life for those willing to work for it. They also extolled the salubriousness of the climate, the pure air and freedom from the epidemics of typhoid, dysentery, tuberculosis, scarlet fever, yellow fever, malaria, and particularly Asiatic cholera, which in the two decades to follow would kill 30,000 Americans.

One charming and often quoted story told of a Missourian asking a man just returned from California if there were fevers and "ague" out there. The man said that there was but one man in all of California who ever got a chill there, and he was the subject of so much wonderment that people in Monterey went eighteen miles out into the country just to see him shake.

3

To Marcus and Narcissa Whitman and Henry and Eliza Spalding, 1841 meant they were entering their fifth year of work at their missions, the Whitmans at the "Place of the Rye Grass" on Mill Creek on the north bank of the Walla Walla River, and the Spaldings a comfortable 110 miles northeast, among the Nez Percé at Lapwai.

The first years of their "Call" to minister to the Indians were devoted more to the physical labor required to make their missions self-sustaining—building, planting, fencing, tending to stock—than to teaching and preaching, giving such a visitor as Lieutenant Charles Wilkes the impression that they were more interested in making money than converts.

This notion was entirely specious, for these families made neither money nor converts. Both missionary families suffered frustrations and failures unforeseen in the days when they dreamed of delegations of savages arriving on their doorstep eager to learn the Christian way of life. Henry Spalding wrote Elijah White, a physician who came out to Oregon in 1836, "I have no evidence to suppose but a vast majority of them [the Nez Percé] would look on with indifference and see our dwelling burned to the ground, and our heads severed from our bodies." This fatalistic thinking was echoed by Congregational missionaries among the Spokane Indians near Fort Colville. Elkanah Walker of Maine and Cushing

Eells of Massachusetts were of the opinion that the natives were more interested in tobacco than in the Testaments. (In 1847, Mrs. Eells wrote home, "We have been here almost nine years and have not yet been permitted to hear the rites of one penitent or the songs of one redeemed soul.")

The mission families did their best against crushing odds. The Lapwai station was commodious and warmed by eleven fireplaces. It had a reception room, a spinning and weaving room, a dining room and bedrooms, and a schoolhouse, all under one roof. The Spaldings had planned and supervised the building of a church, mill, blacksmith shop, granary, warehouses, and farm buildings. They strove for self-sufficiency, the Board of Foreign Missions' *sine qua non*, and worked, taught, and preached tirelessly, in isolation and, at times, in fear. The Nez Percé, even those who sent their children to the mission school and attended the mission church, were fickle in their relationships with the Spaldings, and unpredictable. They pulled down the sawmill on one occasion, with no known motive, threatened Spalding, at least once carrying guns, and repeatedly insulted his wife.

At Waiilatpu, the Whitmans experienced a similar pattern of progress, frustration, and signals of danger in their efforts among the Cayuse's people. With Indian workers and hired hands they planted wheat and potato fields, built a gristmill and a sawmill, and fenced pasturage for a small herd of cattle, some horses, and hogs and sheep imported from the Sandwich Islands. Their story-and-a-half adobe mission house was sixty feet long by eighteen wide with a library, bedrooms, dining and sitting rooms, a kitchen, and schoolrooms where Narcissa taught reading and singing. A second house, forty by thirty feet in size and occupied by the Utica woodworker and "secular agent" for the Oregon missions, William H. Gray, stood a short distance away. The Walla Walla River and a millpond formed one side of the mission grounds, an irrigation ditch the other. Toward the west stretched a pretty meadow and copses of apple trees. The mission sawmill lay twenty miles up Mill Creek.

The Cayuse, the principal natives of the Waiilatpu area, shared a similar language with the Nez Percé, were related to them through intermarriage, and, like the Nez Percé, were master horsemen.* But the two tribes distrusted each other and the Cayuse were reputedly more erratic in their behavior and more "savage," this perhaps growing out of battles with their traditional enemies, the Shoshoni, whose lands lay on the eastern slopes of the Blue Mountains and in Snake River country.

(In a report he sent east, Elijah White said that the insolence of the Cayuse had been growing since the visit of Captain Benjamin Bonneville, who in 1834 paid the Indians for their furs far more than Hudson's Bay agents and that the Indians began making demands ever after.)

Some Nez Percé who visited the Whitmans early upon their settling at the Waiilatpu station warned them that the Cayuse "were not good people," were "morose and treacherous." This signal, perhaps dismissed as intertribal bitterness, seemed much more alarming and premonitory after a series of incidents the Whitmans endured that were even more unnerving than those experienced by the Spaldings. From the outset, the Whitmans had to contend with the Cayuse's peculiar notion that they were owed by the missionaries and not vice versa: They demanded to be paid for receiving religious instruction and for use of the land being cultivated. Split-Lip, chief of the Cayuse of the Waiilatpu area, was a particularly demanding and insulting *bête noir* of the missionaries, so much so that on several occasions Whitman had to seek help from Pierre Pambrun, the factor at Fort Walla Walla, in dealing with him. The natives were careful not to anger the Hudson's Bay Company agents, fearing that they might withdraw their trading posts from the country, and Pambrun was generally able to assist Whitman and manage the menacing natives.

Nonetheless, there were confrontations, and the direst of these occurred in 1840 when a band of Cayuse rode through the mission wheat field and trampled it flat. When Marcus Whitman attempted

---

*Hence "cayuse," an Old West word for an Indian pony.

to reprove them, several of the band threw mud at him, while others dismounted and stood face-to-face with the terrified man, pulling at his beard and ears, cocking and snapping an unloaded pistol at his head, threatening him with an ax, and shouting that they would tear down the mission house and burn it. Whitman, shaken by the confrontation, reported it to John McLoughlin. The factor, who had never trusted the Cayuse and was dubious of any missionary efforts among them, strongly counseled the Whitmans to quit Waiilatpu forthwith.

But they stayed on, and in 1841 withstood another menacing incident, this one involving Gray, the volatile cabinetmaker residing on the mission grounds, who struck an Indian boy for some unknown offense. The boy's uncle was the Cayuse chief Tiloukaikt—described by Bancroft as "a haughty and irascible man"—who sought out Whitman in the mission yard and avenged the insult by striking at the missionary and knocking off his hat.

Narcissa, too, had suffered the insults and ingratitude of the Indians but bore them more stoically than her husband. She had learned to bear the vicissitudes of wilderness life by surrounding herself with children. She had arrived in Oregon pregnant, and on her birthday, March 4, 1837, gave birth to their daughter, Alice Clarissa, the first white American child born in the Oregon Country. The girl, the light of the Whitmans' lives, drowned in the Walla Walla River in June 1838, and Narcissa never recovered from her death nor bore another child. She did persuade Marcus to adopt Helen Meek and Mary Ann Bridger, the half-Indian children of the mountain men Joe Meek and James Bridger. In 1842 she took in an orphaned three-year-old "Spanish-Indian" boy, and when her husband returned from a trip east in 1843, he brought with him his thirteen-year-old nephew to join the household. Finally, in 1844, the Whitmans adopted the seven children of Henry and Naomi Sager, both of whom had died on the Oregon Trail.

For all the reverses in their proselytizing, both the Whitmans and the Spaldings were sustained by their faith and the harsh realization that their Christianizing work would require a lifetime or more to produce a healthy number of converts. They were at least making a start in a noble endeavor. They were also learning that their work not only involved battering down centuries of heathenish spiritual beliefs and teaching the path to righteousness, but overcoming secular hindrances as well. The Indians had been despoiled by the white men who had preceded the missionaries, had been taught the *value* of things, a concept foreign to them before their intercourse with whites. Both the Cayuse and Nez Percé complained often that the missions and fields had been appropriated without permission and that the crops were raised and sold to others with the Indians receiving no part of the profits; that mission gristmills even charged the Indians for grinding their grain. Both tribes wanted the missionaries to share their cattle, hogs, and sheep.

To the Indians these were simple matters. The whites, after all, were intruders—and by 1841 there were nearly 500 of them in the Oregon Country and the number was swelling. To the missionaries and other settlers, the natives were shiftless, intractable, and insolent ingrates, owing much to the whites for teaching them English, the Bible, the value of planting, of livestock, of trading in furs, of *money*. To the whites the Indians were owed nothing, least of all for the land they claimed. The land was American land, there for the taking for those who would "improve" it, and the land claimers and improvers were on the march.

One secular issue that more than any other burdened the missionaries and distracted them from their teaching and religious work was the notion of self-sufficiency. This lodestone seemed so rational and possible in New York, where policies were formulated by men who could not locate the Continental Divide much less divine what obstacles lay beyond it, but in actual practice the idea was chimerical. For the missions to become independent of home support, more churchly people, missionary families, were needed, and above all, more time was needed.

17

SAPLING GROVE

"OREGON OR THE GRAVE"

1

In early May 1841, at a place called Sapling Grove, west of Independence, Missouri, a frontier schoolteacher named John Bidwell paced his camp, waiting for other members of the Western Emigration Society to rendezvous and begin their plunge westward to the Pacific. He was headed for Mexican California; others of the society were interested in the Oregon Country. None knew anything about getting to either place ("The ignorance of the route was complete," Bidwell later wrote), and the only maps of the Rocky Mountain country and beyond were filled with blank spaces and purported but unproven lakes and rivers.

Bidwell seemed an incongruous candidate to lead, or even follow, an overland party of emigrants. He was twenty-two, fit and handsome, but except for a brief stint as a farmer had spent his adult life studying and teaching. Still, he had always been drifting westward. He was a Chautauqua County New Yorker, attended schools in Ohio, and ventured to Missouri in 1839 with seventy-five dollars in cash and "nothing more formidable than a pocket-knife" to protect himself.

He was teaching school in Platte County when he caught the westering fever after hearing of the glories of California from a Santa Fé trader who had been there. Toward the end of 1840, Bidwell and a few like-minded enthusiasts organized the ambitiously named Western Emigration Society. A month after it was publicized, 500 people, most of them from Missouri, Illinois, Arkansas, and Kentucky, responded and signed a pledge to buy a suitable "outfit" and come to the Sapling Grove rendezvous in the first week of May 1841 "armed and equipped to cross the Rocky Mountains to California."

Bidwell himself scraped up enough money to buy a gun, a wagon, and some basic provisions. An associate who said he would supply horses backed out at the last moment, and the schoolmaster had to search Independence and Westport Landing (the future Kansas City) to find another partner. This man owned a good horse and had a few dollars in cash, traded the horse for a yoke of oxen to pull the wagon, and also bought a "sorry-looking one-eyed mule."

When Bidwell reached Sapling Grove a week or so before the departure time, only one wagon had preceded him; indeed, until a few days ago before heading out, the whole scheme seemed to have disintegrated. Some attributed the dampening of enthusiasm among Bidwell's followers to letters appearing in the press written by one Thomas Jefferson Farnham, a Vermont lawyer who had settled in Illinois and attended a Jason Lee appearance at the Main Street Presbyterian Church in Peoria in September 1838. Farnham was enthralled by Lee's tales of the Oregon Country and even more so by the stories told by one of Lee's Chinook boys about the salmon runs of the Columbia and how easily the fish could be caught, dried, and sold. The lawyer began having Nat Wyeth–like visions of a fortune to be made in salmon-pickling, and in the spring of 1839 he put together a party of fifteen wilderness-raw adventurers calling themselves the Oregon Dragoons. Mrs. Farnham even stitched them a flag bearing the legend "Oregon or the Grave." They set out from Independence for the Pacific with the vaulting ambition to plant the flag—the Stars and Stripes, not Mrs. Farnham's banner—in the Oregon Country. They intended claiming sovereignty in the name of the United States, repelling any contrariness by the British and their Hudson's Bay agents, pickling a lot of fish, and returning home with shiploads of kegged salmon and their pockets lined with gold.

Not surprisingly, none of this worked out. The Peorians added several men and two missionary couples to their party in Independence, but others defected en route. They missed the outward-bound caravan carrying supplies and trade goods to the Green River rendezvous and were forced to tag along with traders on the Santa Fé Trail to Bent's Fort on the Arkansas River, arriving there on July 5, where more men deserted. Those remaining bickered over "Captain" Farnham's military strictness. One man was badly wounded in a firearms accident and had to be carried in a wagon and at times in a makeshift litter. Farnham accused some of the Oregon Dragoons of planning to abandon the wounded man on the Colorado prairie, resigned his captaincy, and hired a guide at Bent's Fort to take him and four loyalists west across the Rockies. By the time he reached the Walla Walla River in late September 1839, the lawyer was down to two companions and an Indian guide.

He visited the Whitmans at Waiilatpu and Jason and Daniel Lee in the Willamette valley, and there received from a delegation of settlers a memorial signed by sixty-seven citizens of the United States, which he promised to deliver to the appropriate authorities in Washington. The petition contained familiar grievances, demands, and questions: American traders had been driven from Oregon by the British; they were unprotected and beholden to foreigners even for such necessities as clothing; there was an alarming increase in the crimes of theft, murder, even infanticide, which they were helpless to arrest since they had no legal recourses of any kind. The paper also included an alarming reference to being at the mercy not only of the savages around them but of "others" who would do them harm, the "others" a transparent reference to the agents of the Hudson's Bay Company.

On October 15, accompanied by Daniel Lee, Farnham departed for Fort Vancouver, and at The Dalles, where Lee maintained a small satellite mission station, the two had a run-in with a band of Indians that clearly illustrated the problems the missionaries were having with the "savages." Farnham, in his 1841 book, *Travels to the Rocky Mountains*, described how he and Daniel Lee encountered a party of about forty Dalles natives and tried to recover from them a bridle and some saddle leather that had been stolen from Lee's workshop. The Indians took umbrage at the suggestion of thievery and the chief of the tribe drew a pistol while Farnham raised a rifle. No blood was shed, but the natives were greatly agitated and refused to assist the white men in loading their canoes to continue their journey downriver.

At Fort Vancouver, Farnham paid a call on McLoughlin but cut his visit short, planted no flag and pickled no fish—these ideas seemed to have vanished along with most of his Oregon Dragoons. Alexander Simpson, a clerk at the fort related to Governor George Simpson, described Farnham as possessing much dry humor but added that he "talked grandiloquently and acted shabbily."

Eighteen of Farnham's followers, a few of them members of the original Oregon Dragoons, stayed on in Oregon but their disappointed captain departed on the Hudson's Bay ship *Nereid* on December 3 bound for Oahu. Once there, he dispatched the first of his letters to the secretary of war on the nefarious and monopolistic practices of the British and its Hudson's Bay agents. In this he followed the custom of many Americans before him in partaking of the Company's hospitality, sailing on a Company ship, and, once free of its charity, slandering the Company with a will.

From the Sandwich Islands Farnham proceeded to Monterey, spent a few weeks in California—during one of the province's periodic rebellions against Mexican authority—and returned home after crossing Mexico from San Blas to the Gulf of Mexico and New Orleans.

2

Unlike most who visited the Pacific Northwest before him, Farnham was not impressed with the place. The Willamette valley, which Jason Lee and others had oversold as a wilderness Arcadia, the lawyer found unattractive: unbearably hot in summer, unbearably wet and cold in winter, plagued with mosquitoes and flies and the fevers they carried. Oregon as a whole was too dry in the east, too wet in the west; the forests were too heavy in some places, too sparse in others; the mouth of the Columbia was unfit for commercial use. He wrote even more scathingly of Alta California and its turbulent governance and warned would-be emigrants that the province was no Eden and that life there was harsh. Bancroft took severe issue with Farnham's California views, writing that "in all those parts resting upon his own observations it is worthless trash, and in all that relates to the California people a tissue of falsehoods," but the Peorian's perorations, published as open letters, were influential.

What impact Farnham's work had on the Pacific-bound, specifically those of John Bidwell's Emigration Society, is unknown, but it had some negative effect, along with the cholera epidemic raging through the Missouri countryside, rumors of Indian depredations and associated miseries of overland travel, and the economic gloom in Missouri, where farm prices were still disastrously low. Many of Bidwell's 500 pledge signers were too ill, broke, or scared to go anywhere.

Even so, by the departure date, sixty-nine emigrants, including five women and several children, gathered at Sapling Grove with thirteen mule- and ox-drawn wagons. Among the latecomers was one John Bartleson from Jackson County, Missouri, who fourteen years earlier had helped plan the town of Independence. He brought seven men with him and announced to the others that if he were not named captain of the train, he and his associates would stay behind, presumably to wait for another emigrant group willing to let him lead them.

Bartleson was elected, but he had no more idea of how to get wagons and people to the Pacific coast than any of the others. This realization, and his insufferable self-importance, caused frictions among the fragile, fearful neophytes and were factors in the eventual splitting of the party at Soda Springs in Idaho. There, half the party decided to proceed to Oregon rather than accompany their captain to California.

For the present, the pressing problem was how to get to the Pacific with more specificity than following the sun. The answer fell into their laps when a horseman came into the Sapling Grove camp and announced that three Jesuit priests, five teamsters, and two French-Canadian trappers would be arriving soon in the vicinity. The messenger said the priests were headed for the Oregon Country and that they were being escorted by Thomas Fitzpatrick.

This was heaven-sent news. Broken Hand Fitzpatrick! Who had not heard of this Nimrod of the far West? And who knew the route to the Pacific better than he, who had crossed and recrossed South Pass with such peers as Jedediah Smith and Jim Bridger, who had guided the Whitmans and Spaldings to the Oregon Country?

Some in the Bartleson group "thought we could not afford to wait for a slow missionary party," John Bidwell wrote. "But when we found that no one knew which way to go, we sobered down and waited for them to come up. And it was well that we did for otherwise probably not one of us would ever have reached California because of our inexperience."

The three missionaries who had hired Fitzpatrick to guide them to the Oregon Country, specifically to the Bitterroot valley of Montana, were led by Father Jean-Pierre De Smet, a forty-year-old Belgian who had emigrated to the United States in 1821, entered the novitiate of the Jesuit order near Baltimore, and in 1827 was ordained. He had worked as a missionary among the Potawatomis in Iowa, and in 1840 joined a fur-trade caravan to the Green River and spent two months among the Flatheads in the Three Forks region of Montana. Now he was returning, with two fellow priests, Nicholas Point and Gregory Mengarini, to build the Jesuit Mission of Saint Mary's among the Flathead people.

De Smet was a good-natured Friar Tuck who stood at

five feet seven, weighed over 200 pounds and impressed all who met him, including the Protestant missionaries who hated "Romanism" in all its manifestations. Bidwell said, "He was genial, of fine presence, and one of the saintliest men I have ever known, and I cannot wonder that the Indians were made to believe he was divinely protected."

This assessment was correct. De Smet and his Jesuits were to have a success among the natives of the Oregon Country that contrasted sharply with the frustrations of the Lees, Whitmans, and Spaldings. The Jesuits were genuinely sympathetic to the hardships the Indians endured and found them apt pupils, so eager to learn that when the Flatheads set out in their late-fall buffalo hunt they expressly asked for a "Black Robe" to accompany them and continue their religious instruction. This assignment De Smet delegated to Father Point, who spent six years with the Flatheads, the neighboring Coeur d'Alenes, and the dreaded Blackfeet. He followed their hunting parties, lived with them in their winter camps, made numerous converts (which some said was due to colorful Catholic symbolism, trappings, and rituals), and fought what he called "the avarice and cupidity of civilized man," the "abominable influence of frontier vices," and the "Apostles of Protestantism."

De Smet had identical attitudes and successes. By 1847 he had three missions in the Oregon Country and by 1850 five Jesuit and two Oblate missions serving in the Pacific Northwest.

3

On May 10, 1841, the first emigrant train to set out from the Missouri frontier for the Pacific rolled northeasterly toward the Platte River on a route soon to bear a heavy traffic. The Bartleson-Bidwell party's thirteen wagons followed Fitzpatrick and the Jesuits with their five two-wheeled carts drawn by mules in tandem hitches. In all, there were close to eighty people in the caravan and, as the true pioneers of what became known as the Oregon Trail, they had to work ceaselessly to make a trail out of a dim trapper's path. Wagons* had to be wrestled along at an agonizingly slow pace, boulders rolled away, giant sinkholes spaded over, brush chopped, and trees felled.

Father Point mirrored the relief of the whole party in having Fitzpatrick riding ahead of the caravan, directing the work and doing his share of it, and taking command of every aspect of their passage west. "In these immense solitudes it was necessary to have an experienced guide," Point wrote. "The choice fell not on the colonel [Bartleson], who had never crossed the mountains, but on the captain Father De Smet engaged. He was a courageous Irishman known to most of the Indian tribes as Tet Blanch [White Head] or Broken Hand. He had spent fully two-thirds of his life crossing the plains." The one dissenting voice in the praise for Fitzpatrick was that of Reverend Joseph Williams, a Methodist preacher who caught up with the caravan on May 21, riding up alone, unarmed, and uninvited and attaching himself to the party. "Our leader, Fitzpatrick," Williams later wrote, "is a wicked, worldly man, and much opposed to missionaries going among the Indians. He has some intelligence, but is deistical in his principles." The reverend suspected that nearly all the others in the party were "deists," his favorite word for non-Christians, blasphemers, and those not comporting to his ideas of "Godliness." While his attitude toward the Jesuits is unknown, he no doubt kept his distance from them and all others of Papist inclinations. Fitzpatrick's biographer, Leroy Hafen, said that Williams' statements "may be classed as amusing rather than important."

---

*These were common farm wagons and not, as often depicted, the big (and expensive) Conestogas built in Pennsylvania, which weighed a ton and a half when empty, carried five-ton loads over eastern roads, and hauled the first settlers over the Appalachians. They were too massive for the rain-sodden prairies, river crossings, and mountain defiles of the Oregon Trail. Nor did the 1841 emigrants carry their possessions and foodstuffs in "prairie schooners," although use of this memorable conveyance, perhaps the most enduring single symbol of the Old West, lay just ahead.

Father Point recorded in his diary the daily schedule of the caravan under Broken Hand's captaincy: He signaled the departures, ordered the line of march, selected the rest and meal stops and the camps for the night; he set the sentries (the priests did their stint along with every other adult male) and maintained discipline. When possible the camps were made in wooded areas close to water. The wagons and carts were drawn together in a hollow square, "more or less according to the nature of the terraine," Point said, the tongue of one wagon fastened to the rear of the next, the horses, oxen, and pack animals picketed inside. No cookfires were permitted after nightfall so as to prevent alerting Indians in the camp vicinity.

Fear of "red savages" was a palpable feature of all overland emigrant parties, and while there were few instances of Indian hostility against wagon trains, two weeks after the Bartleson-Bidwell party departed Sapling Grove there was a scare that seemed to justify all the campfire qualms and cautions.

One of the young men in the party, Nicholas Dawson, rode a mule out some distance ahead of the wagons as they neared the Platte River in Nebraska. He was a hunter and hoped to find an antelope or two to bring back for the cookfires. But when he ran back to the camp afoot he told Fitzpatrick that he had been assaulted by an Indian war party and robbed of his mule, guns, and even some of his clothing. The captain immediately ordered the wagons into a square and this was completed just as about fifty Indians rode into view and, to the astonishment of the white onlookers, nonchalantly began setting up their lodge poles and making camp. Fitzpatrick and one of his men rode over cautiously for a parley. The Indians were Cheyenne and told Broken Hand that they had been forced to disarm the white boy after he saw them approach, appeared terrorized, and waved his firearms in their direction. They readily turned over the mule and guns they had confiscated.

Nicholas Dawson never heard the end of it, and the story of "Cheyenne Dawson," festooned with elaborate exaggerations, was told around western campfires for years afterward.

□

Between the South Platte and Sweetwater Rivers, buffalo were in such abundance that the emigrants, few of whom had seen the great beasts before, gorged on them trapper-style, finding the tongue, hump meat, and bone marrow, thumbed out from the split bones in strips, special delicacies. "There is no better beef in the world than that of the buffalo," Bidwell said, but he added plaintively that the animals were slaughtered randomly and needlessly by white hunters who left many untouched carcasses on the prairie for wolves and ravens. He observed the Cheyenne, still traveling two or three miles ahead of the caravan, taking all the meat, the hide, horns, and hooves, wasting nothing.

The animals' numbers were frightening. "I think I can truly say that I saw in that region in one day more buffaloes than I have seen of cattle in all my life," Bidwell wrote. "They seemed to be coming northward continually from the distant plains to the Platte to get water, and would plunge in and swim across by the thousands—so numerous were they that they changed not only the color of the water, but its taste, until it was unfit to drink; but we had to use it."

The prohibition against night fires that might attract Indians gave way in buffalo country to bonfires and men periodically firing their rifles into the night sky to prevent the herds from trampling the camp. "We could hear them thundering all night long," Bidwell said, "the ground fairly trembled with vast approaching bands; and if they had not been diverted, wagons, animals, and emigrants would have been trodden under their feet. One cannot describe the rush and wildness of the thing."

Perhaps second only to the scary grandeur of the buffalo herds, which were often described as an immense brown blanket on the prairie stretching to the horizon, the journeyers were awed by the sudden and spectacular lightning fireworks of the violent thunderstorms that soaked their camps, turned the trail to a muddy gumbo, sank wagon wheels to their hubs, and caused horses, mules, and

oxen to bolt and scatter. The storms usually formed in the afternoon sunlight with the tops of billowing western clouds flattening,
followed by light breezes popping the wagon covers and thunder
rolling across the prairie. The wind then began screaming at them,
frequently reaching eighty miles an hour in force, pummeling man
and beast off their feet, upsetting wagons, and driving uprooted
trees and brush along in dense clouds of dirt. Often the storms
produced hailstones as big as turkey eggs—big enough to knock a
man unconscious—and created a panicky run for cover under wagons or in whatever trees were available. Animals in the open were
always injured by the plummeting stones.

The caravan forded the South Platte at what was called the Old
California Crossing, near Brule, Nebraska, and followed the North
Platte to Fort Laramie, arriving there on June 22. The course was
now westerly and the party crossed the North Platte near Casper,
Wyoming, and South Pass, descended to the Green River, thence to
Soda Springs, in Idaho, at the northernmost bend of the Bear River.

By now, the Bartleson-Bidwell group, sixty-nine in number at
Sapling Grove, had been reduced by five men. One man (mordantly
named Shotwell) accidentally killed himself, presumably while
cleaning his rifle; another left the party at Fort Laramie; and three
others turned back after crossing South Pass. Those remaining divided evenly at Soda Springs. Thirty-two elected to follow Fitzpatrick and the Jesuits to Fort Hall, about forty miles distant, and
move on via the Snake and Columbia to Fort Vancouver. The other
thirty-two, Bartleson and Bidwell among them, plunged into the
terra incognita toward California.

The California-bound remnant of the Western Emigration Society struggled across the Utah and Nevada deserts, their draft and
pack animals dropping in the waterless, grassless wastes, their wagons left behind as grim sentinels for those who dared to follow. In the
middle of October the travelers reached the eastern escarpments of
the Sierra Nevadas. They had eaten the last of their mules and oxen
and were progressing little more than ten miles in a day when they
stumbled across the mountains just ahead of the worst of the killing
winter snows. They walked into the San Joaquin valley ranch

of an American squatter named John Marsh on November 1, 1841.

Those Oregon-bound from Fort Hall, guided by Nez Percé, also surrendered their wagons but came safely into the Willamette valley in the fall of 1841, the first organized emigrant party to travel the 2,000-mile Oregon Trail. After they made a stop at Waiilatpu, Marcus Whitman, the veteran wagon wrestler, wrote, "They have left their wagons at Fort Hall, but very soon others will discover that they can bring them through to the Columbia." He saw the newcomers heralding a great American migration to Oregon. "Lapwai and Waiilatpu will become supply stations to thousands of travellers," he wrote, "and the objectives of the committee [the American Board of Foreign Missions] will be removed. Help can be obtained from the immigrants; a settlement can be formed and a strong Protestant influence brought to counter the efforts of the Catholics."

Holding Romanism in check was a strong argument and one used forceably by Whitman and Spalding in their correspondence with the eastern supervisors. Above all, they said, they needed time to attain the persistently stated aspirations of the Mission Board: self-sufficiency and a record of success in Christianizing Indians. Five years in the Oregon Country was not time enough to accomplish either of these purposes. They were still building and planting, and they needed more people, more funds, more time.

In Boston, the board's commissioners were deaf to these appeals; indeed, in the summer of 1842 they were preparing a plan to dismantle the Oregon stations and recall several missionaries. This drastic departure from the bright and hopeful days of the Macedonian Cry resulted from too-high expectations and inevitable disappointments. Their correspondence revealed that the missionaries seemed more occupied with bickering among themselves than with doing God's work (Elkanah Walker's wife, Mary, wrote that "None of them love one another well enough to live in peace together"); the stations were far more expensive to build and maintain than had been anticipated; and for five years there had been no optimistic word from Waiilatpu, Lapwai, or the smaller mission at Kamiah, opened in 1839 sixty miles up the Clearwater above

Lapwai, that the natives were interested in learning of Jesus and the Scriptures.

No matter how loathsome the incursions being made by the Papists in Oregon, the board could not afford to continue its high-minded experiment there. They decided to close the missions at Waiilatpu, Lapwai, and Kamiah, recall the Spaldings and William Gray, and send the Whitmans to Chemakane, the station among the Spokanes operated by Cushing Eells and Elkanah Walker. With this consolidation and house-cleaning, Chemakane would become the sole Presbyterian-Congregationalist outpost in Oregon.

4

These devastating orders were to be hand-delivered to Marcus Whitman and Henry Spalding by Dr. Elijah White of Tompkins County, New York. Bancroft described this singular man as having manners that "were of that obliging kind which made him popular, especially among women, but which men often called sycophantish and insincere." He gained a reputation as a busybody, was greatly "fond of oratorical display and of society, affectedly rather than truly pious, not altogether a bad man, though a weak one. He had no talent, as Heinrich Heine would declare, but yet a character. And strange to say, the longer he dwelt upon this [the Oregon] coast, the more he became smooth and slippery like glass, and flat withal, yet he could be round and cutting on occasions, particularly when broken on the wheel of adversity."

White, about thirty-three, had originally gone out to the Pacific coast on the brig *Hamilton* in 1836 among Jason Lee's first reinforcement. The characteristics Bancroft described, and his penchant toward argumentativeness, were not found to be helpful by the volatile Lee and his Willamette flock. Inevitably, the two men clashed and White had returned home in 1840 aboard the *Lausanne*, the vessel that had carried Lee, his new wife, and his "Great Reinforcement" to the Columbia in 1840.

The *Lausanne* was commanded by Josiah Spaulding, with whom

White struck up a friendship. The captain had transmuted from a merchant skipper to an Oregon specialist in his voyages. He seems to have shared his views with Dr. White, who found them so compelling he offered to assist Spaulding in writing them down for the purpose of delivering them to Congress. The lengthy document born of this collaboration was a compendium of rumor and purplish prose describing Indian depredations and massacres and, among other libels, accusations that the Hudson's Bay Company had incited the Oregon tribes to attack American settlers and missionaries.

Spaulding's scuttlebutt-filled report found an audience in Washington, as all anti-British opinions did. It was among the testimonials employed by Senator Linn of Missouri in his 1841 Oregon bill. That document proposed American military occupation of Oregon and contained a recommendation that an "agent" be appointed to monitor Indian activities in the Northwest and keep an eye on the Hudson's Bay Company.

The bill died aborning, but the Indian-agent idea survived and Elijah White, who was in Washington and therefore handiest of the Oregon veterans, got the job, as "subagent," at a $750 annual salary and the promise that the stipend would be doubled upon the resubmission and passage of Linn's bill. His duties were as vaguely stated as his title, but this did not hamper Dr. White, who was quite capable of filling in the blanks. Historian David Lavender wrote that the missionary-physician believed that "Every person there [Oregon], from McLoughlin on down, would have to heed him. By the time the doctor reached the Willamette, indeed, he would consider himself vested with as many powers as a full-fledged territorial governor."

Before departing for Independence, White, a Methodist, apparently paid a courtesy call at the Presbyterian-Congregationalist Mission Board in Boston, no doubt offering to be of service in his new role as Indian subagent in Oregon. As a result he was asked to deliver a sealed directive to Spalding at Lapwai and Whitman at Waiilatpu. White was not privy to the contents of the letter.

Since he divined that his assignment included encouraging westward emigration, when he made his way to Missouri in the spring of 1842 White launched a publicity campaign, made countless speeches, and wrote newspaper letters drumming up a party to accompany him to the Oregon Country. Over 100 people responded, better than half men over eighteen years of age stirred by his tales that the United States would soon be acting on the Oregon question and his assurance that Senator Linn's bill, with its magnanimous land allotments, would become the law of the land.

On May 16, 1842, White led (there was no question, at first, that he would lead) a train of 100 men, women, and children; eighteen wagons; a hundred horses and pack-mules; and a cattle herd west out of Elm Grove, twenty miles southwest of Independence.

At first those who accompanied him suffered the numerous rules their petulant pilot cobbled together, but they soon broke them as they saw fit. They had not gone far when they booted him out as captain of the train altogether, this after he ordered all dogs to be slain lest their barking attract hostile Indians. Of this incident, Bancroft wrote, "King Herod's edict anent the slaughter of the innocents could scarcely have called forth a louder wail of lamentation from the mothers of Judea than was evoked from the women and children of White's party."

The man who replaced White as wagon master and captain, Lansford W. Hastings, a callow twenty-four-year-old out of Knox County, Ohio, did little better. What harmony remained from White's brief regime vanished under Hastings' guidance, so much so that the column broke into two factions, each marching separately until they reached Fort Laramie on June 23.

With the always dependable Tom Fitzpatrick now their guide to Fort Hall, the Hastings group reached the Sweetwater River on July 13 and, though harassed by a band of Sioux who stole some of their horses, they pushed on. At Fort Hall, on Fitzpatrick's long-standing advice, the Oregon-bound agreed to give up their wagons and trade them for flour and provisions.

Elijah White went ahead with a group of horsemen to Fort Boisé and reached Whitman's mission on September 20, where he delivered the notice of the American board on the mission closings. He told of the hundred emigrants toiling behind him and of the more that would come in '43 dependent on the missions for succor. Then, after dispatching the board's directive to Spalding, he pushed on to Fort Vancouver, with "some feeling of self-importance and exultation on returning as the first officer of the United States appointed in that country," Bancroft said.

□

There is no record of Marcus Whitman's reaction as he read the startling news, but one can imagine him trembling with fury at the officious lines on a sheet of foolscap. A supervisory board 3,000 miles away had expressed a blithe willingness to throw over five years of incessant work, humiliation, and frustration to establish a Christian station in the wilderness among a hateful native people. Until now, he had held out the hope that, given time and resources, the Indians would come in and that the mission would become the haven for the heathen they had envisioned when he and Narcissa first saw Waiilatpu in the winter of '36. Did the commissioners, in the comfort of their Boston boardroom, imagine that they could perform miracles? Did they not realize that five years was a tick of the clock when compared to the centuries the Cayuse and other Northwest tribes had been mired in savage idolatry?

The Spaldings can have felt little differently about their work with the Nez Percé or the Eells and Walkers about theirs among the Spokanes when Whitman met with them to ask their support. He planned to travel east immediately to convince the board to reverse their decision to close the missions.

There were objections: The trip east and back would take a year and the mission would have to make do without its only physician, and it was too late in the year to undertake such a journey. But these arguments could not change Whitman's mind, and he started out on October 3, 1842, with fast horses, a minimum of supplies, a guide, and a newcomer to Waiilatpu, A. L. Lovejoy, who had come in with Elijah White's party. They reached Fort Hall without incident but with winter closing in, and upon learning that Sioux war parties were abroad along the Platte, they swung south into Mexican territory and in Santa Fé joined a trade caravan bound for Bent's Fort, the outfitting oasis on the Arkansas River. The journey south was an awful ordeal in which the two men wandered lost, nearly starved, and fought snowstorms, frostbite, and and fatigue. Lovejoy gave out at Bent's Fort and Whitman went on alone to overtake a fur brigade bound for the Missouri frontier.

He reached the Eastern Seaboard on March 30, 1843, and paused in Washington, where he had a brief audience with President John Tyler, conferred with Secretary of State Daniel Webster on establishing emigrant supply stations along the Oregon Trail, and talked with editor Horace Greeley of the *New York Tribune*.

Whitman then proceeded to Boston, and of the Mission Board's reaction to his unexpected visit Bancroft says it "was not cordial or even kind; it was frigid. They disapproved of his leaving his station, of the unnecessary expense of the journey, and of its object, especially as it asked for more money and missionaries." Whitman, he wrote, spoke against closing the stations at a time when emigrant numbers were increasing by the year—the Oregon contingent of the Bartleson-Bidwell party being the latest example. He said the stations needed more than ever to be ministering to the Indians, who would be greatly affected by the increased white presence in their ancestral lands. To these arguments, even to those on the dreaded Catholic advances, the board was cold—"the savages of the inhospitable north-west were not just then in favor with the Sunday-schools," Bancroft wrote acidly. Nevertheless, the board consented to allow the doctor to return to Waiilatpu and continue his work there, providing he was willing to do so without further support of the board, and even without board payment of his return-journey expenses. The Spaldings could stay put as well, but without board funds.

Whitman, burdened with his failure before the commissioners and with apprehension on returning to Oregon empty-handed, resolved to make the best of it. He paid a visit to his New York home and, with a young nephew accompanying him, reached the western Missouri border on June 1, 1843. There he joined a large emigrant train and returned to what Bancroft called a "smouldering volcano" in Oregon.

18

JUMPING OFF

"BEHOLD, THE PLACE WHICH IS NOW CALLED INDEPENDENCE."

1

On April 13, 1842, at the time when Dr. Elijah White was orating across Missouri to Elm Grove where he would undertake to "lead" a party of emigrants to Oregon, the man who blazed much of the trail White would follow died in Saint Louis.

Wilson Price Hunt, John Jacob Astor's field marshal, had commanded the grueling and adventuresome nine-month trek of the Astor Overlanders from Saint Louis to the Columbia in 1811, and it had been adventure enough for his lifetime. He had reached home, after a detour to China, in 1816, and devoted the rest of his life, twenty-six years, to his merchant enterprises. Those who knew his history must have sought him out to recount the story of that five-year epic when he radically recast his career from that of New Jersey businessman to wilderness journeyer, leading sixty-nine other Astorians to the Pacific just a few years after Lewis and Clark's continental crossing.

Like his employer in New York, Hunt was a businessman and had no interest in the settlement of the Oregon Country except as it might have abetted the fur trade. Yet he lived long enough to witness the death of the fur trade and be honored as a pioneer in breaking the ground for the overland migration to the Oregon Country. Even his mishaps and failures had pointed the way. In the fall of 1811, after he and his footsore and starving party had attempted to negotiate the Snake River in dugout canoes but were battered into surrender, he found a route to the Columbia that filled in a blank: the far western segment of the Oregon Trail.

By the time of his death there *was* an Oregon Trail, a maddening route of zigs and zags, detours and wanderings, but it was becoming defined through the hard-earned work of an Olympian roll call of trailbreakers: Robert Stuart (first to travel it west to east; discoverer of South Pass), Manuel Lisa, the Ashley-Henry brigades, Jedediah Smith, Jim Bridger, Thomas Fitzpatrick, Nathaniel Wyeth, Benjamin Bonneville, Jason Lee, the Whitmans and the Spaldings, the Bartleson-Bidwell party, and Elijah White.

All of these brush cutters, boulder movers, river forders, and mountain climbers crossed the path, almost literally, that led to Wilson Hunt's counting house in Saint Louis, and justly so: The Oregon Trail began there.

□

In 1842, the year Hunt died, Charles Dickens, the thirty-year-old author of *The Pickwick Papers, Oliver Twist, Nicholas Nickleby, Barnaby Rudge,* and *The Old Curiosity Shop,* came to Saint Louis at the end of his six-month American lecture tour. He landed in New York in January with two enormous portmanteaux and a mission: to talk about the detestable habit of American publishers of pirating the work of European authors and the crying need for an international copyright law. This was not a particularly inspiring theme for the man Daniel Webster said had "done more to ameliorate the condition of the English poor than all the statesmen that Great Britain has sent into Parliament." Dickens spoke poignantly of Sir Walter Scott, whose last days of indebtedness, the lecturer said, would have been lightened if the thieves of his work had paid a tithe of what was due him. But on his book-buccaneering exertions the Hartford *Times* spoke for many in editorializing, "It happens we want no advice on this subject." This attitude convinced Dickens, as it had Alexis de Tocqueville before him, that America had far less freedom of expression than the Americans boasted. He also found too little sympathy for his privately expressed views on slavery—"that most hideous blot and foul disgrace."

No matter his message, Dickens was a crowd-pleaser, especially so when he gave his brilliant readings from his works, each character coming alive through the theatrical quality of his voice. Three months into his tour, in every city he visited his admirers came out in enormous levees; he shook 600 hands every day and so enthusiastic were his auditors that they grabbed at his topper and cane and pulled the fur from his coat for souvenirs. After a great ball at the Carlton Hotel in New York he was so exhausted that he spent four days in bed to gather strength to move on.

When Dickens sailed for England in June, he had a six-month journal* of opinions on America and Americans, much of it negative, written in a dubious, seriocomic tone giving the reader the impression that these were the memoirs of a hapless victim of circumstance on a hellish junket of discovery. In truth, he had quickly sickened of America and Americans; he was revolted by the way men bolted their food and spit tobacco; thought it fatuous that women attended so many elevating lectures (presumably including his own); saw nearly every site as dreary and monotonous. Upon returning, after a more comfortable time among Englishmen in Toronto and Montreal, he wrote a friend, "I would not condemn you to a year's residence on this side of the Atlantic for any money,"

---

*The book based on it, *American Notes* (arrangements for which he had made before he sailed), went through four quick printings in a year and earned him £40,000. In this book and in the novel *Martin Chuzzlewit* (1844) Dickens took a literary revenge on the United States for ignoring his copyright pleas. His friend, William Makepeace Thackeray, refused to review *American Notes*, considering it "vulgar and flippant."

and to another who asked about a particular American acquaintance Dickens wrote, "I do not know the American gentleman, God forgive me for putting two such words together."

He traveled as far west as Saint Louis and as his steamer neared the Mississippi what minute traces of beauty and civilization he had seen in New England gave way to an enveloping primeval ugliness: "The trees were stunted in their growth," he wrote, "the banks were low and flat; the settlements and log-cabins fewer in number; their inhabitants more wan and wretched than any we had encountered before. No songs or birds were in the air, no pleasant scents, no moving lights and shadows from swift-passing clouds."

The juncture of the Missouri and Mississippi he found to be "A dismal swamp . . . teeming with rank, unwholesome vegetation, in whose baleful shade the wretched wanderers who are tempted hither droop and die, and lay their bones; the hateful Mississippi circling and eddying before it . . . a slimy monster hideous to behold; a hotbed of disease, an ugly sepulchre, a grave uncheered by any gleam of promise, a place without one single quality, in earth or air or water, to commend it; such is this dismal Cairo." To Dickens, the Father of Waters suffered from an appalling disease, and probably its bank-dwellers as well. He called it "an enormous ditch, sometimes two or three miles wide, running liquid mud, six miles an hour . . . the banks low, the trees dwarfish, the marshes swarming with frogs," and said "the wretched cabins" were few and far apart, "their inmates hollow-cheeked and pale, the weather very hot, mosquitos penetrating into every crack and crevice of the boat, mud and slime on everything."

In Saint Louis he stayed at Planter's House and observed the town's "crazy old tenements with blinking casements, such as may be seen in Flanders." He mentioned its wharves, warehouses, and shops, and found them wanting in comparison even to those in Cincinnati, found its heat and humidity unbearable and its vast tracts of undrained swampland giving off the vapors from which awful fevers were born.

"No man ever admits the unhealthiness of the place he dwells in (unless he is going away from it)," he said, "and I shall therefore,

I have no doubt, be at issue with the inhabitants of St. Louis in questioning the perfect salubrity of its climate, and in hinting that I think it must rather dispose to fever in the summer and autumnal seasons."

When Dickens saw it, Saint Louis had been incorporated as a city for only twenty years, and barely eighty years had passed since a primitive fur-trading post was raised on the site by Pierre de Laclède Liguest and named for the sainted thirteenth-century king Louis IX. From those muddy origins in 1764 and thereafter, Saint Louis was to the American fur trade what Michilimackinac, the Grand Portage, and Fort William were to the Canadian fur trade, a frontier entrepôt where trapping brigades were fitted out to venture to the Rocky Mountains and beyond, where furs were received and shipped out and supplies and goods were received.

In Astor's time, the decade of the Louisiana Purchase, when Saint Louis fell into the American sphere, the town was "the centre of rude bustle and business activity," Bancroft wrote. Its original Creole population, descendants of French colonists, were mixed with "keen, trafficking New Englanders; brawny backwoodsmen of the western frontier; tall, big-boned specimens of the unwashed and untaught corn-bread-and-bacon-fed of Tennessee, Kentucky, Illinois, and Missouri." With these were *coureurs de bois* and *voyageurs* from Canada, Indians of many tribes and half-breeds from the prairies, and some who drifted down from the Rocky Mountains; keen traders from the Atlantic states; vagrants, shopkeepers, speculators, and extravagant, bragging boatmen as well as "lavish, loud-joking, royal American pedlers" who "were then beginning to practice their pistolings, knife exercises, and card-waxing for the forty years of commercial throat-cutting, highway blackguardism, and unique boat-racing and boiler-bursting which were to follow."

This motley populace, which Washington Irving said was prone to pass its time "in idleness and revelry about the trading posts or settlements; squandering their hard earnings in heedless conviviality, and rivaling their neighbors, the Indians, in indolent indulgence and an impudent disregard of the morrow," had changed but little when Dickens' bile rose upon visiting the town. The Canadian

woods runners and canoemen had departed, but most of the others
were still there, following their several bents, among these a new
profession for the old trapper-explorer of the western frontier. By
1842, Bancroft's "leathern-frocked frontiersmen" were now guiding emigrant parties out of the Saint Louis gateway and into the
air and elbowroom of the far West.

2

Once inside the gateway to the West, commonly at Saint Louis or
its environs on the west bank of the Mississippi, the typical Pacific-
bound emigrant followed the Missouri River 250 miles westward
to Independence, a log hamlet on a nicely timbered bluff three miles
inland from the Big Muddy's great northward bend, forty miles
downstream from Fort Leavenworth, and just inside the border of
the United States.

The first cabins at Independence had been thrown up in 1827
and grew into a helter-skelter collection of low-roofed log and
adobe huts, taverns, and stores. The area then became the chief
staging area for trade caravans setting out on the 780-mile-long
Santa Fé Trail and the departure point for fur brigades heading for
the Rockies and beyond. In 1833 its main steamboat landing
washed away and pilots had to find a new one a few miles upstream, at Westport Landing, and the time would come when Saint
Joseph, fifty miles to the northwest, would become the favored
launching place for overland caravans. But Independence had a
running start, and by 1841 it had a permanent population of perhaps 800 and a transient one of 7,000 to 10,000 in the peak spring
season. There were dry-goods stores there, and barbershops, saloons, a church or two, harness-making, wheelwright, and blacksmith shops—all booming businesses. There were even a few
refined homes above the riverbank and a plain where the canvas
tents of the emigrant trains gave off their lantern glow at night.

Nathan Boone, Daniel's youngest son, visited the town early in

its history and called it "Eden," and Joseph Smith, the founding
father of Mormonism, spoke of it in 1831. God had revealed to
him "The land of Missouri," he said, "the land which I have appointed and consecrated for the gathering of the Saints." He had
found the land of promise and the place for the city of Zion: "Behold, the place which is now called Independence." (Joseph Smith
was murdered in Carthage, Illinois, in 1844, and Missouri turned
out to be an earthly hell to Mormons. The Zion he sought became
the city founded on the Great Salt Lake of Utah by his successor,
Brigham Young.)

No one who passed through Independence in the 1830s forgot
its *noise*. Saint Louis had its din, too, but was big enough for it to
thin out and even had genteel places where the loudest sounds were
the click of billiard balls and the tinkling of a piano. Not so in the
tiny Bedlam on the fringe of the immense solitude and stillness of
the western prairies. Independence seemed to have been born in a
cacophony that never let up.

The racket began at the steamboat slips at Independence Landing, where the tall-stacked paddle wheelers offloaded their com-
plements of traders, trappers, and emigrant parties and the
encumbrances of each amid the raucous hooting of steam-whistles,
clanging of bells, and slamming down of landing ramps. The trail
to Independence was a pandemonium of braying mules and
squawking chickens, quarreling emigrants, blaspheming stevedores
and teamsters, the hiss and pop of bullwhips, gunshots announcing
pack-train arrivals, the rattle of buckets and tinware hanging on
creaking wagons—the din rising in volume and tempo in the town
itself.

Francis Parkman, a handsome, long-nosed twenty-three-year-
old Bostonian and Harvard man, came through the town in May
1846, en route to Fort Laramie and the writing of his enduring
classic, *The Oregon Trail*. He had taken passage on a steamer out
of Saint Louis, in a throng, he said, of "Santa Fe traders, gamblers,
speculators, and adventurers of various descriptions," the boat's
steerage "crowded with Oregon emigrants, mountain men, negroes,

and a party of Kansas Indians." Thus laden, the steamer struggled upriver for seven or eight days* against the rapid current of the Missouri, "grating upon snags, and hanging for two or three hours at a time upon sandbars." Close to the landing place he began to see "signs of the great western movement that was taking place. Parties of emigrants with their tents and wagons were encamped on open spots near the bank, on their way to the common rendezvous at Independence."

Parkman watched a train of emigrant wagons from Illinois pass through, saw children's faces peeping out from under the wagon covers, and "Here and there a buxom damsel was seated on horseback, holding over her sunburnt face an old umbrella or a parasol, once gaudy enough, but now miserably faded." He allowed, however, that not all the emigrants were of such innocent stamp. "Among them are some of the vilest outcasts in the country," he said.

He, too, made note of the noise: "A multitude of shops had sprung up to furnish the emigrants and Santa Fe travelers with necessaries for their journey and there was an incessant hammering and banging from a dozen backsmiths' sheds, where the heavy wagons were being repaired, and the horses and oxen shod."

Added to the anvil and animal sounds, the red-clay streets of Independence pulsed with the shouts, curses, buzz, and laughter of its swarming transient populace. J. Quinn Thornton, an observer there at the height of the Oregon Trail migration, called the town "a great Babel of African slaves [probably black stevedores], indolent dark-skinned Spaniards [Mexicans], profane and dust-laden bullwhackers going to and from Santa Fe with their immense wagons, and emigrant families bound for the Pacific, all cheerful and intent in their embarkation upon the great prairie wilderness." He omitted to mention the Indians, mostly Kaws and Shawnee, but also wanderers from other tribes from all points of the compass;

---

*The trip normally took five days or less, depending on the river's height above the mud that gave it its nickname.

and Mormons, soldiers out of Fort Leavenworth, mountain men searching for guide work, and a miscellany of drifters, drunks, and gamblers hanging around the groggeries and camps looking for somebody to rob. Some of the transients, Bernard De Voto said, had as their only motive in being on the edge of nowhere "was to see the elephant* wherever the elephant might be."

There were plenty of idlers in Independence, but not among those who intended having a pretty fair and lingering view of the elephant. The emigrants, many of them farmers who had scraped together every dime they could find for the journey, had no time to waste. They unloaded their dismantled wagons, their animals, chicken coops, plows, furniture, bales, and boxes of supplies at the steamer landing, then reassembled the wagons, hitched their teams, and snaked them to the high ground three miles south of the Independence town square. Some brought their precious cash and sparse belongings and bought their rigs in the town; some, satisfied that they had everything they needed, avoided the town and searched out the rendezvous points, camps with names like Fitzhugh's Mill, Indian Creek, Elm Grove, and Sapling Grove, to await others coming in. At these places the trains were organized, captains and other "officers" elected (often with heated debate), and guides and emigrant leaders pored over their maps and inspected the wagons, ensuring that the draft animals were shod and fed.

Independence and its neighboring outfitting places had their busiest season in April, May, and early June, and for a distinct and critical purpose. The idea was to await the greening of the prairie grass before kicking off the wagon brakes and lurching northwest toward the Platte River. The journey to the Pacific was a 2,000-

---

*This was a popular phrase for the westering adventure. In the 1840s, few Americans had actually seen an elephant and fewer in the country beyond the Missouri frontier. The trails west were thus "paths to the elephant." The "turnarounds," those who went as far as they dared then turned back to civilization, were said to have "seen enough of the elephant." A recently published emigrant memoir by C. G. Hinman is titled *A Pretty Fair View of the Elephant*.

mile treadmill on which the pioneer family and its ox- and mule-drawn wagon averaged fifteen miles a day—barring disasters. Five months out of Independence to Oregon or California was an excellent pace and leaving later than the first week of June was perilous: There were mountains to cross, and winter closed suddenly and with a vengeance in the passes.

3

While the general outline of the Oregon Trail had been emerging for thirty years before John C. Frémont made his first expedition to the Rocky Mountains, he clarified it, popularized it, and dispensed with certain tenacious myths about it.

When he set out from Saint Louis with his exploring and mapping party in June 1842, he was but twenty-nine years old, a barely tested army topographical engineer yet to inspire poets such as Whittier, Longfellow, and Joaquin Miller as Daniel Boone had inspired Lord Byron. Yet even at twenty-nine he had a record of accomplishment, and he now had powerful forces behind him. For one thing, maybe the main thing for his present purposes, he had married well.

The son of a French adventurer and a pretty American teacher, Frémont's unmarried parents moved from his birthplace in Savannah, Georgia, to Nashville, Tennessee, in 1813, and within days of their arrival there occurred one of our history's momentous coincidences: Within a few days of taking rooms in Nashville's City Hotel, baby John Charles received a pistol-shot introduction to a future president of the United States, to his future father-in-law, and to his future wife's namesake.

In the lobby of the hotel that September day, General Andrew Jackson, fresh from his battles against Creek Indians, and the Benton brothers, Jesse and Thomas Hart, both Tennessee soldiers who had fought with Jackson in the late war with Britain, engaged in a gunfight. The origin of the fracas remains obscure, but Jackson had recently served as "second" for a close friend in a duel with Jesse

Benton and while neither duelist had been seriously injured, the Benton brothers saw Jackson's participation as a personal affront and betrayal. In the City Hotel lobby, after some insults and challenges were issued, guns were drawn and Jackson took a ball in the shoulder, following which the general's retinue got into the fight, as did former militia colonel and Tennessee state senator Thomas Hart Benton. More wild shots were exchanged, but somehow order was restored and there were no further casualties.

In the Frémonts' upstairs room, a stray bullet is said to have knocked plaster off the wall where the baby, John Charles, lay sleeping. His mother fainted.

The affair was a splendidly bizarre curtain-raiser for an adventurer's life.

The elder Frémont died in Charleston, South Carolina, in 1818, leaving the family in poverty. John Charles, exceptionally bright, managed to attend Charleston College briefly at age fifteen (he was expelled for "incorrigible negligence") and through the efforts of a family friend, the botanist and statesman Joel Poinsett, won appointment in 1838 as lieutenant in the army's newly organized Corps of Topographical Engineers. In Washington three years later, Frémont was introduced to Senator Thomas Hart Benton, one-time Tennessee politician, soldier, and hotel-lobby fighter. Now representing Missouri, he was among the most persuasive voices in Congress for the exploration of the trans-Mississippi West, known for bellowing "The *facts*! What are the *facts*?" when he rose to challenge what he considered a dubious senatorial issue. He had another noteworthy feature: his towering egocentrism, so pronounced that a journalist described it as "so part and parcel of the man, that it is not at all offensive, but a sort of national institution in which every patriotic American could take a just pride."

Whether the two men exchanged notes on the matter of their peculiar 1813 propinquity is not known, but they became friends, Benton seeing in the dashing lieutenant the pattern of youth, boldness, intelligence, and ambition ideal for an agent of expansionism.

Their long association and friendship faltered seriously only once, when Frémont fell in love with Benton's tomboyish daughter

Jessie, second of his six children. She was seventeen and Frémont twenty-eight when the two eloped and married on October 18, 1841. Jessie soothed her father's anger and John Charles was welcomed into the family.

In Washington, the Frémonts met and charmed the capital elite—Senator Lewis Linn, Benton's expansionist partner; Senator Daniel Webster; General Winfield Scott; and President John Tyler among them. At the time, Tyler was not friendly toward the idea of any government-sponsored move into the Oregon Country; he wanted no confrontation with England to interfere with the matters receiving his closest attention, such as the issue of annexing Texas. Even so, he did not oppose a bill sponsored by Benton, which appropriated $30,000 for a topographical party to be led by the brilliant mathematician and cartographer Joseph Nicollet. The expedition's mission was to reconnoiter the opening stretch of the overland route for Oregon-bound emigrants from western Missouri through South Pass in the Rocky Mountains.

Nicollet had been Frémont's mentor in 1839 during a survey of the Minnesota and Dakota territories, and when the frail scientist's health failed on the eve of his departure to South Pass, his protégé was given the command.

In June 1842 Frémont set out from Saint Louis with twenty-eight men, twenty of them listed as *voyageurs*, together with a German cartographer, Charles Preuss, and, as guide, the Kentuckian Christopher Houston Carson, who in his thirty-two years had tramped and trapped the West from Santa Fé to California, from the Gila River to the northern Rockies. The Frémont-Carson partnership, which would be sustained through many more expeditions and tribulations in the future, would be compared to that of Lewis and Clark, Burton and Speke, Stanley and Livingstone.

The explorers followed the Kansas River and moved northwest to the Platte, thence up the North Platte toward the Rocky Mountains. On August 8, averaging twenty miles a day, they reached South Pass. Frémont was disappointed in this unprepossessing saddle at the Continental Divide, comparing its ascent to climbing Capitol Hill, and hastened on. His instructions from his superiors at Topographical Corps headquarters in Washington called for him to turn back after reaching and mapping the pass, but, not for the last time, he ignored orders. The party pushed on northwest and set up camp in the Wind River Mountains.

On the return trip, Frémont gathered six of his men in a rubber boat to shoot some Platte River rapids, a foolish venture that came to near disaster when the boat hit a submerged rock and flipped over, taking all his scientific papers to the bottom. Fortunately, duplicates of the journals and maps were carried by the main party.

The expedition reached Fort Laramie at the end of August and Saint Louis in October. In Washington, with Preuss turning out a map and meteorological table, Frémont collaborated with his wife in writing a hefty report to Congress. When it was published and offered to the public, it became a sensation, thanks to Jessie Benton Frémont's literary gifts and her husband's voluminous and meticulous observations and eye for poetic detail. Instead of the customary dusty, officious, fact-foundered explorer narratives of the past, Frémont's *A Report of an Exploration of the Country Lying Between the Missouri River and the Rocky Mountains on the Line of the Kansas and Great Platte Rivers* gave the Twenty-seventh Congress something no Congress had received before: a *book*, beautifully organized and written. It contained lovely descriptive passages such as the rendering of the Wind River Range as "a gigantic disorder of enormous masses, and a savage sublimity of naked rock, in a wonderful contrast with innumerable green spots of rich floral beauty, shut up in their stern recesses." Even the text's data on terrain, weather, soil and water, vegetation and wildlife were lively, as was its advice on where forts should be built, and where good campsites might be located. The book also disproved the "Great American Desert" myth of the Great Plains favored by Major Stephen H. Long in 1819–20.

By the time the *Report* was published in March 1843, Frémont had packed his telescope, sextant, and pocket chronometer and was deep in preparations for a return to South Pass, this time to push on to the Oregon Country. He had thirty-nine men, including Kit Carson again as guide and Charles Preuss again as cartographer, and they started west in May 1843, on what became a fourteen-month milestone in American exploration, the most significant expedition since Lewis and Clark.

Frémont's party followed the footsteps of the 1842 journey to South Pass, then turned south and east toward the Great Salt Lake, arriving there on September 9. After a stopover at Fort Hall, they followed the Snake River to Fort Boisé and reached Fort Vancouver on November 8, 1843, where they observed a small but steady stream of emigrants arriving on the Columbia and moving south to the verdant valley of the Willamette.

As was his often near-fatal habit, Frémont ignored orders to lead his men home after reaching the Pacific. In mid-January 1844, he and his men reached an enormous (188 square miles in size, it turned out) and stunningly pristine lake in western Nevada, which he named Pyramid Lake for the rock formations around it, and there planned to cross the mountains into Mexican California. Whether this decision was his own alone or inspired by his father-in-law and the public clamor for information on California, it was a dangerous idea that must have bothered even such a loyalist as Kit Carson. It was winter, and the Sierra Nevada's cold savagery nearly cost them their lives. Their horses slipped on the icy trails, many died of hunger or were slaughtered for food (of their 104 mules and horses, thirty-three survived); their Indian guides wisely deserted them; they suffered from starvation, snowblindness, and frostbite. They were fortunate: That Sierra winter was a mild one, and on February 6, 1844, Frémont and a scouting party climbed on snowshoes to the top of a promontory south of Lake Tahoe. "Far below us, dimmed by the distance," the explorer wrote, "was a large snowless valley, bounded on the western side, at a distance of about a hundred miles, by a low range of mountains, which Carson recognized with delight as the mountains bordering the coast."

The overlook gave them a panoramic view of the Sacramento valley and they reached Sutter's Fort, the oasis at the juncture of the American and Sacramento Rivers, in early March. John Augustus Sutter, the Swiss emigré who had built the fort on the land granted him by the Mexican government, welcomed Frémont and his men, as he did all Americans. Of their arrival, he recorded, "The starvation and fatigue they had endured rendered them truly deplorable objects."

Among the expedition's accomplishments was the exploration and the Preuss map of what Frémont named the "Great Basin," the vast tract of mountains, deserts, and plains between the Wasatch Mountains of Utah and the Sierra Nevadas; the navigation of the "magnificent object," as Frémont called the Great Salt Lake (explored in a leaky rubber boat at a time when the party was reduced to eating stewed skunk); and the first dependable map and description of the surrounding Bear River basin.* They had mapped the waterways, vital to California-bound pioneers, that rose in the desert and then vanished in the sand before ever reaching the ocean: the Humboldt, which meandered across southern Utah before disappearing into a swampy lake bed Frémont named the Humboldt Sink; and the river that flowed easterly from the Sierras to its terminus in the Carson Sink, named for the expedition's scout.

(Frémont *named* the Humboldt—formerly called Mary's River—but only rediscovered it. In 1833, Joseph Reddeford Walker, another of the Tennessee brotherhood of mountain men and at the time an associate of Benjamin Bonneville, led a trapping party of forty men to the river and made an arduous three-week crossing of the Sierra Nevada, descending between the Merced and Tuolumne Rivers. In the same expedition, Walker and his men discovered Yosemite Valley and were the first Americans to see the giant sequoia trees. Frémont was aware of the accomplishments of those who had gone before him and did not claim the "Pathfinder" title overly romantic writers bestowed on him.)

The expedition reached Saint Louis in August 1844.

---

*Charles Preuss's maps were used by Brigham Young, and Frémont's narrative prompted the Mormon leader to move his followers to the Salt Lake valley in 1847.

Frémont would make many westward journeys in his tumultuous life, but his second expedition remained the most momentous, and his second *Report* even more widely read and admired than the first. For the Oregon-bound, Frémont's new book, published in 1845, added an immense amount of data on the emigrant route there: topography, Indian inhabitants, game and plant life, and an optimistic view for the country. "Commercially, the value of the Oregon Country must be great," he wrote, "washed as it is by the north Pacific Ocean—fronting Asia—producing many of the elements of commerce—mild and healthy in its climate—and becoming, as it naturally will, a thoroughfare for the East India and China trade."

He had not discovered the Oregon Trail, but for the westering folk gathering in camps and rendezvous places around Independence and Westport Landing, he had mapped it, fixed on paper its waterways and landmarks, and made a perilous journey safer by telling everything he had learned about it.

Part Five

MEDICINE ROAD

19

TOWARD THE ELEPHANT

"NOTHING IS WISE THAT DOES NOT HELP YOU ALONG. . . ."

1

Getting to Oregon took more than a route, a guide, grit, and work; it took money, and by 1840s standards, and the wage of the average emigrant, a lot of it. Sailing-ship passage was out of the question for most people. It was too expensive, too inaccessible, and too nightmarish for a farm family to contemplate. A thousand dollars was not an unusual fare for the 13,000-mile voyage out of New York or Boston, and the price was not much less from New Orleans. Either way, it was going to take five or six months on a converted merchantman butting the terrifying seas off Cape Horn to the Pacific. In 1846 a treaty opened a shortcut across the Isthmus of Panama, cutting the journey by two months' time but adding new horrors: Passengers had to travel the malarial Chagres River by dugout canoes, the last miles by muleback or on foot to Panama City on the Pacific side, and then wait and hope to catch passage on a vessel heading for the Sandwich Islands, or the Alta California or Oregon coast.

Walking the 2,000 miles or so from Independence or the other frontier settlements to the Columbia was cheaper, even though everything but the walking cost cash.

Bernard De Voto estimated that the average family "outfit"— wagon, draft animals, tools, food, and supplies—was worth from $700 to $1,500, the money deriving from selling a farm, liquidating a small business, borrowing, pooling, scraping together. The really poor man with nothing to liquidate had to hire out as a laborer, camp helper, hunter, or teamster, carrying his kit on his back and working for his meals. Many men, and some families, started out on foot with no wagon or even a horse, toting survival essentials and hoping to attach themselves to an emigrant train. One man became an Oregon Trail celebrity of sorts as he made his way west pushing a wheelbarrow containing a few tools, some spare clothing, and food.

For the farm-seller and family with the money to invest, the immediate matters to attend to, before or after reaching Saint Louis, involved wagons, what to put in them, and the animals to pull them.

By 1843 there were guidebooks, memoirs, and advice aplenty from those who had made the journey (and a great deal of advice from those who hadn't). All these authorities were in general agreement on the ideal of a light load in a light wagon drawn by strong, healthy animals. Like all ideals, this one was easily stated and difficult to practice. Of course dependable authority Marcus Whitman, despite his own failure to take one beyond Fort Hall, believed that wagons were essential for families to reach the Columbia River valley.

Wagon wisdom, refined over the years since the Whitmans and the Spaldings made their overland journey in 1836, drifted toward the ideal. Few of the Oregon Trail wagons of the 1840s resembled the ponderous, big-wheeled, boat-curved Conestogas used by freighting outfits. Whether set aside when farms were sold, or custom built (at a cost of $60–$100), the typical overland wagon was generally light, made of hickory or maple as often as oak, springless and straight-bedded, the wagon box ten to twelve feet long, four feet wide, and two deep. The box, generally overloaded at the start of the journey with 3,000 pounds or more of goods and belongings, was packed four feet deep with a narrow passage down the middle. At the bottom were the big, heavy items, like plows, bedsteads, stoves, chests, and bags of seeds; then a layer of kitchen utensils and clothing; and on top the immediate necessities: water kegs, cooking pots, axes, firearms, bags of flour, salt and coffee beans, blankets, and the like. False bottoms provided extra storage for spare wagon parts, and a jockey box up front or mounted on the side of the bed held tools for repairs.

Wagon wheels were complex structures of carefully fitted components: curved oaken or bois d'arc felloes pegged or clamped together on which the iron tires were bolted; heavy spokes socketed into the felloes; massive hubs; all, excepting the tires, bolts, and supporting strap iron, fashioned of wood, since metal was too heavy and too difficult to repair in the wilderness. The rear wheels were commonly five to six feet in diameter and the front ones smaller, four feet or so, to permit sharp turns and to prevent them from jamming against the wagon box. The wheels were dished outward for stabilization and removed by cranking up the bed with a jack.

The wagon undercarriage was a cunning arrangement keyed to a kingpin, the main front pivot, running through a wooden "box bolster," a support on which the wagon box rested. Brakes consisted of hardwood blocks levered against the rear wheels. The running gear was greased from a bucket suspended from the rear axle.

Wagon covers were made of double thicknesses of canvas (often made of hemp, an important cash crop in Missouri and the deep South), drill, or sailcloth, waterproofed with paint or linseed oil and fixed to hickory bows and puckered with ropes rove through their hems. The grimy white covers, billowing and popping in the wind as the wagons crawled across the grasslands, inspired the image of the "prairie schooner," but the name took on a decidedly unromantic meaning at certain river crossings where timber was unavailable for raft building. On such occasions the wagon boxes were caulked and sheathed in rawhide or tarpaulin coated with oakum and tallow, the running gear removed and placed inside the box, and the box floated across swollen waterways with cursing, sputtering men handling the guide ropes.

On the downhill side of steep mountain slopes, the wheels had to be locked in place by chains threaded through the spokes and fastened to the bed, the wagon then skidded downhill with curved iron shoes attached to the motionless wheels to prevent them from developing flat spots.

People walked alongside their wagons, occasionally taking a rest on a "lazy board," a seat projecting from the side of the box, or on horseback or mule-back. In camp in bad weather a family would sleep on top of the load under the canvas; otherwise, they lived outside the wagon and walked alongside it.

□

The enduring debate among outfitters, teamsters, and overland travelers had to do with the critical matter of the best animals to pull the wagon. Horses were seldom a part of the argument. They were needed by outriders and hunters, but were not practical as draft animals. They were too expensive ($200 for a good one), they did not forage well on the dry grass of the plains so their feed had to be supplemented by grain carried along in the train, they were prone to distemper from drinking alkaline water, too easily plagued by flies and mosquitoes, and they lacked the strength required to pull a heavy wagon.

Both mules and oxen had strong adherents. Oxen covered less ground in a day but were "easy keepers" and cost less: forty to sixty-five dollars for an ox three to five years old, ninety or a hundred dollars for a five-year-old Missouri mule. The ox required no expensive harness, collars, or trees, only a double hickory yoke about four feet long with up-and-over curves at each end, holes bored in it to receive the ends of the oxbow, and a croquet wicket–shaped loop that ran under the animal's neck, kept in place by wooden "keys," wedges, or cotter pins. A swinging iron ring carried the wagon pole.

Oxen worked in pairs, or yokes, with a minimum of two but usually three yokes for each wagon, plus a spare or two. The biggest animals would be yoked just ahead of the wagon for the hardest work.

Some emigrants with enough pooled money hired teamsters, but most managed their wagons on their own. Oxen trained to the yoke as calves were driven by a bullwhacker walking alongside them with an eighteen-foot braided rawhide whip with a "popper" at the end. The bullwhip was held by its two-foot-long handle, and was swung backward, then in a circle over the driver's head, then forward to crack over the animals' ears. Goads, long sticks with a spike at the end, were also used, but sparingly—no good teamster injured his animals with whip or goad—and occasionally the lead ox would have a rope hooked over his horns and jerked to get his attention.

Oxen were controlled with the standard shouts of "Gee!", "Haw!", and "Whoa!" but they were often unresponsive to such orders. A familiar Oregon Trail tableau was that of ox teams straining against their yokes, heads low, snorting and blowing the dust and burned-over prairie grass from their nostrils, heaving their overloaded wagons forward with chains rattling, axles shrieking, and whips popping loud as pistol shots—all this as the grimy, sun-scoured drivers cursed above the din.

Oxen had disadvantages: They tended to recklessness when thirsty or overheated and would sometimes stampede to a water hole or stream. On such occasions nothing could be done to stop them until they were sated and bogged down in mud. In this characteristic they differed from the other animals in the train, including the humans, only in their bulk and corresponding water requirements and capacity.

The greatest problem oxen presented as draft animals was the tendency for their hooves to wear and split on rocky ground. Cracked hooves were "cured" by drawing a string soaked in hot tar through the split. They were shod with small parenthesis-shaped iron shoes nailed on each side of the cloven hoof, but the average ox was uncooperative in this operation and when his hooves needed examining often lay down with his feet tucked under him. Ox-shoeing was a difficult procedure even in a blacksmith's shop, where the animal had to be driven headfirst into a timbered stall, canvas slings placed under its belly so the beast could be hoisted by a windlass, and its feet tied to a rail for shoeing. On the prairie, the whole thing was hellish: A trench was dug and the terrified ox wrestled into it upside down, the kicking feet lashed together and held while the shoes were tacked on. If spare shoes had been used up between outposts on the trail pieces of thick leather were used as substitutes, or the hooves were smeared with tar and grease and buffalo-hide booties fastened on. Some teamsters were able to rope, tie, and shoe the animals without the trench method, but it was a dangerous business either way.

An emigrant wagon required a minimum of six mules to draw 2,000 pounds and in addition to costing more per animal and requiring relatively expensive harness, they had to be driven, meaning relays of men had to sit on the jouncing wagon for hours on end. Mules were faster than oxen and endured the heat better, but they were sulkier too, shying at sudden noises, and even at shadows, and bolting for no apparent reason—"much given to mayhem," in Merrill J. Mattes' felicitous phrase. Mules were tough and durable, and if a wagon broke down beyond repair mules became pack animals, which oxen did not; on the other hand, Indians would steal a mule but not an ox, and a dead ox made better eating than a dead mule.

Peter Burnett of Indiana, who made his Oregon Trail journey in 1843, said, "The ox is the most noble animal, patient, thrifty, durable, gentle. Those who come to this country will be in love with their oxen by the time they get here."

That nobility struck many a westering family on the Oregon Trail as with rags soaked in camphor clapped to their noses they passed the rotting carcasses of hundreds of oxen that had been shot for food or perished from hunger, thirst, and overwork. One such witness wrote, "There ought to be a Heaven for all ox that perish under the yoke, where they could roam in the fields of sweet clover and timothy."

□

Early travelers on the Oregon Trail offered valuable advice to the emigrants moving out from the rendezvous places around Independence: For families with children, take a milk cow (and hang a bucket of milk from the wagon undercarriage—it'll bounce and make butter); take a few head of cattle if possible, and maybe some chickens in a coop lashed to the tailgate. They can be let out in camp to forage on bugs and worms and kids can be given the chore of chicken-wrangler to gather them up before the dawn departure. Above all, take spares and extras: spare horse; spare draft animals; extra shoes, yokes, chains and harness; and wagon parts—axles, tongues, wheels, spokes, oxbows, kingbolts and tonguebolts. Take good water kegs and plenty of rope, light for picketing animals and general chores, heavy for lowering wagons down slopes and towing wagon boxes across water. Take whiskey for dosing animals poisoned by bad water, and a medicine chest for sick humans; take rifles and shotguns, powder, lead and bullet molds, lanterns, extra boots and socks. Take duck trousers, flannel shirts and woolen long johns; ladies take gingham and sunbonnets.

As to provender, experience said to go light on rice and beans—they take too long to cook—and heavy on cornmeal, for johnnycakes, biscuits, and the like. Take flour, dried fruit and vegetables (anti-scorbutics), hardtack, salt, coffee, tea, sugar, molasses, vinegar, saleratus (baking soda), wrapped bacon sunk in a barrel of bran or cornmeal to keep it from spoiling, eggs treated the same way. Take matches sealed in corked bottles and gutta-percha or painted canvas cloths for sleeping on wet ground. Follow Doctor Marcus Whitman's dictum—"Nothing is wise that does not help you along; nothing is good for you that causes a moment's delay"—and take nothing except what is absolutely essential to getting to your destination.

Randolph Barnes Marcy of Greenwich, Massachusetts, an army officer who led emigrant caravans to California in gold rush years, listed in his popular *Prairie Traveller* the minimum "allowance of provisions for each grown person" heading to the Pacific from Missouri, good for four months: 150 pounds of flour or its equivalent in hard bread (hardtack); twenty-five pounds of bacon or pork, and "enough fresh beef to be driven on the hoof to make up the meat component of the ration," fifteen pounds of coffee, twenty-five pounds of sugar, "plus saleratus or yeast powders for making bread, and salt and pepper."

No matter the advice and voices of experience, the wagons crawling west were packed to the sideboards and four or more feet deep with the very superfluities Doctor Whitman and Marcy warned against. Some of these, such as the tools of a farmer's trade—plows, axes, hoes, hammers, kegs of nails, bucksaws, spades, augurs, and whetstones—seemed absolute essentials for one expecting to build a cabin and cultivate a subsistence crop in the wilderness. Other things were carried along because they brought a remnant of civilized life to a savage land: claw-footed tables, heirloom chiffoniers, cast-iron skillets and cookpots, "thunder mugs" (chamber pots), washbowls, rocking chairs, books, churns, bedsteads, feather mattresses, quilts, and bundled clothing.

The opening shake-down miles of the journey determined what the real necessities were and what had to be sacrificed as the ox and mule teams reached rough country and the first serious water crossings. The jettisoning process began a few miles out from the Missouri frontier, took a serious turn near the head of Grand Island, Nebraska, and became more serious by the time Fort Laramie was reached. All along the Oregon Trail load-lightening relics were strewn among the carcasses of oxen and mules: stacks of bacon rotting in the sun—as much as a half-ton in some places—trunks, mattresses, carpenter tools, saddles, sawmill equipment, mining augurs, anvils, bellows, crowbars, scythes, gold washers, plows, grindstones, baking ovens, harness, kegs and barrels, books and furniture, and fatally broken wagons.

Passersby scavaged among these pickings, finding needed wagon parts, tools, and miscellaneous treasures. One posted sign urged HELP YOURSELF, and one pioneer wrote home: "Don't bother to bring cooking stoves. I could pick up one anywhere."

2

Oregon Trail journeyers were a freewheeling lot who were apt to turn their wagons off the roadway with no notice to see the sights or take a rest from eating dust. They wore down their stock, threw up hasty camp corrals that let their animals wander, were late making camp, dallied at starting out in the morning, groused at taking their sentry-duty turn or at doing any other communal chore, argued and fought among themselves, occasionally with real violence. What discipline could be imposed came from their elected train captain and his subordinates or from their guide, but the emigrant trains never abided the rigid marching orders and military order of the Santa Fé trade trains or Brigham Young's Mormons.

They did work assiduously once a campground was selected by the guide, usually on the basis of water, grass, and firewood availability, all three of which were abundant in the early miles of the journey and in the first months of Oregon Trail traffic but became more precious later on.

The Platte River had lush grass along its banks and, early on, plenty of trees on its islands. Its water, brown with suspended silt, had to be filtered through cloth or with a handful of meal in a bucket to settle the mud. Some emigrants boiled their water, not to kill bacteria, which were their unknown, but to get rid of the minnows, "wiggletails"—mosquito larvae—and whatever else was swimming in it. Francis Parkman, in his 1846 journey on the trail, wrote of dipping a tin cup in the Platte after a long ride in the scorching sun and discovering "a troop of young tadpoles sporting in the bottom of my cup." Platte water, called a "Platte River cocktail" when taken straight, warm, brackish, and muddy, had an additional quality: One emigrant wrote home that it "partakes of the same laxative qualities of the Missouri and Mississippi." Where water was scarce clothing could not be washed; when water was found there was great rejoicing, not only to replenish the casks but to bathe, wash clothes, and boil diapers, which in waterless days had to be scraped, dampened, dried, and reused. Unknown to the emigrants, the boiling of water helped check the spread of infectious diseases.

Before the Platte islands were denuded of their trees, willow, poplar, and cottonwood were chopped and gathered by the armload. In tall-grass country, children were dispatched from camp to make twists of prairie grass, slough grass, or hay called "cats," which burned well when dry and burned smokily when green or wet. A better fuel—hotter, slower burning, and odorless—was what the French called *bois de vache*, buffalo "wood," the chips of dried dung gathered by women in their aprons and by kids in large sacks. The gatherers did not at first relish the idea of handling the dung—a trail song said,

> Look *at her now with a pout on her lips*
> *As daintily with her fingertips*
> *She picks for the fire some buffalo chips*

—but the pout soon disappeared of necessity. With the rule that "three bushels make a good fire," the chips were collected, placed in a shallow firehole, lit using dry grass as tinder, and the cookpots were then suspended over the fire. (An extra benefit: One or two smoldering chips brought inside a wagon chased mosquitoes away.)

As the trains moved beyond the Platte to the Sweetwater and buffalo thinned and disappeared, the chips were genuinely missed, being far preferable to knotty chunks of pungent sagebrush, which burned too quickly.

In buffalo country, along the succulent grasslands of the Platte where they thrived, where as late as 1850 emigrants were seeing them in a solid phalanx of so many thousands they took two hours or more to pass, the herds were so frighteningly immense that guns had to be fired to prevent the camp from being trampled. The signal of their advent was always a low, distant thunder-like rumbling followed by clouds of dust on the horizon. Then the ground shook as they passed, 2,000 or 10,000 at a time, so closely bunched their horns clacked and rattled against each other.

Buffalo were easily, and therefore cruelly and wastefully, killed. Shot and wounded, lurching about with broken backs and on mangled legs, blinded by shotgun blasts, spouting blood, they were fallen on by hunters with long throat-slitting knives and often butchered before their hearts were still. Buffalo tongues, rib, and hump meat were prized by most, although not by all. Some found the meat inedible even after hours of boiling or roasting, creating an unswallowable bolus when chewed. Jerky, made by soaking strips of meat in brine and drying them over fires or in the sun, was to many the only way to eat buffalo. In truth, however it was cooked, little of the animal was eaten, usually no more than a few pounds of a beast weighing 800 to 1,200 pounds (full-grown bulls could weigh two tons and more). The rest was left to the wolves and coyotes who always haunted the herds awaiting the chance to hamstring a calf or feast on the bloating carcasses left behind by human slaughterers.

The Platte River valley offered a variety of other game for the hunters, and for a time cookpots and skillets steamed and sizzled not only with the customary daily fare of bacon, cornmeal johnnycakes, stewed apples, and coffee, but with the meat of pronghorn antelope, sage hens, rabbits, plover, pigeons, marsh quails, snipe, and even black bears near the Platte forks. There were also edible greens to be gathered, including onions, which were good for protection against scurvy, and berries—goose, black, blue, serviceberries, purple and black chokeberries—to add to the diet.

On the Oregon Trail, as at home, women carried as much of the workload as the men—and sometimes more. They not only gathered fuel, picked greens and fruit, cooked, and tended the children, but they also helped herd the animals and often marched alongside their wagons with bullwhip at the ready. To perform such work, womenfolk discovered early that the trail required modification of their clothing. Their long cotton or linsey-woolsey skirts dragged on the ground, became tattered by brush and rock, were rendered drab by soaking rains and river crossings, and were scorched by cookfires. Some wives wore their husbands' spare trousers,* flannel shirts, brogans, and floppy wide-brimmed hats, but most were guided by the admonition in Deuteronomy 22:5: "The woman shall not wear that which pertaineth unto a man." (But apparently not by 22:11: "Thou shall not wear a garment of divers sorts, as of woollen and linen together"). They pinched the wings of their sunbonnets together, sewed rocks along hemlines to keep skirts down in the wind, and went about their never-ending work.

☐

To the emigrant family or individual starting out on the Oregon Trail, everything seemed conquerable except Indians and disease. Storms and bugs (mosquitoes, buffalo gnats, grasshoppers, flies, something called a "black gallinipper") were hated, but injuries, sickness, and Indians (the latter the subject of the direst warnings in the overland "guides" read so assiduously in the 1840s, of overheated columns in eastern newspapers, and of word-of-mouth horror stories told in the Missouri camps) were truly feared.

But in reality the Indian scare, perhaps the deepest dread of overland families in the early years of the migration west, turned out to be the least worrisome. The Indians of the plains and mountain country of the Trail had been warring against one another since before recorded history, and fur traders—often the source of the bloodiest of camp-told Indian tales—had battled with many tribes, bands, and horse-stealing parties on the Missouri, Platte, Snake, Columbia, and virtually in every nook and cranny between. Most emigrants, however, saw the Indians as beggers, not warriors, coming to the camps trading trinkets and looking for food, occasionally helping in river fordings and other labors, and stealing some horses and cattle at night—the Pawnee were particularly

---

*In 1851 Amelia Bloomer's skirt-and-trouser outfit was introduced, but few emigrant women ever wore them.

adept at this. The emigrant trains were always overarmed for Indian threats; the Indians almost never approached an emigrant caravan with hostility.

While the overlanders learned that they would probably not have to combat Indians, they fought injuries and disease—often before they departed the Missouri border. An estimated 20,000 people died on the Oregon Trail in the decade of 1841–50, most by accidents and Asiatic cholera. This strain of the cholera reached epidemic proportions during the California gold rush years, in 1848 to 1850, but it struck western Missouri camps and emigrant trains moving along the Kansas–Nebraska prairies in the early 1840s, the fatal bacteria thriving in garbage and in springs polluted by latrines built too near them.

Occasionally the cholera-stricken miraculously survived. An emigrant named M. L. Wisner wrote in his diary that he "passed a man by the side of the road who had been attacked by cholera, when his company, panic struck, inhumanly left him to die one hundred and fifty miles from any house. He had a sack of provisions by his side, and lying on the ground, could hardly speak. . . . He could not be moved. . . . All I could do for him was to bring him one of my pint tin cups of water. . . . We learned by a man on horseback the next day, that he had recovered."

But such cases were rare, and as a rule no clyster, poultice, or dose of laudanum helped.

While cholera killed more overlanders than all other diseases combined, others also took a toll: measles, typhoid, whooping cough, smallpox, chickenpox, diphtheria (called "Putrid Sore Throat"), grippe, rheumatism, scurvy, malaria and many nameless "mountain fevers," "slough fevers," and agues. Emigrant diaries are filled with mysterious "bilious complaints," "inflammation of the bowels," "congestion of the brain," "intestinal inertia," "excessive vomiting," "childbed fever," "lung fever," and "bloody flux." These homemade diagnoses covered everything from cholera to ulcers, blocked bowels, food poisoning, puerperal fever, peritonitis, strokes, appendicitis, tuberculosis, pneumonia (common from sleeping in wet bedding, enduring freezing winds and sudden temperature changes), and dysentery, which killed the weak and malnourished.

There were also references to hydrophobia (rabies, always fatal), vertigo, "died of exertion" (probably heart attack), trachoma (endemic among the Indians), alkali poisoning, delirium tremens, and gangrene.

After disease, accidents and mishaps of every description took the most lives on the Trail. Drownings were commonplace, as were broken bones and mashed flesh, and frostbite turned gangrenous. There were accidental (and occasionally purposeful) gunshots; a few homicides;* countless falls from heights, horses, and wagons with attendant broken spines and necks; snakebites; lacerations; infections; blood poisoning; and shock from field amputations.

Edwin Bryant, a Kentucky newspaperman who ventured west on the Oregon Trail in 1846, wrote of a boy who developed gangrene from a compound leg fracture. A drover with the boy's party had been a hospital orderly, and after whetting some butcher knives served as surgeon. The boy was dosed with laudanum and camphor held to his nose as the incision was made above the knee. A gush of foul-smelling pus burst from the swollen flesh and the drover cut the bone through with a common handsaw. The boy died as the stump was cauterized and the flap sewn shut.

The emigrant medicine chest, even the sophisticated ones carried by physicians, were filled with nostrums and dubious "cures" mixed with genuinely useful substances: "physicking pills," rum and peppermint "essences," hartshorn, tartar emetic, belladonna, zinc sulphate, Peruna, beef tonics, turpentine, sulphur, camphor, calomel, cayenne pepper, tincture of rhubarb, tamarack syrup, bitters, asafetida, ipecac, Seidlitz and Dover's Powders, Jayne's Car-

---

*There were twelve murders recorded on the Oregon Trail and several executions, by hanging or firing squad. Merrill Mattes wrote of a drumhead trial and execution of a Missouri teenager found guilty of an ax murder. According to an eyewitness, the boy "was hyung on the limb of a basswood tree."

minitive Balsam, Ayer's Pain-Killer, and Epsom and Glauber's
Salts.

3

In a Christian journal review of Reverend Samuel Parker's *Journal of an Exploring Tour beyond the Rocky Mountains*, the writer called the Oregon Trail a road "excavated by the finger of God," the Indians called it "the White Man's Medicine Road," and those who made the journey and survived it had good reason to think they had accomplished something epic, even biblical, in its testing of human will and endurance. In an 1885 address to the annual reunion of the Oregon Pioneers Association in Salem, Oregon, a Trail veteran named E. L. Eastham said:

> Where else in the history of man, civilized or not, do you read the story of a 2,500-mile march through hostile country, over unexplored desert and mountain? The host led by Moses and Aaron wandered for years, but only accomplished a direct journey of a few hundred miles. Xenophon in his famous retreat from the Euphrates had a less distance to go before he reached safe harbor at home. No crusade ever extended over so great a distance, and most of the way through Christian and friendly countries. Napoleon on his disastrous trip to Moscow only essayed a march of 1,500 miles.

The Trail, which started at Saint Louis for those east of the Mississippi, began again in the camps around Independence, Westport Landing, Saint Joseph, and even farther north, at Council Bluffs, Iowa, or Omaha, Nebraska. What had been a trappers' path and road to Astoria carried only small numbers of emigrants and missionaries up to 1841, when the sixty-nine-member Bartleson-Bidwell company followed it from Sapling Grove to Soda Springs in Idaho, and there split up, half heading on to Oregon, half to

California. In 1842, when Frémont and his first expedition were examining South Pass, close to 200 people were trudging along the Trail, and upwards of 1,000 made the trek the next year, during the "Great Migration." In the twenty-five busiest years of its history, when it had evolved into a true route—actually a series of routes—to the Pacific, the Oregon Trail was the longest thoroughfare in America. And until 1846, when the United States and Great Britain settled the Oregon boundary, its travelers defined the word *emigrant*—people traveling out of their native country into a foreign land—as surely as those sailing from Europe to America.

□

The first few miles of the journey followed the Santa Fé Trail into Kansas, the caravans following the Little Blue River into Nebraska until it made a southward bend, then making their way across the prairie to a ridge of sandhills from which the Platte River, their conduit for the next 600 miles, could be seen.

Among rivers, Bernard De Voto said, the Platte was "one of the most preposterous in the world," for its width, a mile or more, and its frivolous nature. In spring rains and with plenty of snowmelt from the mountains to the west, the river ran high and crashed and tumbled about its braid of islands; but it was most often little more than a mile-wide trickle so muddy it was said to flow from the bottom up, its quicksand so deep it could swallow a wagon and the ox team pulling it.

After a week following the south bank of the river the caravans had to ford the south branch to follow the North Platte drainage, a crossing that often occupied four or more toilsome days of fashioning bull boats from green buffalo hides stretched over willow frames, dismantling the wagons, and ferrying them and countless tons of goods, people, and animals across.

Once across, the wagons were scaled up a rise called California Hill to a wide, high benchland that dropped off to the North Platte valley. Another twenty miles or so from the fording lay Windlass

Hill, where the teams had to be unhitched, the animals led down a forty-five-degree grade, and the wagons with their brakes locked scooted down at the end of guy-ropes into Ash Hollow, which lay 500 miles out and was the first shady place the pioneers had seen in weeks. Of the descent one emigrant wrote, "I cannot say at what angle we descend but . . . some go as far as to say, 'the road hangs a little past the perpendicular!' "

The nights were growing colder as the trains followed the packed-sand riverbanks into higher altitudes and began encountering celebrated Oregon Trail landmarks: Ancient Bluff Ruins; Courthouse Rock, a tall volcanic mound said to resemble a municipal building in Saint Louis; Jail House Rock, four miles off the main trail but so interesting that many rode or hiked to it and climbed to its summit to catch a glimpse of yet another odd formation, a great inverted funnel on the western horizon fourteen miles away. This was the 500-foot-high Chimney Rock, mentioned in pioneer diaries more often than any other site on the Medicine Road. A Dr. A. H. Thomasson (his doctorate clearly not in English composition) saw it in 1850 and noted in his journal, "We went up it about 4 hundred feet then it became so steep they was feet holts cut in so we could clime up about 25 feet further then we could see where some had cut noches and drove little sticks to clime abot 20 feet further but did not venture up that. I suppose that there is not less than 2 thousand names riten in difrin plases."

Thirty-five miles west of Chimney Rock lay Scotts Bluff, another of the Platte's geological curiosities, a Nebraskan Gibraltar looming over the western horizon and hugging the river so closely that wagons had to detour to the south over what became known as Robidoux Pass. Journalist Edwin Bryant, who saw the formation in the mid-1940s, described it as the "ruins of some vast city erected by a race of giants, contemporaries of the Megatherii and the Icthyosaurii." Nile explorer and traveler Richard Burton called it "a massive medieval city . . . round a colossal fortress."

The caravans now entered Wyoming and, ideally in mid-July, reached Fort Laramie, 650 miles from the Missouri border and a point where one overland guide informed his charges, "It is discouraging to tell you that you have not yet travelled one-third of the long road to Oregon."

The fort lay at the junction of the Laramie River with the North Platte, and had been named for an early French-Canadian trapper, Jacques LaRamee, said to have been killed by Indians on the site and his corpse thrown into the river. A hollow square of whitewashed adobe walls six feet thick, fifteen feet high, and about 130 feet on each side, the fort had blockhouses at opposite corners and inside were apartments, storage rooms, corrals, a trading post where supplies were sold at outrageous prices, a blacksmith shop, and even a post office. An old trapper named James Bordeaux, a veteran of the Upper Missouri trade who was married to a Brulé Sioux woman, ran the place and kept peace with the Indians. Laramie was located in prime buffalo country, and there were often as many as 600 Oglala and Brulé lodges—and 2,000 Indians—in the vicinity. A green meadow east of Laramie served as a favorite wagon campsite and there the journeyers rested, mingled with the Indians, reshod their animals, and bought needed supplies. There, too, the travelers, especially those heading for California by the roundabout detours west of South Pass, became mindful of falling behind schedule and being shut out of the mountain passes by winter snows.

Eight miles west of Fort Laramie the trail passed a tall sandstone-and-white-chalk bank called Register Cliff, which required only a nail or knifepoint to inscribe a name and date on it, and for several miles beyond it the wagons left tracks in the sandstone hills that so deepened over the years they would be visible a century and a half afterward.

The steeper westward tilt of the continent toward the Rockies tried man and beast, and the heavy cargo items—anvils, chiffoniers, sheet-iron stoves, and the like—became daily roadside casualties as the wagons rejoined the North Platte near Casper, heading due west, fording the river again near where Brigham Young's Mormons would build a ferry in 1847. The Trail took them over Emigrant Gap, past Poison Springs, identifiable from the animal carcasses surrounding it, to Willow Springs, an excellent campsite with good water, and on to Independence Rock overlooking the Sweetwater. This landmark, named by fur traders who discovered it on July 4, 1824, and called it the "Register of the Desert," was an oval-shaped granite boulder 128 feet high. Messages were scratched or painted on it, and names and dates, by nearly all who reached it. Some indicated their relief that they were "half-way" to the Pacific when in fact they were but 815 miles out from Independence and had 1,200 miles or more to travel.

After passing Independence Rock, the caravans made the first of no less than nine crossings of the maddeningly meandering Sweetwater, bypassed the awesome 400-foot gash through the rocks known as Devil's Gate, reached "Three Crossings," where the wagons thrice crossed the Sweetwater in a gate-like canyon, and came upon Ice Slough. Here water collected beneath an insulating layer of peat moss and froze in the harsh winters, remaining frozen through the summer when travelers could dig it out and use slabs of ice to cool water barrels.

The wagons negotiated South Pass, 914 miles out, with little effort, the grassy gap in the Wind River Range at the Continental Divide sloping so gently "that the traveler would scarcely perceive that he was ascending were it not for the great change in the atmosphere," one traveler wrote. The air continued thinning to its summit at 7,412 feet, the Trail then emerging into Oregon Country near Little Sandy Creek and continuing on through desert country to Pacific Springs, a memorable place in that it was the first water the pioneers encountered that flowed toward the western ocean.

Upon reaching the Green River there was a choice of routes to follow. Some took the Sublette Cutoff, named for one of the fur-trading brothers, which cut straight across a fifty-mile alkaline lake bed and grassless, gravelly benchland with the only water available at its far western side. This scary path was eighty-five miles shorter than the drop southeast to Fort Bridger, the trading post on the Green built by mountain immortal Jim Bridger and his partner Lewis Vasquez in 1843, but most were unwilling to chance the Sublette and took the detour, with its ample water and grass.

Joel Palmer, an Indiana legislator who joined an 1844 wagon train to Oregon, described Bridger's post as "a shabby concern built of poles and daubed with mud," but it was a place where a few supplies could be purchased and where "recruited" oxen, ones whose health and strength had been restored by rest and good pasturage, could be obtained by trading in footsore and weary ones and paying a fee.

It was at Fort Bridger, a thousand miles out of Independence, that the Mormons following the Oregon Trail veered off to the southwest into Utah.

From Bridger, the Trail returned northwest to Soda Springs, one of a series of iron-laden carbonated waters, which some travelers said tasted like small beer and made an excellent lemonade when mixed with citrus syrup and sugar. Fifty-five miles beyond the springs lay Fort Hall, the Hudson's Bay post originally built by Nathaniel Wyeth in 1834. Here many wagons had been abandoned over the years and were cannibalized to repair the ones now heading toward Oregon and California.

The Trail out of Fort Hall followed the left bank of the Snake River, tributary of the Columbia, through "a melancholy and strange looking country," Frémont said, "one of fracture, and violence, and fire," the crossing of the Snake eased somewhat by two islands, which enabled wagons to cross in three laborious stages.

A few miles west of Fort Hall, at the American Falls of the Snake, those heading for California left their wagons and mounted horses and mules. Now, with a train of pack animals they followed their pilot southwestward toward the Great Basin of Utah and Nevada, a known killer of man and beast, 200,000 square miles of white salt beds, sand, lava, alkali, sage, and clay wastes circled by mountains that reflected the sun's heat like a mirror. The Hudson's Bay factor at Fort Hall recommended that emigrants take the California route, hoping to delay the time when Oregon could be invaded by Americans. While playing down the dangers of the southward journey, he warned the Oregon-bound about ravaging Indians, the likelihood of famine, how the Snake River threw itself and its passengers suicidally down its yawning gorges, and how mountain blizzards lay waiting in the Blue Mountains. Much of what he described required no exaggeration.

The Oregonians listened to the stories and moved on anyway, down the Snake to Salmon Falls, across the sage plains to Fort Boisé, and on to the Grand Ronde valley, a gorgeous campground of piney hills, rich pasturage, and abundant watercourses just east of the snow-shrouded Blue Mountains. They crossed the mountains, often in blizzards, visited the Whitmans' mission at Waiilatpu, and continued west to Fort Walla Walla with only the Cascades and sixty-odd miles separating them from the Willamette valley but no wagon road to reach it.*

The more cautious of the emigrants completed their journey down the Columbia banks on horseback. Many took their wagons and struggling animals the 250 miles across the Cascade Range into the forests around Mount Hood, to stagger into the Willamette on their literal last legs. Many more traveled in *bateaux*, dugouts, and canoes on the Walla Walla and Columbia to The Dalles, where they felled trees, made rafts, dismantled their wagons and placed them aboard, and faced the worst stretch of their 2,000-mile journey. The sixty miles of the Columbia to the mouth of the Willamette River rocketed down a basalt gutter that breached the Cascades, a mountain chain sixty to eighty miles wide with canyons 3,000 feet deep, a roller-coaster ride in icy winds blowing upstream that killed many so near the end of their journey and the beginning of their new lives.

After recovering from their Columbia passage, the newcomers crossed the river to the mouth of the Willamette. They hugged the shore for about twenty miles to Oregon City, a village on the east bank just below the falls of the Willamette.**

---

*At least until 1846, when Illinois emigrant Samuel Barlow and workers completed a ninety-mile road over the Cascades to a point south of Mount Hood, which became the standard route into western Oregon.

**By 1846 Oregon City had a population of 1,000; flour mills and sawmills; a foundary; a circulating library; a temperance society; a debating club; Catholic and Methodist churches; two saloons; a weekly newspaper, the *Oregon Spectator*; and had become the center of the American populace of the Oregon Country, ten times the size of Portland, which lay fifteen miles downstream.

Most of the emigrants eventually paid a visit to Fort Vancouver, where John McLoughlin received them courteously and at no charge provided them with rooms to rest, salmon, potatoes, firewood, and whatever they required—within reason and usually within the rules of the Hudson's Bay Company—before they left his domain to travel on south to the land they were claiming.

THE GREAT MIGRATION

"MAY WE NOT CALL THEM MEN OF DESTINY?"

1

By 1843, even the European press took notice of the Oregon Trail "movers," the pioneer families who were pointing their wagons west. British papers and journals, protective of their interests in the Pacific Northwest, saw the whole business as inexplicable. In a July 1843 editorial, the venerable *Edinburgh Review* informed its readers that for six months of the year the territory between the western boundary of the United States and the Oregon Country was "a howling wilderness of snow and tempests" and the remaining six months a wasteland "of hopeless sterility" infested with Indians "of more than Sythian savageness and endurance, who cannot be tracked, overtaken, or conciliated." The writer praised the energy of the American emigrants but predicted that "Oregon will never be colonized overland from the United States."

The view was shared by many influential Americans, among them Horace Greeley, editor of the *New York Daily Tribune*, the very man who urged, "Go west, young man, and grow up with the country!" (by which he meant west to the far country of Erie

County, Pennsylvania). In 1843 he was in his "Stay east" mode, in which, receiving reports of the extraordinary gathering of wagons and pioneer families on the Missouri frontier he railed, "This migration of more than a thousand persons in a body to Oregon wears an aspect of insanity." He acknowledged that the United States had a rightful claim to Oregon but cautioned against making unnecessary trouble with the British by an emigrant invasion of the Northwest. The place was too distant, he said, and not nearly as fertile and rich in resources as the paeans of the propagandists would have it.

He urged caution. The Oregon boom was a sickness, infecting otherwise sensible folk into febrile acts, such as leaving comfortable homes, good farmlands, and markets, leaving their churches and friends and responsibilities. He wrote in his paper on July 19, 1843, "For what, then, do they brave the desert, the wilderness, the savage, snowy precipices of the Rocky Mountains, the weary summer march, the storm-drenched bivouac, and the gnawings of famine? Only to fulfill their destiny! There is probably not one among them whose outward circumstances will be improved by this perilous pilgrimage."

Nor was that all. Greeley wrote of starvation and savages, warning would-be pioneers who were so accustomed to the comforts and safety of their civilized lives that they could expect Indian attacks, perhaps several, during their journey between Missouri and Oregon, as well as other dangers and privations. He attempted to soften his panicky editorializing by assuring his readers that he was actually in favor of American settlement of the lands beyond Missouri, and looked in favor at the American pioneer spirit. But, he said, a *mass* movement to Oregon was too extreme, and he called upon all prudent men to "stop this side of the woods"— meaning at the Missouri boundary—because it was "palpable homicide to tempt or send women and children over this thousand miles of precipice and volcanic sterility to Oregon."

Greeley's shaky sense of distance and topography improved in 1859, when he made an overland trip to California and en route invented the Q&A newspaper interview after having a chat with Brigham Young in Salt Lake City. However, even as late as 1845, when 10,000 overlanders were clogging the Medicine Road, he was still calling the enterprise "foolhardy," still warning against Indian depredations and famine. He cautioned on the consequences of depending upon the Hudson's Bay Company to be of assistance if the emigrant miraculously got to Oregon, sick, shrunken to a skeleton, with his belongings strewn along the trail and his animals done in or dead. The Hudson's Bay people, he said, could not be expected to provide succor to "a horde."

While Greeley was among the most persistent and eloquent of the lemmings-to-the-sea school of observers of the Great Migration, he had company in his views. The *North American Review* compared Oregon to Siberia and said the roads to each were similarly perilous. The *New Orleans Picayune* advised in 1846, after the Oregon Trail had conveyed thousands to the Pacific, that emigrants, if they insisted on hazarding the journey west, do so via the Isthmus of Panama "to divert the travels to Oregon by the long, dangerous and expensive route across the prairies and Rocky Mountains." Even the *Daily Missouri Republican* in Saint Louis counseled menfolk to "stay home and earn an honest living."

In Congress, reactions to the growing traffic on the Trail were mixed. In January 1843 Senator George McDuffie of South Carolina thanked God "for placing the Rocky Mountains in such a way as to thwart Americans from reaching the Pacific." That same month, Lewis Linn of Missouri, surgeon in the War of 1812, Jacksonian Democrat, and party warhorse, died, indefatigable to the end in introducing bills for the settlement of Oregon. In one of his last addresses to the Senate he spoke of the "easy" passes across McDuffie's thwarting Rockies and expressed envy at the "wild and strange rapture" Daniel Boone must have felt when he penetrated the forests and first cast his eye upon Kentucky. The Oregon pioneer would experience such a rapture, he promised, and, never at a loss for biblical precedent, said the journey of the westward pioneers recalled those going "to the wilderness, like our first parents, when God sent them forth from the Garden of Eden to subdue the earth." Representative Orlando Bell Ficklin of Illinois took this a step further, speaking of the emigrants of the 1840s in allusions to Abraham and Lot, Moses and Aaron, and said he dreamed of the day he could climb the mountains to see and hear "with wild delight" the roar of the mighty Columbia as it crashed into the western sea.

Those whose dreaming had turned to doing were propelled west in 1843 for practical reasons. The residue of the economic Panic of '37 lingered; prices for farm goods remained depressed, as did those who raised the goods, who scratched out a meager subsistence from their Mississippi valley or Ohio valley acreage. Fresh reports from witnesses as reliable as Marcus Whitman, Jason Lee, Elijah White, and John C. Frémont told of open markets, fertile land, and limitless opportunity for "industry" and the industrious in Oregon.

"Hurry on," many who had seen the elephant were writing home, and warnings filtered eastward that the journey was becoming most costly for those who tarried and who did not provision themselves adequately. Post traders, capitalizing on the surge of traffic on the Trail, were charging exorbitantly for supplies. Frémont's cartographer Charles Preuss wrote in his diary in 1843 that "Carson [Kit Carson] was sent ahead to Fort Hall to secure provisions for us. If the emigrants get ahead of us, we shall not find much there." Marcus Whitman, who served as a guide for many of the Oregon-bound that year, wrote of the booming business and high prices at the four principal Oregon Trail posts—Forts Laramie, Bridger, Hall, and Boisé.

(The pitiless scalping escalated: At Fort Laramie in 1846 Francis Parkman seethed that the traders had become the "natural enemies" of the overlanders who, he wrote, "were plundered and cheated without mercy." He told of "one bargain, concluded in my presence," in which "I calculated the profits that accrued to the fort, and found that at the lowest estimate they exceeded *eighteen hundred per cent*.")

□

On May 18, 1843, at Elm Grove, the rendezvous place twelve miles out of Independence, recognizable for its one large elm tree and one small one, a concourse of wagons, ox and mule teams, horse and cattle herds, and people from every part of Missouri, Iowa, Illinois, Indiana, Ohio, Kentucky, Tennessee, and farther-flung hamlets and towns awaited the signal to begin the long walk to the Pacific. They had trickled in for weeks, "relying only on the fertility of their invention." One notable man among them, Jesse Applegate, later wrote, "Always ready and equal to the occasion and always conquerors. May we not call them men of destiny?"

The men, women, and children of destiny numbered between 875 and 1,000 with 150 wagons, an immense cattle herd, and a collection of spare horses, mules, and oxen—all told as many as 5,000 animals. The assemblage was late in starting—a cold spring had kept the bluestem grass in hibernation—and impatient. They were oblivious to the stragglers pouring into their bustling camp every day who jockeyed for lead spots in the line of march. There was much quarreling over the cow herd, which the cowless felt would drag them all down and delay them reaching the mountains before winter.

At the head of the caravan, which moved west on May 22, was Captain John Gantt, a Marylander and former army officer in his early fifties. A tough, no-nonsense guide, he had found his own second chance and a new life in the West after being court-martialed and dismissed from the service in 1829 for falsification of pay accounts, and he had close to twenty years' experience in Indian country. He had been recruited as pilot at the rate of one dollar per emigrant and agreed to lead the caravan as far as Fort Hall, where he would then continue on to California.

Another experienced hand who signed on to assist Gantt, Joseph Ballinger Chiles of Kentucky, had gone to California in '41 with the Bartleson-Bidwell train and had returned home with permission to build a grain mill in the Napa valley north of San

Francisco Bay. He had recruited thirty men and had eight wagons loaded with mill equipment.

News arrived at Elm Grove that Dr. Marcus Whitman would be joining the caravan after he finished some business at Shawnee Mission, the Methodist Indian school at Westport Landing. He had returned to Boston the year past to convince the Board of Foreign Missions to save Waiilatpu and the Spaldings' mission at Lapwai.

When Whitman caught up with the Gantt train on the Platte, he calmed such anxieties as those created by many Trail veterans who warned the party that their wagons could not be taken beyond Fort Hall. Whitman said they could be taken all the way to the Columbia because the caravan had the combined manpower, which he lacked in '36, to get them there.

Also hurrying along toward the Missouri border was Lieutenant John C. Frémont, with a new expedition of forty men, pack animals, carts, and even a twelve-pounder cannon to impress any belligerent Indians on his line of march. He was heading toward South Pass again, but this time he intended pushing on to Oregon.

Notable among the tyros in the 1843 caravan was Peter Hardeman Burnett, one-time storekeeper in Weston, Missouri, a self-taught lawyer who was hopelessly in debt and had an ailing wife and six children. Taken down with Oregon fever, he had spent a year lecturing in western Missouri, calling for the other fever-stricken comrades to join him in Independence to start the journey. He had patched together the funds to buy two wagons and the oxen to pull them and by the time he arrived in Independence he had many followers and seemed a natural leader.*

Also eager and impressive were the Applegate brothers, Jesse, Lindsey, and Charles, from the Osage valley of Missouri. The Applegates were originally Kentuckians, having moved to Missouri

---

*As he turned out to be. In 1849 Burnett left Oregon, where he had been appointed a territorial judge, for the California gold fields, and in 1850 he was elected the first governor of the state. James M. Nesmith, Burnett's orderly sergeant in the 1843 journey, became a judge, a brigadier general of militia, and, in 1860, a United States Senator from Oregon.

when the boys were young to farm corn and cotton and raise hogs and cattle. Jesse had studied surveying and was known to have walked up to sixty miles a day in his work. He was tall, rawboned, and "so homely," David Lavender wrote, "he avoided mirrors all his life." He had gone broke farming and surveying, sold his property, and enlisted his brothers, who were little better off, to sell out. They all brought their wagons, cows, and families to Independence.

2

The train rolled out of Elm Grove on May 22, 1843, heading southwest along an old trace that intersected the Santa Fé Trail, by now a broad roadway pounded flat from two decades of heavy trade-wagon traffic. A day out of Fitzhugh's Mill, near Gardner, Kansas, they turned due west to the Wakarusa River, the first of many river obstacles that would try the patience and endurance of the tenderfeet, a steep-banked stream that required a path to be spaded down for the wagons' passage. The next crossing, the Kaw (or Kansas) River, was far worse. Gantt led the caravan thirty miles along its banks before finding a suitable fording place, then supervised the building of cross-timbered rafts to ferry the wagons, and people, across. The operation, including swimming the horses, draft animals, and cattle herd to the far bank, occupied five days.

Meantime, stragglers continued coming up. On May 31 Frémont and his expedition reached Elm Grove, where he observed ragged files of wagons bumping along toward the Kaw nine days behind the main train. Among the others who caught up were two Jesuit missionaries bound for the Flathead villages of the Bitterroot valley, and William Drummond Stewart, the Waterloo and Fifteenth King's Hussars veteran. Sir William had been hunting and taking part in the fur traders' rendezvous for a decade and was now returning to his beloved American West for the last time, accompanied by a party of sportsmen friends, heading for the Green River. Stewart was popular for his stories of Wellington in the

Iberian Peninsula and fighting Napoleon's Grand Armée at Waterloo. Stewart's guide, Bill Sublette, had endless campfire tales of his
experiences as one of Ashley's "enterprising young men" in '23: his
narrow escape in the Arikara fight on the Upper Missouri, his journey with Jedediah Smith into Crow country and all the way to Hudson's Bay territory in Oregon, recollections of Nat Wyeth in 1832,
and his wound in the Blackfoot battle at Pierre's Hole on July 18 that
year. Sublette, now ailing and with only two years to live, was, like
his employer, making his last journey into the mountains.

Past the Kaw and into rolling hills covered with wildflowers the
train crawled northwest amidst daily thunderstorms and whipping
winds that blew the rain horizontally into their faces, scattered
tents and camp gear, and chased the terrified stock into the brush.

The long passage of the Kaw signaled the need for a better
organization of the caravan, one along military lines for better discipline and order. This probably resulted from Captain Gantt's
counsel and, perhaps because he brought the most people to the
Elm Grove rendezvous, Peter Burnett was elected captain and
James M. Nesmith, a bachelor, "orderly sergeant" for the train.
Burnett lasted eight days before resigning due to "ill health," but
he more than likely succumbed to the squabbles between the cattle
haves and have-nots. The big cow herd, ponderously slow crossing
the waterways, spooking and scattering in thunderstorms, was de-
laying the entire party, the have-nots said, and they clamored to
have the column split, with those owning only a few head of stock
to move ahead while the big herd followed with its drovers in the
rear. The Applegate brothers, majority cow owners, undertook to
mind the "cow column" with Jesse in overall command.

Jesse Applegate, of whom James Nesmith would write, "As a
frontiersman, in courage, sagacity, and natural intelligence he is
the equal of Daniel Boone," managed to keep a colorful record of
the journey west and in *A Day with the Cow Column, 1843*, described one eighteen-hour day that advanced his party twenty miles
toward Oregon.

At four A.M., Applegate wrote, "sentinels on duty fire their rifles in the air and every wagon and tent pours forth its occupants;

60 men spread out to form the cattle in a semicircle around the camp; corral formed by wagons connected to each other by tongue and ox-chains, entrenchment against Indians and impenetrable by a maddened ox or cattle stampede."

From six to seven, breakfast fires were extinguished, tents struck, wagons loaded, teams yoked and brought forward to be attached to their wagons. At seven a bugler signaled the march to begin and "those unready," Applegate said, "have to take their place at the rear of the column and eat dust."

He described how the wagons were divided into platoons of four abreast, each platoon moving forward at the start of each day's march so that all took a turn in the lead. The pilot (John Gantt) and a squad of men struck out ahead of the lead wagons with picks and shovels to "prepare the trail," filling in chuckholes and moving boulders, while a party of hunters rode out in search of game.

Toward midday, Gantt would "measure the ground," judge the speed of the wagons, and walk his horse along to select a "nooning" place, as close as possible to good graze and water, for the party to rest after five hours of travel.

At one, the bugler announced the march to resume. The day wore on tediously with the wagons bumping along old buffalo paths and wallows, the oxen lamed by the needles of burned grass stubble, some wagons straggling out of the line for a brief respite from the choking dust.

With the sun low in the west, Gantt would find a good campsite, whereupon wagons were circled, cookfires lit, and tents pitched. All adult men were formed into companies and divided into watches, with each company standing guard duty every third night.

Applegate wrote of fiddle music and impromptu dances among "the youths and maidens" before the deepening night called the travelers to their tents and bedrolls to a bone-weary sleep after "a prosperous day" of twenty miles' progress.

In July they reached the Platte, always wide, generally shallow and murky, with its notorious shifting beds of quicksand, "an infernal liar," as some Oregon Trail veteran called it, "hardly able to float a canoe." The 1843 emigrants had heard the tales of times when eighteen yoke of oxen were required to drag a single wagon across its mud, but they were faced with a high Platte, swirling with currents, that required ferrying by bull boats made of caulked wagon boxes before they could reform and swing along its southern bank through prickly pear, yucca, prairie-dog towns, and dry grass in the hammering heat of the prairie summer.

Ash Hollow . . . Courthouse Rock . . . Chimney Rock . . . Scotts Bluff . . . rafting across the Laramie River to the adobe fort, 640 miles out of Independence, 1,400 miles to the Columbia . . . the awful last fording of the Platte and the alkali plains beyond it that gave the cattle "scours" (diarrhea) until the trail broke toward the clear, cold Sweetwater.

The days blended into one ceaseless crawl. "Groaning, they fell once more into their dusty line," David Lavender wrote memorably of the awful daily desuetude of the Oregon Trail. "That was the heroics of the migration: not Indian scares or thrilling buffalo hunts or flooded stream crossings but rather this remorseless, unending, weather-scoured, nerve-rasping plod on and on and on and on, foot by aching foot."

At turtle-backed Independence Rock they climbed and painted on its granite face their names and a record of having plodded to this spot:

> *The Oregon Co.*
> *arrived*
> *July 26, 1843*

The 400-foot slit in the rocks called Devil's Gate they detoured via a trail to the south; they surveyed the Wind River Range running north beyond their eyesight, left the Sweetwater for a twenty-mile-wide sagebrush plain, crossed South Pass into Oregon Country, and reached Fort Hall on the Portneuf River of Idaho. There, the Hudson's Bay Company trader in charge, Richard Grant, a burly six-foot-tall Canadian with thirty years' wilderness experience, said it would be impossible for them to take their wagons on to the Columbia and urged them to turn south to Mexican California with Captain Gantt and Mr. Chiles. But the Oregon people had been hearing the wagon warning since gathering at Elm Grove and were assured, again, by Dr. Whitman that they had the muscle of hundreds of men to push the wagons on.

At Fort Hall, John Gantt, having fulfilled his contract, and Joe Chiles collected their partners and wagons laden with grain-mill equipment and departed toward the Humboldt River, the Sierra Nevada, and California. Gantt had done good work and was much respected by his 875 wards. Nesmith spoke of him as "our respected pilot," and Jesse Applegate wrote that the captain "has spent his life on the verge of civilization" and had been chosen to lead the 1843 caravan "from his knowledge of the savage and his experience in travel through the roadless wastes."*

The Oregonians took up a collection and offered Marcus Whitman $400 if he would guide them to the Columbia and to this he readily agreed, and no doubt would have done so without the welcome offer of cash. He led the train down the Snake to Salmon Falls and across the sage plains to Fort Boisé, arriving there on September 20, 1843. After a brief rest he guided the wagons on to the Grand Ronde valley on October 1, and crossed the Blue Mountains in mounting snowstorms to camp, on October 10, within three miles of Waiilatpu.

The Applegate brothers left their cattle at Fort Walla Walla; whipsawed driftwood and timber into rafts; climbed into dugouts, canoes, and *bateaux*; floated to the Celilo Falls; and portaged across to The Dalles. During the harrowing trip through the rapids Jesse and Lindsey Applegate both lost ten-year-old sons to

---

*Gantt died in California on February 14, 1849, of a heart ailment, at age fifty-nine. He had crossed the Rockies eight times in various trapping journeys and was said to have explored every river between the western settlements of Missouri and the Pacific. Among his other accomplishments, he was the first to see the opportunity for a prosperous trading post on the Arkansas River in southeastern Colorado, a project carried out with immense success by William Bent and his Bent's Fort.

drowning, and Charles Applegate's son was crippled when a boat overturned in the current.

In all, of the approximately 875 men, women, and children of the Great Migration caravan headed for Oregon, sixteen died en route to the Willamette.

3

In 1844, three new groups of Oregon-bound emigrants formed up on the Missouri frontier, between 700 and 800 people with 150 wagons and 1,500 head of cattle; in 1845, the number westering was about 3,000, and there were fewer in 1846 because of the threats of war against both England and Mexico. The figure rose in 1847, to 4,500 emigrants.

Among the 1845 emigrants was a high-domed, self-styled "intelligent farmer" named Joel Palmer. Born in Canada in 1810 of Quaker parents, he had lived in Pennsylvania before settling in Laurel, Indiana, where he had some success as a canal contractor and farmer. He served a term in the state legislature, but after reading up on the Oregon boundary dispute decided to try his hand at something new in a new place. He left his wife and children behind in Laurel "with a truly melancholy heart" and took a steamer to Independence "with a view of satisfying myself whether Oregon's advantages were sufficient to make it my future home."

He had a magnetic personality and a politician's polish and employed both in getting elected captain of a twenty-five-wagon train that reached Fort Laramie on June 24. There his party made a layover to mend wagons and harness, shoe animals, write letters, and replenish supplies at the outrageous prices then prevalent and going up by the day—fifteen dollars for a hundredweight of flour, a dollar for two cups of sugar or coffee beans. Palmer, a meticulous chronicler of the 1845 migration, recorded counting 145 wagons in four separate trains camped within a few miles of each other on the Platte.

He had an interest in Indians, too, and wanted to know what

they had to say of the whites coming into their country in such
rising numbers. With the blessing of the people of his party and
after enlisting an interpreter, he arranged a banquet for the hundred or so Oglalas camped near the fort on the bank of the Laramie
River. Each emigrant family provided two dishes of food and the
feast was arranged on buffalo robes at the edge of the village. The
Indians seated themselves in two concentric semicircles, the pioneers making up a single one opposite. The Oglala chief was asked
to speak and did so, bluntly: "This country belongs to the red man
but his white brethren travels through, shooting the game and scar-
ing it away. Thus the Indian loses all that he depends upon to
support his wives and children. The children of the red man cry
out for food, but there is no food." He asked for guns to kill game
like the white man since the game that survived the whites' incursions were now too skittish for bows and arrows.

Palmer later wrote, "As it devolved upon me to play the part
of the white chief, I told my red brethren that we were journeying
to the great waters of the west. Our great father owned a large
country there and we were going to settle upon it. For this purpose
we brought with us our wives and little ones. We traveled as
friends, not as enemies." He said he and his companions were
farmers and had no guns to trade. He urged the Oglalas to feast
on the meat, rice mush, cakes, bread, and coffee spread out before
them. The eating went well; Palmer's words, which would be repeated countless times, with countless variations, in the years
ahead, often with howitzer and rocket displays and peace pipe
sharing, were unsatisfactory to the "red brethren."

On November 1, 1845, after 200 days on the Oregon Trail,
the Palmer train reached Oregon City. The intelligent farmer recalled in his *Journal of Travels Over the Rocky Mountains* that the
town had among its civilized establishments "a neat Methodist
church, a splendid Catholic chapel, two grist mills, two sawmills,
four stores, two taverns, one hatter, one tannery, three tailor shops,
two cabinet makers, two silversmiths, one cooper, two blacksmiths,
one physician, three lawyers, one printing office, and a good brick
yard."

Palmer returned to Indiana in 1846, satisfied that Oregon indeed had sufficient advantages to make a home, collected his family, and returned. Among his accomplishments as an Oregon pioneer, he became superintendent of Indian Affairs where he was directed to prevent the Cayuse and Nez Percé tribes from joining forces for hostile purposes. Bancroft said wryly that he "bent his enormous energy and personal magnetism to the difficult task of obtaining all their lands from the Indians without creating enough dissatisfaction among them to cause a war." Even so, Palmer was genuinely sympathetic toward the Indians and respectful of their rights to the point that he came under severe censure by white Oregonians.

He negotiated treaties with the Umpquas, Shastas, Walla Wallas, Cayuse, and Nez Percé, and is said to have diligently sought and found good reservation lands for the dispossessed tribes. Bancroft, conceding that Palmer made "some errors," judged his efforts on the whole to be "humane and just." His faults, the historian said, "were those of an over-sanguine man, driven somewhat by public clamor, and eager to accomplish his work in the shortest time. . . . He succeeded in his undertaking of removing to the border of the Willamette Valley about 4,000 Indians, [and] for his honesty and eminent services, he is entitled to the respect and gratitude of all good men."

Palmer was removed from office in 1857 because of white impatience with his solicitude toward his Indian charges. After his discharge, he opened a route to the British Columbia gold fields, engaged in many business enterprises, and served as a state representative and state senator. He died at Dayton, a town he founded southwest of Oregon City, in June 1881.

21

THE PARALLEL

"FIFTY-FOUR FORTY OR FIGHT!"

1

The man who would at last answer the Oregon question, James Knox Polk, came to the presidency by a fluke, announced early that he would serve but a single term, set forth a number of goals for his administration, and left office after accomplishing all of them, something remarked on 100 years later by Harry S. Truman: "James K. Polk, a great president; said what he intended to do and did it."

Born on the family farm in Mecklenburg County, North Carolina, in 1795 and the eldest of ten children of a prosperous planter, Polk came to Tennessee with his family in 1806 and received a university education in classical studies—Latin, Greek, mathematics, philosophy—as well as law. He served in the Tennessee legislature, was admitted to the state bar in 1825, and began his rise in national politics that year as a congressman from Tennessee and a staunch supporter of Andrew Jackson, with whom he had a close personal friendship. Polk served as Old Hickory's floor leader in the House of Representatives, and became Speaker in

1835, serving two years in the office before returning to Tennessee to campaign for, and win, the governorship.

"Young Hickory," as his adherents called him, actually had none of Jackson's charisma, daring, physical stature, or stamina, but the two men shared other characteristics: a combative nature, a thin skin, an obduracy, and a passion for politics.

Polk was short, slender, high-browed, and thin-lipped, with deep-set gray eyes, his unruly graying hair brushed behind his ears. He had a dignified carriage and was always scrupulously dressed. He suffered ill health most of his life, a delicacy worsened by living in Washington amid the Potomac swamps and their disease-laden miasmas, and he tired easily. He was exceedingly ambitious, and for the most part well liked, although he had few close friends and only one confidante, his wife, Sara Childress Polk, a lively and charming adjunct to her dour mate.

Many, even Polk's admirers, regarded him as historian Bernard De Voto did: "rigid, narrow, obstinate . . . pompous, suspicious, and secretive." Abraham Lincoln, in his single term in the House of Representatives, said in 1848 that Polk "is a bewildered, confounded, and miserably perplexed man." But others saw beneath his granitic exterior and humorlessness a thoroughly honest and incorruptible man, a better man than Jackson in many respects, and while "in no sense a man of brilliant parts," as Woodrow Wilson would say of him, he was "a sturdy, upright, straightforward party man."

Polk sprang from party-workhorse obscurity to national prominence at the 1844 Democratic Party convention. What happened in the Odd Fellows' Hall in Baltimore between May 27 and 30 that year surprised the most acute prognosticators among the party faithful.

The frontrunner nominee of the Democrats was Martin Van Buren of Kinderhook, New York, who had served as Jackson's secretary of state and vice president and had succeeded Old Hickory as president in 1836, serving one term. As expected, he won a majority in the first ballot voting in Baltimore. But he failed to win the necessary two-thirds majority of the delegate votes for the nomination, and after the first ballot other party hopefuls—Lewis Cass of Michigan, Richard M. Johnson of Kentucky, and James Buchanan of Pennsylvania—eroded the Van Buren margin. The former president's cause was doomed by his opposition to one of the party platform's strongest planks, the annexation of Texas, at a time when the American people (or so said their representatives in Washington) were ardently "expansionist," lusting after Texas, California, Oregon, and whatever else was occupied by foreigners west of the Mississippi. Van Buren had opposed Texas annexation, over the slavery issue, when he was president, alienating southern Democrats, the heart of Jackson's party, and continued to oppose the proposition in 1844 just as the southerners continued to oppose him.

Polk stayed home in Nashville during the Baltimore convention. He had been mentioned as potential vice presidential timber for whoever was selected to head the ticket, but he had no inkling that he might be placed in nomination. His name appeared on the eighth ballot and he won the nomination, with 233 votes, on the ninth, becoming the first "dark horse" in American political history.

He accepted by letter, thanking Jackson for his endorsement and the convention delegates for their confidence in him. He pledged a one-term presidency (which he believed was implicit in Jacksonian ideology, although Jackson served two terms) and set out to win the general election.

Polk's Whig opponent, Henry Clay of Kentucky, who had thrice before been a presidential candidate and had been thrice rejected, now had to endure a final, failed, hurrah. He sought to appease all factions of his party by equivocating on the Texas and Oregon questions while Polk advocated both the annexation of Texas and the assertion of American "rights" to the "whole of Oregon," from the 42nd parallel, the border with Mexican California, and the 54th, considerably north of Edmonton, Canada, and taking in all of Vancouver Island.

Polk narrowly won the election, becoming the eleventh, and at age forty-nine, the youngest, president, carrying fifteen states to Clay's eleven (including Polk and Jackson's Tennessee), and the popular vote by 37,000 votes out of the 1.7 million cast.

He had a remarkably clear and deceptively simple vision of what he wanted to accomplish as president: revision of the protective tariff, acquisition of California, and settling the Oregon question. In foreign affairs he hoped to avoid war, but in his inaugural address on March 4, 1845, he pugnaciously embraced the Monroe Doctrine: "The people of this continent alone have the right to decide their own destiny. . . . No future European colony or dominion shall with our consent be planted or established on any part of the North American continent." And he reasserted American rights to Oregon in his first annual message to Congress the following December, when he recommended that measures be taken to protect American claims to the "whole of Oregon" and proposed abrogation of the joint occupation agreement.

Polk's enduring distrust of the British he confided in his diary in this period: "The only way to treat John Bull," he wrote, "was to look him straight in the eye."

2

Before 1845, Americans had no name for the precept they believed was inscribed on some heavenly scroll: that the United States (twenty-six of them in Polk's era)—that is the white portion of its population of 20 million—was destined by God's decree to occupy the continent.

The idea, an article of faith dating from the dawn of civilization when one state desired the territory of another and found a providential inspiration in taking it, received a memorable designation four months after James K. Polk took office.

In the July–August 1845 issue of the New York–based *United States Magazine and Democratic Review*, lawyer-editor John Louis O'Sullivan wrote a strengthy editorial favoring the annexation of Texas. This joining to the Union, he wrote, would serve as a warning against foreign interference and would have the effect of "checking the fulfillment of our manifest destiny to overspread the continent allotted by Providence for the free development of our yearly multiplying millions."

What the editor wrote of Texas and California applied to Oregon as well: "The Anglo-Saxon foot is already on its borders. Already the advance guard of the irresistible army of the Anglo-Saxon emigration has begun to pour down upon it, armed with the plough and the rifle," and this admirably matched the new president's pronouncement that "our title to the whole of Oregon is clear and unquestionable."

In Polk's day, Manifest Destiny was no idle slogan; it was an operating principle, especially when combined, as Polk combined it, with certain tenets of the Monroe Doctrine of 1823: that the United States would not countenance further occupation by European powers, and that it would regard as dangerous to its peace and safety any attempt at colonization in the Western Hemisphere. The one point of the doctrine expansionists studiously ignored was the part that said the United States would not interfere with existing colonies or dependencies of European powers in the New World. Annexations, such as that of Texas, had been used before as a means of halting "foreign influences" and their nefarious underminings of peace and security in the neighborhood of the United States. Diplomacy and purchase were the desirable means of expansion, but annexation, by war and by conquest, was a workable alternative.

Few questioned that the annexation of Texas would mean war with Mexico and indeed, by the end of 1845, with Texas admitted to the Union, an American army was poised above the Rio Grande to do battle with a Mexican force marching north. The war with Mexico preoccupied the president, but he regarded its rewards as vastly outweighing all sacrifices: Texas was won; now he turned his attention to the other Mexican provinces north of the Rio Grande, New Mexico, and Alta California, and to the Oregon Country.

In his editorial manifesto, John Louis O'Sullivan wrote that "the day is not far distant when the Empires of the Atlantic and the Pacific would again flow together into one," and President Polk intended to fulfill this vision with his mighty one-term agenda, the most ambitious in American expansionist history: Before he left office he intended to add over 1 million square miles of territory to the United States.

3

President Polk's "whole of Oregon" inaugural credo and his avowed intention to end the joint occupancy agreement troubled the Tory government in England, then mired in colonial wars against the Maoris in New Zealand and the Sikhs in the Punjab region of India. The *Times* of London called for "resolute determination" and suggested sending a naval squadron to Oregon waters to keep the sun from setting on the British enclave in the American Northwest. Gunboat diplomats in London succeeded in having the fifty-gun warship *America* broken away from the British Pacific Squadron and dispatched to Juan de Fuca Strait under the command of Sir John Gordon, brother of British foreign secretary Lord Aberdeen. Gordon and Lieutenant William Peel, third son of Prime Minister Sir Robert Peel, traveled to Fort Vancouver in September 1845 to reassure British subjects there of the "firm protection of their rights."

In touring the Willamette valley, where the American farms and settlements were almost entirely confined, Lieutenant Peel met Jesse Applegate and observed that the immigrants, had they chosen the profession of arms, might have made "the best soldiers in the world." Applegate acknowledged that his farmer-comrades "were probably brave enough, but would never submit to discipline as soldiers." Recalling the rivalries and problems of his own overland journey, he said to Peel, "If the president himself had started across the plains to command a company, the first time he should choose a bad camp, or in any other way offend them, they would turn him out, and elect some one among themselves who should suit them better."

Bancroft believed the visit of the *America* and Peel's tour and talks with John McLoughlin, other Hudson's Bay employees and officials, and Americans in the Willamette valley averted a war between the two nations contending the Oregon Country. A decisive matter, the historian said, was McLoughlin's "joining the compact." This referred to the provisional government set up by the settlers at Champoeg after Ewing Young's death in 1841. Applegate had invited McLoughlin to participate, and since the oath of loyalty pledged to support the laws while remaining "a dutiful citizen of the United States or a subject of Great Britain," he took the pledge.

When Gordon and Peel came to Fort Vancouver, Bancroft wrote, "they expected to maintain England's hold on the north side of the Columbia River" but unexpectedly found the Hudson's Bay Company working with rather than against the Americans and "learned the fearless and resolute character of the colonists, and their rapidly increasing numbers." McLoughlin, Bancroft said, "constantly checked" any expressions of hostility toward the Americans, stating to his various visitors and "spies" (often one and the same), as he had openly averred in letters to England, that the country "was not worth a war."

Not all listened to the factor's admonitions, however, or approved of his fatalistic attitude or his generous assistance to the colonists. Chief among these disapprovers was Governor George Simpson, who regularly reported on the American invasion of Oregon to Whitehall.

□

At the time of the Gordon-Peel visit, Simpson and McLoughlin had been associates for over twenty years, a relationship that began eroding almost from the moment the two met in the Canadian wilderness en route to old Fort Astoria in 1824. Simpson was the ideal Hudson's Bay governor. He was brusque and ruthless, kept his eye on the ledgers, roamed about his domain in his *canot du maître*, dressed in a black suit, neck-stock, tartan-lined cloak, and tall beaver hat as he slashed staffs, closed unprofitable trading posts, and issued edicts and orders. McLoughlin, always wary of his ostentatious superior, could never keep a distance. Simpson visited Fort Vancouver frequently and when not at the fort was forever assailing the factor with correspondence and urgent memoranda.

In 1842 a rift opened between the two men that would never close. In June of that year McLoughlin received a letter from Simpson stating that John McLoughlin, Jr., had been murdered at Fort Stikine, the Hudson's Bay trade center near Wrangell, Alaska. Oldest of McLoughlin and Marguérite's four children, John Jr. had been left in charge of the remote post, which was surrounded by hostile natives and what a contemporary called "a gang of miscreant workers" and, according to Simpson's chillingly matter-of-fact letter, had died in a "drunken fray, by the hand of one of his own men." The governor said the young man's conduct at the post had been "exceedingly bad" and that when he drank he showed violence "amounting to insanity" and had driven his men to such a degree that he had been killed "under the influence of terror, as a measure of self-preservation" by one of his employees. Simpson added that any "Tribunal by which the case could be tried, would find a verdict of 'Justifiable homicide' " and advised McLoughlin not to press charges.

The White Eagle, at once devastated by the news and furious at Simpson's brutally accusatory account of the murder, decided to conduct his own investigation into the matter. He found many of his son's workers willing to testify that John Jr. rarely drank (indeed, fort records showed his liquor allowance had been scarcely touched) and that the problem with the men had erupted over Company rules discouraging liaisons with Indian women. John Jr. had quite correctly punished some men who had "scaled the Picquets" after stealing items from the post to give as gifts to their Indian paramours.

The factor also learned that the killer, a man named Heroux, after firing the shot and with his victim "writhing in the agonies of Death," had walked up and smashed in John Jr.'s head with a rifle butt. For this, Simpson coolly informed McLoughlin, the murderer had been turned over to the Russians, from whom Fort Stikine had been leased. When the Muscovites announced that they had no jurisdiction in the matter, Heroux was released from custody.

McLoughlin wrote Simpson bluntly, "Instead of conducting the examination so as to endeavor to find out what had led to the murder, you conducted it as if it had been an investigation into the moral conduct of the Deceased, and as if you were desirous to justify the conduct of the murderers."

After his findings, which he communicated to Hudson's Bay authorities, the official version of the story began to change from that reported by Simpson, so much so that a Company official wrote, "I have come to the conclusion that McLoughlin was not a habitual drunkard, that the punishments he inflicted were not of excessive severity; and that he was very vigilant and strict in keeping the men to their duty day and night."

That was the only satisfaction McLoughlin was to have in the tragedy. He requested that authorities at York Factory send Heroux and his henchmen to England for trial but was notified that if it were done he would have to bear the cost, more than £10,000. He had to abandon the case.

Soon after this awful summer McLoughlin returned to the Catholic faith of his youth and had his marriage to Marguérite sanctified.

□

As a result of one of George Simpson's memoranda to England in 1845, the government sent two officers out to Fort Vancouver as "observers" to scout military sites in the event of war and to gather information on the colonists. The men, Lieutenant Henry J. Warre of the Fifty-fourth Regiment and Lieutenant Mervin Vavasour of the Royal Engineers, traveled to the fort by the transcontinental route from the Red River to Fort Colville and reached Vancouver even before Captain Gordon and Lieutenant Peel of the Royal Navy departed for England that fall. The officer-emissaries posed, rather too ostentatiously, as tourists by wearing beaver hats, figured vests, and tweed trousers, and they lounged about the fort partaking of McLoughlin's hospitality. He knew they were spies but had to endure them as they made notes for their report to London.

The two gathered little information to support a military defense of Oregon lands, particularly those south of the Columbia, but they did make damaging accusations against Hudson's Bay's handling of the American influx, charging McLoughlin with welcoming the colonists to the country in such numbers that they now outnumbered British residents. Warre and Vavasour reported that they had personally observed immigrants arriving at Vancouver who were sold goods from the Company's stores at cheaper rates than those offered British subjects, and said that McLoughlin was also "overly friendly" to American missionaries. Without his aid, they said, "not thirty American families would now have been in the settlement."

The factor's good deeds were not to go unpunished. The two army lieutenants, and in his more moderate report, Peel of the Royal Navy, were critical of the Company's overly generous relationship with American colonists, directing them to the farmlands south of the river and assisting them with men, equipment, and transportation instead of discouraging their settlement and perhaps advising that they move on south to Mexican California. Hudson's Bay directors had repeatedly warned McLoughlin not to give more than minimal humane assistance to the Americans, their missionaries in particular. They knew, probably from Governor George Simpson's reports, that the factor not only sold the clerics all the supplies they needed to start their mission stations, but even extended the Company's protection over their little enclaves situated among unpredictable natives.

"What would you have?" McLoughlin responded. "Would you

have me turn the cold shoulder to the man of God who came to do that for the Indians which the company had neglected to do?"

Yes, he had assisted the colonists and the missionaries, had assisted Americans long before their numerous arrivals in 1843, '44, and '45, he said. Yes, he had provided food for them, and boats and boatmen to transport them to the Willamette before the Columbia iced over. Yes, he had taken care of their sick and injured at the fort hospital and gave them seeds if they could not afford to buy them so they could plant a crop and stave off starvation. (These matters Bancroft called "Christ-like Deeds.") Had he and his officers refused such humanitarian succor, he said, the Company would have been "covered with obloquy."

While touching lightly on the ingratitude of those who neglected to pay their debts and the rudeness of those who made him despair for American honor, McLoughlin nonetheless defended the Americans from what he considered to be the ignorant slurs of government spies.

"They have the same right to come that I have to be here," he insisted, and repelled the notion that the Company was duty-bound to defend British territorial rights. His responsibility, he said, was to Hudson's Bay directors, not to colonial or military affairs. Those were in Whitehall's province, not his. And as to being in league with the colonists' rudimentary government, he produced copies of letters he had written to England in 1843 describing the potential American threat to Fort Vancouver and asking for protection he never received.

The "White Eagle of the Old Northwest" admitted that British lands had been invaded, but said pointedly, "I have found British subjects just as keen at catching at an opportunity to benefit themselves, in some instances to my cost, as these American backwoodsmen."

McLoughlin had been keen to catch such opportunities himself, having a large property interest in Oregon City, terminus of the Oregon Trail south of the Columbia, and he had been wise to invest in it. He had grown weary of his responsibilities and thankless burdens, and had become desolate over the Company's plan to quit Fort Vancouver. He had first heard of the idea during one of Governor Simpson's visits. Sir George said Hudson's Bay headquarters would likely be moved to Vancouver Island, that the old post had outlived its usefulness, that the bar of the Columbia was too dangerous and the new headquarters would be more central to the northern operations. Now, in 1845, with the fur trade in a steep decline along the Columbia, the region was no longer prized. Moreover, the Company's directors were alarmed at the numbers and aggressive nature of the American settlers in the Willamette valley and feared for the safety of its stores and property at Vancouver.

McLoughlin, seeing that his life work was to be thrown away, tendered his resignation from the Hudson's Bay Company in the fall of 1845—the year the American population of Oregon reached 5,000—and took up residence in Oregon City the following spring. He had intended to seek American citizenship, but with the news in the spring of 1845 of the election of President Polk and the threat of war with England, he could not change his allegiance without being branded a traitor and forfeiting his retirement stipend.

He would have to await settlement of the boundary issue.

4

The Oregon boundary question had first surfaced as a diplomatic issue during the War of 1812, when Fort Astoria was sold to the North West Company. It cropped up again in 1818, when the United States negotiated with the British and fixed the Canadian-American border at the 49th parallel between Lake of the Woods and the crest of the Rocky Mountains. No boundary was established for the region west of the Rockies, and since both nations claimed the Oregon Country, in compromise negotiators decided to leave the territory "free and open" to both nations in what was termed "joint occupation."

Meantime, President James Monroe's secretary of state, John Quincy Adams, sought to pressure Spain to relinquish her claims to all territories north of the 42nd parallel, the northern border of

California. Weakened by colonial revolutions, Spain dragged out the negotiations but capitulated in 1819 with the Adams-Onís Treaty, which established the 42nd parallel as the northern boundary of California and turned over to the United States all claims to the Oregon Territory.

Adams said, "the remainder of the continent should ultimately be ours," and warned that his government "considered this hemisphere closed to any new European colonial establishments." In truth, the government considered the hemisphere closed to *old* colonial establishments as well, and with Spanish claims settled, diplomatic attention turned to Russia. In the late eighteenth and early nineteenth centuries, Russian traders had moved south of their holdings in Alaska and established outposts as far south as San Francisco Bay, but this expansionism ended in 1825. In that year, Adams negotiated a treaty with the czar's ministers providing that Russia would lay no claim to territory south of 54 degrees 40 minutes, a line eastward from the southern tip of Prince of Wales Island. The United States agreed in turn to make no claim to lands north of that line.

With only Great Britain and the United States remaining to contest the territory between the 42nd parallel and 54 degrees 40 minutes, in 1827 the joint occupation agreement between the two nations was extended indefinitely. The document carried the proviso that either power could terminate it after giving the other a year's notice.

The issue lay more or less dormant for a decade, but by the early 1840s, with the first emigrant trains entering Oregon, the boundary question again rose to prominence. Commercial interests became sensitive to the importance of establishing trade ports on the Pacific for business with the Far East, American migration to the Oregon Country was leaping forward (in 1841 there were about 500 Americans scattered throughout the region; by 1845, 5,000), and militant expansionism, the idea expressed in John O'Sullivan's "Manifest Destiny," was taking wing. The idea that Oregon should be annexed by the United States had been gaining momentum since Robert Gray discovered the mouth of the

Columbia River in 1792, and after a half century, the time had arrived to settle the matter.

Britain's case for superiority over the Oregon Country rested on the Nootka Sound Convention of 1790, under which Spain relinquished its claims, the discovery voyage of Captain James Cook in 1778, various explorations such as those of Vancouver in 1792 and Alexander Mackenzie in 1793, and the establishment, beginning in 1821, of fur-trading posts controlled by the Hudson's Bay Company.

The United States pointed to its own explorations: Gray; Lewis and Clark in 1804–06; the acquisition of Spanish rights north of the 42nd parallel via the Adams-Onís Treaty, and to the coast south of 54 degrees 40 minutes by treaty with the Russians; the fur-trading post at Astoria, established in 1811, and the first permanent settlement in Oregon; the actual occupation by American settlers, most of them in the Willamette valley; and the fact that Oregon was contiguous to American soil.

In his inaugural address President Polk had referred to America's claim to Oregon as "clear and unquestionable," but he at least nodded politely toward John Bull by saying that "every obligation imposed by treaty or conventional stipulation should be sacredly respected." He had no intention of risking war with England—he already had an impending war on his hands, with Mexico over the Texas annexation—and he wanted to resolve the matter expediently and peacefully by extending the 49th parallel west to the Pacific. Despite all the talk of "54-40 or Fight!" and the use of it as an unauthorized campaign slogan, the 54th parallel was never seriously in contention. Nor for that matter did England aspire to the whole region as far south as the California line, but early in the dispute did want to make the Columbia River, which meandered through Oregon to the sea several hundred miles south of 49 degrees, the southern border of Canada. The British, specifically its Hudson's Bay directors, believed control of the river essential to maintain hegemony over the interior fur trade. Without some adjustment to the 49th parallel, the British insisted, they would be cut off from the southern end of Vancouver Island and denied access to the Juan de Fuca Strait.

A few months after Polk's inaugural, Richard Pakenham, the British minister in Washington, was instructed to reopen negotiations of the Oregon question. He said his government was willing to accept the 49th parallel boundary but with some modifications of the line as it reached the sea and retention of rights to navigate the Columbia.

On September 12, 1845, Polk replied through his ineffectual secretary of state, James Buchanan (who, Bernard De Voto said, "had the greatest possible shrewdness but no backbone whatever"), proposing extending the 49th with all of Vancouver Island ceded to the British, but he refused to offer use of the Columbia.

Polk could not resist writing into the document a statement that the United States was making the concession even though its claims to *all* of Oregon were patently valid.

Pakenham rejected the offer without submitting it to his government and Polk, angered by this, broke off the talks.

In December, in his first message to Congress, the president placed the failure of the negotiations entirely on Britain, stating that the United States had acted in "a spirit of liberal concession" and "will be relieved of all responsibilities which may follow the failure to settle the controversy." He referred to the Monroe Doctrine, asked Congress to provide armed escorts for wagon trains heading for Oregon, and said it would be desirable to serve England a one-year notice that the joint occupancy agreement would be terminated.

Senator Thomas Hart Benton of Missouri, the most voluble expansionist in Congress and a tireless promoter of an all-American Oregon, originally supported compromising with Britain on the boundary issue, but after the failure of the opening parley he suggested that the government muster "thirty or forty thousand American rifles beyond the Rocky Mountains that will be our effective negotiator." And in the January 1846 issue of the news magazine *Niles' Register*, the editorial titled "Are We to Have

Peace or War?" had to do not with war with Mexico but war with England, which the editor believed the more likely of the two; he also thought that an Anglo-American war would be precipitated by the Oregon boundary question.

In London the American president's bellicose language distressed the Peel ministry, which was juggling problems ranging from the potato famine in Ireland to colonial campaigns in New Zealand and India. Peel's foreign secretary, Lord Aberdeen, long a proponent of compromise, told the American minister in London that "the possibility of a rupture with the United States" had to be "considered."

On April 16, 1846, a resolution was introduced in the Senate to "abrogate the convention of 1827" and give notice to the British government that the United States would terminate the Oregon joint occupancy agreement.

Benton of Missouri filibustered on behalf of the measure for three days; it passed both houses, the president signed it, and on April 28 he sent the notice by special packet to the sovereign of Great Britain.

During these difficult days fortuitous news arrived in London that the Hudson's Bay Company had moved its main depot from the Columbia to Fort Victoria on Vancouver Island. Now Lord Aberdeen and other moderates in the government were able to counter the argument among their colleagues in Parliament that the Columbia River was indispensable, not only for Hudson's Bay trade but for the western provinces of Canada. Aberdeen quietly informed the American secretary of state that the 49th parallel was acceptable to England. The memorandum asked only that when the line reached saltwater it would swing through the main channel of the Strait of Georgia to Juan de Fuca Strait and westward to the Pacific.

The Oregon treaty, signed by both nations on June 15, 1846, recognized the 49th parallel as the international boundary from the Rocky Mountains to the middle of the channel between Vancouver Island and the mainland, thence along a line running southward through Juan de Fuca Strait to the Pacific. Free navigation of the channel and strait by both signatories was stipulated.

Senator Benton made a speech upon the treaty ratification, pointing out that the 49th parallel had been tendered to Britain for nearly forty years; by Jefferson in 1807, Monroe in 1818 and 1824, Adams in 1826, Tyler in 1842, and Polk in 1845.

□

When news of the settlement reached the Columbia on November 12, 1846, not all the Americans there greeted it with approval. Some expressed dismay that Washington had retreated from its "All of Oregon," "Fifty-Four Forty or Fight!" battle stance; others pointed to the few American farms located near Hudson's Bay posts north of Forty-nine, lands now in British control.

To these malcontents H. H. Bancroft devoted one of his finest polemics. "Man is a preposterous pig," he wrote, "probably the greediest animal that crawls upon this planet." He continued:

Here were fertile lands and temperate airs; meadows, forest, and mountains; bright rivers and broad ocean seaboard, enough of earth for half a dozen empires; and all for nothing—all stolen from the savages and never yet a struggle, never yet a dollar in return, only fevers, syphilis, and the like by way of compensation; and yet these colonial representatives of the great American nation grudge their brethren, but little later than themselves from Great Britain, a few squares of land round the posts which they had built and occupied for so long . . .

Instead of falling on their knees for the blessings bestowed upon them, he said, "they fell to cursing; they cursed the British, and particularly President Polk, for failing to carry out his policy avowed before election." They had believed in that promise, had painted "54-40" on their wagon covers, "and poverty-stricken and piggish, had wended their way to the Pacific in the faith that they were helping to accomplish this high destiny for the United States, this broad destiny for themselves."

The Americans had won five degrees of latitude, he said, yet, preposterous pigs that they were, wanted more.

But since they were not to get more, the colonists of the Willamette valley turned their energies toward increasing their numbers, petitioning for territorial status and what the most ambitious thought was an eventuality: statehood.

Increasing the population of the Oregon Country by encouraging and aiding new emigration was not a point of argument, but granting territorial status proved to be bitterly disputatious. The provisional government set up by Oregon settlers in 1843 had made a point of excluding slavery in the region, and when a similar ban was included in the Oregon territorial bill in 1846, pro-slavery forces in Congress defeated it, which they did again in 1847, despite support of the legislation by President Polk and Senator Benton.

The idea of instant post–boundary settlement statehood was regarded as even more of a distant dream. Even had slavery not been an issue, granting statehood to an unmapped wilderness as remote from civilization as Timbuktu seemed laughable. The matter of distance had been elaborately, amusingly, and indelibly expounded upon as far back as an 1825 Senate debate in which Senator Mahlon Dickerson of New Jersey (subsequently secretary of the navy in the Jackson and Van Buren administrations) rose with some statistics he had worked out for his colleagues.

"The whole distance from Washington to the mouth of the Columbia River is 4,650 miles," he said. "The distance, therefore, that a member of Congress of this 'state of Oregon' would be obliged to travel in coming to the seat of government and returning home, would be 9,300 miles. This at a rate of eight dollars for every twenty miles, would make his traveling expenses amount to $3,720." He said that at the rate members of Congress travel according to law, twenty miles per day, "it would require, to come to the seat of government from Oregon and return, 465 days. . . .

But if he should travel at the rate of thirty miles per day, it would require 306 days. Allow for [rest on] Sundays it would amount to 350 days. This would allow the member a fortnight to rest himself at Washington, before he should commence his journey home."

The senator said, "It would be more expeditious, however, to come by water round Cape Horn, or to pass through Behring's Strait round the north coast of this continent to Baffin's Bay, thence through Davis' Straits to the Atlantic, and so on to Washington. It is true, this passage is not yet discovered, except upon our maps; but it will be as soon as Oregon shall be a state."

Actually, the impatient Oregonians did not have to wait for discovery of the west-to-east Northwest Passage before their new home was declared a territory of the United States. In fact, they had less than two years to wait.

22

THE BOSTONIAN

"GREAT CHANGES ARE AT HAND. . . ."

1

On June 15, 1846, the day the United States and Great Britain signed the Oregon boundary treaty, Francis Parkman rode into Fort Laramie on the North Platte below the mouth of Laramie Creek. He had departed Boston early in April on a gentlemanly "Summer's Journey Out of Bounds" to observe the Indians of the Plains and perhaps write something about them before their way of life disappeared, a casualty of the advent of the white man. In truth, he did not know precisely what he was doing on the Oregon Trail or what he would do when he returned. He was twenty-three and Harvard educated, and had the luxury of a wealthy bachelor's aimlessness.

Parkman had been a familiar, respected name in Massachusetts for a century or more when Francis was born on Boston's Beacon Hill in 1823. His grandfather had risen to become one of the city's wealthiest merchants; his father, an 1806 Harvard graduate, served as minister of the New North Church for thirty-six years; his mother was Caroline Hall of Medford and her father owned a farm bordering 3,000 acres of timberland known as the Middlesex Fells where young "Frank" hunted, trapped, and hiked.

At age twelve Parkman attended private school in Medford and demonstrated an aptitude for composition and literature; in 1840 he entered Harvard, earned a Phi Beta Kappa key, became a popular clubman, and fell in love with a girl from Keene, New Hampshire, who turned down his entreaties and married another.

He tramped alone in the Berkshires and made many excursions into the mountains and forests of New England, Montreal, and Québec; became adept at woodcraft; sharpened his rifle and horsemanship skills. "I was haunted with wilderness images day and night," he later wrote.

During his undergraduate work at Harvard and as a law student later, his health faltered. He began having heart palpitations, migraine headaches, swellings in his joints, insomnia, weakening eyesight, and the general diagnostical grab bag labeled "nervousness." His friends attributed the problems to his "Spartan life," his incessant hiking, canoeing, and camping in the back country of northern New England, sleeping under the stars in wet and cold weather, wading through frozen streams, and pushing himself to exhaustion in the college gymnasium.

In his senior year at Harvard Parkman suffered a physical collapse and since he abhorred idleness, he convalesced by sailing for Europe, then part of the education of every wealthy gentleman, well or ill. He reached Gibraltar on a barkentine out of Boston loaded with fruit, traveled on to Sicily and wandered for weeks in the island's western wilds, spent time in a Passionist Fathers retreat in Rome in hopes of gaining some insights into Catholicism, and tramped about Switzerland, France, and England.

He returned to Cambridge in June 1844 and received his degree in August, then spent eighteen more months studying law, earning his jurisprudence degree in January 1846. He never applied for admittance to the bar and seems to have given little thought to actually practicing in the profession. History and literature (they were attached in Parkman's time, great histories rising to great literature) had taken command of his imagination.

He did not have to earn a living, but since it would have been unthinkable for a Parkman not to do something constructive with his life, he began thinking of combining his literary interests with his love of the outdoors. He began by publishing articles on his trips to New Hampshire in *Knickerbocker Magazine* in New York, something his family and friends believed was more a harmless hobby than anything leading to a profession, but soon he cast about for a bigger project. When he was eighteen and at Harvard, he had made an exploration into the northern New Hampshire woods and out of the experience felt an inspiration to write a history of the last French war in America and the conquest of Canada. That great project now returned to mind: Since he had conceived a great admiration for Pontiac, the Ottawa chief who conspired against the British, perhaps he could begin a history of the French and Indian Wars with a scholarly book on Pontiac's rebellion of 1763. To do so he would have to visit many libraries, read original documents, and make voluminous notes, but he had strained his eyes studying law and his physician warned him that he must take a respite from reading and research. What to do until he could resume scholarship?

He was considering his options when a cousin, one with the perfect Bostonian name of Quincy Adams Shaw, came visiting and said he was preparing to depart for the Rocky Mountains on a hunting expedition and would Frank like to come along?

Parkman's darkening days suddenly brightened. The seasoned if somewhat insular outdoorsman had been handed the opportunity to travel west of the Mississippi with a trusted and lively companion for a season among the savages such as Herman Melville— whose first novel, *Typee*, was published in 1846—had experienced in the South Seas. Here was a chance to witness Indian life first-hand. He realized that the Plains natives differed markedly from the forest tribes of the Eastern Seaboard, but even the differences could be important grist for preparation of the book he intended to title *The Conspiracy of Pontiac and the Indian War after the Conquest of Canada.*

Parkman visited Nathaniel Wyeth of Cambridge, Oregon Trail

pioneer and one-time *bourgeois* at Fort Hall, then bid his parents
and friends farewell, and took a riverboat down the Ohio to Saint
Louis, where on April 28, 1846, he and Shaw set out up the Missouri by riverboat to Westport Landing.

The things he saw with his tired eyes, no matter how lovely or
awful, invigorated him and soothed, if not cured, whatever ailed
him, stimulating his ability to remember and describe. Everything
interested him, especially the people—the emigrant farmers, the
traders, soldiers, and frontiersmen—he squinted at and who peered
back at the handsome, long-nosed Bostonian with the shock of
brown hair curling over his ears and collar who wanted nothing
more than to learn from them and jot things in his notebooks.

At Westport, Parkman and Shaw completed outfitting for their
journey and hired as guide Henry Chatillon, an intelligent, illiterate
plainsman, "a natural gentleman," Parkman said, who had spent
two decades trapping and hunting in the Rockies and, as the Bostonian delightedly learned, was married to the daughter of Bull
Bear, principal chief among the Oglala Sioux. The party was completed by the hiring of a good-natured Canadian named Deslauriers
to serve as cook, wagon driver, mule skinner, and general factotum.

As they collected their horses and supplies to move out on the
Trail, Parkman heard the pilots shouting at the emigrant men to
get their wives, children, dogs, horses, chickens, cow herds, oxen,
mules, and wagons ready to begin moving west by daybreak;
watched trade wagon convoys coming in from the Santa Fé Trail;
listened to the rumors of war with Mexico. One thing about Westport that concerned him more than the war talk: "Whiskey," he
wrote, "circulates more freely in Westport than is altogether safe
in a place where every man carries a loaded pistol in his pocket."

Parkman and Shaw decided to avoid traveling with an emigrant
train, too slow for their purposes, but did find themselves linking
up with a party led by Captain Bill Chandler, an Irishman retired
from Her Majesty's Army, out to see the West with a vast amount
of superfluous baggage and a variety of arms to kill the West's
animal life. With the captain were his brother Jack; three *engagés*
hired as bearers, muleteers, and general handymen; and a fop

named Romaine, said to be a Templar and graduate of Trinity College. This man, Bernard De Voto said, was "a faintly literary gentleman who bossed everything, knew nothing, was inept in all things, and expressed his type at the very beginning by leading them off the trail for a full week."

The ten men made their first stopover at Fort Leavenworth and there met General Stephen Watts Kearny of the First Dragoons Regiment, who was just then gathering his troops for the long march to Bent's Fort, Santa Fé, and Alta California.

2

For one setting out with only a vague idea of linking the Plains tribes with future research on Pontiac of the Ottawa, there was a weird precision in Francis Parkman's plans. Although he was trained for law, history had a hold on him, and it swirled in the wake of the steamer he took down the Ohio to the Mississippi and in the tracks of the horses he rode to Fort Laramie. Indeed, in the six weeks he took to reach that out-of-bounds place on the Laramie River, he quite literally rode into history, then made some of it himself.

This was the summer of 1846 and, only a month after the Bostonian had departed the salons, soirées, eligible ladies, and intellectual causeries of Boston and Cambridge society, a leathery, tobacco-chewing American general named Zachary Taylor fought and won two battles against a Mexican army. These occurred on May 7 and May 9 among the cactus and chaparral at Palo Alto and Resaca de la Palma, places nobody could find on a map but that belated newspaper reports said were "just north of the Rio Grande," and they took place a week *before* the United States and Mexico were officially at war.

Then, at about the time Parkman and Shaw were chatting at the rail of the steamer taking them from Saint Louis to Westport Landing, a prosperous Illinois farmer named George Donner, age sixty-two, thrice married and with thirteen children, rode out in front of an Oregon Trail caravan bound from Independence to California. Accompanying him were his newest and last wife, Tamsen, forty-five; their five youngest children; and Donner's older brother Jacob and his family. In Springfield, Donner's neighbor James Frazier Reed, a furniture factory proprietor who had fought with Abraham Lincoln's company in the Blackhawk War, also set out for the Missouri border. With him were his wife, Margaret, their four children, and Margaret's mother, Mrs. Sarah Keyes, age seventy-five. While her husband was away attending to circuit court duties, Mary Todd Lincoln and her son Robert came out to see the Reeds' departure. James Reed had fabricated a huge "two-story" wagon fitted out with bunks and even a stove drawn by eight Durham oxen, and he had two accessory wagons stocked with "fancy goods" and liquor, plus spare draft animals and horses.

The Donner brothers had twelve yoke of oxen, five saddle horses, a small herd of milk and beef cattle, several hired hands, a dog, and a fortune of $10,000 in cash sewn into a quilt.

Parkman saw the Donner-Reed wagons corralled on the prairie beyond Fort Laramie that June as he stood on a bluff above the fort and watched other emigrant trains cross the Laramie River. He may also have encountered some of the party when he wrote of entering a log-and-mud "apartment" at the fort full of men "all more or less drunk" on Missouri whiskey apparently carried by "a company of California emigrants." These had unencumbered the liquor at great loss to the fort's traders, he said, and were getting rid of the rest of it by drinking it on the spot.

At the time he saw them, the Donner-train occupants were otherwise unremarkable, not much different from the other emigrant parties departing the frontier.

But the Donners were making mistakes at the commencement of their journey: They were getting a late start, rushing to catch up with the rear guard of the '46 migration, and they were over-burdened with "fancy goods." Their gravest miscalculation lay in their decision to take an untested shortcut to California recommended in a popular guidebook written by a zealot named Lansford

Warren Hastings. This Ohioan had gone out to the Mexican province in 1842 and dreamed of a flow of American pioneers and adventurers, a revolution, and perhaps himself as president of an independent republic. In his *Emigrant's Guide to Oregon and California*, published in 1845, a year before he saw the route himself, Hastings recommended that overlanders depart the Oregon Trail at Fort Bridger instead of taking the customary turnoff at Fort Hall. He advised them to travel directly across the Wasatch Range into the Salt Lake valley, thence across the Great Basin to pick up the California Trail at the Humboldt River of Nevada. The route, he said, would save 400 miles.

Nearly six months would pass before any news of the Donners reached California, and it would be many months later that Parkman would learn their fate.

3

Although Parkman, Shaw, and the others preferred to ride at their own pace, hunting and resting at their leisure and observing no timetable, they did occasionally attach to an emigrant train and sometimes made a night camp among the circled wagons. There the men gathered at the cookfires and told the "news," mostly rumor amplified in the retelling, brought in by riders from the Missouri settlements: that bands of Kaw Indians were lurking in the brush along the Kansas and Platte Rivers eager to fall upon the trains for loot and scalps; that a party of Englishmen—perhaps a reference to Captain Chandler's group—were on the move under Her Britannic Majesty's orders to incite the natives to, as Parkman wrote, "rob, murder, and annihilate" travelers on the Oregon Trail; and that thousands of "Saints"—Mormons—were gathered near the emigrant camps, armed with rifles, knives, and brass field-pieces. These people, the stories said, had blood in their eyes after being chased out of Nauvoo, their settlement in swampy Illinois country bordering the Mississippi, and then evicted from Missouri as well.

Parkman fell in with this latter fantasy, writing, "No one could predict what would be the result when large armed bodies of these fanatics should encounter the most impetuous and reckless of their old enemies on the prairies."

The few Mormons in the vicinity were, in fact, 100 miles north, near Kanesville, Iowa, and while it was true that they kept their guns loaded and eyes narrowed for the sighting of any hated Missourians—whom they called collectively "pukes"—they were not interested in the innocent "Gentile" travelers on the Oregon Trail.

Bernard De Voto said that Parkman's experiences on the Oregon Trail, and what he wrote of them, were hampered by his "Brahmin snobberies," and that he "almost felt the emigration" but "succumbed to a parochialism of his class" and failed to have the empathy for the pioneers needed to write a great work. In his unyieldingly disapproving approach to the Mormons, whom he consistently dismissed as "fanatics," Parkman mirrored a majority attitude but he missed one of the epic stories within the epic of the Oregon Trail.

The Mormons he saw that summer were the vanguard of thousands searching for a new Zion and but a year distant from finding it. They had vacated their homes in Nauvoo during the winter before Parkman saw the first of their number and eighteen months after the murder of Joseph Smith, founder of their Church of Jesus Christ of Latter-Day Saints. Smith's successor, the forty-three-year-old Vermont-born farmer-carpenter Brigham Young, had supervised the Nauvoo exodus in February 1846, leading 1,600 of his "peculiar people" across the ice-blocked Mississippi to a "Camp of Israel" at Sugar Grove, Iowa, while the others in Illinois waited to cross the river. By June, at about the time Parkman reached Fort Laramie, Young had covered the first 400 miles toward Zion by leading the Saints across Iowa to a place on the Missouri River where no town yet stood, but which became known as Kanesville and later as Council Bluffs.

In the winter, while Parkman was warming his feet at his Beacon Hill fireplace, 12,000 Mormons had established quarters at Florence, Nebraska, near Omaha, where 600 of them were to die

in the snows. And in April 1847, after the first three parts of Parkman's Oregon Trail memoir had appeared in a New York magazine, Brigham Young took a "Pioneer Band" of 143 men, 3
women, and 2 children and pushed west along the north bank of
the Platte (to avoid contact with emigrant Missourians on the south
bank). The band had seventy-three wagons; 211 horses, mules, and
oxen; six months' rations; and a small brass cannon to frighten off
hostile Indians. This vanguard reached Fort Laramie and crossed
South Pass in June, bore southwest to Fort Bridger, and moved on
over the rugged Uinta Mountains and then across the desert into
the eastern spur of the Wasatch Range.

On the last fifty miles of their journey, they followed a narrow
and tortuous trail across the Wasatch that had been broken the
year before by the Donners and the Reeds. On July 19, 1847, after
the sixth of Parkman's twenty-one Oregon Trail memoir installments had appeared, Young's scouting party caught the sun's glint
of a great silvery body of water in the distance, and on the twenty-
fourth the Mormons entered the valley of the latter-day Dead Sea
known as the Great Salt Lake. They were 1,400 miles from Nauvoo, "thrown like a stone from a sling," Young said, "and we have
lodged in this goodly place just where the Lord wants his people
to gather."

Within a month of their arrival the Saints had cleared a seven-
mile wagon road to bring fir and pine logs to build a fort and frame
and roof houses, and had thrown up a stockade that enclosed
twenty-nine cabins, a smithy, communal storehouses, and corrals.
So much was done in that month that Young and an escort were
able to retrace their route to the Iowa-Nebraska frontier and point
the 13,000 others waiting there toward the Mormon Trail and their
new home.

□

Four days out on the Platte, a country Parkman, apparently infused
with Stephen Long's old exploration reports, called "the Great
American Desert," the party spotted a buffalo herd and made their

first serious "hunt," the white man's euphemism in buffalo country for "slaughter." Parkman's horse Pontiac had not been broken to such exertions, and the Bostonian was armed with only a pistol, but these were not hindrances. Buffalo were big, dull-witted targets with poor eyesight, and they tended to bunch up: A hunter merely kept shooting into the herd until one or more fell, blood frothing at mouth and nostrils from lung-shots (their deeply buried hearts were rarely hit and bullets glanced off the plates of their skulls). The more their numbers increased, the more were killed—and wasted. Often only the tongue and a few steaks carved from the hump were taken. Parkman's guide Henry Chatillon, the only real marksman in the party, was averse to sport killing and in deference to him the Americans stopped it.

By the time Parkman's party reached the South Platte, they stopped something else: They had had enough of the Englishmen. Captain Chandler "was by no means partial to us," Parkman said, and seemed determined to retard the journey "we were anxious to quicken" by calling a halt at unreasonable hours, often when they had traveled but fifteen miles. The Americans resolved to travel on to Fort Laramie on their own, a matter Captain Chandler said was "an extraordinary proceeding, upon my word!" However, his officer-as-gentleman remonstrances did not change the decision.

Parkman reached Fort Laramie on June 15, 1846, the day of the Anglo-American treaty settling the Oregon boundary question and the day before a band of American squatters captured the town of Sonoma, raised their homemade Bear Flag Republic banner, and signaled the beginning of the conquest of Mexican California.

In 1846, Laramie was a fur-trader's oasis, a decrepit but busy log-palisaded adobe fort on the North Platte adjacent to 600 lodges and upwards of 2,000 Oglala and Brulé Sioux. The Americans arrived there just as a band of Oglala, headed by a chief named Old Smoke, rode in from their village at a watering place called Horse Creek. This event, a happening common to the habitués of the fort, proved eventful to Parkman. Chatillon, who was married to a Sioux woman, made a visit to the Indian camp and introduced his Boston friends to Old Smoke. The chief agreed to let them stay.

In the two weeks that followed that July of 1846, Parkman found the "savage adventure" of his Oregon Trail journey. The experience was not to be without cost. He had come out West to study Indians and improve his health, and he had in fact strengthened on the journey to Laramie. But once there he had contracted dysentery and was so weakened he could scarcely walk, and it was in this frail state he was given the opportunity to study the Indians and live among them.

When he and Shaw joined them, Old Smoke's people were preparing to go to war against the Shoshoni to punish some obscure outrage committed the year before, but for reasons equally obscure the war party became a buffalo hunt, a safer venue for Parkman to observe the Indians in their daily survival work. He was dangerously ill, still battling dysentery, taking six grains of opium at a dose, feeble, giddy, and often doubled over with the agony of stomach cramps. Nor did the Oglala diet help. Early in his stay with Old Smoke's band he visited the chief's lodge and was invited to stay for a meal. Outside, one of the chief's wives knocked a puppy in the head with a stone mallet, chopped the dog to pieces, singed its hair off over the fire, and threw it all, entrails included, into a stew pot. Parkman ate his share. "A dog-feast," he said, "is the greatest compliment a Dakota can offer to his guest; and, knowing that to refuse eating would be an affront, we attacked the little dog, and devoured him."

He joined the hunters even when mounting his horse exhausted his ebbing strength. "To have worn the airs of an invalid would certainly have been an indiscretion," he wrote, and in any event he felt he had to go. If he lay abed, he said, "a horse, a rifle, a pair of pistols, and a red shirt might have offered temptations too strong for aboriginal virtue." While hunting buffalo on horseback over a broken country when "he could scarcely sit upright in the saddle" was not strictly necessary for maintaining prestige, he believed "that to tame the devil it is best to take him by the horns."

He had a sharp eye for the divergence of cultures around Fort Laramie: the Indians; the French-Canadians who married into their bands; the trappers, hunters, and guides; and the American emigrants camped in the meadows along the river.

Parkman knew there could be but one end to it. The Indians were a dying race and he saw the Oglala as representative of a culture that could never withstand the white invasion. At Horse Creek he once stood with Old Smoke and one of his young wives, who sat astride a fine mule caparisoned with whitened deerskins and held her husband's feathered lance and shield. Not far from them were other tribal leaders, "stately figures, their white buffalo robes thrown over their shoulders, gazing coldly upon us," and behind them, their camp, swarming with warriors, women, children, and dogs, and "close at hand, the wide, shallow stream was alive with boys, girls, and young squaws, splashing, screaming, and laughing in the water." For a thousand summers such a carefree and peaceful tableau had taken place there, but Parkman saw something that augured the end of it. Approaching and crossing Horse Creek came a long train of emigrant wagons, "dragging on in slow procession by the encampment of the people whom they and their descendents, in the space of a century, are to sweep from the face of the earth."

He tried to depict the Indians he saw with honesty: They were at once noble and petty; they had great courage and physical prowess; they lived in a disorderly society, rudimentary in its greatest moments; they were preoccupied by internecine warfare; they were dogged and doomed by such ancient traits as their inabilility to make a plan and abide by it.

"Great changes are at hand," he wrote. "The buffalo will dwindle away, and the large wandering communities who depend on them for support must be broken and scattered. The Indians will soon be abased by whiskey and overawed by military posts; so that within a few years the traveller may pass in tolerable security through their country. Its dangers and its charms will have disappeared altogether."

As his stay among the Oglala lengthened Parkman became an insomniac—the warriors drummed and sang at all hours and his host had dreams that forced him to get up at midnight to join in a long song-chant. He wrote of being "hipped"—depressed—a condition that would plague him throughout his life. But when the Sioux exhausted their stock of buffalo meat and moved north toward the Black Hills, he accompanied them. Away from the camp, in the open wilderness, afoot as often as on horseback, he seemed to recoup his strength and after two weeks with Old Smoke's band was ready to return to Laramie.

He distributed his few remaining gifts among his hosts and then, with a couple of Indian companions and one of the French-Canadians in the camp, took his leave of them and returned on August 3 to Fort Laramie, where Shaw and the others had preceded him.

They decided to return to Saint Louis by a different route, a 300-mile drop straight south to the Arkansas River, east to Bent's Fort and to the Missouri frontier along the Santa Fé Trail. They joined a party of trappers and hunters and set off.

En route to Bent's they learned that the expected war with Mexico was no longer a rumor, and at a dilapidated village in Colorado called the Pueblo they picked up some details of Zachary Taylor's first victories, encountered a scattering of Mormons and learned of their desperate winter crossing of the Mississippi from Nauvoo into Iowa. Parkman continued to regard the Saints as "blind and desperate fanatics."

Bent's Fort, the great oasis on the Arkansas River, showed the effects Kearny's expedition had in passing through en route to Santa Fé, the Gila River, and California: His dragoon horses, draft animals, and cattle herd had consumed the grass around the fort.

Parkman and Shaw returned to Westport Landing, paid off Deslauriers, and, with Chatillon accompanying them, took a steamer downriver to the Mississippi, an eight-day voyage with one-third of the time spent fast aground on a sandbar. Once they reached the crowded Saint Louis levee, the Bostonians took rooms at Planter's House, sought a tailor, and bought clothing appropriate for the return home.

Henry Chatillon paid them a last visit at the hotel. "No one who met him in the streets of St. Louis," Parkman wrote, "would have taken him for a hunter fresh from the Rocky Mountains. He was very neatly and simply dressed in a suit of dark cloth; for although since his sixteenth year he had scarcely been a month together among the abodes of men, he had a native good taste which always led him to pay attention to his personal appearance." Both Bostonians had a high regard for their guide—"He had served us with a fidelity and zeal beyond all praise"—and in addition to the salary he had been paid at Westport, Shaw had given Chatillon his horse and Parkman presented him with his favorite rifle.

A fortnight later, in mid-October, they were home, and in February 1847 in *Knickerbocker Magazine* appeared the first of twenty-one installments of "A Summer's Journey Out of Bounds By a Bostonian," under the general heading "The Oregon Trail."

WAIILATPU

"IS THERE ANYTHING I CAN DO TO STOP THE BLEEDING?"

1

On the Oregon Trail and its busy tributary into California, 1847 opened and closed in lamentation.

The year began with a story of a calamity in the snowdrifts of Truckee Pass in the eastern foothills of the Sierra Nevada Range. There were no details in the early reports received at John Augustus Sutter's fort on the west side of the mountains, only sketchy information on an emigrant party of Illinoisians said to have been shut out of the passes by wind and blizzard. The details, when they did become known, were terrible beyond imagination.

□

When Francis Parkman saw their wagons on the meadow beyond Fort Laramie in June, the Donners and the Reeds and the others making up their California-bound train were getting a late start toward reaching the Sierras before the onset of winter, but they were confident. They planned to reduce travel time by 400 miles by departing the Oregon Trail at Fort Bridger and taking the "Hastings Cut-off." This route would take them south along the Wasatch Range, past the Great Salt Lake, and across the Utah-Nevada desert to the Sierra foothills in time to cross the mountains before winter closed them out.

Their party had swollen to eighty-seven, forty-one of them children, and twenty-three sagging wagons when it set out from Bridger on the last day of July 1846. Within a few days' crawling travel, they learned the awful truth of the shortcut described in Lansford Hastings's guidebook; the Donner-Reed train took twenty-one days to make the thirty-six-mile crossing of the Wasatch Mountains.

They reached the Humboldt River on September 30, after a nightmarish crossing of the desert, which killed most of their oxen and forced abandonment of all but a few of their wagons, and they approached the Sierra Nevada foothills a month later. By now they had exhausted their rations and were eating wild onions and dabs of tallow from their tar buckets. Many of their cows and horses were stolen in a raid by Paiute Indians; they hoped to salvage the remaining animals against the prospect of a starving time before reaching the Sacramento valley.

On October 20, eleven killing weeks out of Bridger, they reached the lush meadows of the Truckee River and rested, grazing their pitifully reduced animals for five fatal days with an early winter snow falling on the mountain ridges before them. The party moved on to a big lake on the thirty-first, just beyond which lay Truckee Pass, the last major barrier between them and their destination.

But they could not cross. The blizzards, snowdrifts, and murderous winds of the pass closed the corridor. They found an old cabin, threw another one together from timber and driftwood along the lake, made lean-tos and brush shelters, and erected tepees and tents to huddle in against the snow and cold. Snowshoes were fashioned for futile attempts to cross the mountain range. The last animals, including the Reeds' dog, were killed for food. They made gruel for the babies from precious handfuls of flour; ate owls, wolves, and whatever other starving animals strayed near enough to be killed with a rifle shot; boiled hides and drank the gluey broth; and, on the day after Christmas, began roasting and eating strips of flesh from the dead.

By the time the first rescue party reached them on February 4, 1847, Jake Donner and three of his hired hands were dead; George Donner was dying from exposure, starvation, and a gashed hand turned gangrenous; and the others were reduced to wraiths, several teetering on the brink of insanity. Rescuers stumbled through snowdrifts to come upon scenes more chilling than any Sierra gale. In one appalling camp where a woman named Elizabeth Graves and her five-year-old son Franklin had died, parts of their bodies were found boiling in a pot as her infant daughter, a miraculous survivor, lay wailing near Elizabeth's carved-up corpse. Two members of the rescue team, William Eddy and William Foster, who had struggled over Truckee Pass with a few others to seek help at Sutter's Fort on the Sacramento River, returned to an unutterable horror. Each had left a young son behind at Truckee Lake in the care of others, and both boys had died. A big, well-educated German named Lewis Keseberg, who had emigrated to the United States only two years past, told Eddy and Foster that he had found the boys' bodies in the snow and eaten them. He was discovered lying beside a pot containing the liver and lungs of one of the boys and said he had subsisted entirely on human flesh despite the nearby ox quarters lying in the snow, which he claimed were "too dry for eating."

Of the eighty-nine members of the train who crossed the Wasatch Mountains, five had died before reaching Truckee Lake; thirty-six others perished in the camps below Truckee Pass or in attempting to cross it, and one died after the rescue: The toll was forty-two dead, forty-seven alive.

After her ordeal, twelve-year-old Virginia Reed, daughter of James and Margaret, all of whom had survived the ordeal without resorting to cannibalism, wrote a cousin back home, "Never take no cut ofs and hury along as fast as you can."

2

Marcus and Narcissa Whitman were not sure what they had accomplished in their eleven years in the Oregon Country. They had come out in '36, before any migration, great or small, filled with inspiration and fervent to do the Lord's work "among the heathen." They had carved out their mission station among the Cayuse people at their Place of the Rye Grass with the expectation that if they made the Bible and its message available the people would come, just as the Flatheads and Nez Percé had journeyed all the way to Saint Louis to find out about the white man's God.

They were not expecting miracles; the work would take time, supreme physical and mental effort, and forbearance, and this, they knew, would take a toll on them. But they would make progress even if as water dripping on a stone. They would convert the savages to Christianity, send the saved out to proselytize among others of their tribe and bring them in to Waiilatpu in ever-increasing numbers. They were prepared for every exigency but failure.

The sheer joy over their prospects and the daily labors building the mission house, schoolrooms, outbuildings, and mill; tilling the soil and planting; teaching and ministering to the bodies as well as the souls of those who drifted to them masked any foreboding they had after hearing Dr. John McLoughlin's early warning that the Cayuse were a "bad people," not to be trusted. At first the Whitmans could not countenance such an idea—there were no "bad" Indians, only ignorant ones awaiting the salvation the missionaries were bringing to them. But they came to see, with the passage of months and years, little evidence that their religious work was making a difference; they had made a few converts but those few seemed listless and irresolute, with none of the humble gratitude and fervor expected of the newly saved.

Whitman had made an arduous return east in the spring of 1843 to appeal directly to the Board of Foreign Missions not to close his Waiilatpu station, Henry and Eliza Spalding's place among the Nez Percé at Lapwai, or any of the others. He made no professions of success in converting the Indians but set before the board's directors other compelling arguments: The Indians ought not to be abandoned at a time when the immigrant population was increasing almost daily; the stations were needed to provide medical aid and assistance to the emigrant trains; the Catholics were moving in in numbers and would fill any vacuum left if the Protestants departed.

He won but a small triumph: The missions could stay open but without further monetary assistance from the governing board.

He returned disconsolately to Oregon with the Gantt-Applegate train in May 1843 and learned that in his absence Narcissa had suffered indignities at the hands of the increasingly truculent Cayuse. On an October night during his absence, a man named Tamsucky, believed to have been a subchief under Tiloukaikt of the Cayuse, tried to enter her bedroom but was run off. When he heard of the incident, Archibald McKinley, the Hudson's Bay factor at Fort Walla Walla, drove a carriage to the station and insisted that she accompany him back to the fort. Subsequently she spent time with the Methodists at The Dalles, the inland port on the Columbia, and with friends in the Willamette. While she was away, the Waiilatpu grain mill was burned to the ground. Marcus heard the stories, surveyed the ruins, and became convinced that McLoughlin had been right all along.

As the only physician in an area extending from Fort Walla Walla to The Dalles, Whitman was away from Waiilatpu more often than not, riding hundreds of miles on horseback to provide medical aid to settlers and Indian villages. In the first few years of their work Narcissa accompanied him, but as the numbers of emigrants on the Oregon Trail increased, she was left alone to manage the mission and its farm, to run the school for Cayuse Indian boys she had started, to assist newcomers, and to entertain such distinguished visitors as John C. Frémont, John A. Sutter, up from his "New Helvetia" land grant in northern California, and Charles Wilkes.

After a few years of lonely work at the mission, Narcissa's letters home devolved from youthful exuberance and naïveté to de-

spondency over the "proud, wayward" natives she had come out
to serve. She was an "indefatigable instructress," T. J. Farnham
said after visiting the mission in 1839, and a Wilkes expedition
member reported in 1841 that she had 124 natives on the school
rolls (although the average attendance was but twenty-five). She
tried to teach Cayuse women to sew, knit, and spin, but with little
success. She wrote a friend, "The Kayuse women are too proud to
be seen usefully employed." Nor did she have better luck with the
Walla Walla women, a related people.

She confided to her family that the Indians sought the "Book
of Heaven" as a source of white man's power rather than for its
Christian inspiration, and said that they were becoming distrustful
of the missions and missionaries. Her letters were filled with her
health concerns, and with an overall graveness and melancholy that
worried her family.

The Whitmans' apprehension of the Cayuse began before Marcus made his Boston journey and grew apace after he returned. The
Indians had always seemed indolent, selfish, and ungrateful, but
these were ancient traits that simply had to be dealt with patiently.
There were more ominous developments: The natives began stealing horses and cattle, sought to extract payment from the missionaries for everything from "language lessons" to use of their land
for farming. They raided the gardens, stole vegetables, fruits, and
grain so blatantly that William Gray, the "secular agent" who accompanied the Whitmans and the Spaldings to Oregon, decided to
respond by poisoning some melons he knew would be stolen. The
violently ill culprits learned no lesson from this extreme measure
but they promised revenge.

"The savages of the Upper Columbia were very good men, for
savages," H. H. Bancroft wrote. "It is true they were thieves, and
if their natural benevolence prompted them to relieve the necessities
of the white strangers, they rewarded themselves the first opportunity. Thieving was a legitimate means of securing themselves
against want, and lying only a defence against discovery and loss."
The mistake the missionaries made, he said, was believing that such
behavior was proof of the Indians' need for spiritual guidance,

"when it was, in fact, an evidence of a natural emulation, to put themselves on a footing with the superior race." In this, he said, "both teachers and pupils were deceived; the savages in expecting to acquire in a single lifetime the civilization which was the slow growth of unknown ages; the missionary in believing that he could graft on this wild stock a germ whose fruit would not be tinctured with the bitter sap of the uncultivated tree."

At the root of the mission failures, he said, lay the "characteristic covetousness of the aboriginal, and his inability to understand that he could not at once become the equal of his teacher. Here his self-love was mortified. He began to suspect that his teachers were governed by selfish and sinister motives in intruding into his country. The more white men he saw, the more this conviction grew."

At their Lapwai station, Henry and Eliza Spalding grew worried about the spreading Indian unrest, worried more for the Whitmans than for themselves. Even the Nez Percé distrusted the Cayuse people, and Henry made a point of warning emigrants coming through his mission lands to avoid them. After the boundary settlement he also began asking newcomers if the United States might be sending army dragoons to keep the peace.

The Spaldings, like the Whitmans, had initial successes at their station, with good school attendance, a sawmill and gristmill in operation, and families working in the fields, but by 1842, with the first sizable force of emigrants arriving on the Oregon Trail, they saw the crumbling of the edifice they had so laboriously built. The Indians began deserting the mission, and classroom and worship-service attendance dwindled.

Joel Palmer, among the 1845 emigrants, visited Lapwai in the spring of 1846 to buy horses, and while he admired the work done by the Spaldings, he wrote that "it is impossible for one family to counteract all the influences of bad and designing men, of whom there are not a few in the country."

The Spaldings' plight was eerily similar to that of their counterparts at Waiilatpu. The Nez Percé had their own share of dangerous renegades, not just those demanding payment for use of the wood and water on their lands and those who vandalized the mills, broke machinery and windows, cut down precious fruit trees, and disrupted the schoolrooms, but also those threatening physical violence against the white intruders. Spalding wrote in January 1847 that "At one time probably 500 people were collecting threatening to go to my house tie & whip my wife." He said the Indians were furious because Eliza had summoned a Nez Percé chief to remove from the mission premises two men "who had just presented themselves before the school naked & painted with the most horrible figures, & continued their indecent jestures till Mrs. S. was obliged to leave the house."

Elsewhere he wrote of the sad state of their religious work. "I know not there has been a conversion for the last two years," he wrote in February 1847. "The sabbath which was once very strictly observed, is now generally desecrated."

3

Eighteen forty-six ended with New Mexico conquered and Americans on the march to occupy Los Angeles. The annexation of California would take place six weeks into the new year. There were still nine months of battles to be fought deep into Mexico, but few doubted the outcome of President Polk's war.

In the Oregon Country the boundary was settled, and the Governor and Company of Adventurers Trading in Hudson's Bay had removed to their new post of Victoria on Vancouver Island. The liege lord of the Oregon Country, Dr. John McLoughlin, had retired to private life in Oregon City, and Peter Skene Ogden had taken charge of what Company business remained north of the Columbia. The Americans in the Willamette were preparing memorials to Congress seeking immediate territorial status, composing contracts to bring supplies on American merchant ships coming to the northwest coast, requesting confirmation of the settlers' land

claims, and requesting a railroad, military troops, and steam tug-
boats and lighthouses for the Columbia estuary.

News of the boundary treaty had reached the Columbia in the
winter that killed half the Donner party in the Sierra Nevada foothills, a winter that proved disastrously bitter on the Columbia as
well. The Nez Percé and Cayuse people lost half their horse herds in
the arctic-like days, game grew scarce, people starved, and all the
while territorial talk spread along the Willamette and to the Whitmans' station. The suffering Indians were learning that the British
had moved out and the Americans were now claiming sovereignty
over their lands. Year after year, white men in an endless army were
marching in. As yet they had not tarried in Cayuse or Nez Percé
country, but how long could the Willamette valley contain them?

This simmering unrest frowned in the air like a storm cloud.
The Spaldings had felt something dire spreading toward them for
years and began writing to friends that they might have to move
to the Willamette for the safety of their four children. The Whitmans had similar thoughts. In the spring of 1847, fearing that a
rising of some kind might be in the offing, the doctor was able to
scrape together the funds to purchase the vacated Methodist mission station at The Dalles, intending to move Narcissa and the
Waiilatpu furnishings there. The Dalles site was but two days by
canoe to the safety of Fort Vancouver, now American property.

Yet, for all his suspicions and forebodings, Whitman hesitated.
The Catholic fathers were building a mission on the Umatilla
River, only thirty miles from Waiilatpu, and he could not abide
the idea of his Cayuse and Walla Walla students and converts,
small in number as they were, falling into the hands of the Ro-
mans. He and Narcissa had invested eleven years in their mission
and soon, if they held on, an Indian agent of the United States
would arrive, perhaps even a military force, and the natives would
be quieted, the Protestant missions secured under a real territorial
governance.

Meantime, he was moving milling machinery to his rebuilt
gristmill to make flour for the new wave of immigrants. He had
much to do, and Narcissa did as well. They would wait awhile.

□

The first wagons of the 1847 emigration crossed the Blue Mountains in late August, detoured north to the Whitman mission for a rest, and continued on to make camp at The Dalles. They brought with them news gathered on the journey, including estimates that as many as 5,000 settlers would be coming in before the year ended.

The newcomers, and those who flowed in daily in their wake, had suffered on the Trail, particularly the last few hundred miles of it, and had buried some of their number en route. They spoke of "mountain fever" as the ailment that had claimed the lives. They were much less concerned over the measles contracted by many of the children and a few adults during the journey; the measles victims ran fevers but recovered.

What followed, as wagon after wagon rolled across the Blues in the fall and winter months, was unaccountable: The measles, a particularly virulent strain it was said later, became a scourge among the Oregon tribes, obeying what Bancroft called "that inscrutable law of nature which makes it fatal to the dark races to encounter the white race." The disease spread from The Dalles to Puget Sound and before it ran its course killed thousands of Oregon's "dark races," including half of the Cayuse people.

While nothing could stop it, it became Marcus Whitman's fate to be the lone physician, and a white one, among a native populace plagued by a white man's disease. He ministered as best he could with his primitive bag of nostrums, cold compresses, and prayers, but the efforts were futile. No amount of white doctoring cured the white affliction and yet, as quickly became clear to the Indian, the white people were not dying from the disease they called "measles"; only the Indians died of it.

While Whitman worked himself to exhaustion, his efforts earned no gratitude; the Cayuse regarded him as a failed medicine man and, worse, a sorceror, pretending to help but secretly poisoning their people with his potions so that he, in league with other whites, could steal Indian lands.

In this spreading conviction the natives were assisted by a number of what Bancroft called "dissolute characters, half-breeds from the mountains to the east, hanging upon the skirts of the travellers." These men, "whose wild blood was full of the ichor of hatred of religion and civilization, and poisoned with jealousy of the white race, the worst traits only of which they had inherited," were likened to a white-hot brand being towed through the tinder of the stricken Indian villages.

Chief among these firebrands was a French-Canadian drifter with the Americanized name of Joe Lewis, who was said to have come to Oregon from Maine. He appeared at Waiilatpu in the fall of '47, destitute and with his clothing in rags. Whitman fed and outfitted him and tried to find employment for him, but Lewis seemed content to be a hanger-on and soon came to be regarded as a troublemaker. This idea was proven when the idler fastened himself to the Cayuse and became instrumental in spreading the calumny that the measles epidemic could be traced to Dr. Whitman's blueprint to steal the Indians' lands.

Lewis was said to have met with a tribal council and reported that Whitman, and Henry Spalding at the Lapwai mission, were writing to friends in the East to have fresh supplies of poison shipped in to kill the Cayuse and Nez Percé people. Lewis even reported to the council a conversation he claimed to have overheard between the two missionaries. Spalding, Lewis said, asked Whitman why he was so slow in his killings among the Cayuse and the doctor replied, "Oh, they are dying fast enough; the young ones will die off this winter, and the old ones next spring."

The source of Lewis's alleged remarks was William Craig, a forty-year-old Virginian who had come out to Oregon in 1829 after trapping in Blackfeet country with Jedediah Smith. Following a peripatetic career as a fur trader, he recrossed the Rockies and established a farm eight miles north of the Spalding mission. He was distrusted by Henry Spalding, who believed Craig the ringleader of a group of malcontents causing problems among the Nez Percé. But Craig's account of the Joe Lewis–Cayuse council conversation bore the stamp of truth despite the fact that he was the second bearer of it. The story had been told to Craig by a Cayuse who swore by it and added that Lewis told the tribal council that "unless they killed Dr. Whitman and Mr. Spalding quick, they would all die."

4

John McLoughlin's warnings, the pre-epidemic trepidations of the missionaries that the Indians might one day rise, the massive increase in emigrant traffic, and the scourge accompanying it all rushed to a fatal conclusion in November 1847.

The third week of the month began routinely when Henry Spalding rode down to Waiilatpu with his ten-year-old daughter Eliza (named for her mother) to put the girl in the Whitmans' school. Accompanying the Spaldings was a Mr. Jackson, who led a string of mules loaded with grain to be milled. En route they paid a visit to a familiar figure in the valley, Chief Peupeumoxmox, "Yellow Serpent," of the Walla Wallas, whose camp lay near the river and fort bearing the tribal name. The chief was an intelligent and dignified man related by forebears and marriage to the Cayuse, Yakima, and Nez Percé tribes, and he was influential among all the native people of the Oregon Country. He had sent his son to be educated among the Methodist missionaries in the Willamette valley, but in 1844, after the young man was murdered at Sutter's Fort, Yellow Serpent had entertained the idea of a war against the whites, in California and even along the Willamette. He was eventually deterred from this plan by John McLoughlin, who told the chief that such an action would result in the extermination of his people.

Still regarded as "friendly" to whites even after some of his tribe died in the measles epidemic that winter, the chief confided in Spalding that he had heard the rumors about the Americans trying to destroy the Cayuse but said he did not believe them.

Spalding and his daughter reached Waiilatpu on Monday, November 22, and spent the week with the Whitmans. On Saturday, a messenger arrived from the Cayuse camps in the Umatilla valley, thirty miles south, asking for assistance. The missionaries mounted up and rode out in a rainstorm. Spalding later remembered that they talked about how they had entered the valley in '36 along the same route they were now riding, and about the disturbing Indian threats both were hearing. At one point Whitman said, "But my death will probably do as much good for Oregon as my life can."

They rode to the villages on the south edge of the Umatilla, visited the Cayuse chiefs Five Crows and Tauitau, and ministered to some sick villagers. Then, on Sunday afternoon, November 28, they reached the lodge of a chief named Sticcas, considered a friend of the missionaries. He warned Whitman that Joe Lewis was stirring up trouble among the Cayuse and advised the doctor to leave Waiilatpu "until my people have better hearts." This alarmed Whitman enough that he decided to break his own rules against working or traveling on the Sabbath to hasten back to his mission. Spalding stayed behind for the day, and, at dawn on Monday, as he prepared to mount his horse not far from the chief's lodge, a native woman warned him to avoid the Place of the Rye Grass. This was something Spalding could not do: He had left his daughter there and so hurried on, his path leading directly from the north side of the Umatilla past the camps of Tiloukaikt, a Cayuse chief who had troubled Whitman in the past, and a younger man named Tomahas.

Whitman arrived home at near midnight on the twenty-eighth. He was exhausted from the ride but stayed up to relieve Narcissa, who was nearly as fatigued from nursing three of their adopted children, Helen Meek and Louise and Henrietta Sager, who were ill. He ate breakfast alone. Narcissa remained in her room and when one of the Sager girls took a tray of food to her, she found her sitting on a chair, sobbing into a handkerchief.

In the dawn chill Whitman went outside the mission house to supervise the butchering of a beef, then made his rounds to check on his patients at the station hospital. On that day, November 29, three more Cayuse children were discovered dead, one belonging to Chief Tiloukaikt, who had earlier lost two others to the disease.

They were quickly buried, with Whitman presiding with prayers, this a depressing, daily occurrence.

School opened at nine.

The T-shaped Waiilatpu mission house lay on an east-west axis with the crossbar of the T at the west end. It consisted of a parlor, a sitting room with stairs leading to a small loft, and an "Indian Room" with sleeping quarters. At the southern end of the neck of the T was a half-completed addition to the building, and running north lay the schoolroom, bedrooms, and a spacious kitchen next to the crossbar with doors opening into the sitting room, the Indian room, and outside. The house was spacious and comfortable, warmed by three large fireplaces, and except for some low fencing, open and unprotected.

As the twenty-ninth wore on, Whitman, after two days without sleep, walked through the kitchen to the sitting room of the house and sat by the fire to read and rest. At about two o'clock in the afternoon, as he nodded there, Tiloukaikt, Tomahas, and some other Cayuse men knocked on the outside door that led into the kitchen. Narcissa answered and turned toward the sitting-room door. "Doctor, you are wanted," she said.

What occurred in the next few minutes remains, a century and half later, confused by the several survivor accounts, but it appears that Tiloukaikt demanded some medicines and, as the doctor came through the door, he tried to push him back into the sitting room. Whitman resisted, shut the door behind him, and went to the cabinet to fetch the medicines, telling Narcissa to leave the room and close the kitchen door behind her. There were two children in the kitchen, Mary Ann Bridger, Jim's daughter, adopted by the Whitmans, and, just recovering from the measles, seventeen-year-old John Sager, one of the seven Sager children whose parents had died on the Oregon Trail. The two youngsters saw Dr. Whitman hand some medicines to Tiloukaikt, saw Tomahas step behind the doctor, swing a brass tomahawk, and strike Whitman on the head, and saw the doctor crumple to the floor as one of the Indians shot at him while Tiloukaikt and Tomahas hacked at his face and head with their war axes.

John Sager drew a pistol but was shot before he could fire it; Mary Bridger shrieked, climbed out the kitchen window, and ran to the west end of the station house yelling, "The Indians are killing Father and John!" Whitman, blood gouting from his wounds, staggered out the kitchen door, where he was clubbed down again. Either Tiloukaikt or Tomahas jammed a rifle muzzle against his throat and pulled the trigger. Narcissa ran forward and with the help of some other women dragged Marcus back through the kitchen to a settee. She tried to stanch the blood with a towel and ashes from the fireplace, ordered the children to bolt the doors and shutters and hide in closets.

"Do you know me?" she said to her husband.

"Yes." His voice was a whisper.

"Is there anything I can do to stop the bleeding?"

"No."

Outside, the Cayuse, led by Tiloukaikt, Tomahas, and the half-breed Joe Lewis, had dropped the blankets that hid their rifles. A man named William Marsh was gunned down as he ran from the gristmill; another, Isaac Gilliland, working at his tailor's table, fought back with an ax long enough for some mission folk to escape before he was cut down; L. W. Saunders, a schoolteacher, was hacked to death while trying to climb a rail fence as his daughter watched from a school window.

Narcissa walked to the sitting-room window and saw Joe Lewis and the others running amok. "Is it you, Joe, who are doing this?" she cried out. At that moment, a young Cayuse named "Frank" Escaloom fired his rifle into the sitting room, the bullet striking Narcissa under her left arm. She fell but staggered up, helped by the others to a seat while she prayed to God to protect the children.

As the attackers broke windows and smashed at the door, an immigrant named Andrew Rodgers, wounded in the arm, got the women and children, and one other wounded man, upstairs. There Narcissa was placed on a bed, her blood soaking the blankets. No attempt was made to move Marcus, who lay unconscious on the settee below.

When the Indians broke into the sitting room Rodgers met them aiming an old rifle he had found. For a time the intruders were cowed. Then Tamsucky, the Cayuse who had attempted to break into Narcissa's bedroom five years past, promised that no harm would come to the whites if they would surrender. One of the women in the upstairs bedroom recognized Tamsucky as the man who had killed L. W. Saunders and warned the others, but they had no choice but to descend the stairs and hope for mercy.

Narcissa, weak from bleeding, was helped down to the sitting room and nearly fainted at the sight of her husband, still lying on the settee, eyes closed, hideously mutilated, breathing stertorously.

The Indians moved all the captives to the Indian room at the northwest corner of the house and there debated their fate, Tamsucky's promise forgotten. Eliza Spalding, the daughter Henry had brought only a week before to enroll in school, understood enough of their language to know they were arguing over whether or not to kill all the captives. Finally, their decision was to spare the children and all the women except Narcissa.

She was carried out on a settee, Andrew Rodgers, despite his wounded arm, lifting one end of it, and the ringleader of the attack, Joe Lewis, the other. Outdoors, Lewis dropped his end of the couch and stood back as several Cayuse opened fire, killing Rodgers and Narcissa Whitman instantly. One Indian stepped forward and slashed Narcissa's lifeless body with a whip, after which her corpse was dumped into an irrigation ditch.

Soon after these murders, Frances Sager, who had been hiding in the attic above the schoolroom, came down and was dragged outdoors by Lewis and shot to death. She was the third of four of the Sager orphans killed and the ninth white killed before nightfall.

Marcus Whitman, mercifully unconscious, died of his wounds in the sitting room.

Five other Waiilatpu residents would also die, including Helen Meek and Louise Sager, before the end of the siege on December 5.

The bodies of the Whitmans and Andrew Rodgers lay in the dirt outside the Indian room for nearly three days before the Cayuse would permit them to be buried in a common grave.

Six men escaped the massacre. One drowned in the Columbia in flight, another, W. D. Canfield, fled on foot to Lapwai, 120 miles northeast, and warned Eliza Spalding of the horrific events at Waiilatpu. She was frantic for the safety of her husband and daughter and sent two Nez Percé men to the Whitman station to do what they could to rescue them.

Henry Spalding meantime was riding toward Waiilatpu when on the thirtieth he learned of the massacre and that his daughter had survived but was a captive of the Cayuse. He pushed on toward Lapwai—and probably passed without seeing the Nez Percé his wife had sent down on the rescue effort. He rode wildly thirty miles before he fell exhausted from his horse and slept fitfully a short time, during which interval his horse wandered off and he was forced to walk, covering the last ninety miles to Lapwai in six days.

When he reached the outskirts of his mission, Spalding saw a crowd of Indian looters milling about and believed for an instant that he was gazing upon another Waiilatpu, a scene of murder and perhaps other nameless atrocities. Were either of his Elizas alive? His other children? Had any of his mission workers survived?

He was rescued from the shock of these thoughts by one of the Nez Percé faithful who told him his wife and the others were safe, that they had taken refuge at the William Craig farm eight miles north. He was reunited with them on December 7, but his mind had been "injured" by the ordeal of the past week, Bancroft states, so much so that "all his subsequent writings show a want of balance." Thereafter, when relating the events of that experience, "his forehead was covered with great drops of sweat, and his eyes had a frenzied expression."

His manner on such occasions was compared to that of Donner party survivors recollecting their winter ordeal at Truckee Lake.

□

At Waiilatpu, the Cayuse held captive forty-seven whites—thirty-four children, eight women, and five men. Several of the women were "taken for wives" by the Indians, and Spalding later wrote that they were compelled to cook for a large number of the savages and that his daughter Eliza had been forced to taste the food to prove it unpoisoned. The women also sewed garments from goods looted from the mission, and it was reported that the women and girls were subjected to many more "revolting brutalities."

On December 19, Peter Ogden, the Hudson's Bay Company's finest troubleshooter, a clever and forceful man not unused to or even avoiding violence when he deemed it necessary, arrived at Fort Walla Walla. He gathered the chiefs together and announced, "The company have nothing to do with your quarrel. If you wish it, on my return I will see what can be done for you; but I do not promise to prevent a war. Deliver me the prisoners to return to their friends, and I will pay you a ransom, that is all."

The ransom was too alluring to refuse, and in return for $500 worth of shirts, blankets, guns, ammunition, flints, and tobacco provided by the Company, the prisoners were handed over by the Cayuse at Waiilatpu.

Henry and Eliza Spalding arrived at Fort Walla Walla from the Craig farm on New Year's Day 1848, with an escort of fifty loyal Nez Percé, and were reunited with their daughter.

They had closed their mission, taking only a few household goods with them and an inventory for the Board of Missions to employ in making a claim for government restitution. Spalding listed eleven buildings, 100 head of cattle, thirty-nine horses, thirty-one hogs, two wagons, a carriage, two carts, a feather bed, two rocking chairs, four settees, two spinning wheels, fifty-six apple trees, four peach trees, and one pear tree.

He estimated the property and belongings to be worth $10,048.11. It worked out to $913.46 for each year the unsalaried and unappreciated missionaries had spent at Lapwai.

24

LAST TRAILS

"...THE IMAGE OF AN IRREVOCABLE PAST."

1

In February 1848 Joe Meek, the big, shag-bearded, good-natured "bull buffalo" mountain man from Virginia, rode into Waiilatpu with an escort of militia men and some pack animals. He was heading out from Oregon City on a mission to deliver certain important papers to President Polk in Washington and wanted to see again the place where so many of his friends had died, and where his daughter had suffered. Helen Meek, "adopted" by the Whitmans and schooled by them at their mission, had died in December, not long after being freed by the Cayuse and delivered with the other captives to Peter Ogden at Fort Walla Walla.

The ruins of Marcus and Narcissa Whitman's eleven years of labor and hope lay before him: the burned-out shell of the T-shaped house; piles of melted adobe bricks, charred timbers, lintels, roof beams, and planking; and, littering the grounds, shards of china and pottery, snow-stained books and letters, and the rubble of household items the marauders deemed of no value. All the orchard trees had been hacked down, the fields trampled, and the wolves had been at work among the graves. Gnawed bones and rags of clothing had to be gathered up and reburied. Meek found Narcissa Whitman's remains and snipped a lock of her hair as a keepsake before placing her in a deeper grave than before.

As he and his escort rode down to the Umatilla to pick up the Oregon Trail and head east, the Waiilatpu killers remained at large. Tiloukaikt, Tomahas, Joe Lewis, and all the others had vanished. Some said they were still lurking somewhere near their terrible handiwork, and others claimed they had fled into the Blue Mountains. Meek had to contain his great hunger for revenge; he had other work to do, and in any event, the Cayuse' days on the run were closing. The killers could not stay free long when the countryside was swarming with men hunting them down. He only wished he could be in on the kill.

He would be, but two and a half years would pass before the raiders, some of them at least, would be brought to justice.

□

Joe Meek, now thirty-seven and as tough, durable, and dependable as he had been in the days when he headed trapper brigades to rendezvous on the Green River of Wyoming, had been the settlers' choice to deliver an assortment of petitions and papers to Washington. He had served his offices well from the time of the pioneering governmental meetings at Champoeg in '43 when he acted as auctioneer of Ewing Young's estate. He had been the provisional government's choice for sheriff and later marshal, and for his new assignment had another advantage: He was related to the Childresses, Sara Childress Polk's people, and might thereby have an entrée to the president that was denied to others.

One memorial Meek carried was from the officers of the provisional legislature beseeching the federal government to extend to Oregon "the benefit of its laws and protection." The authors of the document were adamant: They had "called upon the government of the United States so often in vain," had received too many empty promises, and now, with legislation pending to grant territorial status to Oregon and the Whitman tragedy underscoring the limits to which the Americans there could protect themselves or punish criminals, stated, "We have the right to expect your aid, and you are in duty bound to extend it." The authors also expressed confidence in the federal government to send them "men of the best talent and most approved integrity" to serve as governor and in the courts regardless of their residency in Oregon or any office presently held. Among the other papers in Meek's saddlebag was a petition signed by 250 settlers and government officials requesting that the president, upon passage of the territorial bill, appoint Joseph Lafayette Meek United States Marshal of the new Territory of Oregon.

Meek's orders originally called for him to take a route to California, to deliver messages asking the American military government there for a requisition of arms, and to request that a warship from the United States Pacific Squadron be sent to the Columbia. The mountain man knew his mountains, however, and, to the annoyance of his dispatchers, decided he could not cross the passes into California in the winter snows and would ride east on the Oregon Trail.

He reached Saint Louis on May 17 and proceeded to Washington by steamer and rail purposely wearing his filthy trail outfit of buckskins and moccasins, presenting himself as a ragged but genuine "Envoy Extraordinary and Minister Plenipotentiary from the Republic of Oregon to the Court of the United States."

The president received Meek immediately. The normally dour Polk was lighter-hearted, enjoying the final nine months of his term. The war had been won and a treaty signed in which Mexico ceded 40 percent of its territory to the United States. With the Oregon settlement, the country had doubled in size, with 1,200,000 square miles added in three years of war and diplomacy. The paper Joe Meek brought from the place Polk had won but would never see must have seemed a pleasant diversion from the toils of his office. The president saw no obstacle in presenting to Congress the memorial Sara Polk's reeking relative delivered from the provisional government in Oregon, especially since the matter it contained was by now moot. As for the marshal's appointment, Meek was told to wait. The president had a job for him.

On August 13, 1848, Polk signed the long-awaited bill creating Oregon Territory.* There had been some division over it. South Carolina Senator McDuffie said he would not "give a pinch of snuff for the whole territory" but he was in the minority, and the bill sailed through Congress. Five days after the signing, Joe Meek was sworn as United States Marshal and on the twenty-seventh he was given the honor of delivering the governor's commission to Joseph Lane, a forty-six-year-old brigadier general and hero in the late Mexican War who had started his military career as a private in the Second Indiana Volunteers.

Meek presented the commission to Lane in Indiana, and the two started for Fort Leavenworth on September 10. They avoided the winter snows of South Pass and beyond and turned southward with ten wagons and a party of trappers, wagon masters and teamsters, and twenty-five soldiers, down the Santa Fé Trail. In the New Mexican capital, now American territory, they left the wagons and switched to pack mules as Colonel Stephen Watts Kearny had done in marching his dragon force to California two years earlier, and followed Kearny's route down the Rio Grande valley, swinging west to Tucson and the Colorado River. In Los Angeles the Meek-Lane party caught an American warship for passage to San Francisco and reached the mouth of the Columbia on March 3, 1849, one day before President Polk's term expired.

□

The ashes of the Whitman station were still warm when the provisional government of Oregon issued proclamations and posted notices calling for volunteers to form a punitive expedition against

---

*The Territory included what would become the states of Oregon and Washington (which gained its own territorial status in 1853) plus portions of Idaho, Wyoming, and Montana.

the Cayuse. Two hundred and thirty men responded to the first call, and 500 would eventually be formed into companies of a regiment of Oregon Mounted Riflemen to take part in the campaign. They were loosely organized and poorly led, as might have been expected of a force of volunteer farmers, hunters, trappers, clerks, mill workers, drifters, and militiamen, but they had a single nine-pounder cannon contributed by Oregon City and a single-mindedness in their mission to punish the savages behind the Waiilatpu atrocities.

The "Cayuse War" consisted of a strung-out series of horseback pursuits and small scuffles from The Dalles, headquarters for the volunteers, along the Umatilla into the Snake River country, southeast into the Blue Mountains, and north beyond Fort Walla Walla, close to the juncture of the Snake and the Columbia, where the Palouse tribe harbored some of the fleeing marauders. The volunteers had no supply train and had to live off the country until returning to headquarters or reaching a farmhouse along the route. The wildest of the skirmishes lasted minutes and resulted in little more than an expenditure of precious ammunition. The war itself produced more rumors than casualties. The Nez Percé, Walla Wallas, and Yakimas were said to be in league with and harboring the outlaws. The Cayuse miscreants were sighted as far east along the Snake as Fort Hall, as far west as the Pacific coast, hiding among the Chinooks. Some suggested the culprits may have gone into Utah to seek protection among the Mormons.

Governor Lane made the difference. The year following his arrival in Oregon, he devoted to bringing the killers to justice, negotiating with tribal elders for the voluntary delivery of the culprits for trial. He was a skillful diplomat and his work reached fruition in the spring of 1850, when he traveled to The Dalles with a military escort to receive the prisoners. There were five of them: Tiloukaikt, Tomahas, the best known of the raiders; and men named Klokamas, Isaiachakalis, and Kiamasumpkin. To the infinite regret of all, Joe Lewis had escaped capture and disappeared from Oregon and from the historical record. Some Oregonians believed he was killed in one of the punitive raids, others say he died at the hands of the Nez Percé, or, even more satisfactory, was killed by the Cayuse for sowing the seeds of their destruction.

The Cayuse prisoners were questioned closely en route to Oregon City, where they would stand trial. When offered food by Lane's escort Tiloukaikt said, "What hearts have you to offer to eat with me, whose hands are red with your brothers' blood?" and when asked why he surrendered, said, "Did not your missionaries teach us that Christ died to save his people? So we die to save our people."

The trial opened on May 22 with the Indians defended by the secretary of the Territory and three army legal officers, and prosecuted by the newly arrived district attorney. John McLoughlin, who had warned the Whitmans of the perils of trying to work among such truculent savages, appeared to testify against the condemned.

The proceeding was brief but dignified; the defendants were all convicted and sentenced to death by hanging by the trial judge, O. C. Pratt, originally of Ontario County, New York, a distinguished lawyer with, according to H. H. Bancroft, "analytic intelligence" and "fine sensibilities."

On June 3, 1850, before much of the white population of Oregon City and some who had traveled far for the witnessing, the condemned men mounted a scaffold built to hang them simultaneously. A Catholic father, who had given the men the sacraments of baptism and confirmation in their cells, attended them on the gallows with the prayer, "Onward, onward to heaven, children; into Thy hands, O Lord Jesus, I commend my spirit."

Joe Meek, United States Marshal of Oregon Territory, served as executioner and years later recalled the moment.

"I brought forth the five prisoners," he said, "and placed them on the drop. Here the chief, who had always declared his innocence, Kiamasumpkin, begged me to kill him with my knife—for an Indian fears to be hanged—but I soon put an end to his entreaties by cutting the rope which held the drop with my tomahawk. As I said, 'the Lord have mercy on your souls,' the trap fell and the five Cayuses hung in the air."

Three of the five died instantly; the other two struggled, Meek said, "the Little Chief, Tomahas, the longest. It was he who was cruel to my little girl at the time of the massacre; so I just put my foot on the knot to tighten it, and he got quiet."

Most of the surviving Cayuse people, weakened by disease and reduced to small, scattered groups, were moved to a reservation with the Umatillas in 1855; others melded into the Nez Percé, Ya-kima, Palouse, and other tribes.

The Cayuse had lived in the region between the Walla Walla and Umatilla Rivers for five centuries before, in Bancroft's words, the "Juggernaut of an incomprehensible civilization" under "whose wheels they were compelled to prostrate themselves to that relent-less law, the survival of the fittest, before which in spite of religion or science, we all in turn go down."

2

An important postmortem to the Whitman tragedy came about when Narcissa Whitman's sister, Miss Jane Prentiss, wrote a letter in 1849 seeking an answer to the question that had caused her family such anguish: "Why did the Indians kill my sister and her husband who had done so much for them?"

She directed her inquiry to Reverend H. K. W. Perkins, Meth-odist missionary at the Waskopum station at The Dalles, with whom Marcus Whitman often visited in his travels to and from the Willamette valley. Perkins had visited Waiilatpu as well, and seems to have known both Whitmans intimately, the reason, no doubt, that Jane Prentiss sought his counsel.

Perkins answered her question with great clarity, underlining words and phrases for emphasis, and with forthrightness; more of it, perhaps, than Miss Prentiss anticipated.

He said the Whitmans "were out of their proper sphere" in mission work. Marcus was "perfectly fearless and independent" but had no talent for patient talk with the Indians, "could never stop to parley," and saw no gray areas between yes and no. The

Indians feared him, Perkins said, but he "never identified himself
with the natives as to make their interests <u>paramount</u>." Dr. Whitman, he said, had "no sense of personal dignity—manners, I
mean," presumably referring to Whitman's habitual slovenliness of
dress, and was "always at work," but not necessarily at religious
and educational efforts among his Indian charges. The result, he
said, was that the Cayuse "began to suspect that he was more
interested in the white man than in them."

Narcissa, Perkins wrote, "felt a deep interest in the welfare of
the natives," but was considered by them to be "haughty" and
"very proud." He concluded that she "was not adapted to savage
but <u>civilized</u> life. She would have done honor to her sex in a polished & exalted sphere." Her death, he said, "was her <u>misfortune</u>,
not her <u>fault</u>. She was adapted to a different destiny. She wanted
something exalted—communion with mind. She longed for society,
<u>refined society</u>."

He concluded his extraordinary analysis by saying of Narcissa,
"The self-denial that took her away [from refined society] was suicidal. . . . She was not a <u>missionary</u>, but a <u>woman</u>, a highly gifted,
polished American lady. And as such she died."

❑

After the Waiilatpu massacre and the closing of their Lapwai mission, Henry and Eliza Spalding took up residence in the Willamette
valley. He seemed to be searching for answers to the question Jane
Prentiss posed when, with a group of Presbyterian adherents, he
opened an attack on those he considered to be at the source of the
tragedy: the Catholic clergy.

Spalding's letters appeared in the *Oregon American*, a small
monthly paper printed in Oregon City on a handmade press. He
asserted that not only the nefarious Joe Lewis but also certain Jesuits who arrived at Fort Walla Walla in September 1847 had
spread the lethal lie among the Cayuse that the Americans had
brought the measles plague to kill them so that their lands could
be confiscated. The missionary, and others supporting his

viewpoint, maintained that the Jesuit clergy had conspired with the Indians to destroy all the Protestant missions.

"All were termed Jesuits," Bancroft wrote angrily on this episode, "whether Jesuit, secular, or Oblate; and fertile imaginations, half crazed by horrors, were sown with suspicions the foulest and most unnatural."

The charges, examples of the dread of "Romanism" and "Popish designs" among the Protestant missionaries, did not reflect well upon Spalding's otherwise excellent record of work and sacrifice among the Nez Percé, Bancroft said; indeed, he wrote, "The mere intimation of such atrocity exposes the heart of those who made them." Nor did the campaign in the short-lived *Oregon American* (it lasted six issues) come to anything, least of all an investigation. "The Presbyterians blamed the Catholics, and the Catholics blamed the devil," the historian summed up, "for what the exercise of ordinary good judgment ought to have averted, but which sectarian pride and obstinacy resolved to dare rather than avoid."

When Eliza Spalding died at the age of forty-eight on January 7, 1851, the 200-word epitaph her husband composed for her tombstone told of her birth and marriage, their crossing of the Rocky Mountains with the Whitmans in 1836, Eliza and Narcissa being the first women to do so, and their devoted labors among the Indians until "Dr. and Mrs. Whitman and 12 others were cruelly massacred by the Cayuse Indians." She hoped that their mission might be resumed, the inscription went on, "but the shock of the massacre and the trial and suffering occasioned by those sad events, laid the foundation for the sickness, which finally caused her death." All this was followed by the sentence, "She always felt that the Jesuit missionaries were the leading cause of the massacre."

Henry Spalding remarried in 1853 and returned to Lapwai in 1871 at the behest of the Presbyterian Board of Foreign Missions. He was greeted enthusiastically by the Nez Percé and claimed to have baptized 1,000 Indians during his tour.

He also paid a memorial visit to the Waiilatpu ruins and saw that it had become a place of rye grass again.

At his home in Kamiah, Idaho, he baptized a Cayuse chief with the Christian name Marcus Whitman, and the chief's wife as Narcissa Whitman.

Spalding died at Lapwai on August 3, 1874, and in 1913, Eliza's remains were moved there and reburied alongside her husband's. The old accusatory tombstone had been destroyed and a new monument placed over their graves.

3

Francis Parkman's "A Summer Journey Out of Bounds by a Bostonian" began appearing serially in *Knickerbocker Magazine* in February 1847, at the time when rescuers were reaching the appalling camp of the Donner party in the Sierra Nevada foothills, and completed its twenty-one-issue run in February 1849. By then, the Mormons had reached their Salt Lake valley Zion, the Whitmans and Waiilatpu were no more, Oregon had been declared a Territory of the United States, the War with Mexico had ended, John Jacob Astor had died,* and the argonauts were on the march to the gold diggings in California.

Parkman had returned in October 1846, and for a time he had no trails to follow other than the dimly lit paths through his Beacon Hill home, those between the furrows of his rose garden, and, when he became Harvard's first professor of horticulture, the walkway to his office in Cambridge.

The Oregon Trail adventure had not revived his failing health as he had hoped. His eyesight had worsened; impaired during his law studies, it had become permanently damaged, his physicians said, by the merciless prairie sun. His heart palpitations had

---

*Having lived not only to see the settlement of the Oregon Country but to read of the great migrations to the Pacific in the 1840s, some years after the western fur trade had dwindled to near extinction and long after he switched his investments to New York real estate. He died in New York City on March 29, 1848, at age eighty-one, leaving a fortune of $30,000,000 and in his will many philanthropical bequests.

returned too, and he had agonizing headaches—suspected at first
to derive from a cranial tumor—and insomnia.

But while his eyes never improved, Parkman's other problems
seemed intermittent. He regained his strength after periods when
he had to lie abed or hobble about on two canes to tend to his
garden or find his research materials for his daily writing stint, then
he would lose it again. He became resigned to a life as a semi-
invalid and bore it with courage and humor. Once, when a doctor
remarked on his "strong constitution," he said sadly, "I'm afraid
that's true."

Outwardly, at least, he seemed resigned to his handicaps and
serene, and found ways to work. In writing his Oregon Trail series
for the *Knickerbocker*, his sister and his friend and traveling companion Quincy Shaw read his rough journal notes to him as he
convalesced. He digested them, composed paragraphs in his head,
and dictated them to his volunteer scribes. In later years he most
often wrote in semidarkness using a contraption he devised and
called a "noctograph" consisting of a wooden frame with wires
stretched across it to support is hand and guide his pen so that he
could write with his eyes closed. There were times when headaches
and listlessness from insomnia kept him from writing more than a
half-hour in a day, times when his daily production was as little as
six lines, and times when he wrote prodigiously.

He remained frail all his life, his health and strength fluctuating
from despairing periods in bed with his writing frame propped before him to periods when he could work outdoors, teach at Harvard, make research voyages to Europe, and even have a social life.
His students and friends saw him as a convivial host, an uncom-
plaining, modest, and friendly man.

Few of those close to Parkman in the early years following his
Oregon Trail experience believed he would live to write the books
he planned in his Harvard days; indeed, many of his close associates believed he would soon tire of chronic invalidism and welcome
death, and the journal of his one great exploit would be his first
and only book, monument enough for this courageous man.

What no one counted on was his obstinacy, his ability to discover new passions that invigorated him and to rediscover old ones that inspired his will to live and work.

Even so, probably no one was more surprised than Parkman that he would outlive his Oregon Trail journey by forty-three years and write all the books, and a few others, he aspired to write. There were to be twelve volumes under the general title *France and England in America*, the first of which, *History of the Conspiracy of Pontiac*, appearing in 1851, he had mentally outlined before he set out with Quincy Shaw for Fort Laramie. He wrote seven other historical books, including *Montcalm and Wolfe* generally regarded to be his finest work in 1884, *The Book of Roses*, and even a novel.

Parkman's histories were hailed as classics by Henry Adams, James Russell Lowell, Herman Melville, and Henry James, and at his death at age seventy on November 8, 1893, he was hailed as "the Herodotus of American history."

□

Of all his books, only *The Oregon Trail** reached a popular audience and would remain in print, to date, for 150 years. The author's youthful grit and ingenuousness, his being "haunted by wilderness images night and day," and the magic of his eye for detail contributed to its endurance. Above all, his first book was the only book he wrote from a firsthand, participatory viewpoint. The sense he had that what he was seeing had long-lasting historical importance was vastly different from the books he wrote about events whose historical importance had long been established.

"The narrator must seek to imbue himself with the life and spirit of the time," he wrote in an era when history was literature and not yet as dismal a science as economics. "He must study events in their bearings, near and remote; in the character, habits,

---

*It appeared in book form in March 1849, three months before the death of President James K. Polk, on June 15, in Nashville, at the age of fifty-three, three months and twelve days after he left office.

and manners of those who took part in them. He must himself be, as it were, a sharer or a spectator of the action he describes."

Only in *The Oregon Trail* was Parkman a sharer and a spectator, accountable to no research sources, depending only upon his senses and his ability to assimilate what he experienced and to put on paper what Bernard De Voto called "one of the exuberant masterpieces of American literature."

□

Parkman returned west of the Mississippi but once, a visit to Saint Louis in 1867, where in the nearby town of Carondelet he was reunited with his noble old guide, Henry Chatillon. "Time hung heavy on his hands," the Bostonian said of his "brave and true-hearted" friend, "as usual with old mountain-men married and established."

They met two years before the Union Pacific and Central Pacific rails linked up at Promontory Point, Utah, at a time when a government "peace commission" was concluding treaties at Medicine Lodge Creek in Kansas, with the Arapaho, Cheyenne, Comanche, and Kiowa. These papers were to establish reservations and provide the Indian with everything he abhorred: a fixed residence, farms, schools, allowances of food and clothing, restrictions on areas he could hunt.

Among the snippets of news Parkman learned from Chatillon was the fate of Old Smoke and his people, that "band of the hated Sioux" at Horse Creek, "with whom," the Bostonian said, "I had been domesticated." The guide told him "they had nearly all been killed in fights with the white men."

Parkman kept abreast of western affairs and lamented the "Great changes" he had seen coming in '46. In 1872, in the preface for a new edition of *The Oregon Trail*, he expressed gratitude that his book had not been allowed to fall into oblivion and ascribed its extended life to the interest attached "to the record of that which has passed away never to return . . . the image of an irrevocable past."

He recalled a time when he and Quincy Shaw rode together by the foot of Pike's Peak on their return journey from Fort Laramie. Shaw said the time would come when the plains would be transformed to a grazing country, the buffalo giving place to cattle, farmhouses springing up along the watercourses, and wolves, bears, and Indians "numbered among the things that were." He and his companion knew, Parkman wrote, that gold lurked in the seams of the pristine mountains before them, "but we did not foresee that it would build cities in the waste, and plant hotels and gambling-houses among the haunts of the grizzly bear." They knew in 1846 that the Mormons—"a few fanatical outcasts"—were "groping their way across the plains seeking asylum from gentile persecution," but did not imagine that "the polygamous hordes . . . would rear a swarming Jerusalem in the bosom of solitude itself.

"We knew that, more and more, year after year, the trains of emigrant wagons would creep in slow procession towards barbarous Oregon or wild and distant California," he wrote, "but we did not dream how Commerce and Gold would breed nations along the Pacific, the disenchanting screech of the locomotive break the spell of weird, mysterious mountains."

Even in '46 Parkman wrote in a melancholy mood about the dwindling of the buffalo, the end of the Indian way of life as they became abased by liquor and harried by the military, and the disappearance of the west he saw in all "its dangers and charms." Twenty-six years later he reflected on these inexorable changes. The Indian, whom he tried to depict honestly in his journal, and the mountain man, whom he saw somewhat more romantically, symbolized for Parkman the sad passage of the Old West he knew.

"The wild cavalcade that defiled with me down the gorges of the Black Hills, with its paint and war-plumes, fluttering trophies and savage embroidery, bows, arrows, lances, and shields, will never be seen again," he said. "Those who formed it have found bloody graves, or a ghastlier burial in the maws of wolves. The Indian of to-day, armed with a revolver and crowned with an old hat, cased, possibly, in trousers or muffled in a tawdry shirt, is an

Indian still, but an Indian shorn of the picturesqueness which was his most conspicuous merit."

Of the Henry Chatillons he had known, he said, "The mountain trapper is no more, and the grim romance of his wild, hard life is a memory of the past."

He said he had gone out to Fort Laramie in 1846 "in great measure as a student," without a fixed purpose and with somewhat of a youthful rashness. "My business was observation," he said, "and I was willing to pay dearly for the opportunity of exercising it."

4

After twenty-two years as chief factor at Fort Vancouver, John McLoughlin took his leave of the Hudson's Bay Company's service on January 6, 1846. The Company provided him a generous £500 salary for the first year of his retirement, to be followed by a two-year "leave of absence" at full pay, then full retirement at "half-pay," similar to the British army custom for unemployed officers waiting for a war and an active service assignment. Only in McLoughlin's case there would be no more wars, and his services were no longer sought.

He had been forced out and it disturbed him, even though he was quite aware that he had assisted significantly in his own downfall.

He had been at loggerheads with Governor Sir George Simpson almost from the beginning of their relationship, when the two came down from Canada to old Fort George in 1824. They had quarreled frequently, often rancorously, and often about the factor's tendency to bend or break Company regulations and orders or twist them to meet what he believed were immediate needs. One such episode was the time Simpson sent HMS *Beaver* to the Columbia, the first steam-powered vessel on the northwest coast. It did not impress the factor and he ordered the removal of its engine to run a Company sawmill.

But the worst moment in their stormy relationship, and the one McLoughlin could never forgive, was Simpson's officious and abrupt announcement of John McLoughlin, Jr.'s murder at Stikine in '42 and his willingness to accuse young John of drunkenness and cruelty, and of creating the mood of violence that ended his life.

There were other rankling matters as well: Simpson's imperious orders closing certain of the Company's trading posts that McLoughlin had labored to open and which had not been given time to show a profit; Simpson's overbearing anti-American pronouncements; the accusations, both intimated and bald, that the White Eagle not only disobeyed Company policy and the policies of Whitehall, but that he aided and abetted the American takeover of the Oregon Country.

Then there was the matter of the spies Simpson sent to Fort Vancouver: Peel and Gordon, Warre and Vavasour, the latter a pair of layabouts who had accused him of encouraging American settlement. They had revealed that he had extended credit to the immigrants over the years in the amount of about $32,000 American, a sum that Simpson said horrified him and which he reported somewhat too gleefully to London.

McLoughlin's generosity had yielded a cruel irony. For all the help and hospitality he had extended to the Americans, from rescuing Jedediah Smith in '28 and Hall Kelley in '32, down through the arrival of the Protestant missionaries, the Whitmans, the Spaldings, and others, and the starving, desperate settlers thereafter—for succoring them all he had been rewarded with was betrayal. The Americans had wickedly short memories: So many of those he befriended, took into his home, loaned or gave necessities from the Company's stores—so many of them had turned their backs on him. They lied to the British spies, and even to their own spies (of whom there had been many, Kelley, Bonneville, Slacum, Wilkes, and Farnham among them), and besmirched the Company's name, and thereby his name.

McLoughlin had property, and that too had been used against him. In 1829 he had claimed land at a place he called the Falls, a considerable tract south of Fort Vancouver at the falls of the Willamette River, and built a sawmill there and some log houses. Eventually he hired a surveyor to lay out the town that became Oregon City, sold some lots, donated others for churches and schools, built a gristmill and a two-story clapboard house on the property. The house was almost ready for occupancy when McLoughlin departed Fort Vancouver for the last time. He and his beloved Marguérite, his widowed daughter Louisa and her children, would all enjoy the place, and his freedom, together.

□

A man named Samuel R. Thurston became McLoughlin's final nemesis and deprived the White Eagle of the peaceful old age and family joys he sought.

Thurston was a lawyer, from Maine originally, a graduate of Bowdoin College, a Methodist, and a one-time editor of the Burlington, Iowa, *Gazette*. He emigrated to Oregon toward the end of 1847 and in the raw new territory aligned his political ambition and gift for hortatory on a single issue: the Hudson's Bay Company's continued "presence" in and possession of American lands. The perfect embodiment of the problem, in Thurston's thinking, was John McLoughlin.

"Much has been said about the rude and violent manners of western men in pursuit of an object," Bancroft said of the upstart, "but Thurston was not a western man; he was supposed to be something more elevated and refined, more cool and logical, more moral and Christian than the people beyond the Alleghenies . . . and yet in the canvass of 1849 he introduced into Oregon the vituperative and invective style of debate, and mingled with it a species of coarse blackguardism such as no Kentucky ox-driver or Missouri flat-boatman might hope to excel."

Thurston's career had a quick and high trajectory and as sudden a collapse.

After the first official meeting of the Territorial Legislature in July 1849, just eighteen months after his arrival in Oregon City,

Samuel Thurston, age forty-three, was on his way to Washington as the territory's first delegate to Congress. He fell ill when being escorted across the Columbia bar in a small boat and had not recovered during the sailing to San Francisco and on to Panama. On the Chagres River, in the crossing to the Atlantic side of the isthmus, his baggage was stolen. Despite these travails, in June 1850 he was able to propose a pioneer land bill in the House of Representatives that carried with it provisions to declare John McLoughlin's claims to his Oregon City property null and void.

Thurston wrote other members of the House that McLoughlin had taken the land illegally, forced Methodist missionaries off the tract by threatening to have Indians attack them, and held the claim by threat of violence while making huge profits by selling lots and from other business enterprises. He also accused McLoughlin of refusing to take American citizenship and holding on to the property for the benefit of the Hudson's Bay Company. Among his "infamous lies," Bancroft wrote, was Thurston's statement that the Company "has been warring against our government for forty years," that "Dr. McLoughlin has been their chief fugleman, first to cheat our government out of the whole country, and next to prevent its settlement." He stated that McLoughlin "has driven men from claims and from the country to stifle the efforts at settlement."

Thurston's work did not win the endorsement of all Oregonians or former Oregonians. Nathaniel Wyeth of Cambridge warned Senator Winthrop of Massachusetts to be cautious in reacting to the freshman congressman's diatribes, and in Oregon, McLoughlin learned that many American settlers were indeed grateful for his efforts on their behalf when fifty-six pioneers put together a memorial defending the factor against Thurston's charges.

Unfortunately the petition did not reach Washington until after the congressman's land bill, and most of his charges against McLoughlin, were received and adopted in Congress.

Thurston next prepared a sixteen-page recounting of his services in Washington on behalf of the territory—careful "to leave no possible means by which the man who had founded and fostered Oregon City could retain an interest in it," Bancroft said. He also submitted himself for reelection while the victim of his malice "began the painful and useless struggle to free himself from the toils by which his enemies had surrounded him, and from which he never escaped during the few remaining years of his life."

But Thurston died first, in April 1851, aboard the steamer *California* off Acapulco en route to Oregon from Washington. His death was attributed to "natural causes from chronic ill health." Bancroft said, "Thus while preparing boldly to vindicate his acts and do battle with his adversaries, he was forced to surrender the sword which was too sharp for its scabbard."

In 1852, after McLoughlin had completed his application for United States citizenship, the territorial assembly passed an act accepting his Oregon City property as a gift for the purposes of endowing a university but, with Thurston and his democratic party out of power, there was no movement to evict the White Eagle and his family from the land and they remained at the big whitewashed house until his death.

In his last, relatively calm, years McLoughlin was often seen walking the Oregon City streets in his brass-buttoned swallow-tail coat, ruffled shirt, and black cravat, baggy trousers stuffed into long-legged, beaded Indian moccasins, carrying the gold-headed cane he had once laid alongside the head of Reverend Herbert Beaver and tipping his tall beaver hat to the ladies. He still looked the Laird of the Pacific Northwest, but toward the end he became more house-bound, suffering from diabetes, and had developed a palsy in his hands that ended his ability to answer correspondence. As his granddaughter wrote for him from dictation, he checked each sheet of foolscap with his eagle's eye. If any were blotted she knew she would have to make a clean copy.

In the summer of 1854, Peter Ogden fell ill and was forced to retire from Hudson's Bay and take up residence with his wife, daughter, and son-in-law in Oregon City. McLoughlin visited him regularly and urged Ogden to legalize his marriage to his Indian wife. This idea did not appeal to the leathery brigade leader, who said their devotion to one another, and to their several children, was testimony enough to the sanctity of their relationship.

Ogden died in Oregon City on September 27, 1854, at age sixty.

In the summer of 1857, McLoughlin met an American lawyer named Lafayette F. Grover of Maine who, ironically, had come to Oregon at the suggestion of Samuel Thurston. The White Eagle told the young future district attorney, "I am an old man and just dying, and you are a young man and will live many years in this country. As for me, I might better have been shot like a bull; I might better have been shot forty years ago." He asked Grover to "give your influence, after I am dead, to have this property go to my children. I have earned it, as other settlers have earned theirs, and it ought to be mine and my heirs'."

Grover promised to do all he could.

On September 3, 1857, McLoughlin's nephew, Dr. Henri de Chesne, came to look in on his patient and greeted the old man with his usual salutation, *"Comment allez-vous?"* This time McLoughlin answered *"A Dieu,"* and died at eleven that morning, from "gangrenous diabetes," at the age of seventy-three.

He was buried in an enclosure in the Catholic church of Oregon City and on his tombstone was inscribed the legend, "The Pioneer and Friend of Oregon; also the Founder of this City."

Marguérite McKay McLoughlin died on February 28, 1860, and was laid to rest beside her husband of forty-five years.

The Oregon legislature restored the McLoughlin property to his heirs in 1862.

☐

Herbert Howe Bancroft, who admired McLoughlin above all the great figures in the 300-year Oregon journey, wrote the most eloquent tribute to him:

I think of him as if present; and so he is, though he were dead this quarter century and more. I never saw him, and yet I see him; I never heard him, and yet he speaks to me now; I never grasped his hand, but I feel his presence, and am the better for it. The good that a man does lives after him, saith the seer.

EPILOGUE

In 1844 the *American Agriculturist* of New York carried an editorial inspired by the success of the "Great Migration" the year before—the one that Horace Greeley said "wears an aspect of insanity." The magazine writer, carried aloft by the spirit if not by the eloquence of Manifest Destiny, opined that "we might as well undertake to stay the sun and moon in their course over the peaks of the Rocky Mountains, as emigration to the west by the hardy nomadic population of our country." He went further: "Who will not take the risk of being scalped by Indians, or devoured by grisley [*sic*] bears, to say nothing of sustaining innumerable hardships for a succession of years, and living free from all moral and civil restraints, to emigrate to the Ultima Thule . . . the El Dorado of the final borders of the great illimitable west!"

By Ultima Thule and El Dorado the writer meant Oregon, but within four years of the writing the words were being applied to California.

□

The first book edition of Francis Parkman's masterpiece appeared with the title *The California and Oregon Trail: Being Sketches of Prairie and Rocky Mountain Life*. The author had not authorized inserting "California" into the title since he had made no reference to the California Trail in the book, but the publisher clearly intended making the most of the public fixation on the road that led to the goldfields.

Parkman may have been fuming, but George Putnam's publishing firm knew what would boost sales.

At the time the book appeared in March 1849, over a year had passed since the first silt-like gold and small nuggets had been found in the race of a sawmill owned by John Augustus Sutter on the south fork of the American River in northern California. For a time the discovery was kept localized, but word of it inevitably spread to San Francisco, then shot eastward.

At the uppermost estimate, there had been 1,000 emigrants in the "Great Migration" of '43; 4,000 in 1844 and 5,000 in 1845, a very small trickle of these rolling south at Fort Bridger or Fort Hall to the California Trail. There had been some slight falling off in the emigrant numbers during the Mexican War years, but by 1849, 25,000 to 30,000 people, including 1,000 children, 2,000 women, and 60,000 animals, were clogging the Oregon Trail between South Pass and Fort Bridger, most of them bound for the goldfields—and this represented only about a third of those being somewhat ambitiously called "argonauts." The majority chose alternate routes: southwestern trails such as that followed by Colonel Kearny in his march from Santa Fé to Los Angeles; deadly desert paths across Mexico; isthmian crossing of the fever swamps of Panama and Nicaragua (six weeks from New York to San Francisco and in 1849, $400–$500 per person); and the old Cape Horn sea route. Fully 16,000 people reached San Francisco by sea in 1849, and 12,000 in 1850. The average voyage from eastern ports or New Orleans via Cape Horn took 200 days, and the cheapest ticket cost $200.

The overland argonauts followed the traditions of their Oregonian predecessors. They were struck by a cholera epidemic in western Missouri that killed 1,000 of them before they got a fair start, and they overloaded their wagons. They learned what was essential and what was not, heaved overside expensive gold-washing machines sold to them by fast-talking entrepreneurs in Saint Louis and Independence, plus weighty tools, furniture, and similar impediments. Even wagons, some of them perfectly workable, were left behind in the rush to get to California and dip gold out of the streams and chip it off the mountains. Wagons and oxen were traded for pack animals as hopeful miners threw together a few belongings and supplies and made up a pack train or rode on across the prairies with a single horse or mule for company.

Along the south bank of the Platte the Trail was strewn with wagon hulks, the boxes, wheel-spokes and anything burnable broken up for firewood, and a detritus of other abandonments—piles of rancid bacon, yokes and horse collars, wheelbarrows, household goods, rusting machinery—as the Forty-niners fled toward their end of the rainbow.

Beyond South Pass, more than half of the gold seekers followed the well-traveled Oregon Trail routes that led south to Fort Bridger, or north to Fort Hall, from these points aiming toward the Humbolt River valley. Some struck due west across the sagey wastes between South Pass and the Green River, and others, desperately short of supplies, followed the Mormon Trail to Salt Lake City. There they swapped their bags of beans, rice, and oats for fresh vegetables and meat, and traded their wagons and oxen (at a common rate of six trail-worn and skinny animals for two fresh and fat ones). They then proceeded around the rim of the Salt Lake to trudge across the desert wastelands that would take them to the Humboldt, the place where the California trails, detours, and cut-offs merged.

When the winter of '49 closed in, there were 10,000 argonauts at the foot of, or struggling across, the Sierra Nevada passes, a potential Donner party of such staggering proportions that $100,000 was appropriated for the army in California to mount rescue and relief work. In the end, miraculously, few lives were lost.

By 1850, the California-bound overlanders, as well as the dwindling number trekking to Oregon, were traveling light, depending upon the Trail's booming trading posts between western Missouri and the Snake or Truckee valleys for outfitting. These trailside emporia ranged from tented or brush-and-board gambling hells to hammered-up plank buildings with windows and large-lettered signs selling food, whiskey, draft and pack animals, placer gold mining equipment, repair and even mail services.

The Oregon and California Trail traveler of 1850 also found ferries in operation, with prices escalating from forty cents each for wagons crossing the Sweetwater to sixteen dollars to cross the Green.

By then there were even bridges going up across the Platte, the Laramie, the Bear, and the Portneuf below Fort Hall, although there were few similar luxuries for the Oregon-bound between Hall and the Willamette valley. Fort Boisé and Fort Walla Walla remained virtually unchanged since the days when the Hudson's Bay Company ruled the Oregon Country.

In 1850, the third year of California gold, the number of Oregon Trail travelers increased to 55,000. (At Fort Laramie, now an army post, a tally was made of the people, wagons, and livestock passing through that year: 7,472 mules; 30,616 oxen; 22,742 horses; 5,270 cows; 8,998 wagons.) Of that crush of 55,000, only about 400 were headed to Oregon.

Even Oregonians were going to California in the gold rush years, thousands of them, and only half returned. During the trial of the Whitman massacre defendants, Governor Joseph Lane, mysteriously absent, was widely rumored to be at his gold diggings on California's Tuolumne River.

California gold ended Oregon's supremacy as the Ultima Thule of westward emigration and transformed, for the rest of its history, the White Man's Great Medicine Road. The Oregon Trail served for seven or eight years as the main overland thoroughfare in the

300-year journey to the Pacific Northwest; after 1848 it became the trail that intersected the trail to California.

□

In 1890, an assemblage of pioneers, children and grandchildren of pioneers met in Portland. The group debated a resolution that would extend membership in the organization to those who arrived in Oregon (or Washington, which gained territorial status in 1853, statehood in 1889) on or before February 14, 1859, the date of Oregon statehood. The old bylaws had established January 1, 1855, as the terminal date for those who could be considered "pioneers."

One of the 1849 pioneers present at the meeting drew a distinction between the overlanders and those arriving on shipboard:

> The word pioneer meant foot-soldier, foot-traveler; it properly represents the condition of those who came to this country as foot-travelers, and that word prepares the way. . . . I am very much opposed to extending the time beyond 1854. A pioneer is not a pioneer when he can get on a steamship in the port of New York, pay his passage, get three good meals a day, get a berth to sleep in at night, and be landed here with all his bag and baggage, without effort on his part; he is not a pioneer in any sense of the word.

Not until 1894, at the twenty-second annual reunion of the pioneers association, was the amendment passed extending the date to 1859.

□

By 1869, when the transcontinental railroad was completed, something on the order of 400,000 men, women, and children had made the 2,000-mile journey from the Missouri frontier to the Pacific

Coast on the Oregon Trail and fulfilled the ambition of presidents from Thomas Jefferson to James K. Polk, and visionaries from Hall Jackson Kelley to Jesse Applegate, who saw the United States stretching "from sea to shining sea."

SOURCES

The literature of the old Oregon Country and the Oregon Trail—scholarly material, first-person accounts by participants in the saga, popular works—is massive and, for any new writer of the story, rich beyond imagining.

Some illustrative examples:

• In the 1930s, Philip Ashton Rollins, a New York lawyer, followed virtually every footstep of Robert Stuart's epic journey from Astoria to Saint Louis for the purpose of editing and annotating a new edition of Stuart's journals. The result was a breathtaking work of scholarship, *Robert Stuart's Narratives of His Overland Trip Eastward from Astoria in 1812–1813* (1935), available in a recent edition from the University of Nebraska Press. The opening sixteen-page biography of Stuart has 174 footnotes.

• The eminent Nebraska historian Merrill J. Mattes (1910–1996), in writing *The Great Platte River Road*, examined over 700 eyewitness overland narratives (only about half of which had been published) and listed at least 1,000 sources for his masterwork.

• *The Plains Across: The Overland Emigrants and the Trans-Mississippi West, 1840–60* was published in 1979, three years after the tragic death from a brain tumor of its thirty-nine-year-old author, John D. Unruh, Jr., of South Dakota. His magisterial book, indispensable to any writer on the mid-century West, contains such meticulous data as the average travel time for overlanders to California in the period 1841–48 (157.7 days) and those to Oregon (169.1 days).

• Francis Parkman, a formidable scholar himself, would have admired the work of E. N. Feltskog, whose edited edition of Parkman's *The Oregon Trail* (1849) is a model, if not *the* model, for reintroducing such classics to new generations of readers. The recent University of Nebraska·Press edition of Feltskog's Parkman contains a staggering 314 pages of notes and bibliography, not a line of which is unimportant.

In recounting the Astor experiment in Oregon, I have made extensive use of Washington Irving's *Astoria, or Anecdotes of an Enterprise Beyond the Rocky Mountains* (published in 1836 in two volumes), recognizing that it was a work-for-hire, a collaboration, said Irving authority Alfred Powers, between "the nation's Midas and the nation's Homer," and therefore predictably pro-Astor. Irving was paid $5,000 by the financier to write the book, and earned another $12,000 in royalties from its substantial sale. James Fenimore Cooper, when he heard of the Astor-Irving alliance, predicted that Irving would make Astor "greater than Columbus," and H. H. Bancroft declared that the book contained "a current of unqualified sycophancy, trickery, sentimentality, and maudlin praise." In scattered places, Bancroft said, Irving's language was often "strange" and filled with "effeminate inconsistency," but, worse than that peculiarly phrased charge, declared that "many of its most brilliant passages are pure fiction."

Whatever the case for these accusations, Irving interviewed all the central characters and had access to Astor's correspondence and papers as well as the great nabob himself, and his book is much more trustworthy than Bancroft would have us believe. It is ironic that Bancroft was so trenchantly critical of Irving and De Voto so persistently critical of Parkman, because the most eloquent of the old writers on the old Oregon Country are Washington Irving and Herbert Howe Bancroft, Francis Parkman's is the best book on the Oregon Trail written by a contemporary, and De Voto's work on the entire era remains indispensable.

Of modern writers of Oregon and the Oregon Trail, David Lavender has few, if any, peers; of modern publishers, the University of Nebraska Press (through its Bison Books reprints) has contributed more to the overland epic than any other, with the University of Oklahoma Press, the Arthur H. Clark Company, and Caxton Printers of Caldwell, Idaho, all having a significant share in the imposing literature of the era.

As always, the late Dan L. Thrapp's masterly *Encyclopedia of Frontier Biography* has saved countless hours in the writing of this book. I recommend the University of Nebraska Press CD-ROM version (1995) for quick reference, and the hardbound or paperback versions for a leisurely reading and education.

BIBLIOGRAPHY

John Bakeless, *Lewis and Clark: Partners in Discovery*. New York: William Morrow, 1947.

Bancroft, Herbert Howe. *History of the Northwest Coast*. New York: The Bancroft Co., 1884; two volumes.

————. *History of the Pacific States of North America: California*. San Francisco: The History Company, 1886–1890; seven vols.

Batman, Richard. *The Outer Coast*. New York: Harcourt Brace Jovanovich, 1985.

Bergeron, Paul H. *The Presidency of James K. Polk*. Lawrence: University Press of Kansas, 1987.

Bidwell, John. *Echoes of the Past*. New York: The Citadel Press, 1962; reprint ed.

Billington, Ray Allen. *Westward Expansion: A History of the American Frontier*. New York: The Macmillan Co., 1967.

Blacker, Irwin R. *Westering*. Cleveland, Ohio: The World Publishing Co., 1958.

Blevins, Winfred. *Give Your Heart to the Hawks*. Plainview, New York: Nash Publishing Co., 1973.

Case, Robert O. *The Empire Builders*. Portland, Oregon: Binfords & Mort, 1949.

Clark, Keith, and Lowell Tiller. *Terrible Trail: The Meek Cutoff, 1845*. Bend, Oregon: Maverick Publications, 1993.

Delano, Alonzo. *Life on the Plains and Among the Diggings*. Auburn, New York: Miller, Orton & Mulligan, 1854.

Denton, V. L. *The Far West Coast*. Toronto: J. M. Dent & Sons, 1924.

De Voto, Bernard. *Across the Wide Missouri*. New York: Houghton Mifflin Co., 1947.

———. *The Year of Decision: 1846*. Boston: Little, Brown, 1943.

Dickens, Charles. *American Notes*. Introduction by Christopher Lasch. Greenwich, Connecticut: Fawcett Books, 1961.

Doughty, Howard. *Francis Parkman*. New York: The Macmillan Co., 1962.

Drury, Clifford Merrill. *Marcus and Narcissa Whitman and the Opening of Old Oregon*. Glendale, California: Arthur H. Clark Co., 1973; 2 vols.

Drury, Clifford Merrill, ed. *On to Oregon: The Diaries of Mary Walker and Myra Eells*. Lincoln: University of Nebraska Press, 1998. Reprint ed.

——. *The Mountains We Have Crossed: Diaries and Letters of the Oregon Mission, 1838*. Lincoln: University of Nebraska Press, 1999. Reprint ed.

Du Pratz, Antoine LePage. *The History of Louisiana*. London: T. Becket, 1774. (Reprinted in New Orleans by J. S. W. Harmanson, n.d.)

Egan, Ferol. *Frémont: Explorer for a Restless Nation*. New York: Doubleday, 1977.

Eggenhofer, Nick. *Wagons, Mules and Men*. New York: Hastings House, 1961.

Farragher, John Mack. *Women and Men on the Overland Trail*. New Haven: Yale University Press, 1979.

Ferris, Robert G., ed. *Soldier and Brave*. Washington, D.C.: U.S. Department of the Interior, National Park Service, 1971.

Franchère, Gabriel. *A Voyage to the Northwest Coast of America*. Chicago: R. R. Donnelley & Co., 1954. Reprint of 1854 edition.

Franzwa, Gregory M. *The Oregon Trail Revisited*. Tucson: Patrice Press, 1997.

Frémont, John C. *Memoirs of My Life*. New York: Belford, Clarke & Co., 1887; two volumes.

Gilbert, Bill. *The Trailblazers*. New York: Time-Life Books, 1973.

Gulick, Bill. *Roadside History of Oregon*. Missoula, Montana: Mountain Press, 1991.

Hafen, LeRoy R., ed. *Fur Trappers and Traders of the Far Southwest*. Logan: Utah State University Press, 1997. Reprint ed.

————. *Mountain Men and Fur Traders of the Far West*. Lincoln: University of Nebraska Press, 1982. Reprint ed.

————. *Broken Hand: The Life of Thomas Fitzpatrick: Mountain Man, Guide and Indian Agent*. Denver: Old West Publishing Co., 1973.

Hafen, LeRoy R., and Carl Coke Rister. *Western America*. Englewood Cliffs, New Jersey: Prentice-Hall, 1950.

Hawgood, John A. *America's Western Frontiers: The Exploration and Settlement of the Trans-Mississippi West*. New York: Alfred A. Knopf, 1967.

Hill, William E. *The Oregon Trail, Yesterday and Today*. Caldwell, Idaho: The Caxton Printers, 1987.

Holliday, J. S. *The World Rushed In: The California Gold Rush Experience*. New York: Simon & Schuster, 1981.

Holmes, Kenneth L., ed. *Covered Wagon Women: Diaries & Letters from the Western Trails, 1853–1854*. Lincoln: University of Nebraska Press, 1998. Six volumes, reprint ed.

Horn, Huston. *The Pioneers*. New York: Time-Life Books, 1974.

Irving, Washington. *Astoria*. Portland, Oregon: Binfords & Mort Publishers, n.d. (Original edition, 1836).

Jackson, Donald, and Mary L. Spence, eds. *The Expeditions of John Charles Frémont*. Urbana: University of Illinois Press, 1970. Two volumes.

Jackson, John C. *Children of the Fur Trade: Forgotten Metis of the Pacific Northwest.* Missoula, Montana: Mountain Press, 1995.

Johansen, Dorothy O. *Empire of the Columbia: A History of the Pacific Northwest.* New York: Harper & Row, 1967.

Lavender, David. *The Fist in the Wilderness.* Garden City, New York: Doubleday, 1964.

————. *Land of Giants: The Drive to the Pacific Northwest.* Lincoln: University of Nebraska Press, 1979.

————. *The Overland Migrations: Settlers to Oregon, California, and Utah.* Washington, D.C.: U.S. Department of the Interior, National Park Service, n.d.

————. *The Way to the Western Sea: Lewis and Clark Across the Continent.* New York: Harper & Row, 1988.

————. *Westward Vision: The Oregon Trail.* New York: McGraw-Hill, 1963.

Lyman, Horace S. *History of Oregon.* New York: The North Pacific Publishing Co., 1903. Three volumes.

McDougall, Walter A. *Let the Sea Make a Noise: A History of the North Pacific from Magellan to MacArthur.* New York: Basic Books, 1993.

McGlashin, Charles F. *History of the Donner Party.* Ann Arbor, Michigan: University Microfilms, Inc., 1966. (Original edition, 1879.)

Marks, Paula Mitchell. *Precious Dust: The American Gold Rush Era, 1848–1900.* New York: William Morrow, 1994.

Mattes, Merrill J. *The Great Platte River Road*. Lincoln: University of Nebraska Press, 1987. Reprint ed.

Morgan, Dale L. *Jedediah Smith and the Opening of the West*. Lincoln: University of Nebraska Press, 1964. Reprint ed.

Morris, Richard B. *Encyclopedia of American History*. New York: Harper & Brothers, 1961.

Morrison, Dorothy N. *The Eagle & the Fort: The Story of John McLoughlin*. New York: Atheneum, 1979.

Moulton, Candy. *Roadside History of Nebraska*. Missoula, Montana: Mountain Press, 1997.

Murphy, Virginia Reed. "Across the Plains to the Sierra Nevada with the Donner Party." *Century Magazine*, July 1891.

Nevins, Allan. *Frémont: Pathmarker of the West*. New York: Longmans, Green, 1939.

Noy, Gary, ed. *Distant Horizon: Documents from the Nineteenth Century American West*. Lincoln: University of Nebraska Press, 1999.

Parkman, Francis. *The Oregon Trail*, edited by E. N. Feltskog. Lincoln: University of Nebraska Press, 1994.

Paxon, Frederic Logan. *The Last American Frontier*. New York: The Macmillan Co., 1924.

Peavy, Linda, and Ursula Smith. *Pioneer Women: The Lives of Women on the Frontier*. Norman: University of Oklahoma Press, 1998.

Pelzer, Louis. *The Cattlemen's Frontier*. Glendale, California: Arthur H. Clark Co., 1936.

Reinfeld, Fred. *Trappers of the West*. New York, Dell Books, 1964.

Robertson, R. G. *Competitive Struggle: America's Western Fur Trading Forts, 1764–1865*. Boise, Idaho: Tamarack Books, 1999.

Ronda, James P. *Astoria and Empire*. Lincoln: University of Nebraska Press, 1990.

Rollins, Philip Ashton, ed. *The Discovery of the Oregon Trail: Robert Stuart's Narratives of His Overland Trip Eastward from Astoria in 1812–1813*. Lincoln: University of Nebraska Press, 1995. Reprint of 1935 ed.

Ross, Alexander. *Adventures of the First Settlers on the Oregon*. New York: The Citadel Press, 1969. Reprint of 1848 edition.

———. *The Fur Hunters of the Far West*. Norman: University of Oklahoma Press, 1956.

Rumer, Thomas A. *The Wagon Trains of '44*. Spokane, Washington: Arthur H. Clark Co., 1990.

Rumer, Thomas A., ed. *The Emigrating Company: The 1844 Oregon Trail Journal of Jacob Hammer*. Spokane, Washington: Arthur H. Clark Co., 1990.

Russell, Carl P. *Traps & Tools of the Mountain Men*. New York: Alfred A. Knopf, 1967.

Stegner, Wallace, et al. "The Oregon Trail," in *Trails West*. Washington, D.C.: National Geographic Society, 1979.

Stewart, George R. *The California Trail*. New York: McGraw-Hill, 1971. Reprint ed.

———. *Ordeal by Hunger: The Story of the Donner Party.* New York: Henry Holt & Co., 1936.

Stokesbury, James L. "Francis Parkman on the Oregon Trail," *American History Illustrated,* December 1973.

Sullivan, Maurice S. *Jedediah Smith: Trader and Trailbreaker.* New York: Press of the Pioneers, 1936.

Thrapp, Dan L. *Encyclopedia of Frontier Biography.* Glendale, California: Arthur H. Clark Co., 1988. Three volumes. (CD-ROM version by University of Nebraska Press, 1995.)

———. *Encyclopedia of Frontier Biography: Supplemental Volume.* Spokane, Washington: Arthur H. Clark Co., 1994.

Unger, Irwin. *These United States: The Questions of Our Past.* Englewood Cliffs, New Jersey: Prentice-Hall, 1989.

Unruh, John D., Jr. *The Plains Across: The Overland Emigrants and the Trans-Mississippi West, 1840–60.* Urbana: University of Illinois Press, 1979.

Van Orman, Richard A. *The Explorers: Nineteenth Century Expeditions in Africa and the American West.* Albuquerque: University of New Mexico Press, 1984.

Vestal, Stanley. *Joe Meek: The Merry Mountain Man.* Caldwell, Idaho: The Caxton Printers, 1952.

Victor, Francis Fuller. *The River of the West: The Adventures of Joe Meek.* (Volume I: The Mountain Years). Missoula, Montana: Mountain Press, 1983. Reprint of the 1870 ed.

Wagner, Henry R., and Charles L. Camp. *The Plains & Rockies: A Critical Bibliography of Exploration, Adventure and Travel in the American West, 1800–1865*. San Francisco: John Howell Books, 1982.

Webber, Bert, ed. *Dr. John McLoughlin, Master of Fort Vancouver, Father of Oregon*. Medford, Oregon: Webb Research Group, 1994.

Williams, Lucia. "A Letter Home." Text and photographs by Jerry Gildemeister. *American History Illustrated*, January 1988.

Winther, Oscar Osburn. *The Old Oregon Country*. Lincoln: University of Nebraska Press, 1969. Reprint of 1950 ed.

INDEX